Catching Up on The Chronicles of Narnia

The following books, which I recommend reading in the order I've listed here, make up *The Chronicles of Narnia*:

- *The Lion, the Witch, and the Wardrobe* tells of the Pevensie children's trip to Narnia and how Aslan frees the enchanted land from the White Witch.
- *Prince Caspian* chronicles the adventures of the Pevensies and Prince Caspian in their battle against the Telmarines.
- *The Voyage of the "Dawn Treader"* takes you on an odyssey as King Caspian and his shipmates travel to the End of the World.
- *The Silver Chair* tells of the quest to free Prince Rilian from the evil Green Witch.
- *The Horse and His Boy* explores the adventures of a boy and a talking horse as they attempt to save Narnia from invasion.
- *The Magician's Nephew* takes you back to how it all began, showing how children from our world first ventured into Narnia.
- *The Last Battle* chronicles the final defeat of evil in Narnia and the start of the real Narnia.

Highlights of the Life of C.S. Lewis

- **1898:** Born in Belfast, Ireland.
- **1908:** Lewis's mother dies.
- **1917–1918:** Fights in World War I.
- **1925:** Named don in the English department at Magdalen College, Oxford.
- **1931:** Converts to Christianity after several years of searching for truth.
- **1933:** Along with J.R.R. Tolkien, forms the Inklings literary group.
- **1940-1946:** Publishes his best known Christian works, including *The Screwtape Letters, The Problem of Pain,* and the series of three BBC broadcast talks that later were published together as *Mere Christianity.*
- **1950–1956:** Publishes *The Chronicles of Narnia* at the rate of one book per year.
- **1956:** Marries Joy Davidman Gresham in a civil ceremony. They're married in a church wedding in 1957.
- **1960:** Joy dies after a long battle with cancer.
- **1963:** Lewis dies of a stroke at age 64 on the same day John F. Kennedy is assassinated.

The Best and Wittiest of the Chronicles

In Chapter 5, I hand out some "best of" awards for the Chronicles. Here's a sampling of the list:

Wittiest opening line. Humor can be found throughout *The Chronicles of Narnia,* but there's no wittier line than the opening line of *The Voyage of the "Dawn Treader:"* "There was a boy called Eustace Clarence Scrubb, and he almost deserved it."

Best theological line. Summing up perfectly the role of Aslan in the lives of all Narnians, King Tirian says to Jill Pole in *The Last Battle:* "Courage, child: we are all between the paws of the true Aslan."

Best line to use at a party. When Puddleglum introduces himself in *The Silver Chair,* he quips, "Puddleglum's my name. But it doesn't matter if you forget it. I can always tell you again."

Best "glass is half full comment." In *The Silver Chair,* when Eustace, Jill, Rilian, and Puddleglum appear to be stuck underground forever, the Marshwiggle reasons, "And you must always remember there's one good thing about being trapped down [in Underland]: It'll save funeral expenses."

Best-Loved Books by C.S. Lewis

Fiction

- *The Chronicles of Narnia*
- *The Screwtape Letters*
- Space Trilogy (*Out of the Silent Planet, Perelandra, That Hideous Strength*)
- *The Great Divorce*
- *The Pilgrim's Regress*
- *Till We Have Faces*

Nonfiction

- *Mere Christianity*
- *The Problem of Pain*
- *Miracles*
- *The Abolition of Man*
- *The Four Loves*
- *Surprised by Joy*

C.S. Lewis & Narnia For Dummies®

Cheat Sheet

Who's Who in Narnia

Narnia is filled with an eclectic cast of characters that fit into four main groups.

Children

- **Peter Pevensie:** The eldest of the Pevensie children; a strong leader who becomes High King of Narnia
- **Susan Pevensie:** The second eldest of the Pevensie children; becomes Queen Susan the Gentle
- **Edmund Pevensie:** A traitor in *The Lion, the Witch, and the Wardrobe;* restored by Aslan and later named King Edmund the Just
- **Lucy Pevensie:** The first child to enter Narnia through the wardrobe; later named Queen Lucy the Valiant
- **Digory Kirke:** Travels to Narnia in *The Magician's Nephew;* is the older professor in *The Lion, the Witch, and the Wardrobe*
- **Polly Plummer:** Digory Kirke's next-door neighbor in *The Magician's Nephew;* travels to Narnia with Digory
- **Eustace Scrubb:** Spoiled and self-centered kid in *The Voyage of the "Dawn Treader;"* is eventually transformed by Aslan
- **Jill Pole:** Drawn into Narnia with Eustace Scrubb in *The Silver Chair*

Divinities

- **Aslan:** The creator and ruler of Narnia; symbolizes what Jesus Christ would have been like if he had come to a world called Narnia
- **Emperor-over-the-sea:** Father of Aslan; symbolizes God the Father in the Christian Triune God (Father, Son, and Holy Spirit)

Narnians and friends

- **Mr. Tumnus:** Faun whom Lucy encounters when she first enters Narnia in *The Lion, the Witch, and the Wardrobe*
- **Mr. and Mrs. Beaver:** Talking beavers who provide assistance to Peter, Susan, and Lucy in *The Lion, the Witch, and the Wardrobe*
- **Caspian X:** King of Narnia during *Prince Caspian* and *The Voyage of the "Dawn Treader;"* father of Rilian
- **Rilian:** Son of Caspian X; kidnapped for ten years by the Green Witch in *The Silver Chair*
- **Puddleglum the Marshwiggle:** Memorable Narnian creature who helps Jill and Eustace in *The Silver Chair*
- **Shasta:** Runs away from Calormen in *The Horse and His Boy;* later discovers he's one of King Lune of Archenland's twin sons
- **Bree:** Talking horse from *The Horse and His Boy*
- **Aravis:** Daughter of Calormene leader; runs away from home in *The Horse and His Boy*
- **Tirian:** Final king of Narnia, as depicted in *The Last Battle*

Enemies

- **White Witch (Queen Jadis):** Evil witch who destroys Charn in *The Magician's Nephew* and later casts a spell over Narnia in *The Lion, the Witch, and the Wardrobe*
- **Maugrim:** A large wolf and captain of the White Witch's secret police in *The Lion, the Witch, and the Wardrobe;* also known as Fenris Ulf
- **King Miraz:** Wicked king of Narnia in *Prince Caspian*
- **Telmarines:** Originally pirates from our world who stumble into Narnia and later inhabit Telmar; conquerors of Narnia, as depicted in *Prince Caspian*
- **Green Witch:** Villain of *The Silver Chair;* entrances Prince Rilian and holds him in her Underland
- **Prince Rabadash:** Haughty prince of Calormen who tries to invade Narnia in *The Horse and His Boy*
- **Shift the Ape:** The great deceiver in *The Last Battle;* lulls Narnia into an attack by the Calormenes

Where's Where in Narnia

- **Narnia:** Enchanted land of Talking Beasts; where the Narnian Chronicles take place
- **Archenland:** Mountainous land south of Narnia; a traditional ally of Narnia
- **Calormen:** Hot, arid land south of Narnia and Archenland; traditional enemy to Narnia
- **Telmar:** Land west of Narnia
- **Underland:** Home of the Green Witch in *The Silver Chair*
- **Stone Table:** The table on which Aslan is slain by the White Witch
- **Aslan's How:** A mound built over the Stone Table on which Aslan was sacrificed
- **Cair Paravel:** Capital of Narnia and the seat of Peter, Susan, Edmund, and Lucy during their golden reign
- **Lantern Waste:** The empty world that Digory and Polly enter in *The Magician's Nephew;* the children see Aslan's creation of Narnia here

For Dummies: Bestselling Book Series for Beginners

C.S. Lewis & Narnia

FOR DUMMIES®

by Richard Wagner

Wiley Publishing, Inc.

C.S. Lewis & Narnia For Dummies®

Published by
Wiley Publishing, Inc.
111 River St.
Hoboken, NJ 07030-5774
www.wiley.com

WILEY

About the Author

Richard Wagner is author of *The Gospel Unplugged* and several books in the *For Dummies* series, including *Christianity For Dummies* and *Christian Prayer For Dummies*. He is also publisher of Digitalwalk.com, a Web site for challenging and encouraging Christians living in a digital, postmodern age. Richard has been an avid student of C.S. Lewis's works for over 20 years. He lives in Princeton, Massachusetts, with his lovely wife and three zany but terrific boys.

Dedication

To Jack, the master himself . . . Further up, further in.

Author's Acknowledgments

When you look at the works of C.S. Lewis, you can see the influence that other people — authors, colleagues, and friends — had on his writing. I feel much the same about *C.S. Lewis & Narnia For Dummies*. There are several people that I'd like to acknowledge who helped shape and guide this book, sometimes directly and sometimes indirectly.

Three other authors contributed their expertise to this book. I'd like to express my thanks to them for their involvement and acknowledge their contributions:

David Gentleman (Anna Marie College) wrote Chapters 15 and 18, focusing on *Mere Christianity* and Lewis's perspective on major topics.

Dr. Ian C. Story (Trent University) is an expert on *Till We Have Faces* and as such wrote Chapter 14.

Amy Vail (Baylor University) wrote Chapter 12 on the Space Trilogy.

I would also like to thank several others who were involved in this project. I must begin with the editing team: Chrissy Guthrie, for her masterful job of handling the project and her keen instinct for knowing what was essential and not so essential to include in the book; Elizabeth Rea, for her editing prowess and for ensuring that the text spoke well to modern readers; and Dr. Dave Neuhouser, for his thoughtful insights and ever-watchful eye that ensured the accuracy of all things Lewis.

Thanks also go to Kathy Cox for working with me for over 18 months to get this project off the ground.

My good friends Flip and Cherri Burrer deserve special mention as being the people who suggested this book idea in the first place. (You never know what's going to happen if you give me a book idea.)

Finally, my wife and boys were far more than just spectators in the writing of this book. Their zeal and interest in seeing this book come to fruition was such an encouragement throughout the writing process. Kimberly is always the first person to proof my chapters and provides the feedback that I trust the most. My boys were my in-house Narnia fanatics who continually tried to stump me with Narnia trivia. (Sorry boys, your dad is just too good!)

Publisher's Acknowledgments

We're proud of this book; please send us your comments through our Dummies online registration form located at www.dummies.com/register/.

Some of the people who helped bring this book to market include the following:

Acquisitions, Editorial, and Media Development

Project Editor: Christina Guthrie

Acquisitions Editor: Kathy Cox

Copy Editor: Elizabeth Rea

Editorial Program Assistant: Courtney Allen

Technical Editor: Dave Neuhouser, PhD

Editorial Manager: Christine Meloy Beck

Editorial Assistants: Hanna Scott, Melissa Bennett, Nadine Bell

Cover Photos: © Daniela Richardson/2005

Cartoons: Rich Tennant, www.the5thwave.com

Composition Services

Project Coordinator: Shannon Schiller

Layout and Graphics: Jonelle Burns, Andrea Dahl, Lauren Goddard, Stephanie D. Jumper, Heather Ryan, Julie Trippetti

Proofreaders: Leeann Harney, Jessica Kramer, Carl William Pierce, TECHBOOKS Production Services

Indexer: TECHBOOKS Production Services

Special Help
David Gentleman; Ian Storey, PhD; Amy Vail, PhD

Publishing and Editorial for Consumer Dummies

Diane Graves Steele, Vice President and Publisher, Consumer Dummies

Joyce Pepple, Acquisitions Director, Consumer Dummies

Kristin A. Cocks, Product Development Director, Consumer Dummies

Michael Spring, Vice President and Publisher, Travel

Kelly Regan, Editorial Director, Travel

Publishing for Technology Dummies

Andy Cummings, Vice President and Publisher, Dummies Technology/General User

Composition Services

Gerry Fahey, Vice President of Production Services

Debbie Stailey, Director of Composition Services

Contents at a Glance

Table of Contents

Introduction

When most people today are introduced to C.S. Lewis, they know him initially as the author of the best-selling *The Chronicles of Narnia*. Not so with me. My parents — apparently bypassing all sense of parental, moral, and civic responsibility — never introduced me to the classic children's series. Perhaps they thought I'd be scared of the White Witch? Maybe they thought I'd want a lion for a pet? Or perhaps they thought I'd try and jump into a picture on the wall? Only my mom and dad know the real story.

Consequently, I got to know C.S. Lewis in a more roundabout way — through my roommate in college. He began his sophomore year as a normal enough guy, but after reading *Miracles, The Screwtape Letters,* and *The Chronicles of Narnia,* my roommate turned into a something of a C.S. Lewis fanatic. Before long, he was attempting to walk through wardrobes and take voyages down a nearby creek in a canoe he christened the *Dawn Treader.* He even started talking like C.S. Lewis; when, for example, I asked him if it was my turn to clean the room, he'd reply with something like: "Its intrinsic reasonableness shines by its own light."

When I was convinced my roommate would change his first name to "Clive," I knew I had to do something — and quick! So, in haste, I started reading Lewis — to pick up the lingo and talk some sense into my friend. However, after opening the cover of my first book, I was hooked as well and found myself devouring my roommate's collection of Lewis's works, abandoning all thoughts of "fixing" my friend.

Reading Lewis strengthened the relationship I had with my roommate, but more significantly, it transformed my relationship with God. Despite my long-held Christianity, as I entered college I began struggling with intellectual doubts: Does God really exist? Why would a loving God allow evil to take place? How do I know that what I've been taught and believed all my life is really true? Books such as *Mere Christianity* and *The Problem of Pain* gave my faith the intellectual muscle that I was so desperately looking for. Because of Lewis, I began to realize that my beliefs were based on far more than just wishful thinking — they were actually the most reasonable explanations on the market for the major questions of life.

If you don't share my Christian beliefs, though, you can still appreciate the works of C.S. Lewis. In fact, you may be attracted to him simply because he was a great fantasy and sci-fi writer. So, whatever your background — Christian or non-Christian, academic or average Joe, human or Narnian — I invite you to explore the life and works of C.S. Lewis and discover the world of Narnia.

About This Book

While writing *Christian Prayer For Dummies,* I led a church group in a study of Lewis's *The Screwtape Letters.* When some of the group expressed their puzzlement with the text, one couple casually suggested that I write a *For Dummies* book on C.S. Lewis. Their basic idea was that I should take the writings of Lewis and make them more understandable and approachable for normal folks. Great idea, I thought.

Bewilderment is a common reaction to Lewis's works. Apart from *The Chronicles of Narnia,* many readers find Lewis challenging to read. For example, although Lewis targeted *Mere Christianity* at the average British man or woman of the 1940s, the book's philosophical nature and the intellectual level at which it's written can still require a strong effort from even well-read contemporary readers. What's more, some of Lewis's most compelling arguments explaining and defending Christianity are buried deep inside his most theoretical works such as *The Abolition of Man.* Yet, these books are written at a level that doesn't appeal to a large mainstream audience. The result: Some of Lewis's best thinking is read by a small group of people. Even Lewis's less-difficult fictional books — such as *The Chronicles of Narnia, The Great Divorce,* and the space trilogy — leave readers with questions about the author's extensive use of symbolism.

C.S. Lewis & Narnia For Dummies is designed to serve as your guide and traveling companion as you journey both to the world of C.S. Lewis and to a fantastic land called Narnia.

Conventions Used in This Book

When you travel to another city or country, you probably want to speak or at least understand the local lingo. With that idea in mind, note the conventions and definitions detailed in this section, and you're sure to understand the lingo used throughout the book.

Christian definitions and conventions

Several definitions and conventions pertaining to Christianity are particularly noteworthy, and your familiarity with them should make this book and Lewis's works all the more informative. These definitions and conventions include

- *Church* with a capital *C* refers to the *Body of Christ,* or the collective body of Christians throughout the world. Church with a lowercase *c* refers to a local church congregation.

- *Historical Christianity, biblical Christianity,* and *orthodox Christianity* are interchangeable terms. Each speaks of beliefs that historically have been upheld by the Church for 2,000 years. Some of these key beliefs include: God came to Earth as Jesus Christ, who was crucified for the sins of the world and was literally resurrected; the Bible is the authoritative Word of God and is the "bottom line" for matters pertaining to the Christian faith; and people who repent of their sins and believe in Jesus Christ as their savior receive the gift of eternal life.

- *Apologetic* may sound like it refers to a paramedic watching *Apollo 13,* but actually it's a term that means a rational defense of the Christian faith. C.S. Lewis is often considered the most important modern-day *apologist.*

- Bible passages are cited using the standard convention: book chapter:verse. For example, John 3:16 refers to John as the book of the Bible, 3 as the chapter of the book, and 16 as the verse of the chapter.

- Bible verses quoted in *C.S. Lewis & Narnia For Dummies* are from the World English Bible translation (on the Web at `www.worldenglish bible.com`). In this book, I sometimes paraphrase passages to make them more readable.

Formatting

In order to set apart or draw your attention to particular words and phrases, I use the following formatting conventions throughout this book:

- *Italics* are used for emphasis and to highlight terms being defined.
- **Boldface** is used to indicate keywords in explanatory bulleted lists.
- `Monofont` text is used for Web addresses.

What You're Not to Read

In this book, I explore the basics for gaining a deeper understanding of the works of C.S. Lewis and his world of Narnia. However, I do cover some topics that you can feel free to skip over, at least on your first reading of this book. The sections that you have permission to skip are

✔ **Paragraphs marked with the Technical Stuff icon.** Any text shown beside this icon is more technical or philosophical in nature. It's really quite interesting (Hey, I wrote it!), but you don't miss out on anything essential if you skip over it.

✔ **Sidebars.** The shaded boxes you see scattered throughout the book are kind of like rest stops on an interstate highway: They're great breaks from the normal flow, but you're not obligated to read each one.

Foolish Assumptions

In writing this book, I made the following assumptions about you:

✔ You may or may not have read Lewis before. If you have read Lewis, you want to know more about the meaning behind what you've read. If you've never cracked any of his books, you'd like to know what Lewis is all about but have neither the time nor the inclination to read through his books in their entirety.

✔ You may or may not know anything about Narnia, C.S. Lewis, or his works.

✔ In chapters that discuss specific books, you have either read those books and know the endings, or, if you haven't read them, you don't mind being clued in on what happens. In other words, I include "spoilers."

✔ You may be a Christian, or you may know little about Christianity and the Bible.

✔ You think that "Clive Staples" is an absolutely horrible name that Lewis's parents inflicted on him. (Don't feel bad. C.S. Lewis agreed with you — he much preferred the nickname "Jack.")

How This Book Is Organized

C.S. Lewis & Narnia For Dummies is divided into five parts, which are described in the following sections.

Part 1: C.S. Lewis: Christian Apologist and Storyteller

In Part I, I introduce you to C.S. Lewis, and you get to know who this gifted scholar and author was and how his life's experiences shaped his writings. This part chronicles how this dyed-in-the-wool atheist was transformed into arguably the 20th century's most brilliant defender of Christianity. The chapters in this part also examine the close relationship that Lewis had with J.R.R. Tolkien and other intellectual and literary giants of England in the mid-20th century.

Part II: All Things Narnia: Voyaging to the World of Aslan

Part II transports you to the fantasy world of Narnia. You get a peek at the meaning behind each of the books in *The Chronicles of Narnia*. You also discover the ideas that shaped Lewis's writings and understand the symbolism behind Narnian history, geography, events, and characters. Finally, you explore the many parallels between the Narnian Chronicles and the Christian faith.

Part III: Tell Me More Stories: Lewis's Other Novels and Fantasies

Although Narnia was Lewis's best-known children series, he wrote many stories for adults as well. In Part III, you explore Lewis's other novels and fantasies, including *The Screwtape Letters, The Great Divorce*, the space trilogy, *The Pilgrim's Regress*, and *Till We Have Faces*.

Part IV: Getting Real: Discovering Lewis's Nonfiction

C.S. Lewis is considered by many to be the most significant modern-day defender of the Christian faith. Part IV focuses on Lewis's major nonfiction Christian apologetic books, all of which are considered classics today: *Mere*

Christianity, The Problem of Pain, and *The Abolition of Man.* As you dive into each of these works, I make it easy to understand the essential points that Lewis makes in them. Also, in this section, you delve into some of the topics discussed in Lewis's other nonfiction works, including *Miracles, The Four Loves,* and *Letters to Malcolm: Chiefly on Prayer.*

Part V: The Part of Tens

In Part V, I provide a variety of resources to help round out your understanding of C.S. Lewis, Narnia, and his other writings. You discover ways to better read Lewis as well as where to go to explore Lewis and Narnia even further. Finally, because Lewis was an avid, lifelong reader, I include his recommendations on authors you should read if you like his works.

In addition, an appendix, located at the end of the book, provides a complete list of all Lewis's books.

Icons Used in This Book

Throughout the book, you'll discover nifty little icons beside certain paragraphs. In addition to their artistic appeal, they indicate particular kinds of information that you'll find useful:

The Remember icon is much like having a yellow highlighter built right into the pages of the book. These sections contain key ideas to keep in mind in order to better understand Lewis's works.

The Tip icon marks a section that contains practical tidbits of information.

The Technical Stuff icon indicates information that's technical, philosophical, theoretical, or in some way complicated. You can read these sections, but don't lose sleep if you feel like skipping 'em.

If you ever watch quiz shows on TV or play board games, you know many people are fascinated with trivia — interesting, non-essential facts about a particular subject. The Trivia icon marks a section that contains information that may not be essential to know, but these sorts of details can enrich your overall appreciation of Lewis and his books.

Heed the Warning icon. These sections help you steer clear of misunderstandings that you may run into when reading Lewis.

Where to Go from Here

It's perfectly okay to read *C.S. Lewis & Narnia For Dummies* from cover to cover. If you do, you'll find the topics are ordered logically. I start with a look at the life of C.S. Lewis and then move on to his fictional and nonfictional works. However, this book is designed as a reference book, so you don't have to read it from start to finish. If you prefer, you can jump to a specific subject. Consider, for example, the following topics for exploration:

- For a mini-biography of C.S. Lewis, read Chapters 2 and 3.

- For an all-expenses paid trip to the world of Narnia, read Chapters 4, 5, 6, and 7.

- For an examination of the Christian symbolism found in Narnia, read Chapters 8 and 9.

- If you think your life sucks and you'd like a glimpse of heaven, check out Chapter 11.

- Are you a skeptic of Christianity or have many probing questions about the faith? Explore Chapters 15 through 18.

Part I
C.S. Lewis: Christian Apologist and Storyteller

The 5th Wave   By Rich Tennant

In this part . . .

I know you're anxious to jump off into the fantasy world of Narnia and better understand the cool logic and reasoning of this master Christian apologist. But before you do so, let me introduce you to the man himself, C.S. Lewis. With a crash course in Lewis as an author, scholar, and Christian, you can better appreciate his fictional and non-fictional works.

Chapter 1

C.S. Lewis's Gift to the World

Great authors usually become so by achieving greatness in a particular genre of writing. J.R.R. Tolkien, for example, is revered for his fantasies *The Hobbit* and *The Lord of the Rings*. William Shakespeare will forever be known as the master of the dramatic play, and Lord Byron is heralded for his romantic poetry. C.S. Lewis, however, has done what so few have done before: write classic works across a number of genres. John Ruskin once said, "All books are divisible into two classes; the books of the hour and the books of all time." Time has proven that a large part of the Lewis collection falls into the latter category.

What's more, Lewis's influence extends beyond the pages of his books. Modern films explore not only his fantasy world of Narnia but also his short-lived romance with his wife, Joy. And, in one of America's most prestigious universities, perhaps the most popular class for several years has been one that contrasts Lewis's and Sigmund Freud's views on God. Finally, as Chapter 19 outlines, various C.S. Lewis Societies, Web sites, festivals, and annual conferences both in Britain and North America allow people to cultivate their appreciation of his books as well as explore connections between what Lewis wrote in his time and today's pressing issues (see Chapter 18 for details).

As you start your journey into the world of C.S. Lewis, this chapter introduces you to the author and scholar, highlights his many works, and considers his legacy, which grows more significant with each passing year.

Catching a Glimpse of C.S. Lewis

Before you explore the world of Narnia and Lewis's other Christian writing, take a moment to get to know C.S. Lewis (shown in Figure 1-1) and find out what made him tick. I provide a sound bite type of summary here, but if you want to get a much fuller picture of Lewis's fascinating life, check out Chapters 2 and 3.

Growing up and losing faith

C.S. Lewis was born in 1898 in Belfast, Ireland. His given name, which he wasn't particularly fond of, was Clive Staples. Lewis decided at an early age that he liked the name Jack much better, and his friends came to know him by that nickname throughout his life. Lewis and his older brother Warnie were extremely close when they were young and enjoyed a strong relationship throughout their lifetimes.

Unlike other kids his age, Jack didn't spend his free time playing ball in his backyard or hanging around on the street corner with neighborhood pals. Instead, he usually kept himself busy playing indoors for hours on end. (Warnie had been sent to boarding school by this time, so Jack was on his own for entertainment.) He conducted countless explorations of his family's large and rather eccentric house, insatiably read his parents' library of books, and wrote about an imaginary world of talking animals called Animal-Land (which, as Chapter 4 discusses, wasn't anything like Narnia). These childhood experiences helped give birth to a rich imagination and a deep love for fantasy and fairy tales. Lewis later called this inner part of him "the imaginative man," and it was something he never outgrew.

Lewis's childhood wonderland fell apart suddenly when he was ten years old. His mother died of cancer, leaving Jack and Warnie in the care of their father, Albert Lewis. Unfortunately, Albert was so distraught by the loss of his wife that he really didn't know what to do with Jack. Feeling unable to care for him, Albert sent Jack to join Warnie at boarding school. Over the next few years, Jack and Warnie found themselves in a series of different boarding schools, some of which made negative and even traumatic impressions on young Jack. Eventually, Lewis's father allowed him to hop off the boarding school merry-go-round and instead be taught during his high school years by a personal tutor named William Kirkpatrick. Kirkpatrick was a no-nonsense academic, relentless in teaching Lewis how to think and reason. Under his tutelage, Lewis not only excelled in a classical education, but he also developed an amazing knack for logical argument, which he used throughout his life. This period of learning gave birth to that other core part of Lewis, what I call "the logical man."

Figure 1-1:
Author and
scholar
C.S. Lewis.

renounced his faith during his teen years and began calling himself an atheist. Some of the factors that led to his decision included the disillusionment resulting from his mother's death, various literary and artistic influences, and negative peer and teacher influences at boarding school.

Lewis was ready to enter college during the height of World War I, but like other British young men of his age, he did his patriotic duty and enlisted in the army to fight the Germans. His time on the front lines in France was devastating in that he lost close friends and became sufficiently injured to return to England. After the war ended, Lewis entered University College at Oxford University (Oxford is comprised of many smaller "colleges") and later graduated in 1923.

Discovering real Christianity

Feeling suited to the academic life, Lewis decided to try to attain a position at Oxford following his graduation. In 1925, he was hired by Magdalen College, Oxford, where he served as don (teacher) in English until 1954. (In 1954, he left Oxford to become professor of Medieval and Renaissance English at Cambridge and held this position for the rest of his life.)

By the time Lewis was in his thirties, his search for truth brought him back again to Christianity's doorstep. Through a combination of books and late night discussions with friends including J.R.R. Tolkien, Lewis became convinced of the truth of Christianity and converted to the faith in 1931. (Chapter 3 takes a much closer look at Lewis's journey from atheism to the Christian faith.)

Lewis wrote two books of poetry before becoming a Christian, but his literary career really took off a few years after his conversion. Starting in the mid-1930s, he went on a publishing spree that is almost unparalleled, publishing one great and memorable book after the other for nearly 30 years. (Check out the appendix for a complete listing.) It was during this period of his life that he formed the famous Inklings literary group, which is discussed in Chapter 3.

Leaving behind a legacy

Lewis's health deteriorated significantly in his last years, making it difficult for him to maintain his work at Cambridge and his prolific writing career. Then, on November 22, 1963, on the very same day the world had their eyes on the assassination of John F. Kennedy in Dallas, Texas, Lewis quietly passed away while sitting in his armchair at his countryside home in Oxford. Lewis was 64 years old when he died, just a week away from his 65th birthday.

Lewis was popular during his lifetime, but as the past decades have shown, his stature and renown have only increased since his death. Yet, as you discover throughout this book, the seeds of what makes Lewis so revered and loved today lie not as much in his scholarly successes at Oxford or the influence of his "big league" literary friends. What makes him such a unique author are those two parts of him that he developed during his early, formative years — the imaginative man and the logical man. Upon these blocks his literary legacy is built. Lewis is a logical, calculating intellectual who never outgrew fairy tales.

Tipping a Hat to the Six Hats of Lewis

Younger readers know C.S. Lewis as the Narnia guy. Christians see him as a modern-day knight, an ardent defender of their faith. Oxford and Cambridge students during the mid-20th century saw him as the charismatic English lecturer and debater whom no one wanted to challenge. His friends knew him simply as Jack, the personable, witty man they liked to hang around. Clearly, Lewis was a man who wore several different hats in his life.

By looking at each of the facets of Lewis's life highlighted in this section, you get a stronger grasp on Lewis as a person and a professional.

Lewis as children's author

With the success of *The Chronicles of Narnia,* both in print and on TV and movie screens, mainstream audiences may assume that Lewis is best known for his classic children's series. Ironically, Lewis turned to writing Narnia only after he was already well entrenched as a top-selling Christian author and "popular theologian."

Lewis first dreamed up the idea of what became *The Lion, the Witch and the Wardrobe* in 1939. But he never completed the story and ended up putting the idea on the back burner for more than ten years. Eventually, after his flurry of Christian nonfiction books in the 1940s, the idea of a children's book resurfaced in his mind. His interest in publishing the book received little support from his publisher, who thought such a move into children's fare could damage Lewis's reputation. What's more, as I discuss in Chapter 3, some of Lewis's closest friends were also less than enthusiastic. J.R.R. Tolkien, in particular, disliked *The Lion, the Witch and the Wardrobe* from the start and never developed an appreciation for the Narnian tales.

Eventually, Lewis's publisher said that if Lewis was actually going to write a children's book, at the very least he should make it part of a children's series. In so doing, *The Chronicles of Narnia* was born. From 1950 to 1956, Lewis published one book each year as part of the Narnian series: *The Lion, the Witch and the Wardrobe* (1950), *Prince Caspian* (1951), *The Voyage of the "Dawn Treader"* (1952), *The Horse and His Boy* (1953), *The Silver Chair* (1954), *The Magician's Nephew* (1955), and *The Last Battle* (1956). You can read all about *The Chronicles of Narnia* in Chapters 4 through 9.

Lewis as popular Christian spokesman

In the 1981 film, *Chariots of Fire,* Eric Liddell — the man who wouldn't run on Sundays — is challenged by his brother to run in the Olympics as a Christian witness: "What we need now is a muscular Christian. To make folks sit up and notice." Similarly, I like to imagine someone around C.S. Lewis exhorting him in the same way before he started writing his popular Christian books. "What we need now is an intellectual Christian," the person might say. "To make folks sit up and notice. Write in God's name and let the world stand back in wonder."

Lewis was exactly what the Christian Church needed in the mid-20th century. He was the person who could "make folks sit up and notice." In a world barraged by "isms" — Darwinism, Communism, theological liberalism, relativism, and secularism — that attacked biblical Christianity, Lewis provided intellectual beef to the idea that Christianity was every bit as true and relevant in the mid-20th century as it ever was.

Lewis's emergence as a popular Christian spokesman may have begun with his book *The Problem of Pain* (see Chapter 15) in 1940, but his broadcasts on the BBC in the early 1940s are what made him known to the mainstream public. These talks allowed him to connect with people who wouldn't have dreamed of reading his books otherwise. Always articulate, yet entertaining and down-to-earth, Lewis had a natural talent for live radio and connected well with audiences. Eventually, these broadcast talks became the basis for *Mere Christianity,* the most popular of his apologetics works (see Chapter 16). During the 1940s, Lewis wrote other nonfiction works as well, such as *The Problem of Pain, The Abolition of Man* (see Chapter 17), and *Miracles.*

At this time, Lewis's popularity began to spread beyond the borders of Britain as American readers discovered his writings. In fact, by 1946, Lewis had gained enough notoriety in the United States that he was featured on the cover of *Time* magazine as well as *The Atlantic Monthly,* the latter of which dubbed him the "apostle to the skeptics."

What made Lewis so popular was not his intellect — there were plenty of smart Christians already — but rather his ability to effectively communicate his thoughts to the average Joe (and little Joey, with his Narnian tales). He had an uncanny ability to make his ideas approachable and understandable without watering them down or appearing to talk down to his audience.

Lewis as fiction author

Lewis loved writing fiction more than anything else. He obviously used his imaginative side in *The Chronicles of Narnia* (covered in Part II of this book), but he also turned out several adult fiction books over the course of some 25 years.

His first fiction work published after his conversion to Christianity is *The Pilgrim's Regress,* an allegorical look at the search for Joy and truth. I focus on this work in Chapter 13. Lewis also wrote a science fiction trilogy (*Out of the Silent Planet, Perelandra,* and *That Hideous Strength*) that remains highly popular. Chapter 12 examines this trilogy. His other fictional books include *The Screwtape Letters* (see Chapter 10), *The Great Divorce* (see Chapter 11), and *Till We Have Faces* (see Chapter 14).

Lewis as scholar

Given the impressive array of books written by Lewis, you may think that he was a full-time author. However, amazingly, he wrote only in his spare time, usually in the evening after a long day at work. As I explain earlier in this chapter in the section "Introducing C.S. Lewis," Lewis's day job was teaching at Oxford (see Figure 1-2) and later at Cambridge. He was an extremely popular lecturer and regularly addressed halls that were standing room only.

Figure 1-2:
Lewis spent
much of his
professional
life stomp-
ing the
grounds of
Magdalen
College,
Oxford.

Topical Press Agency/Stringer

To the surprise of many contemporary readers, Lewis also wrote several books on English literature and literary criticism, most notably *English Literature in the Sixteenth Century Excluding Drama.* Many of these works remain in print; you can find a description of them in the appendix.

Given the high regard to which Lewis is held today as an intellectual and aca-demic, you'd think he was the toast of Oxford in his day. Yet many academics at Oxford looked down on the "popular theology" and evangelistic fervor in many of Lewis's books.

Lewis as friend

With the fragmented, transient nature of today's society, most people place less and less importance on maintaining lifelong friendships. In contrast, Lewis valued friendship very highly, and he had many relationships that he cultivated throughout his life.

Most interesting to people today is Lewis's relationship with a circle of friends known as the Inklings. The Inklings, discussed in detail in Chapter 3, were made up of many of Lewis's closest friends, including authors J.R.R. Tolkien and Owen Barfield and novelist Charles Williams. The group met once a week to discuss various topics of interest and read aloud chapters of books as they were being written.

Five interesting aspects of Lewis

Throughout this book, you find out a lot about C.S. Lewis. But as you begin your journey, some lesser known facts are helpful to sizing up Lewis and getting a grasp on what sort of man he was and why he wrote what he did.

✔ **Lewis was a guy who liked to have a good time.** If you know his title, "Professor of English Literature," and watch the portrayal of Lewis in the film *Shadowlands,* you may conclude that he must have been a reserved, stoic scholar. But his friends would tell you otherwise: Jack was a guy who loved to laugh and had a keen sense of humor. He loved to chum around with friends and spend time drinking pints at the Eagle and Child pub, where the Inklings regularly met.

✔ **Lewis was a fanatical reader.** Lewis was a man who loved books. He obviously liked writing them, but he probably enjoyed reading them even more. With no television or video games to distract him, he began reading at a very young age and never lost his love for it. Over the course of his lifetime, he read his favorites over and over again, discovering something new to appreciate each time. (Chapter 21 lists several of Lewis's favorite and most influential authors.)

✔ **Lewis distrusted the latest and greatest of anything.** Lewis was wary of the latest trends or fashions of the day, whether they be in culture, literature, philosophy, or technology. He recognized the potential danger of fashionable things: People become enamored with what's hip and plunge "into it because it seem[s] modern and successful." You may call Lewis "old school," but he was never out of touch with what was true. (See Chapter 10 for Lewis's thoughts on how Satan uses fashion as a tool.)

✔ **Lewis and Tolkien were friends, but they were very different men.** Given their enduring friendship, shared Christian beliefs, mutual love for fantasy literature, and academic backgrounds, you may assume that Lewis and Tolkien were like the "Bobbsey twins." Yet, as I explain in Chapters 3 and 6, both were quite different, both as individuals as well as in their approaches to writing.

✔ **Although Lewis's books sold millions, he lived frugally.** When you look at the sales figures for Lewis's books, you may think that he could have been featured on Lifestyles of the Rich and Famous (assuming that program even existed during his day). In reality, Lewis lived a very modest life; he was something of a tightwad when it came to spending money on himself or the Kilns, but he was incredibly generous to others, giving away two-thirds of his income to the Church and various charities.

Lewis as bachelor turned hubby

On the home front, Lewis had quite an unusual lifestyle for the better part of two decades. During World War I, one of his closest friends in the army, Paddy Moore, was killed in action. Primarily out of loyalty to his fallen friend, Lewis looked after Paddy's mother and his sister Maureen for more than twenty years. After a series of rentals, Lewis, his brother, and the Moores purchased a relaxed country residence called the Kilns in 1930. The Kilns became Lewis's permanent home for the remainder of his life.

During the 1950s, the lifelong bachelor began corresponding with an American woman named Joy Davidman Gresham, who was a fan of his books. Through letters and eventually face-to-face visits, Lewis and Joy became dear friends. After Joy divorced her abusive husband, Lewis agreed to marry Joy as a way to enable her and her children to stay in Britain and out of her ex-husband's reach. The relationship between Lewis and Joy may have started as civil marriage, but it eventually blossomed into a deep, passionate love. Sadly, Joy died of cancer just four years into their marriage, striking a blow that Lewis never fully recovered from.

Lewis's Lasting Gift to Readers of All Ages: *The Chronicles of Narnia*

The Chronicles of Narnia is a series of seven children's books that, over the years, has emerged as Lewis's most enduring literary treasure (in spite of his already legendary success in the Christian apologetic and sci-fi genres). The series has sold a staggering 85 million copies in 29 languages — easily out-selling all of Lewis's other books combined.

It's no mere coincidence that the Narnian Chronicles sit comfortably on the bookshelf next to the other classic fantasy series written in the past century: J.R.R. Tolkien's *The Hobbit* and *The Lord of the Rings*. As you can read Chapter 3, C.S. Lewis and J.R.R. Tolkien were good friends and collaborated throughout much of their careers. Although they didn't always agree on what made a great story, Lewis and Tolkien had a mutual love for fairy tales and shared a desire to create mythical worlds that would stand the test of time.

Most best-selling children's books are popular for a season or two but then go out of style quicker than you can say "leisure suit." But the Narnian Chronicles have displayed true staying power for decades now, in part because of the following factors:

- ✔ **Narnia is magical.** Lewis was a master at creating the enchanted world of Narnia and making it a place that people long to return to time and time again. It's beautiful, full of wonder, and inhabited by talking animals, heroic humans, menacing villains, and one-of-a-kind creatures, such as the Marshwiggles and the monopod Duffers.

- ✔ **The stories are adventurous.** Each of the seven books in the series features a thrilling, high-stakes adventure in which good is pitted against evil. The plots engage readers, and Lewis's pace keeps everyone turning the pages.

- ✔ **Narnia reveals something about ourselves.** Readers, old and young alike, identify with the principal characters of the story. Not only do the characters have to defeat evil enemies, but, just as often, they also have to overcome themselves as they face temptations, moral dilemmas, and crises of belief. Like you and I, they aren't just one-dimensional people without fault. For example, I've succumbed to temptation like Edmund does in *The Lion, the Witch and the Wardrobe.* Like Lucy in *Prince Caspian,* too often I've gone along with the crowd rather than done what I know to be right. And like Eustace in *The Voyage of the "Dawn Treader,"* I sometimes find myself whining and complaining.

✔ **Narnia deals with the big issues.** The Narnian Chronicles may be fairy tales, but they aren't escapist or unrealistically imaginative. The stories center around the major issues of life: how the world started and how it's going to end; how sin and evil came into the world; how we can overcome sin and receive redemption; and how we can life lives that matter.

✔ **Narnia assumes "the Tao."** In a world of relativism, in which no one's sure what's good or bad, Narnia is a breath of fresh air for many readers. In Narnia, good is good, and bad is bad. Bravery, chivalry, and honor really do matter, and pride, betrayal, and evil are stomped upon. Narnia is a land built upon what Lewis liked to call the *Tao,* or, as he defines elsewhere, "the belief that certain attitudes are really true, and others really false." (See Chapter 5 for more on absolute values in Narnia and Chapter 17 for a full discussion of the *Tao.*)

✔ **Narnia reveals Christianity.** Although *The Chronicles of Narnia* isn't an allegory (see Chapter 6), Lewis does use characters and plot lines to symbolize Christian truth inside the stories (see Chapters 8 and 9). As a result, many readers have been able to grasp Christianity's core teachings in a way they never would have been able to understand by reading nonfiction alone.

In a world where so much of what you and I watch or read feels like a TV sitcom, Lewis's works stand apart. The Narnian Chronicles have endured because Lewis, like Tolkien with *The Lord of the Rings,* understood that fairy tales capture our sense of wonder in ways that "modern" books do not and therefore never go out of style. In the foreword to Dennis Quinn's *Iris Exiled: A Synoptic History of Wonder* (University Press of America), James V. Schall agrees:

> *The Lord of the Rings and the Chronicles of Narnia arouse our wonder in a way Stephen King or MTV do not . . . This is a world that might not have existed at all or might have been otherwise through human or divine choices that poets and artists can imagine. They do not "create" other worlds, but they can see how this world might have been otherwise.*

Chapter 2

Getting to Know Jack

*I*n person and in print, C.S. Lewis was called many things, but the one name he would prefer you not call him was his given name: Clive Staples. From an early age, Lewis realized that name had to go. So, at the age of four, he insisted on being called "Jacksie," though he later shortened it to simply "Jack." The nickname stuck, and close friends throughout his life called him Jack. In this chapter, you get to know Clive Staples . . . er, Jack . . . by looking at the major milestones and events in his life and exploring how they influenced and shaped his books.

A Lewis divided cannot stand!

In the classic sitcom *Seinfeld,* George Costanza tells his best friend Jerry about the fear he has of letting his girlfriend hang around with his circle of friends. George has divided himself and his life into Relationship George and Independent George, and he's terrified at the prospect of having these two worlds collide. In desperation, he exclaims, "If Relationship George walks through this door, he will kill Independent George. A George divided against itself cannot stand!"

At various times during his life, C.S. Lewis had a similar tendency to compartmentalize different aspects of his life and personality. In his adolescent years, he kept an Inner Lewis all to himself while showing the rest of the world an Outer Lewis. Later, during his teaching days, the Oxford Lewis coexisted with the Country Homeowner Lewis; most people who knew him at the university had no idea of this non-academic side of his life. Even as he gained recognition as an author, his books often led readers to compartmentalize him even more; Christians saw him as Apologist Lewis, children as Narnia Lewis, and scholars as Literary Critic Lewis.

Like George Costanza, a Lewis divided against himself would not have stood. As you explore the multi-faceted life of C.S. Lewis in this chapter, you discover how the various "compartments" worked together to complete the man and enable him to become a legendary author.

Growing Up in Belfast, 1898–1908

C.S. Lewis, shown as a young boy in Figure 2-1, was born on November 29, 1898, to Albert and Flora Lewis. Living in Belfast, Ireland, Albert was a successful attorney known throughout the city for his conviction and integrity. He provided well for his family, although he had a lifelong fear of going "belly up," a phobia that passed on to Jack and persisted even after he was a best-selling author. Living in a region long torn by Catholic and Protestant infighting, the Lewis family was staunchly Protestant. They went to church every Sunday, not so much for the worship but as a statement of the fact that they were Protestants, not Catholics. Jack picked up on his parents' bias and struggled early on with anti-Catholic sentiment.

Figure 2-1:
Jacksie or Jack are fine, but don't call him Clive Staples.

Used by permission of The Marion E. Wade Center, Wheaton College, Wheaton, IL

Albert and Flora were also avid readers who spent their evenings reading for hours on end, and over the years, they developed an extensive library. Although they didn't read to Jack themselves — that duty fell to their nursemaid — they passed on to their children an insatiable love of reading.

Like peas and carrots

Jack's one sibling was a brother three years older named Warren, often called "Warnie." As Forrest Gump would say, Jack and Warren were "like peas and carrots," best friends who even lived in the same house for much of their lives. Lewis writes of Warnie in his autobiography *Surprised by Joy,* "We were allied, not to say confederates, from the first."

The magical world of Little Lea

The Lewis family's first home, Dundela Villas, was within sight of Belfast Lough, which always saw many ships coming and going. Both Jack and Warren spent hours watching the ships move through the lough, and Warren, in fact, developed a love of boats while at Dundela Villas that would last his lifetime. When Jack was 7 years old, however, the Lewis family moved to another Belfast house they called Little Lea, shown in Figure 2-2. Little Lea was a large three-story house that was anything but "cookie cutter." With a large sprawling attic spanning the entire house, tunnels here and there, and various nooks and crannies, Little Lea was totally impractical. And Jack and Warren loved it! They played throughout the house, climbing in the attic and burrowing in the tunnels. Undoubtedly, some of Jack's memories from Little Lea contributed to his ideas for *The Magician's Nephew,* the first book in *The Chronicles of Narnia* series. Lewis said that Little Lea was far more than a house — it was a character in the story of his life.

As a child, Jack was a homebody. If you've read Frances Hodgson Burnett's classic *The Secret Garden,* think of Jack as Colin Craven without the leg braces. Jack played outside and rode his bike occasionally, but much of his childhood days were spent playing indoors at Little Lea. Jack was stuck inside primarily because his parents felt he was a sickly kid, overly suscepti-ble to the common childhood diseases of the day, such as typhus and typhoid. Therefore, cold or dreary weather meant "Little Lea lock-up" for Jack. And given the fact that Lewis lived in Ireland, he had to stay indoors almost year-round.

Little Jack, however, never really considered being stuck indoors a bad thing. It have gave him plenty of time to let his imagination run wild. In addition to his adventures around the house, he read voraciously and quickly became a fan of Beatrix Potter's books (particularly *Squirrel Nutkin*). However, Jack usu-ally bypassed children's books in favor of the ones in his parents' collection. To further amuse himself, he also started writing stories. Warnie and Jack dreamed up an imaginary country that they called Animal-Land, with talking animals and gallant knights. Although these stories were simplistic, they helped prepare Jack for the enchanted world of Narnia that he would create later in life.

Figure 2-2:
Little
Lea, the
childhood
home of
Lewis.

Used by permission of The Marion E. Wade Center, Wheaton College, Wheaton, IL

Tragedy strikes Little Lea

Jack's childhood of wonder, however, didn't last. The bubble burst when he was 10 years old and Flora died of cancer, an event that forever rocked the Lewis household.

The death of their mom brought Jack and Warnie closer than ever, but the tragedy also distanced the brothers from their father. Albert had a terrible time dealing with his grief, and instead of considering the impact of the loss on his sons, he became lost in his own world.

By the time of his mother's death, Warnie was already attending boarding school. Given his problems with his father, Jack became convinced that the best thing that he could do would be to join Warnie at school and get out of Little Lea.

As the boys grew older, Albert (see Figure 2-3) proved to be a clumsy father. He usually meant well and worked hard to be a friend to his sons, but Albert seemed to have the knack of always saying or doing the wrong thing. When the boys returned for visits to Little Lea, Albert invariably suffocated them, invading their personal space and making them anxious to leave. Over the years, Jack developed a strained relationship with his dad and never really got on well with him, as much as they tried.

Used by permission of The Marion E. Wade Center, Wheaton College, Wheaton, IL

School Daze, 1908–1916

After his mother's death and up until he was ready for college, Lewis attended a series of boarding schools before being home-schooled by a tutor during the final years of the British equivalent of high school.

Wynyard: The school from Hell

After Albert Lewis decided it was best for Jack to go to boarding school, he enrolled his son in 1908 at the same English school that Warren was attending, Wynyard School in Hertfordshire. It's almost impossible to imagine a worse choice: Wynyard was an awful school, something right out of a Dickens novel. The building itself was dreary and physically run-down, but worst of all, the headmaster was a cruel, sadistic tyrant. If you've read another Frances Hodgson Burnett classic, *A Little Princess,* think of the Wynyard headmaster as Miss Munchkin on steroids. Warnie eventually was pulled out by his father, but for some reason, Jack's pleas to withdraw from Wynyard fell on deaf ears. Jack was finally able to leave the "school from Hell," as he called it, after his second year, but only because the school had to close due to lack of funds. (Evidently, evil, brutal school principals were as bad for marketing then as they are today.) Looking back on his experience at Wynyard, Jack always maintained that he learned little academically during his tenure at the school. However, Lewis did say one good thing about the headmaster. In *Surprised by Joy,* he writes, "I can also say that though [the headmaster] taught geometry cruelly, he taught it well. He forced us to reason, and I have been the better for those geometry lessons all my life."

Quick camping at Campbell

After leaving Wynyard, Jack returned to Ireland and enrolled (in July of 1910) at Campbell College, a Belfast boarding school close to Little Lea. But that winter, just as Lewis adjusted and started to like the place, he developed a bad cough, prompting his father to withdraw Jack from school due to his poor health.

Coming of age at Cherbourg

As soon as Jack was fit as a fiddle, Albert enrolled him at another English boarding school named Cherbourg, in Malvern. At Cherbourg, several changes occurred in Jack's young life. First, because Cherbourg was far better than the other schools he previously attended, his education began in earnest, and his academic prowess (when compared to his peers) started to surface. Beyond academics, Jack also was exposed to the temptations and issues of the wider world. A young, fashion-conscious schoolmaster set Lewis onto everything that was popular and hip. While at the school, Jack began a lifelong habit of smoking, and most significantly, he moved away from his Christian beliefs and became an all-out atheist.

In the vacuum created by his loss of faith, a thunder appeared from the north. As he dove into reading Norse mythology and listening to different kinds of music, Jack became obsessed with all things northern — or "northernness," as he called it. Over the next three years, northernness was the focus of Lewis's life. Related to his love of Norse mythology, he became fascinated by northern lands. He judged anything from the north — whether it was northern Britain or Scandinavia — as inherently superior to anything from the south.

While at Cherbourg, Jack became enamored with the music of Richard Wagner. (Not me, goodness, no! I can't even hold a tune. I'm speaking of the *other* Richard Wagner, the 19th-century German composer.) To Jack, Wagner was the "Official Composer of Northernness," because in his music, Jack experienced the mystery, power, and vigor that he associated with the north. (I recall a similar time in my life when I was lost in the world of Milli Vanilli. Lost, that is, until I discovered they lip-synched their songs.)

Ultimately, it was in northernness and Wagner that Jack experienced "Joy," which he considered a deep yearning for something unattainable. (See the "Exploring Lewis's Lifelong Journey Towards Joy" section at the end of chapter.) Through his obsession with northernness, Jack became two different people: an Inner Lewis that was obsessed with his inner imaginative life and an Outer Lewis that the rest of Cherbourg saw.

Malvern bound

After finishing up at Cherbourg, Jack was old enough to go to Malvern College in September of 1913. (Don't be confused by the name; Malvern was a boarding school for high school–age students.) Warren had attended Malvern and loved it, but Jack did not. In fact, he stayed at Malvern for only one school year. Although the academics were solid and he learned a great deal about poetry, Jack despised the relentless social pressures to be popular and the abuses of power by older students. Looking back years later, Jack admitted he became a "prig" (an uppity, stuck-up person) there, assuming an attitude that would take some time to drill out of him.

While at Malvern, Lewis didn't waste his time playing video games or watching *SpongeBob SquarePants,* like many of today's teenagers. Instead, he wrote an opera libretto called *Loki Bound.* (A *libretto* is an opera's story.) Influenced by Norse mythology and the style of Greek dramas, *Loki Bound* tells the pessimistic story of a smart slave boy who rebels against his master Odin and the other gods. If you get the Malvern connection, the evil gods were the older boys at the school, and Loki represented Jack.

Jack desperately wanted out of Malvern. Perhaps learning from his failed attempt to talk his father into withdrawing him from Wynyard years before, Jack actually threatened suicide if his father didn't take him out of the school. His ploy worked, and Albert reluctantly withdrew him after only one year.

Cramming with the Great Knock

When Jack returned home from Malvern College, Albert was unsure exactly what to do with his youngest son. He eventually came to the decision that the best solution was to turn to his own former headmaster, William T. Kirkpatrick. Kirkpatrick (nicknamed "Kirk" or the "Great Knock") was a "crammer" (a tutor) and agreed to take Jack on as a student. For the remainder of his high school years, Jack stayed in the village of Great Bookham in Surrey and worked under the ever watchful eye of the Great Knock. At least this once, Albert had made a wise decision concerning Jack.

Kirkpatrick, pictured in Figure 2-4, was quite a character. Although well into his sixties, he was an imposing figure — tall, lean, and muscular — and had a gruff, bold personality to match. Kirkpatrick was always direct and didn't tolerate meaningless chitchat. In his biography *Jack,* George Sayers tells the story of Lewis's arrival at Great Bookham. Jack quipped on the ride that the scenery was "wilder" than he had expected. Kirkpatrick responded by demanding to know what Jack meant by "wildness" and what his original assumptions were based upon. Lewis admitted that he had no basis "to have any opinion whatever on the subject."

Figure 2-4:
William T. Kirkpatrick, the Great Knock.

Used by permission of The Marion E. Wade Center, Wheaton College, Wheaton, IL

If Lewis cultivated his imaginative self at Cherbourg and Malvern, he developed his logical self at Great Bookham. Kirkpatrick was a logician with a brilliant mind. Lewis wrote that "if ever a man came near to being a pure logical entity, that man was Kirk." Indeed, Kirkpatrick's influence on Jack for the next two and a half years was profound and laid the foundation for much of what Lewis achieved later in life as an academic, debater, and apologist. Above all, from Kirk Jack acquired both a love and an ability for logical argument that he carried with him the rest of his life.

Great Bookham proved to be the ideal learning environment for Lewis. Kirkpatrick didn't need to hold Jack's hand through his studies; rather, he gave Jack considerable independence and only provided occasional steering or guidance. Lewis devoured classic literature and developed literary tastes that lasted his lifetime. He even learned Greek, Italian, and French — not for speaking, but so that he could read classic literature in its original languages.

As brilliant as Lewis was, however, the monkey on his back was science and math. He was weak in these subjects, and Kirkpatrick was never able to make much progress with Jack on these fronts. In fact, math nearly became a stumbling block that would have prevented Jack from ever pursuing an academic and writing career. He might have been the most brilliant gas station attendant ever if it hadn't been for World War I.

A Great War and a Great College, 1916–1925

Jack may have lived in a learning cocoon at Great Bookham (see the previous section), but the world around him was rapidly changing with the start of World War I. In fact, his brother Warren, who had already enlisted with the Royal Army Service Corps, went to France with the British Expeditionary Force soon after the war began.

Duty-bound: Entering the O.T.C. through Oxford

By the time Jack graduated from high school, the Great War was in full throttle and dragging on with no end in sight. Jack wanted to go to Oxford for his collegiate education, and because he was Irish, he actually could have avoided serving in the British army and begun his studies immediately if he had so chosen. But like other British young men his age, Jack felt the call of duty and decided to enlist. However, he knew that gaining acceptance to Oxford before enlisting would make him eligible to join the Officer's Training Corps and receive a commission.

In December of 1916, Lewis took the entrance exam to Oxford. University College awarded him one of its three open scholarships for studying the classics. However, actually getting accepted into the school required another step: a second test called Responsions. As brilliant as Lewis was in the classics, he failed miserably in the math portion of the test on two separate occasions.

Nervous in the service

In spite of not passing Responsions, Jack was able to live at Oxford and pursue some studies as he began training in the O.T.C. (Officer's Training Corps), preparing for military service. He soon moved over to Keble College, Oxford, and joined a cadet battalion in training for gaining a commission. The most significant event during this time was the formation of his close friendship with his roommate Edward Francis Courtnay "Paddy" Moore, a friendship that would change Lewis's life for years to come.

Jack was eventually given the rank of second lieutenant of the Third Battalion of the Somerset Light Infantry as he headed out to France in November of 1917. In France during the winter of 1917 to 1918, Jack saw some action and had a brief bout with trench fever. But it was the spring of 1918 that proved to be a difficult time for him. Paddy Moore was killed in action, and what's more, Lewis was seriously injured with shrapnel wounds during the Battle of Arras in April. He was hospitalized and eventually had to be transferred back to London in May. He didn't realize it at the time, but his fighting days were over, because the Great War ended before he was fully recovered.

Interestingly, Jack loved to share war stories with friends, but he never wrote about his wartime experiences.

Studying at Oxford

After the war officially ended and he was released from the army, Jack (shown as a young adult in Figure 2-5) eagerly returned to Oxford to pursue his studies. Amazingly, if Oxford hadn't waived the requirement for Responsions for returning servicemen, the brilliant Lewis would have been up a creek without a paddle, on the short end of the stick, at the end of his rope . . . well, you get the idea. (See the section "Duty-bound: Entering the O.T.C. through Oxford" for more info on Jack's Oxford acceptance.) Jack thus owed his entrance into Oxford (and, frankly, his entire future as a scholar and legendary author) to his rather undistinguished military service.

Lewis's writing career officially kicked off when he was still a first-year undergraduate. Writing from 1915 to 1919, Lewis produced a collection of poems that was good enough to be published as *Spirits in Bondage* in 1919. He used the pseudonym "Clive Hamilton," a combination of his own given first name and his mother's maiden name. These poems reflect his atheistic worldview at the time. The major themes of the poems are that nature is terrible and that if there's any God, he's powerless in this world. *Spirits in Bondage* received generally positive reviews but didn't generate enough buzz to sell many copies. Expecting more, Jack was quite disappointed with the response and abandoned his dream of becoming a poet.

Keeping his head in his books, Jack graduated with honors in Greats (classical philosophy) in 1922. After graduating, he tried unsuccessfully for a fellowship in Greats at Magdalen College, Oxford. He toyed with the idea of looking for a job as schoolmaster but ultimately decided to return to Oxford to get a master's degree in English Language and Literature.

Figure 2-5:
All the world's before a young Jack.

Used by permission of The Marion E. Wade Center, Wheaton College, Wheaton, IL

While Jack dashed off to Oxford, Warnie remained in the Royal Army Service Corps until his retirement in 1932.

How Lewis "transcended" himself

I once heard Sting say on *Larry King Live* that he didn't much care to listen to other popular music because he always found himself listening to it with a critical ear; he couldn't just enjoy a song for music's sake. When it came to reading other authors, C.S. Lewis sure never had this problem. Hardly anything gave him greater joy than reading a great book. In fact, he read his favorite books dozens of times over the course of his life. "My own eyes are not enough for me," Lewis wrote in *An Experiment in Criticism*, "I will see through those of others." He continued, "Here, as in worship, in love, in moral action, and in knowing, I transcend myself; and am never more myself than when I do."

Oxford and Mrs. Moore, 1925–1940

Following his graduation from Oxford (see the previous section), Jack spent over a year job hunting before he finally secured the position of don (see the next section for an explanation) in the English department at Magdalen College, Oxford, in 1925. A picture of Magdalen appears in Chapter 1.

Life as an Oxford don

In case you "don know," a *don* is a teacher responsible for lecturing and tutoring students one-on-one. In his three decades in this role, Lewis emerged as master of both disciplines. When he met with a student, Jack was always well prepared and expected the student to be ready to defend his paper or argument. Students who worked hard and were willing to be taught invariably loved Lewis. Cocky and lazy students, however, had a much different take: He could be relentless when he wanted to be. Over the years, Lewis finely tuned his lecturing skills, so much so that he became the most popular lecturer in his heyday at Oxford. And, although he spent much of his life working in this role, the truth is that he actually didn't love teaching much, particularly tutoring, and considered it more of a duty. Like a true professional, however, he never communicated that attitude to his students.

When Lewis began his career at Oxford in 1925, several years had passed since he published his collection of short poems, *Spirits in Bondage*. In his spare time, he had been working on an extended narrative poem called *Dymer* and was able to get it published in 1926, once again under the pseudonym Clive Hamilton. The reviews were positive, but sales were a flop, even worse than those of his book of poetry. However, looking back, one shouldn't be surprised at *Dymer*'s public reception. *Dymer* was plum out of fashion — a traditional long poem published at a time in which readers were looking for something far more modern and in vogue.

Life on the home front

While Jack's life teaching at Oxford was standard professorial stuff, his home life was anything but normal: He was living with the mother and sister of his late friend Paddy Moore. You see, after Jack and Paddy became close friends (see "Nervous in the service"), Paddy asked Jack to look after his mother (who was estranged and subsequently divorced from her husband) if he was killed during the war. Lewis took this duty seriously and followed through on the commitment.

Duty was certainly the major factor in this arrangement, but Jack also felt a strong bond with Paddy's mother, Mrs. Janie King Askins Moore, a woman

27 years older than he was. The connection between the two was forged before Paddy and Jack headed off to war, when Paddy invited Jack to spend time at his mother's house in Ireland. Later, when Jack returned injured from France, Mrs. Moore visited him often in the hospital during his recuperation period. His attachment and dependency on her must surely have been magnified considerably by the fact that his father failed to visit him in spite of an earnest plea from Jack to do so.

The exact nature of Jack's feelings towards Mrs. Moore is a matter of speculation. Some believe the attraction was infatuation with an older woman, while others contend Jack viewed her as a surrogate mother, a feeling certainly exacerbated by the dysfunctional nature of his relationship with his father. Around the house, Jack referred to her as "mother," and Mrs. Moore referred to Jack and Warren as "the boys." Figure 2-6 shows a picture of Jack and Mrs. Moore.

Figure 2-6:
Jack (left)
and Mrs.
Moore (far
right).

Used by permission of The Marion E. Wade Center, Wheaton College, Wheaton, IL

It may seem unusual that Lewis lived with Mrs. Moore and her daughter Maureen, but those who spent time at their home never seemed bothered by it or sensed that anything out of the ordinary was going on.

While Jack was still in school, Mrs. Moore and Maureen moved to a rental house just outside of Oxford, and Lewis moved in with them. At the time, Lewis was living on his scholarship money and a modest allowance from his father. The funds would have been sufficient for a single man, but Jack had three people to support. As a result, money was extremely tight, and they often found themselves in dire straights. Their poverty lasted up until the time Jack started teaching at Oxford. Although his new position eventually made things more comfortable, their financial close calls left a lasting impression that he never overcame.

For 11 years, the trio lived in a series of rental houses but finally decided to buy a house for themselves in 1930. By this time, Warnie, who was close to retiring from the military, also joined the party. The unlikely foursome purchased a house in Headington Quarry, three miles from Oxford center. They named the house the Kilns because it had an old, rundown kilns that was at one time used for brick making. You can see a picture of the Kilns in Figure 2-7.

For their share, Jack and Warnie used proceeds from selling their family home, Little Lea (their father Albert had died in 1929). Legally, the Kilns was in Mrs. Moore's name, although she willed it to the Lewis brothers, who in turn left it to Maureen after their own deaths. They paid £3,300 for the house and eight acres of surrounding land. Sadly, if they could have drummed up £300 more, they could have bought a large field beside the house. Years later, this land was filled with rows of houses, detracting from the otherwise pristine nature of the Kilns.

Figure 2-7:
The Kilns was Jack's home for over thirty years.

Used by permission of The Marion E. Wade Center, Wheaton College, Wheaton, IL

A day in the life

If you could have peeked at C.S. Lewis's PDA (that's a Personal Digital Assistant, for my less gadget-obsessed readers) during his time at Oxford, his typical work day would have looked something like this:

✔ 7:15 a.m.: Morning tea

✔ 8–8:15 a.m.: Chapel

✔ 8:15–9 a.m.: Breakfast and correspondence

✔ 9 a.m.–1 p.m.: Tutorials and/or lectures

✔ 1–5 p.m.: Lunch, afternoon walks, and tea at the Kilns (usually picked up at Oxford by Maureen)

✔ 5–7 p.m.: More tutorials and/or lectures

✔ 7:15–8 p.m.: Dinner

✔ After 8 p.m.: Society gatherings

Mrs. Moore had a kind nature and was quite hospitable to house guests, but she also had a very controlling personality. She seemed to have little concern for the writing and other work that Lewis tried to do at the Kilns and constantly asked Jack to do one chore after another around the house. (Hmmm . . . this scenario sounds hauntingly familiar to this author.) His time-consuming responsibilities at home must have handicapped his work to some extent. However, on the positive side, his complicated home life provided a broader perspective on the everyday life of common folk than he would have gotten as an academic living 24/7 at Oxford.

Jack lived in these two distinct worlds — academic and domestic — and kept them isolated from each other. He stayed at school during weekdays (except for regular afternoon visits home) and then came to the Kilns on weekends. He rarely discussed his home life while at school. In fact, many students thought he was a single guy living full-time at the college!

New friends, new outlook

At Oxford, Jack started developing new friendships with people like J.R.R. Tolkien and Hugo Dyson, out of which arose the Inklings literary group in the mid-1930s. For more information on Tolkien and the Inklings, flip to Chapter 3.

During this period of his life, Jack underwent the most significant change in his life. From 1926 to 1931, he gradually became a believer in Christianity. This change is discussed fully in Chapter 3.

Lewis's writing career finally began to take off during the 1930s. He wrote about his journey to Christianity in the 1933 book *A Pilgrim's Regress,* which

I cover in depth in Chapter 13. In 1935, Jack wrote his first scholarly work, *Allegory of Love.* With *Allegory of Love,* he began to gain a reputation as a top literary critic. Folks within Oxford sat up and took notice of this rising star from the English department. Later, in 1939, Lewis wrote his first largely successful mainstream book, *The Problem of Pain* (see Chapter 15).

Popular Christian Spokesman, 1940–1951

As Jack continued to teach and write, the start of the Second World War brought great change to the Kilns. Warnie, who had been in the Reserves, was called back into duty. Given that he was in his mid-40s, Warnie wasn't thrilled about returning to wartime conditions. In the end, however, he only served 11 months and was eventually discharged due to illness.

At the start of the war, Jack was 40 years old, and because all British men under 41 years could be called into service, Jack anticipated being called up. However, the government allowed him to remain at Oxford. To serve his country, he joined a part-time home security battalion that would be called upon in the event of a full-scale Nazi invasion.

It was during the World War II era that Lewis emerged as a widely popular Christian spokesman, through his talks on BBC radio, his popular apologetic books written during this six-year period, and his activities at Oxford.

Radio star

Around this time, James Welch, director of religious broadcasting at the British Broadcasting Corporation (BBC), was planning a series of radio talks on Christianity. He had picked up a copy of *The Problem of Pain* and loved it, and he decided that Lewis was the perfect person to do four 15-minute talks in August of 1941. Jack hated radio but decided to do the talks as a way to reach out to people who would otherwise never read his books. Lewis was a natural talent — intelligent, entertaining, and charismatic — and quickly became a smash hit and something of a radio celebrity. By 1942, the name "C.S. Lewis" was a household name, and his books, such as *The Problem of Pain* and *The Screwtape Letters,* were selling briskly. Riding the wave of popularity, Jack soon received an invitation to address the Royal Air Force. Although his early talks were shaky, he soon proved popular among servicemen.

Jack's fame soon began spreading across the Atlantic Ocean as well, and his books started selling well in the United States. Figure 2-8 shows Lewis during this period, when his fame and popularity grew.

Figure 2-8:
C.S. Lewis
became a
household
name on
both sides
of the
Atlantic in
the 1940s.

Lewis continued to appear in a series of radio segments until 1944. The BBC was anxious for him to continue his talks (they knew a good thing when they had it!), but Jack declined, believing he'd said everything he had to say. He put together three books (*The Case for Christianity, Christian Behavior,* and *Beyond Personality*) based on his radio talks, and these three were combined into one book entitled *Mere Christianity* (discussed in Chapter 16) in 1952.

Debate central

During the early 1940s, Lewis not only defended Christianity through his books and radio talks, but he also did so through the most popular society at Oxford, the Oxford Socratic Club. The club was a forum for debate and dealing with people's doubts about Christianity. Weekly club meetings consisted of over two hours of debate and discussion. Club members regularly invited an atheist to speak and then debated the merits of the Christian and atheist worldviews. Lewis served as club president and was the star debater of the group, winning debate after debate with his wit, quick thinking, and brilliant logic.

Phases of Lewis's writing career

C.S. Lewis wrote across several literary genres at various times in his life. While it isn't a hard and fast rule, clear boundaries to some aspects of his writing career are apparent. At certain points, he seemed to stop, take stock, and then consciously move on to the next phase of his writing. The following figure illustrates these phases and how they overlap.

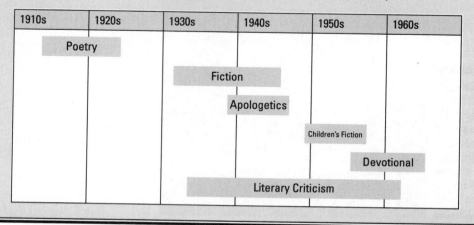

Over the years, Lewis became something of a legend at the university, much like an undefeated heavyweight prize fighter. On one occasion, however, he met his match. Elizabeth Anscombe debated him in 1948 on one of the points that he used to refute naturalism in his book *Miracles*. No one was quite sure exactly who won the debate; some attendants felt Lewis narrowly squeezed by while others thought Ms. Anscombe clearly scored the upset victory. Interestingly, in a later edition of *Miracles,* Jack actually revised one of his arguments, likely as a response to Ms. Anscombe.

Square peg in a round hole

Given Lewis's worldwide popularity during the 1940s, you may assume that he was well-liked and well-respected by his colleagues. In fact, many Oxford teachers and professors didn't much care for him. You see, Lewis was different. Being a popular personality and mainstream author often wasn't considered a positive thing by stuffy professors at the college. And Jack disliked the university politics and intrigue that many other senior professors thrived upon.

Perhaps most significantly, however, he was an outspoken Christian in his books and in the Oxford Socratic Club, and most of his colleagues believed that he should have kept those beliefs to himself. (However, as much evangelistic fervor as Jack may have expressed in his books, he never tried to convert anyone in the context of classes or tutoring.) Perhaps one of the key reasons why Lewis formed the Inklings was to insulate himself from the negative attitudes and anti-Christian bias that he experienced from others at Oxford.

During his time as a student and teacher at Oxford, Lewis never seemed to be comfortable with the "powers that be" amongst his peer group and colleagues. Instead, he thrived when he was able to insulate himself from all that, both at Great Bookham working with Kirkpatrick (see "Cramming with the Great Knock") and at Oxford when he was surrounded by his Inkling friends (see Chapter 3).

Out with the Old and In with the New, 1951–1960

The 1950s brought major changes to nearly every part of Lewis's life. In his writing, apologetics were out and Narnia was in. In his career, Oxford was out and Cambridge in. And on the home front, Mrs. Moore was out and Joy Davidman Gresham in.

Narnia time

Following his blitzkrieg of apologetic books in the 1940s, Lewis seemed to lose interest in trying to combat the postmodern philosophical movements that came into fashion after World War II. Lewis saw that these movements got sidetracked on peripheral subjects (such as the meaning of the language we use) instead of dealing with the core issues. As a result, Lewis believed a substantive logical debate on the issues was virtually impossible.

Logical Lewis was beginning to give up his leadership role to Imaginative Lewis. He began writing his most endearing work, *The Chronicles of Narnia,* a series that kept him busy for seven years. (See Chapter 4 for full details on how Lewis came to write his Narnia books.)

When duty calls

It appears that duty always played a major part in Jack's decision-making processes over the years. Although he could have avoided military service during World War I, he served willingly. When he gave his word to Paddy Moore that he'd care for Moore's mother if Paddy was killed, he followed through with the promise, as impractical and financially tenuous as it was.

Although teaching wasn't his first love, he felt it was his duty and did so without complaint. And finally, when his good friend Joy Davidman risked being sent back from England to the United States, he felt duty-bound to marry her even though he likely had no romantic feelings for her at the time.

Cambridge

For years, Lewis had pursued a full professorship at Oxford, but time and time again, he was passed over. Finally realizing that such a position would probably always elude him at Oxford, Lewis moved across town in 1954 to the other famous university in England — Cambridge — and accepted a position tailor-made for him: Professor of Medieval and Renaissance Studies at Magdalene College. It was a great move for Jack. Cambridge reinvigorated him; he loved the smaller environment, which reminded him of the way Oxford was in his younger days. His new position also freed him from tutoring and enabled him to handpick the lecture subjects that were most interesting to him. What's more, people at Cambridge appreciated him like those at Oxford never did.

Surprised by Joy . . . Davidman Gresham

As the 1940s drew to a close, Mrs. Moore, now in her 70s, was an invalid and confined to her bed at the Kilns. In 1948, Mrs. Moore moved to a nursing home to live out her remaining years under supervision. She died at age 79 in 1951.

In 1950, Jack started corresponding with an American woman named Joy Davidman Gresham, a woman who would eventually rock the placid world of this life-long bachelor. Joy had recently become a Christian and was a big fan of Lewis's work. Jack and Warnie were amazed by how well-written and intelligent her first letter to Jack was, and they began exchanging letters, which subsequently led to visits by Joy to meet Lewis. Fleeing an abusive husband, Joy eventually moved to England in 1954 with her two sons, David and Douglas, and divorced her husband.

Jack and Joy got along well; Jack found her engaging to talk to and nearly every bit his equal in wit and intelligence. But, as enjoyable a time as he had with her, Jack probably didn't have any romantic feelings for her at this time in their lives.

Casting a shadow over *Shadowlands*

Shadowlands is a 1993 film about the relationship and marriage of C.S. Lewis and Joy Davidman, starring Anthony Hopkins and Debra Winger. The film can be an entertaining look into Lewis's life, but only if you take its depiction with a very large grain of salt. The intention of writer William Nicholson was to dramatize the uniquely loving relationship between Lewis and Davidman, not to provide an accurate biographical portrayal of the couple.

Although it succeeds on the dramatic front, several shortcomings cast a large shadow over *Shadowlands*. First, the film completely ignores Jack's and Joy's reliance on their Christian faith during her suffering and death. (This oversight is much like making a movie about George Patton and portraying him as a mild-mannered, timid pushover.) Second, the film suggests that Lewis lost his faith as a result of Joy's death. Yet, as Chapter 15 explains, in spite of the grief and struggles that he went through, Lewis's faith ultimately grew stronger following the tragedy. Third, friends of Lewis who saw the film didn't see much of the *real* Lewis in Anthony Hopkins's solemn portrayal. Hopkins may bear some physical resemblance to Jack, but he never conveys the wit, sense of humor, love of life, and boyish charm that the real C.S. Lewis had.

In 1956, Joy's visa renewal was refused by the British authorities. She faced the prospect of returning to the United States unless she married an Englishman. Once again, Jack's sense of duty kicked in and changed his life. (See the sidebar "When duty calls" for more on this part of Jack's personality.) He entered into a civil marriage with Joy in April of 1956, enabling her to stay in the country. At this point, their marriage was one of convenience only — they didn't even live under the same roof.

Within a year, however, their convenient little arrangement began crumbling. After a period of sickness, Joy was diagnosed with bone cancer that had spread to several parts of her body. She began treatment for the disease and spent considerable time in the hospital.

"Write two books and call me in the morning"

C.S. Lewis often used writing as a vehicle to produce change or cleansing in himself. Early in his life, he had a tendency to live in an imaginary world. So he wrote the long poem *Dymer* as a way to help him with what he called "Christina Dreams," a preoccupation with daydreams that took him out of reality into his own isolated fantasy world. His space trilogy was primarily an effort to "exorcise" himself from his fascination with space. He wrote his autobiography *Surprised by Joy* in part to help him free himself from the difficulties of his childhood, both with his father and at boarding schools. Finally, after Joy's death, Lewis penned *A Grief Observed* as a way to cope with the despair of his loss.

Surprising, interesting, and even perplexing Lewis facts

To round out your knowledge of C.S. Lewis, the man, consider the following facts that are sometimes surprising, sometimes perplexing, but always interesting.

- In spite of his vivid imagination and love of "northernness," Lewis wasn't a traveler. He left the shores of Britain just three times in his life: as a child on holiday to northern France, as a soldier in World War I to wartime France, and finally, to fulfill his wife's lifelong dream to visit Greece. He once remarked that going to a place he loved to imagine would only spoil the wonder and mystery of the place for him.

- Lewis had only one joint in each of his thumbs, which made working with his hands difficult. He never was good at mechanical or hands-on tasks around the house and therefore tended to avoid them. (I'll have to try that excuse around my house.)

- Lewis never learned to drive a car, so he had someone chauffer him any time he needed a lift.

- Lewis suffered a wound to his wrist during World War I that caused him discomfort for the rest of his life.

- Lewis acquired the habit of smoking as a teenager while at prep school, and he smoked pipes all his life.

- Most certainly not a technology guru, Lewis hated radio and television — and those were the days before sports radio, *Gilligan's Island,* and reality TV.

- Lewis would have felt right at home in medieval times because he despised most things modern. In addition to technology, he hated modern trends in poetry, literature, and philosophy. As Chapter 10 describes, Lewis saw dangers in modern fashion.

- Lewis had an uncanny memory. During lectures and tutorials, he could recite lengthy Greek and Latin passages from memory or pull a quote from some obscure book. His brother Warren said that Jack would often memorize a book just so that he wouldn't have to purchase it.

- When Lewis wasn't memorizing books, he was buying them. If he liked a book, he usually wanted to own it so that he could read it again and again and again.

- Lewis enjoyed reading while walking outside. (I'm not making this stuff up, folks.)

- Lewis loved the sea, but he didn't enjoy swimming.

- Lewis had a difficult time acting interested in anything that bored him.

- Lewis wasn't one for small talk and avoided parties and other social functions. In his words, he had a "distaste for all that is public."

- Lewis may have struggled in his younger years with being a "prig," but after he matured and became a Christian, he took on a humble character. He was never a snob and never felt a need to call attention to himself.

When Joy was laid up in the hospital, Maureen (Moore) Blake, who had maintained contact with Lewis, helped out by inviting the two Gresham boys to stay at her family's home during the school holidays.

Given Joy's condition, Jack insisted that she move into the Kilns so that she could be cared for. However, if they were going to live together under the same roof, Jack felt the two should be married by the Church. Therefore, they had a Christian wedding at Joy's bedside in March of 1957. Joy's health was grave after the ceremony, but then she slowly began to rally. And after several months, she was moving around by herself, and the cancer seemed to be gone for good.

In the period from 1957 to 1958, Jack started to fall head over heels in love with his wife. Looking back, this brief period was probably the happiest time of his life because he found the love that had always that eluded him. But, in October of 1959, just when Jack and Joy had convinced themselves that her cancer had disappeared, the sky fell in. Routine tests showed that her cancer had returned, and although there was some hope, her odds for a second recovery seemed improbable.

One of Joy's lifelong dreams was to travel to Greece, and so, in spite of her suffering and pain, she and Jack visited the Greek Islands in April of 1960. It was Jack's first trip out of Britain since he was a soldier in World War I.

Just three months after their trip to Greece, Joy died in July of 1960, uttering the last words, "I am at peace with God."

Jack's love for Joy may have slowly smoldered for several years, but by the end, it had turned into a blazing fire. And even though it was expected, Joy's death nearly destroyed Jack and left his Christian faith reeling in the aftermath. In response to his pain, he wrote *A Grief Observed* under the pseudonym N.W. Clerk, chronicling his struggle with his loss. Chapter 15 examines the battle that Lewis had trying to reconcile this tragedy with his belief in an all-powerful and all-loving God.

Final Years, 1960–1963

Jack's final years were marked by a steady deterioration of his health, but he retained his wit and humor to the end. In 1961, he had prostate problems, but his doctors were reluctant to operate until his kidneys and heart were more stable. He had a difficult time getting around, but his vigor never seemed to dissipate.

TIP

Bio diversity

If you'd like to read even more about the life of C.S. Lewis, I recommend two biographies, both of which were written by people who knew Lewis well:

✔ *Jack*, by George Sayer, is an endearing, personable account of Lewis by an old friend.

✔ *C.S. Lewis: A Biography*, by Roger Lancelyn Green and Walter Hooper, is a well-chronicled account of the Oxford don that deftly interweaves firsthand stories into the flow of the narrative.

Over time, Jack started to feel better and resumed his normal responsibilities at Cambridge, but by the summer of 1963, his health had again grown worse, and he was forced to retire from his seat at the university.

Maureen Blake came to visit Jack in the hospital in July of that year. A few months before, she'd unexpectedly been granted the title of Lady Dunbar of Hempriggs after a distant relative had died unmarried. As Maureen came into Jack's room, there was uncertainty as to whether Lewis would remember her because he'd been having a hard time recognizing others during that period. After she introduced herself as Maureen, the ever witty Lewis responded by saying, "No, it's Lady Dunbar of Hempriggs."

On November 22, 1963, Warren discovered Jack on the floor of his bedroom. He had died of a stroke, at 64 years old.

Warren was distraught over the death of his brother and best friend and perhaps never fully recovered from his grief. He lived ten years after Jack's death, during which he had many struggles with alcoholism. Despite his troubles, Warren was able to edit the *Letters of C.S. Lewis* in 1966, which included a personal memoir.

Lewis's stepsons, David and Douglas Gresham, were nearly adults at the time of Lewis's death and were living fairly independently at different schools. Soon after Jack's death, 19-year-old David began studying Judaism and related studies. (Following the passing of his mother, David had embraced his Jewish heritage.) He went on to several years of academic study in the United States, Jerusalem, and eventually Cambridge studying Biblical Hebrew and Oriental Studies. Douglas Gresham, who was 18 at the time of Lewis's death, had been attending a small private school called Applegarth in Surrey. He soon went to work on a farm to gain experience in agriculture, and, while there, met his future wife. They were married a few years later in 1967.

Although David Gresham hasn't been active in the C.S. Lewis literary estate, Douglas has played a central role in the estate for many years. In fact, Douglas, a committed Christian, serves as co-producer for the Narnia films.

Exploring Lewis's Lifelong Journey Toward Joy

From a young age, Lewis was captivated by the quest for what he called "Joy." Joy was one of the central ideas that shaped his early life, and strains of the concept show up in many of his fiction and nonfiction works. In fact, when the time came to write his autobiography, Lewis entitled it, appropriately enough, *Surprised by Joy.*

To Lewis, Joy is an intense desire or romantic longing for something that nothing on earth ever truly satisfies. You can catch a glimpse of it, but it always remains just out of your reach. As Lewis writes in his poem *Dymer,* "Joy flickers on the razor-edge of the present and is gone." Yet Lewis believes that this longing, though always unfulfilled, is more marvelous than any happiness or earthly pleasure that can be satisfied. "This hunger is better than any other fullness; this poverty better than all other wealth," he explains in *The Pilgrim's Regress.* He writes elsewhere, "For even to have wanted it is what makes life worth having." Joy isn't merely wishful thinking in Lewis's mind. In fact, Lewis believes it's exactly the opposite, calling it "thoughtful wishing."

Lewis's first experiences with Joy were seemingly ordinary incidents when he was growing up; playing with his brother's toy garden and reading Beatrix Potter's *Squirrel Nutkin* are two examples. For Lewis, experiencing Joy in these events isn't just a kid's playful imagination. In fact, Lewis feels so strongly about their importance that he writes in his autobiography, "The reader who finds these [episodes] of no interest need read this book no further, for in a sense the central story of my life is about nothing else."

After Lewis became a Christian, he began to understand that the romantic longing he always had was actually an ingrained desire for God and his "far-off country." He realized, however, that people can easily fall into pitfalls when they misunderstand the nature of Joy. First, most people don't know what these longings mean and often dismiss them as being "romantic" or "nostalgic" fancies. Second, people commonly attempt to substitute earthly pleasures for Joy, but those pleasure ultimately leave individuals unsatisfied and unfulfilled. Third, when you and I taste Joy in life, Lewis warns against making the "conduit" of that Joy into an idol. In the essay "The Weight of Glory," he writes:

> *The books or the music in which we thought the beauty was located will betray us if we trust to them; it was not* in *them, it only came* through *them, and what came through them was longing. These things — the beauty, the memory of our own past — are good images of what we really desire; but if they are mistaken for the thing itself they turn into dumb idols, breaking the hearts of their worshippers. For they are not the thing itself; they are only the scent of a flower we have not found, the echo of a tune we have not heard, news from a country we have not visited.*

Lewis realizes that this longing will someday be satisfied for Christians in Heaven. For when Christians are with God, they finally experience "the healing of that old ache." In the end, Lewis observes in *Letters to Malcolm: Chiefly on Prayer,* "Joy is the serious business of Heaven."

Lewis understands that some people may object to the idea of God implanting an unsatisfiable desire in each person's heart, considering it the equivalent of holding a carrot in front of a donkey's nose. Writing in an essay called "Talking About Bicycles," Lewis offers a different perspective, believing that a wise donkey would look back on life and say "I'm glad I had that carrot tied in front of my nose. Otherwise I might still have thought eating was the greatest happiness." Besides, Lewis understands that this desire is unsatisfiable only in this life: it's evidence that somewhere in the universe there's something that will satisfy it.

Before Lewis accepted Christianity, this romantic longing was pivotal to his whole existence and became almost an obsession for him. Yet, after his conversion, everything changed. He actually lost interest in experiencing Joy as he grew in his relationship with God. He realized that the intense desire that had always been inside of him served as "a pointer to something other and outer."

In *Surprised by Joy,* Lewis compares his pre- and post-conversion perspective on Joy to being lost in the woods. Suppose, for example, you're on a wilderness hike and accidentally veer off the trail and get lost in the middle of nowhere. After walking aimlessly for hours, you stumble across a signpost that points the way back to the path. In the middle of the deep woods, this signpost becomes all-important for you and is probably the supreme object of your attention for a while. However, after you find the main trail, signposts begin to lose their special significance. You still see the occasional signpost as you walk on the path, and they may continue to be exciting reminders of what lies ahead. But you probably don't leave the path to stare at them. Instead, you much prefer to keep walking toward your real goal, home.

For an exploration of Joy in Narnia, see Chapter 9.

Chapter 3

Faith, Friends, and the Inklings

The more you get to know the man behind the books, the more you discover that C.S. Lewis valued two things most in life: his faith and his friends. Interestingly, these two parts of him blended together throughout his life. His friends were a primary factor in his conversion to Christianity, and a shared faith in Jesus Christ was the underpinning for the closest relationships that he had.

This chapter examines both the faith and the friendships of Lewis and explores their interconnectedness. You begin by surveying the Oxford don's road to Christian faith and then discover what friendship meant to Lewis and who his closest friends were. Finally, I share how a circle of friends around him became known as "the Inklings."

A Spiritual Odyssey: From Atheist to Defender of the Christian Faith

C.S. Lewis was the 20th century's most effective defender of the Christian faith and perhaps even the most influential Christian since Martin Luther. But, as I explain in Chapter 2, he wasn't a goody-two-shoes his whole life, studying and preparing to ascend into this role. In fact, Jack came to this role kicking and screaming much of the way. Yet, perhaps it was his initial reluctance that made him a much more effective, enthusiastic, and understanding spokesman for Christianity.

To fully understand the context of the biographical events discussed in this section, I recommend reading Chapter 2 first.

A loss of faith

C.S. Lewis, nicknamed "Jack," was raised in a family that attended church every Sunday. But the brand of Christianity that Jack experienced in childhood left a bad taste in his mouth for years. Church became synonymous with all things dry and legalistic. Lewis writes in his autobiography *Surprised by Joy* that "religious experiences did not occur at all" in his upbringing.

The death of his mother was Lewis's first religious experience and one that left him deeply disturbed. At the time, he thought of God as a magician who waved his magic wand the moment anyone asked him to do something. As a result, young Jack was mystified as to why God didn't answer his prayers to heal his mother. Although this apparent desertion troubled him, Lewis continued to explore his faith while at Wynyard boarding school. He read the Bible, prayed regularly, and discussed issues of faith with other students.

However, nothing took root, and by the time Jack finished up at Cherbourg, his faith had withered away. This change was triggered by a teacher at the school who became fascinated with spiritualism and turned Jack's mind onto beliefs far different than Christianity. In addition, as Jack struggled with adolescent issues, he became disillusioned as his prayers seemed to go unanswered. In response, Jack began to move farther and farther away from Christianity. Over time, he began considering himself an atheist and abandoned faith altogether. His attitude mirrored that of Roman philosopher Lucretius: "Had God designed the world, it would not be / A world so frail and faulty as we see."

This vacuum in Jack's life was quickly filled with "northernness," a fascination with Norse mythology and northern lands (see Chapter 2 for details). Northernness became Lewis's surrogate religion, a substitute that was everything Christianity wasn't: passionate, meaningful, Joy-giving, and imaginative. After his conversion, Lewis looked back and said, "Sometimes I can almost think that I was sent back to the false gods there to acquire some capacity for worship against the day when the true God should recall me to Himself."

Strong influences toward Christianity

Lewis's first taste of genuine Christianity, although he didn't see it as such, came at Great Bookham when he first read George MacDonald's *Phantastes*. Lewis absolutely loved the book, but he didn't see its spiritual significance at the time. Looking back after his conversion, Lewis believed that MacDonald's influence on him was profound because MacDonald created in Lewis a desire to focus his imaginative yearnings on pure rather than sordid things.

The discovery of *Phantastes* proved to be the first step in Jack's journey toward Christian faith. The book served "to convert, even baptize . . . my imagination," reflected Lewis. "It did nothing to my intellect nor (at the time) to my conscience. Their turn came far later with the help of many other books and men."

Despite any "advance work" MacDonald may have done to Lewis's imagination, Jack's logical mind was dead set against Christianity from his high school years until his late twenties. He argued that there was no proof of any religion and believed them all to be myths, much like the Norse myths that he loved. His earliest works, *Spirits in Bondage* and *Dymer,* express this pessimism and antagonism toward God.

Yet after Lewis began his career at Oxford, a slow transformation took place. In 1926, Lewis began a five-year odyssey that would take him out of his atheism and to a belief in some sort of God, ultimately leading him to a belief in, as Lewis concluded, the "one true Christian God."

Several guiding forces influenced Lewis along this path towards faith, each of which are discussed in the following sections.

Christian heroes, friends, and colleagues

While teaching at Oxford, Jack realized that all his heroes in life were Christians. People like George MacDonald, G.K. Chesterton, Samuel Johnson, Edmund Spencer, and John Milton all believed in biblical Christianity. In contrast, the non-Christian people with whom Jack agreed philosophically — such as George Bernard Shaw and Voltaire — he found to have the substance of cotton candy.

In addition, Lewis found that the friends to whom he was becoming the closest and most attached to, such as Arthur Greeves, Nevill Coghill, J.R.R. Tolkien, and Hugo Dyson, were bloody well all Christians. Owen Barfield, as well, was someone Lewis looked up to immensely, and when Barfield shifted his worldview toward supernaturalism, Lewis's movement toward faith was profoundly affected. In *Surprised by Joy,* Lewis confesses that he found himself believing at the time, "Everyone and everything had joined the other side."

A sensible worldview, sort of

During this period of religious reflection, Lewis also became aware that the Christian view of the world was logical and reasonable after all. After reading *The Everlasting Man* by G.K. Chesterton in 1926, Lewis thought that the Christian perspective on history was starting to make sense. However, ever the fighter, he tried to dismiss it by saying, "Christianity was very sensible apart from its Christianity."

Confessions of a fellow atheist

Further nudging him toward conversion, in 1926, Lewis was deeply disturbed by a candid remark made by T.D. Weldon, a tutor in classical studies at Oxford. Weldon was militant in his atheism, but he conceded to Lewis during a conversation that the authenticity of the New Testament accounts of Jesus Christ was amazingly strong. In his autobiography, Lewis tells of Weldon's admission that "It almost looks as if it had really happened once."

Lewis felt himself being trapped in a corner. If Weldon — this atheist of atheists — wasn't safe from the truth claims of Christianity, then Lewis wondered how he could possibly escape intact.

The first reluctant step

Lewis began to realize that he had a real choice of whether to believe in God or deny him. And, as time went on and he was influenced by those factors outlined in the previous sections, Lewis found it impossible to consciously deny God's existence. In 1929, Lewis finally admitted that God was God. In *Surprised by Joy,* Lewis calls himself "the most dejected and reluctant convert in all England."

However, Lewis stopped short of believing in Christianity. He believed in the reality of a deity, but he wanted to go no further. He denied the possibility of any relationship with God. "For I thought He projected us as a dramatist projects his characters, and I could no more 'meet' Him, than Hamlet could meet Shakespeare," writes Lewis. "I didn't call Him *God* either; I called Him *Spirit.* One fights for remaining comforts."

Final steps to faith and Joy

Lewis's longtime process of embracing the Christian faith reminds me of peeling an onion. The many layers of atheism and unbelief took a while to penetrate, but they had gradually started to peel away by the early 1930s. Finally, the last remaining layers were finally stripped away in September of 1931.

Accepting myth as truth

On September 19, 1931, Jack had dinner with friends J.R.R. Tolkien and Hugo Dyson at Magdalen College, Oxford. Later, while walking the grounds of Magdalen, they discussed myths. Lewis told the others that he loved myths as stories but dismissed them as having any validity. Myths were simply "lies breathed through silver," he thought. Tolkien disagreed with his friend; he said that myths almost always have a grain of truth in them, although the truth is usually skewed and distorted. The difference between Christianity and other myths, said Tolkien, is that Christianity is a particular myth that just happens to be true — God really *did* come to earth as a man and died so that those who believed in him could receive salvation. As Tolkien spoke, Lewis suddenly felt a strong breeze come over the threesome as they walked along the path, giving him the sensation of a message from God. Ever the rationalist, Jack didn't want to make too big a deal over this event, but the impeccable timing gave him goose bumps.

Lewis, Tolkien, and Dyson talked until early the next morning. After Tolkien went home, Dyson stayed with Lewis, discussing what forgiveness does to the new Christian.

After this night of extended conversation in mid-September, everything began to come together in Jack's head. In *Surprised by Joy,* he recounts:

> *I was by now too experienced in literary criticism to regard the Gospels as myths. They had not the mythical taste . . . If ever a myth had become fact, had been incarnated, it would be just like this. Myths were like it in one way. Histories were like it in another. But nothing was simply like it . . . This is not 'a religion,' nor 'a philosophy.' It is the summing up and actuality of them all.*

Throwing out all doubt

The last step of Lewis's long journey came a few days later when, of all places, he was riding in the sidecar of his brother Warnie's motorcycle. Within those few moments, Lewis threw his final doubts and hesitations to the roadside and decided that he believed in Jesus Christ as the Son of God.

This decision was far more than an intellectual exercise for Lewis; it transformed his whole life. He experienced a new sense of purpose in his job at Oxford. He focused much of his future writing on defending or articulating the Christian faith. He began to understand that his lifelong pursuit for Joy could be fulfilled through Jesus Christ. Finally, Lewis was able to experience the deeper sense of friendship that had eluded him up until that point.

Friendship through the Eyes of Lewis

Friends were an important influence not only on Lewis's decision to convert to Christianity but also on every aspect of his life. This section explores friendship as Lewis saw and experienced it. Chapter 18 also explores Lewis's perspectives on friendship.

It doesn't get any better than this!

A quick scan of C.S. Lewis's life could reasonably lead you to the conclusion that he must have been a loner. After all, when Lewis was growing up, he played at home by himself most of the time. He never fit in at the boarding schools he attended, thriving only when he worked one-on-one with tutor William Kirkpatrick. As a don at Oxford, he was never part of the "in-crowd" among professors and teachers. To top it off, Lewis was a confirmed bachelor for much of his life.

When you look at these facts by themselves, however, you get a skewed picture. In reality, Lewis valued friendship more than anything else on earth. Writing to his lifelong friend, Arthur Greeves, he explains, "Friendship is the greatest of worldly goods. Certainly to me it is the chief happiness of life." And, on the same note, he writes elsewhere, "Is any pleasure on earth as great as a circle of Christian friends by a good fire?"

Certainly, Lewis was most content and most comfortable being himself when he was hanging out with "the guys," simply enjoying the company of friends.

Sharing truth with "kindred spirits"

Lewis saw a big difference between companionship and friendship. In his opinion, a companion is someone with whom you enjoy doing activities or have some common interests. But a friend is someone far more than that. In *The Four Loves,* Lewis says that friendship springs up when people "discover that they have in common some insight or interest or even taste which the others do not share and which, till that moment, each believed to be his own unique treasure (or burden)." He adds in *Surprised by Joy,* "Nothing . . . is more astonishing in any man's life than the discovery that there do exist people very, very like himself." Or, as Anne Shirley of *Anne of Green Gables* so memorably puts it, Lewis saw a friend as a "kindred spirit."

According to Lewis, at the heart of friendship, friends see eye-to-eye on a key question: Do you see the same truth? Or, if they disagree in their answers to this question, they at least *care* about the same truth.

Lewis believes that you when become a friend with someone, the basic facts of his or her life are non-issues. You don't really care where he lives, who he's married to, or what he does for a living. Lewis quips, "What have all these 'unconcerning, matters of fact' to do with the real question, *Do you see the same truth?*"

Looking at C.S. Lewis before he became a Christian, it's surprising that this dyed-in-the-wool atheist tended to have only Christian friends. Surely, the reason behind this anomaly is that, although he disagreed with them for a while on what the truth was, he cared just as much as J.R.R. Tolkien or Hugo Dyson did about the need to discover what is true. In the end, Lewis's Christian friends were able to help him lift the blinds from his eyes and see that same truth.

The more friends, the better

According to Lewis's philosophy, a friendship should be more than just two people hanging out. When it comes to friends getting together, the more the merrier. When you gather many friends together, one friend brings out something in each other individual that another friend cannot. Reflecting on the give and take of multiple friends, Lewis writes in *The Four Loves* about the friendship between Charles Williams, J.R.R. Tolkien (referred to here as "Ronald"), and himself. He writes, "Now that Charles is dead, I shall never again see Ronald's reaction to [a favorite inside] joke. Far from having more of Ronald, having him "to myself" now that Charles is away, I have less of Ronald."

Christianity enables friendships to blossom

Conversion changed Lewis, and it changed his friendships as well. He had a few good friends before his conversion, but that number grew significantly following his conversion to Christianity.

Harvard professor Dr. Armand M. Nicholi, Jr. suggests in his book *The Question of God* (Free Press) that the shift in both quantity and quality of Lewis's friendships is more than just coincidence. In fact, Nicholi argues that Lewis's newfound faith enabled him to see everything and everyone in a whole new light. He gradually forgot about his own self interest and became more concerned about the needs of others.

Conversion also made Lewis understand that people matter, not just for their few dozen years on earth, but for all eternity. He affirms this idea in his essay "The Weight of Glory," saying that there are no "ordinary people" and no "mere mortals," but only people who are designed and equipped for eternity. Given this new perspective on the world, Lewis was able to focus less on himself and value his friends more than he ever did as an atheist.

Friends are an endangered species

Lewis lamented the fact that, while ancient and medieval cultures embraced friendship, modern society minimizes the need for friends. In an essay called "Membership," Lewis says that modern man "lives in a crowd; caucus has replaced friendship." It's not surprising then that Lewis was never comfortable at boarding schools or aimed to be in the thick of things among the stuffed shirts at Oxford. Even before his conversion, he longed for something more.

Lewis was right: The average adult today has many companions, but few or no real friends. Winston Churchill once said, "We have no lasting friends, no lasting enemies, only lasting interests." Churchill may have been speaking about nation states, but this same truth applies to people as well. In today's transient society, where people commonly experience job-related moves several times in their life, most people don't form permanent friendships. Rather, they establish temporary alliances for a time and then move on when circumstances change. In contrast to reality, Lewis believed friendships were permanent, and it was worth sacrificing most everything else in life, including your career, to live near friends.

Living Under the Influence: Friends of Lewis

C.S. Lewis's address book surely would have made a junk mailer salivate. A quick browse through the dictionary-sized volumes of *The Collected Letters of C.S. Lewis* (HarperCollins) reveals just how many friends, companions, associates, and correspondents Lewis had over the course of his life.

However, a select few had a notably profound influence on Lewis and his writing. These include his brother Warnie Lewis, Arthur Greeves, J.R.R. Tolkien, Owen Barfield, and Charles Williams. All but Greeves were also members of the Inklings, which I discuss in the section "Getting to Know the Inklings," later in this chapter.

Warnie Lewis

Warren (nicknamed "Warnie") Lewis (1895–1973) was the older brother of C.S. Lewis. The two brothers, shown together in Figure 3-1, had a close relationship their entire lives. In fact, except for their school days and Warnie's time in the military, Jack and Warnie always lived under the same roof.

Figure 3-1:
Jack and
Warnie,
brothers
and friends.

Although overshadowed by his younger brother, Warnie was a quick wit, well-read, and an outstanding scholar in his own right. He wrote several books on French history and was a regular at the Inklings gatherings. See Chapter 2 for more information on Warnie.

Arthur Greeves

C.S. Lewis called Arthur Greeves (1895–1966) his first real friend. And while theirs wasn't the closest friendship that Lewis ever had, it was the longest, seeing as they stayed in touch throughout their lifetimes. The decades of written correspondence between Jack and Arthur is compiled in the book *They Stand Together* (Collins).

The two became friends when Lewis was 16 and Arthur was 19. As they got to know each other, Lewis realized that Greeves shared his passion and love for "northernness" and Norse mythology. In his autobiography *Surprised by Joy,* Lewis describes the moment he first discovered this truth about Greeves: "Many thousands of people have had the experience of finding the first friend, and it is none the less a wonder; as great a wonder as first love, or even a greater. I had been so far from thinking such a friend possible that I had never even longed for one; no more than I longed to be King of England." In addition to their love of all things northern, Greeves turned Lewis on to many authors that Lewis would come to love, including Sir Walter Scott.

The similarities between Greeves and Lewis changed as Lewis propelled through Oxford and Greeves stayed put in Belfast. Greeves was a talented visual artist, but he was neither a true intellectual nor a fan of poetry. The friends encouraged each other in their respective interests, but they couldn't relate when it came to their respective strengths. Their emotional bond remained strong, though, and in the 1920s, Greeves provided valuable support for Lewis when he had trying times at Oxford and difficulties at home with Mrs. Moore.

Over the years, their differences may have prevented Lewis and Greeves from being "kindred spirits," but they always got along well and were loyal to each other to the end.

J.R.R. Tolkien

As author of *The Hobbit* and *The Lord of the Rings,* John Ronald Reuel (J.R.R.) Tolkien (1892–1973) has become one of the most influential and endearing authors of the 20th century. Tolkien, pictured in Figure 3-2, was also close friends with C.S. Lewis for almost 40 years. Indeed, the relationship between Tolkien and Lewis, their influences on each other's work, and their collective works makes theirs one of the most remarkable literary friendships in history.

Spiritually speaking, Tolkien was a committed Catholic and was a key influence in Lewis's decision to become a Christian. (See the section "A Spiritual Odyssey: From Atheist to Defender of the Christian Faith" earlier in this chapter for more on Lewis's conversion.)

Meeting at Oxford

Tolkien was a few years older than Lewis when he became a professor of Anglo-Saxon studies at Oxford in 1925, the same year Lewis started as don in the English department.

Lewis became acquainted with Tolkien in 1926 and soon began attending meetings of the Coalbiters society. Lead by Tolkien, this group read stories in Old Norse while they munched on coal fritters and sipped "Coca Coal-a." Okay, I'm kidding. Truth be told, no coal-laced food or drinks were allowed. Actually, *Kolbitar* is an Icelandic term for people who sit around a fire so closely they look as if they're biting coals. Lewis's lifelong love for Norse mythology kept him interested enough to attend regularly.

Figure 3-2:
Tolkien was far more than just a "token" friend for Lewis.

Haywood Magee/Stringer

As time when on, Lewis and Tolkien got to know each other better and valued each other's opinions and respective talents. As early as 1929, they began meeting regularly to chat about Oxford politics and discuss poems and other projects they were working on.

Lewis's first impression of Tolkien was that he was quite opinionated. Lewis wrote in his diary early on, "No harm in him, only needs a smack or so." And, although their relationship developed slowly, they eventually became quite close. In fact, Tolkien, who was scarred by the loss of several good friends during World War I, was very glad to have Lewis for a dear friend.

Dealing with differences

Despite their mutual respect and admiration, Tolkien and Lewis were very different, making their relationship complex and strained at times. Some of their most notable differences include

- ✔ Tolkien was a family man. Lewis was a confirmed bachelor for nearly all his life.

- ✔ Tolkien was Roman Catholic. Lewis was first an atheist and then a Protestant.

- ✔ As an author, Tolkien was a perfectionist and meticulous about everything he worked on. (He invented a complete language, for crying out loud!) He spent decades working on *The Lord of the Rings,* perfecting and crafting his "Magnus Opus." In contrast, in the time Tolkien took to complete four works, Lewis churned out an amazing number of books in a variety of genres, including fiction, children's literature, Christian apologetics, and literary criticism.

If you're interested in finding out more about Tolkien and, more specifically, *The Lord of the Rings,* check out *The Origins of Tolkien's Middle-earth For Dummies,* by Greg Harvey (Wiley).

✔ Although they both valued myth and fantasy, Lewis and Tolkien had opposite perspectives on the use of allegory as a literary device. Tolkien despised allegory, and Lewis saw its usefulness. In Chapter 6, you can see how this showdown between Lewis and Tolkien played out in their different approaches to Narnia and Middle-earth.

✔ Tolkien was a rather strong opponent to Lewis's *The Chronicles of Narnia* series because of its usage of overt Christian symbolism. As Chapter 6 reveals, Tolkien decried *The Lion, the Witch and the Wardrobe* and the other books in the series so much that Lewis chose not to read these manuscripts aloud at meetings of the Inklings.

Tolkien and Lewis were closest during the 1930s, but their friendship cooled off as time passed. The arrival of Charles Williams (see the upcoming "Charles Williams" section) at Oxford in 1939 was the start of the fray. Tolkien was bugged by (and perhaps a bit jealous of) Lewis's enthusiastic embrace of Williams. And after Lewis's "strange marriage," as Tolkien called it, to Joy Davidman, Lewis and Tolkien saw one another even less. For his part, Lewis grew tired of Tolkien's ever strong opinions and had less of a desire to spend time with him as the years passed. Tolkien commented after Lewis's death in 1963, "Many people still regard me as one of his intimates. Alas! That ceased to be so some ten years ago. But we owed each a great debt to the other, and that tie with the deep affection that it begot, remains."

In spite of any interpersonal strain that developed over the years, the influences that Lewis and Tolkien had on one another are undeniable. Tolkien never would have completed *The Lord of the Rings* without Lewis's steady encouragement. "But for the encouragement of CSL," wrote Tolkien to a friend in 1965, "I do not think that I should ever have completed or offered [it] for publication." And, although the Narnia books themselves were a source of tension between the two, Lewis probably wouldn't have developed those stories without the influence of the many discussions that he, Tolkien, and other Inklings had on fantasy and fairy tales.

Owen Barfield

Owen Barfield (1898-1997), author of *Poetic Diction* (Wesleyan University Press) and several other books, became a good friend to Lewis in spite of the fact that they disagreed about many things, viewing life from different perspectives. The two met as undergraduates at Oxford. Lewis thought the world of Barfield and considered him the brightest student he'd come across. The two often talked in depth about subjects close to Lewis's heart, such as poetry, literature, myth, and imagination.

In *The Four Loves,* Lewis argues that you can be good friends with someone you disagree with as long as that person at least "cares about the same truth." My guess is that Lewis was probably thinking about Barfield when he wrote that line. Barfield became a follower of Rudolf Steiner's mystical Anthroposophy movement in the early 1920s. Anthroposophy emphasized education, appreciation of art, and other practical ways to develop spiritually. Because Lewis had little use for Steiner's beliefs, a disagreement ensued. It turned into what Lewis called the "Great War" between he and Barfield in the 1930s, in which the two debated over metaphysics and related issues. Lewis writes in *Surprised by Joy* that, while it was never a fight, "it was an almost incessant disputation, sometimes by letter and sometimes face to face, which lasted for years."

Charles Williams

Though Lewis knew him for less than ten years, the man to whom Lewis was perhaps most drawn in his life was Charles Williams (1886–1945).

Williams was an author and editor for Oxford University Press. In 1936, Lewis read Williams's book *The Place of the Lion* (Regent College Publishing) and was so enamored by it that he wrote Williams a complimentary letter. Serendipitously, when Williams received Lewis's note, he had already started writing to Lewis congratulating him on *The Allegory of Love.* They met soon afterwards, and Lewis said, "Our friendship rapidly grew inward to the bone." Lewis really took to Williams, and the two drew even closer when Williams moved from London to Oxford in 1939 at the start of World War II. Charles Williams died unexpectedly from complications due to an illness in 1945, just after the end of the war.

Getting to Know the Inklings

"The next best thing to being wise oneself is to live in a circle of those who are," explains C.S. Lewis in his *Selected Literary Essays.* As he penned that line, Lewis must have been thinking of the Inklings, an informal circle of his wisest friends that met from 1933 to 1949. This section explores the Inklings and their impact on Lewis and his writings.

Dabbling with books and ideas

"The Inklings" was originally the name of a student reading group at Oxford in the early 1930s. Lewis, J.R.R. Tolkien, and a few other Oxford teachers were invited to participate in the group's discussions, but the group was ultimately short-lived and disbanded after the founder graduated.

During this same period of time (the early 1930s), Lewis and Tolkien began to meet regularly for discussions on various topics (see the "J.R.R. Tolkien" section). As Lewis wrote to his brother Warren, "It has also become a regular custom that Tolkien should drop in on me of a Monday morning and drink a glass. This is one of the pleasantest spots in the week. Sometimes we talk English school politics: sometimes we criticize one another's poems: other days we drift into theology or the 'state of the nation': rarely we fly no higher than bawdy and 'puns.'"

As he and Tolkien grew closer, Lewis dreamt up the idea of group of "like minded" literary minds; such a group could build upon what the two of them had already been doing for a few years. Perhaps Lewis was trying to create a modern version of an 18th-century literary club that would have included such notables as Alexander Pope and Jonathan Swift.

When it came to naming the group, Lewis liked the term "inkling" and decided to reuse it. The name was meant as a pun, a play on the fact that "inkling" means both an idea of something as well as a person who dabbles in ink.

Lewis, Tolkien, Warnie Lewis, and Owen Barfield were among the first Inklings to begin meeting. They convened on Thursday evenings at Lewis's room at Magdalen and met more informally at midday on Tuesdays in the back room of the Eagle and Child bar in Oxford. The Eagle and Child, shown in Figure 3-3, was also popularly known as the "Bird and Baby."

At their meetings, the Inklings discussed literary issues and read works in progress in order to receive honest feedback. Don't confuse them with a mutual admiration society or polite feedback group, however. When a member read from his manuscript, he was on the hot seat and could very well find his work ripped apart by the others.

The group, however, talked about more than just literature. Lewis wrote to friend and former student Dom Bede Griffiths, "We meet . . . theoretically to talk about literature, but in fact nearly always to talk about something better."

Figure 3-3:
The Eagle
and Child
was a
favorite
hangout for
Lewis,
Tolkien, and
the Inklings.

*Used by permission of The Marion E. Wade Center, Wheaton College,
Wheaton, IL*

The group's intended purpose of discussion and criticism was ideally suited
to Lewis's personality. Tolkien once wrote that Lewis "had a passion for hearing things read aloud, a power of memory for things received in that way, and
also a facility in extempore criticism, none of which were shared (especially
not the last) in anything like the same degree by his friends."

Lewis read several of his books aloud to the Inklings, including *The Problem
of Pain, Out of the Silent Planet,* and *The Screwtape Letters.* Tolkien read *The
Hobbit* and *The Lord of the Rings,* and Charles Williams read *All Hallows' Eve.*

Reason for the Inklings

Scholars have long speculated about the reasons behind the Inklings' formation. I suggest three major factors that motivated Lewis to form the group:

✔ Within the literary world, the Inklings lived out Proverbs 27:17, "As iron
sharpens iron, so one person sharpens the wits of another." The Inklings
provided an environment in which each author could sharpen and
improve his works and help and serve his fellow members. The quality
of the literature produced by the group's members during its lifetime
speaks for itself.

- As I discuss in Chapter 2, Lewis didn't gel with many of the powers-that-be at Magdalen College. The Inklings, thus, provided a structure to insulate Lewis and others from university politics and power struggles.

- Arguably as significant a reason as any, the Inklings simply enjoyed being together as friends. Indeed, the group meant the world to Lewis and was filled with people he looked up to. Speaking to this fact, Lewis writes in *The Four Loves* about what a person feels when he's part of such a group:

  Sometimes he wonders what he is doing there among his betters. He is lucky beyond desert to be in such company. Especially when the whole group is together, each bringing out all that is best, wisest, or funniest in all the others. Those are the golden sessions; when four or five of us after a hard day's walking have come to our inn; when our slippers are on, our feet spread out towards the blaze and our drinks at our elbows; when the whole world, and something beyond the world, opens itself to our minds as we talk.

Members only

The members of the Inklings were all friends and shared a Christian worldview. Some members attended most every meeting, but others came only occasionally. Membership into the group was informal but by invitation through general consensus of the members. They knew the type of person that they wanted and didn't want: a good thinker, but not a Prima Donna.

Most scholars believe that Lewis, Tolkien, Barfield, and Williams were the driving force and backbone of the Inklings. However, many different faces appeared at Inklings meetings over the years, including

- **Warnie Lewis,** who began coming in 1933 and, except for his time in the service during World War II, was a regular presence.

- **Hugo Dyson,** a lecturer at Reading University who joined the group in 1935. Being at Reading, he couldn't make it to every meeting. Dyson much preferred talking to listening, which often became a source of irritation to fellow Inklings.

- **Nevill Coghill,** a long-time friend of Lewis since his school years. Coghill was one of the early Inklings, but over time, he attended less and less. His leftist leanings and unorthodox religious beliefs made him to stand out from the rest of the group.

- **Robert Havard,** Lewis's medical doctor. Although he never authored a book, Havard loved the Inklings' discussions and was appreciated by the other members. Lewis nicknamed him "Humphrey" after the doctor in *Perelandra*.

"It must be Tuesday"

Over the years, the Inklings became something of folklore. They're even referred to by Edmund Crispin in his 1947 detective novel *Swan Song* (published in the U.S. as *Dead and Dumb*).

When Crispin's main character sits in the Bird and Baby, he says, "There goes C.S. Lewis. It must be Tuesday."

Others Inklings included: Charles Wrenn (Oxford professor and author), Colin Hardie (Classics tutor at Magdalen), Adam Fox (Dean of Divinity at Magdalen), Lord David Cecil (author and Oxford scholar), Christopher Tolkien (son of J.R.R. Tolkien), James Dundas-Grant, J.A.W. Bennett, Father Gervase Mathew, R.B. McCallum, C.E. Stevens, and John Wain.

Call it a wrap!

The Inklings met regularly until 1949 when, one Thursday evening, no one bothered to show up in Lewis's room at Magdalen College. The no-show meeting signified an end of era, although in actuality the Inklings had been on the decline for a few years. The group's heyday ended with the death of Charles Williams in 1945. This loss hit the Inklings hard, and the group never seemed to be the same afterward. In addition, Lewis and Tolkien were always such driving forces in the group that, when their friendship began to cool off, the Inklings just weren't the same anymore.

Even though the Thursday evening sessions disbanded, what remained of the Inklings continued to meet regularly at the Bird and Baby until Lewis's death in 1963.

Lasting significance of the Inklings

Looking back on the Inklings, you can see that the group wasn't really a "literary movement" per se; however, because each member had a common belief in Christianity and similar interests in fantasy, myth, fairy tales, and imaginative writing, it's not surprising that the body of literature produced by members has a common feel and bond to it. As G.B. Tennyson, an expert on the Inklings, explains, "The Inklings . . . stand for something real and important that speaks to the issue of literature and [Christian] belief and their relation to the modern world."

Part II

All Things Narnia: Voyaging to the World of Aslan

The 5th Wave   By Rich Tennant

THE CHRONICLES OF NARNIA

In the book, a little girl enters a wardrobe to discover the world of Narnia.

I'd have hoped for Chanel or Dior, but to each his own.

In this part . . .

Your journey to Narnia begins now. No, you don't need to bid on an enchanted wardrobe or a shiny ring on eBay in order to enter the world of Aslan and talking beasts. I take you there in this part, even without the magical Narnian "transport devices." In this part, you discover the people, beasts, places, and stories of *The Chronicles of Narnia*. You also go beyond the storyline to examine the symbolism that C.S. Lewis weaves into the seven Narnian books. Finally, you see how the Christian gospel permeates the world of Narnia.

Chapter 4

Unveiling the Wardrobe: Origins and Influences of Narnia

In This Chapter

▶ Uncovering the inside story of how Narnia came to be

▶ Examining the literary and Christian influences of Narnia

▶ Exploring Lewis's love of fairy tales

▶ Debating the correct order of the Narnian Chronicles

▶ Previewing Narnia on the silver screen

Growing up, C.S. Lewis was an avid reader, devouring his parents' library much like a termite in a forest of redwoods. But, never one to follow the crowd, Lewis ignored most children's books at this stage of his life. Instead, he discovered how much he loved fairy tales at an age when most others had outgrown them. He was an adult when he read his favorite fairy tales, including the Bastable children series by E. Nesbit and *The Wind in the Willows* by Kenneth Grahame. However, Lewis never felt as if he missed out on anything by waiting so long to read these types of books. He remarked, "I do not think that I have enjoyed them any less on that account."

I understand exactly how Lewis felt. As I mention in this book's Introduction, I discovered *The Chronicles of Narnia* as an adult after first getting to know Lewis through his nonfiction. Yet, I'm convinced that I appreciate the books in this series as much as my kids do — the constant tugs-of-war over our torn, battered copies serve as strong evidence.

Lewis understood that in order for a children's story to really be worthwhile and continue to be read as the years go by, it must appeal to a broad audience. In a lecture on children's literature in 1952, Lewis spoke to this point, "A children's story which is enjoyed only by children is a bad children's story. The good ones last."

With this chapter, you start your journey into a series of books that have certainly stood the test of time. You get to know *The Chronicles of Narnia* and explore how Lewis came up with the ideas behind this magical land.

Starting with a Faun (Or, How Narnia Began)

Before penning the first Narnia book, *The Lion, the Witch and the Wardrobe,* Lewis seemed to be one of the most unlikely authors of his day to write children's literature. After all, he was a 50-year-old bachelor, an Oxford academic, a literary critic, and a best-selling author known for heady, sometimes philosophical, works. Moreover, he was rarely exposed to children and didn't have the type of personality that drew them to him (or vice versa).

Lewis may not have fit the stereotype for children's author, but he ended up being perfect for the task because of other, more important qualities he had: a child-like imagination, a longing for wonder, and poignant memories of childhood.

As I discuss in Chapter 2, there were two sides to Lewis: the logical and the imaginative. The logical side of Lewis dominated his writing before Narnia. The imaginative side, however, didn't wither away as the man got older; it simply lay dormant, ready to spring into action when the right time came.

An idea is born

Although *The Lion, the Witch and the Wardrobe* wasn't published until over a decade later, Lewis first began brainstorming on the idea of a children's story as early as 1939. During that year, World War II began, and as a result of the Nazi bombings of London, many of the city's schoolchildren were evacuated to safer locations in the country. At his home, the Kilns, Lewis and his friend Mrs. Moore (see Chapter 2 for more on their relationship) housed several girls, usually three at a time, who stayed with them for up to six months. (Read one girl's story in the sidebar "Lewis to the rescue.") He wrote to his brother Warnie in September of 1939 that the children were nice but had a hard time entertaining themselves. "Shades of our own childhood!," Lewis exclaimed.

One of the girls staying at the Kilns during the evacuation become interested in an old wardrobe that Lewis had in one room of the house. She asked Lewis whether she could play in and around it. Perhaps this incident, which was remarkably similar to something he'd read years earlier in E. Nesbit's short story *The Aunt and Amabel,* triggered something in his mind and set the wheels of imagination in motion. In Nesbit's tale, a wardrobe serves as the gateway to a magical world. Lewis apparently began writing down ideas for a children's story around this time but put his work away after failing to make much progress.

Lewis to the rescue

Margaret Leyland was one girl who stayed at the Kilns for six months in 1940. In 1977, a letter describing her brief stay at the Kilns was published in *The Lamp-post of the Southern California C.S. Lewis Society.* Margaret considered herself fortunate to have been placed in the home of Lewis and Mrs. Moore. She described Lewis as "a wonderful story teller" and a "keen astronomer" who showed the girls "many wonders of the universe." He was also "unpretentious, kind, and very human," and he never talked down to her or the other girls. Interestingly, Lewis always seemed to Margaret "unconcerned about the war, his mind being filled with space, the heavens, literature, and his church." Margaret even got a chance to meet J.R.R. Tolkien and learned that he and Lewis were discussing *The Lord of the Rings.*

Mrs. Moore didn't allow the children to eat with the family, but Margaret said that Lewis came to the rescue. The girls were served a meager meal, but Lewis often passed food up to their bedroom (his study was on the floor below) or else helped them sneak into the kitchen to get more food. She reflected, "Without the help of Lewis and the cook we would have spent many a hungry night."

Full steam ahead

After his initial musings on a children's story, Lewis put his logical hat on again for several more years and emerged in the public's eye as a popular Christian author, spokesman, and apologist. But in the late 1940s, he realized that he was ready for a change. He'd said all he wanted to say within the realm of Christian apologetics. As he thought about what to write next, Lewis revisited his children's book idea. The whole plan gained momentum; when he started brainstorming on the book, the imaginative side of Lewis came to life and shoved Logical Lewis into a secondary role. His logic still aided his imagination, of course, just as his imagination had helped his logic while he wrote his nonfiction. Concerning the excitement he had for this book, he said, "A fairy tale addressed to children . . . was exactly what I must write — or burst."

Piecing together the puzzle

When he began what would ultimately become *The Lion, the Witch and the Wardrobe,* Lewis didn't have a storyline all planned out. Instead, he worked from images he dreamed up in his mind; Lewis started with a picture he'd stored away since he was a teenager: a faun (half-man, half-goat) walking through a snowy wood carrying packages and an umbrella. Other pictures, such as a queen riding on a sleigh, started appearing in his mind as well. He then began piecing these snapshots together to form the story. For Lewis, the process of writing fairy tales became much like assembling a jigsaw puzzle, and for the missing pieces of the puzzle, he consciously developed storylines to tie everything together.

The puzzle's final piece: Aslan

Seeing as the lion Aslan is the central figure in all the Narnian Chronicles, one would assume that Lewis had him in mind from the very start. But, in actuality, Lewis was pretty far along into the first story when Aslan, in his words, "came bounding into it." At the time, Lewis had been dreaming of lions in his sleep and realized that was his story's missing element. After the lion entered the scene, Lewis said, everything fell into place, not just for the first story, but for the other six as well.

Early criticism — good and bad

In early 1949, Lewis read the manuscript of *The Lion, the Witch and the Wardrobe* to his friend J.R.R. Tolkien. As I explain in Chapter 3, Lewis's encouragement to Tolkien in writing *The Hobbit* and *The Lord of the Rings* had always been key to Tolkien persevering and successfully getting those works published. If Lewis thought Tolkien would return the favor, he was sadly mistaken. Instead, Tolkien's reaction was much like a vegetarian accidentally biting into a juicy hamburger: Yuck! Ever the purist, Tolkien despised the Narnian story. He considered the book nothing but a hodgepodge of myths — the fauns, Father Christmas, Talking Beasts, the White Witch, and Aslan — from a variety of sources — Roman, Greek, and English traditions. From Tolkien's perspective, Lewis had written the books too haphazardly and wasn't meticulous with the details and overall consistency. Even after all seven books were published and proven successful, Tolkien never altered his disparaging view of *The Chronicles of Narnia*. (Chapter 7 explores the different approaches that Lewis and Tolkien took with Narnia and Middle-earth.)

What's in a name?

C.S. Lewis may have been a world famous author, but he still couldn't get his way when it came to the titles of most of the Narnian Chronicles. Long-time Lewis publisher Geoffrey Bles had a knack for rejecting most of Lewis's title suggestions. The following list compares some final titles with Lewis's proposed titles:

✔ *Prince Caspian:* Drawn into Narnia, A Horn in Narnia

✔ *The Horse and His Boy:* Shasta and the North, Narnia and the North, The Desert Road to Narnia, Cor of Archenland, The Horse Stole the Boy, Over the Border, The Horse Bree, The Horse and the Boy

✔ *The Silver Chair:* The Wild Waste Lands, Night Under Narnia, Gnomes Under Narnia, News Under Narnia

✔ *The Magician's Nephew:* Polly and Digory

✔ *The Last Battle:* The Last King of Narnia, Night Falls on Narnia, The Last Chronicle of Narnia

Lewis was frustrated and hurt by the harsh reaction from a friend whose opinion he respected so highly. He strongly believed that his development of Narnia wasn't careless. He had no qualms about mixing and matching myths from various traditions. After all, he reasoned, if they can exist in harmony inside of people's minds, surely they can coexist in Narnia.

Nonetheless, Lewis seriously questioned the wisdom of continuing work on the book and considered scrapping the whole idea. However, before using his manuscript to fuel an evening fire at the Kilns, he received encouragement from his former student and good friend Roger Green, his doctor and fellow Inkling Robert Havard, and Havard's daughter Mary Clare. Each strongly encouraged him to continue and finish the book.

Narnia goes public

The Lion, the Witch and the Wardrobe was published in time for the Christmas season in 1950, and a new book followed each year until 1956. Early reception for the series was mixed. "Too scary," some parents and teachers argued. "Too Christian," other critics claimed. Yet as the years passed, *The Chronicles of Narnia* grew more and more popular, not only with children but also with critics. Finally, *The Chronicles of Narnia* received the critical recognition it deserved when *The Last Battle* received a prize for outstanding children's literature in 1956.

Over the years, "Chronicles of Narnia" has become the definitive name of the series. But this name came into being only after two books of the series had already been published. Interestingly, neither C.S. Lewis nor the publisher came up with the title. As he shares in his book *C.S. Lewis: A Biography,* author and Lewis friend Roger Green was actually the one who coined the name "Chronicles of Narnia" in 1952; he derived the idea from Andrew Lang's *Chronicles of Pantouflia.*

Surveying Literary Influences on Narnia

Writers are influenced by the world around them, from authors they've read and admired to knowledge they've acquired through research and study to people they know and interact with. C.S. Lewis was no different. Several strands of literary influence can be found within his Narnian Chronicles.

Looking at these influences can be a fun exercise and one that helps you get more from the story, but it's important to remember that Lewis never modeled the Narnian tales after anything. Even when he incorporated outside ideas, Lewis created a world all his own.

In this section, I discuss the various literary influences that can be identified in *The Chronicles of Narnia*.

E. Nesbit

Lewis had an enormous appreciation for E. Nesbit's stories, particularly the Bastable children's series. In fact, when Lewis was writing *The Lion, the Witch and the Wardrobe* in 1948, he was asked by biographer Chad Walsh about his new book. Lewis replied that it would be "in the tradition of E. Nesbit." This comment reveals the kind of story that he was intending to create: Something that would give as much joy to his readers as Nesbit had always given to him.

There are several interesting "Nesbitisms" in *The Chronicles of Narnia:*

✔ Whether intended or not, one remarkable parallel exists between E. Nesbit's delightful short story *The Aunt and Amabel* and Lewis's *The Lion, the Witch and the Wardrobe*. In Nesbit's story, a girl named Amabel discovers a magical world through "Bigwardrobeinspareroom." In Lewis's story, Lucy enters Narnia by stepping into a big wardrobe she finds in a spare room.

✔ Lewis playfully tips his hat to Nesbit (and Sir Arthur Canon Doyle) at the beginning of *The Magician's Nephew*. The book starts out with these words: "In those days Mr. Sherlock Holmes was still living in Baker Street and the Bastables were looking for treasure in the Lewisham Road."

✔ Lewis modeled certain plot lines of *The Magician's Nephew* after *The Story of the Amulet*. Specifically, in Nesbit's story, the Bastable children accidentally bring the queen of Babylon back with them to London, causing a ruckus. In Lewis's story, the evil Queen Jadis comes back to London with Digory and Jill, and all heck breaks loose. Another parallel in these stories relates to the children's parents. The Bastable children's father is in Manchuria, and their mother is sick. Similarly, at the beginning of *The Magician's Nephew,* Digory's father is in India and his mother is ill.

Edmund Spenser

Lewis's love for Spenser's classic long poem *The Faerie Queene* had a notable influence on the world he created in *The Chronicles of Narnia*. The virtue, honor, and chivalry that undergird *The Faerie Queene* are similarly represented inside Lewis's make-believe world. In addition, Lewis features characters from a variety of classical and medieval literary traditions — just like

Spenser does. In *Reading the Classics with C.S. Lewis,* scholar Doris Myers even goes so far as to say that you can think of *The Chronicles of Narnia* as a "miniature *Faerie Queene.*" Myers adds, "Having lived for many years with Spenser's Fairyland, [Lewis] created a parallel universe of his own."

George MacDonald

MacDonald was perhaps the author who left the strongest mark on Lewis over the course of his life and career. MacDonald's fairy tales served to, in Lewis's words, "baptize his imagination." MacDonald's influence perhaps can be most felt in *The Silver Chair,* whose overall plot has several parallels to MacDonald's *The Princess and the Goblin.* In *The Voyage of the "Dawn Treader,"* Lucy "becomes" the character she's reading about just as the hero in MacDonald's *Phantastes* does. So too, Lucy, Edmund, and Eustace travel into Narnia via an enchanted picture on the wall in a similar way that two little girls go through a picture and find themselves in another part of the world in MacDonald's *The Wise Woman.*

Lewis's admiration for MacDonald is also apparent in *The Great Divorce,* which I cover in Chapter 11.

Roger Green

Around the time that Lewis was working on *The Lion, the Witch and the Wardrobe,* his former student and friend Roger Green (who coauthored *C.S. Lewis: A Biography*) gave Lewis a manuscript of a story he'd written called *The Wood That Time Forgot.* Elements of that story influenced Lewis's thinking when it came to writing the first book in his Narnia series.

Real people

Lewis claimed that usually he didn't model characters in his stories after real people. The keyword here is "usually." Professor Kirke in *The Lion, the Witch and the Wardrobe* is loosely modeled on both Lewis's tutor William Kirkpatrick and himself. Puddleglum the Marshwiggle in *The Silver Chair* takes after Lewis's quirky gardener Paxford, and young Caspian's nurse in *Prince Caspian* is much like Lewis's childhood nursemaid Lizzie Endicott.

Boxen: Not a Narnia prequel

When C.S. Lewis was young (see Chapter 2), he enjoyed writing stories about talking animals and chivalrous knights in a country called Animal-Land (which later became part of a larger world called Boxen). On first take, Boxen sounds like an early version of Narnia that Lewis modified or refined later in life to create the Narnian Chronicles. But Boxen had little, if any, influence on Lewis's Narnia. Narnia is a land of magic and enchantment; Boxen, on the other hand, was bland, adult-oriented, and, to quote Lewis, "prosaic," by comparison.

Ancient mythology

In his classical studies at Oxford, Lewis did extensive reading and research in ancient Greek and Roman literature. In *The Chronicles of Narnia,* he brought in mythical creatures from these traditions, such as centaurs, fauns, and minotaurs.

In addition to classic myths, Lewis also incorporated an eclectic set of other characters or creatures from a variety of other mythical traditions, including English, Anglo-Saxon, and ancient Persian ones. Examples include orknies, ogres, Father Christmas, and Tash.

Uncovering Narnia's Christian Elements

Some people, when they realize that *The Chronicles of Narnia* have Christian undertones and symbolism, assume that Lewis intended Narnia to be merely a Christian allegory or morality play. Yet, the truth is actually quite different.

According to Lewis, a successful children's story isn't written by asking what children want or what moral they need to be taught. Instead, he believed that the question to be asked is far more personal for the author: "What moral do *I* need?" He writes, "Let the pictures tell you their own moral. For the moral inherent in them will rise from whatever spiritual roots you have succeeded in striking during the whole course of your life." In other words, Lewis's intent wasn't to hit children over the head with a prepackaged moral or a gospel message; it was simply to tell a good story by writing from within himself.

In fact, Lewis even said that when he first began writing *The Lion, the Witch and the Wardrobe,* "at first there wasn't even anything Christian" about the story, that is until Aslan came leaping into the book. (See the section "Full steam ahead" earlier in this chapter for more on his writing process and that particular book.) Lewis's integration of Christian themes into the Narnian Chronicles is, therefore, simply an extension of himself. His Christian worldview wasn't something he could just turn on or off. In the end, he couldn't have created Narnia in any other way.

Having said that, Lewis believed that your faith shouldn't impact your enjoyment of the stories themselves. With that in mind, he wanted to write great stories for Christians and non-Christians alike. In fact, he didn't really want kids to recognize the Christian symbolism in Narnia. Just as George MacDonald's *Phantastes* "baptized his imagination" when Lewis was young, he wanted the Narnian Chronicles to do the same for his young readers. Then, when they heard about Jesus Christ later in life, they'd recognize him as the Aslan they read about when they were young.

Chapters 8 and 9 dive fully into the Christian symbolism embedded in *The Chronicles of Narnia.*

Seeing the Importance of Fairy Tales

To most adults, fairy tales are "kid's stuff." But to Lewis, the fairy tale's an important way to express truth. In his lecture "On Three Ways of Writing for Children," Lewis speaks of the timeless quality of fairy tales: "When I was ten, I read fairy tales in secret and would have been ashamed if I had been found doing so. Now that I am fifty I read them openly." This idea is reflected in his dedication to Lucy Barfield (daughter of Lewis's good friend, Owen Barfield) in *The Lion, the Witch and the Wardrobe:* "You are already too old for fairy tales . . . But some day you will be old enough to start reading fairy tales again."

Some critics scoff at fairy tales as giving kids an unrealistic picture of the world, but Lewis strongly disagrees with that sentiment. He explains, "I think no literature that children could read gives them less of a false impression. I think what profess to be realistic stories for children are far more likely to deceive them." According to Lewis, so-called "realistic" stories — such as becoming popular in school or getting even with the neighborhood bully — have a much greater danger of producing unrealistic expectations because the stories make it sound as if such things are really achievable within the reader's life.

One of Lewis's all-time favorite books was Edmund Spenser's *The Faerie Queene.* As a literary critic, he spent considerable time analyzing the work and wrote in his *Studies in Medieval and Renaissance Literature,* "It is of course much more than a fairy-tale, but unless we can enjoy it as a fairy-tale first of all, we shall not really care for it." This same principle holds true for *The Chronicles of Narnia.* You can slice and dice the books as you search for symbolism and Christian parallels. But, before doing so, make sure you're enjoying the books as a child does — for the fantasy and wonder of it all. If not, you're missing Lewis's primary intent. (For more on Spenser and *The Faerie Queene,* flip to Chapter 21.)

In What Order Should the Books Be Read?

Ever since the series' release in the 1950s, a running debate has raged on the exact order in which *The Chronicles of Narnia* should be read: the order in which the books appeared in print or the chronological order of the stories themselves.

The traditional order (by publication date) is

1. *The Lion, the Witch and the Wardrobe* (1950)
2. *Prince Caspian* (1951)
3. *The Voyage of the "Dawn Treader"* (1952)
4. *The Silver Chair* (1953)
5. *The Horse and His Boy* (1954)
6. *The Magician's Nephew* (1955)
7. *The Last Battle* (1956)

The updated order (by Narnian chronology) is

1. *The Magician's Nephew*
2. *The Lion, the Witch and the Wardrobe*
3. *The Horse and His Boy*
4. *Prince Caspian*
5. *The Voyage of the "Dawn Treader"*
6. *The Silver Chair*
7. *The Last Battle*

The updated order originates from Lewis's response to a young reader's letter in 1957. An American boy named Laurence Krieg was having a debate with his mother over the best reading order; he argued for the chronological order while his mother believed in the order of publication. So Laurence wrote to Lewis asking him which order he, the author, recommended. Lewis replied:

> *I think I agree with your order for reading the books more than your mother's. The series was not planned beforehand as she thinks . . . so perhaps it does not matter very much in which order anyone reads them. I'm not even sure that all the others were written in the same order in which they were published. I never keep notes of that sort of thing and never remember dates.*

In the past, the books were physically numbered according to their publication dates. However, recent editions of *The Chronicles of Narnia* published by HarperCollins (1994 and later) have switched to the chronological order based on the recommendation of Lewis's stepson, Douglas Gresham.

If you're a new reader of *The Chronicles of Narnia,* I, along with many Narnian experts, recommend the traditional order — by publication date. Here are three reasons for reading the books in this order:

✔ *The Lion, the Witch and the Wardrobe* is the book that sets the tone and focus for the entire Narnian series. Because Lewis wrote this book first, it's the most natural introduction to Aslan and the world of Narnia.

✔ *The Magician's Nephew,* which deals with the origins of Narnia, is far more exciting and interesting when read as a flashback story following *The Lion, the Witch and the Wardrobe.* By the time you get to *The Magician's Nephew,* you deeply care about the background information of Narnia and how it came to be.

✔ *Prince Caspian* is a more natural follow-up to *The Lion, the Witch and the Wardrobe* than *The Horse and His Boy* because it picks up again with the four Pevensie children in England just a year after you leave them at the end of *The Lion, the Witch and the Wardrobe.*

Perhaps the most revealing argument for approaching the books in the traditional order is that the makers of the upcoming Narnia film series (see the "Catching up to Frodo: Narnia Goes Hollywood" section below) chose *The Lion, the Witch and the Wardrobe* when deciding which book to transfer to the screen first.

In the end, however, don't get overly concerned about the book order. The truth is that you can read the seven Narnia books in any order and still enjoy each of them for their own sake.

Catching Up to Frodo: Narnia Goes Hollywood

Up until the release of filmmaker Peter Jackson's adaptation of *The Fellowship of the Ring* in 2001, fantasies like *The Chronicles of Narnia* and *The Lord of the Rings* seemed relegated to low-budget TV or animated adaptations. The common belief in Hollywood was that people wanted realism, not fairy tales. However, the record-breaking and award-winning success of Jackson's *The Lord of the Rings* trilogy changed everything. Due in large part to the films' successes, Narnia fans now have the opportunity to see *The Chronicles of Narnia* the way it was meant to be seen: as a high quality, live-action motion picture.

"Please Dad, just one more chapter?"

The Chronicles of Narnia is a perfect children's series to read aloud to your kids. The style, cadence, and flow of C.S. Lewis's writing lends itself well to oral reading. The adventures in the books are also exciting enough to keep your kids interested and ready for more. Not only is reading aloud with your kids a chance to spend quality time with them, but it also has lasting educational value. Here are some tips to keep in mind:

✔ Find a quiet, comfortable setting so your kids can relax and concentrate as you read.

Sitting on the family room couch or reading to them while they're in bed are both great ideas. Be sure to turn off the stereo, television, and other distractions.

✔ Read aloud in a way that Lewis would have wanted you to — with expression! Don't read the book in a monotone voice; be creative and animated as you speak. Also, if you're up to it, give unique voices to each of the characters.

The Lion, the Witch and the Wardrobe is the first book of the series to appear on the silver screen. Fortunately, the film's production company has acquired the rights to all seven books and is expected to film the entire series. Best of all, the first film adaptation (and hopefully the six that follow) promises to hold true to Lewis's original vision for the story, even its Christian symbolism. Douglas Gresham, stepson to C.S. Lewis, is serving as co-producer and working to ensure the integrity of the original story. Gresham has vowed not to "change the words of the master."

Chapter 5

Tour De Narnia: Themes and Literary Approaches

. . . .

In This Chapter

▶ Looking at the major themes of *The Chronicles of Narnia*

▶ Exploring time and politics in Narnia

▶ Uncovering the series narrator

▶ Noting Lewis's approaches to characterization

▶ Identifying colloquialisms in the series

. . . .

A few years ago, my wife and I had a chance to visit Venice, Italy, a place we'd always dreamed of exploring. The romance, the rich Italian history, the candy-striped poles, and the gondolas were just as we expected. Our Italian escapade did have some setbacks, though, namely two travel-weary toddlers and my six-months-pregnant wife's premature labor pains. When we arrived in Venice, our vision of a magical ride into St. Marks Square on a gondola was smashed by the harsh reality that our two port-a-cribs, double stroller, multiple suitcases, and other kid necessities would have sunk the most sea-worthy outrigger. Despite the fact that our dreams for a romantic getaway were thrown out the window, with a trusty guidebook in hand and background reading fresh in our minds, we had a grand time touring Venice anyway.

Because we came prepared, my family got the most out of our trip to Venice. Oh sure, we could have enjoyed the city without doing all the prep work, but we would have undoubtedly missed out on many adventures that added meaning and substance to the visit. In the same way, whether you're reading *The Chronicles of Narnia* solo or with your entire family, don't just wing it. C.S. Lewis does a remarkable job of presenting seven enchanted stories that are easy for kids and adults to read and understand. However, because the stories are so rich in detail, texture, and underlying meaning, you need a guidebook in tow as you head into the wardrobe. Therefore, use this chapter (along with Chapters 6 through 9) to get the most out of Lewis's tales.

Exploring the Major Themes from The Chronicles of Narnia

Even though each of Lewis's ventures into Narnia is unique, several ideas and themes resurface throughout the series. As you read through the books, pay special attention to these underlying themes and details.

The Lion, the Witch and the Wardrobe

The Lion, the Witch and the Wardrobe chronicles the Pevensie children's trip to Narnia and recounts how Aslan frees the enchanted land from the White Witch. As you read it, keep in mind the following points:

- **Major theme:** *The Lion, the Witch and the Wardrobe* is a Narnian Passion play in that it depicts, in memorable fashion, Aslan voluntarily giving up his own life to save Edmund from the White Witch.

- **Crisis of belief:** Mr. Tumnus and Edmund face a similar crisis of belief on whether to side with Aslan or the White Witch. Tumnus makes the right choice, and Edmund makes the wrong one.

- **Key spiritual journey:** Edmund goes from villainous traitor to fully restored king of Narnia. (Jump to Chapter 9 for more on Edmund's transformation.)

- **Key role of Aslan:** Redeemer (parallels Jesus Christ's role discussed in Hebrews 2:14 and Romans 5:8).

- **Evil and sin portrayed:** The White Witch is the personification of evil; she symbolizes Satan in many ways. Edmund is depicted as a Judas-like traitor, but he's restored by Aslan to Narnia and his siblings.

- **Beacons of faith:** Mr. and Mrs. Beaver and Lucy.

- **Biblical parallels:** Aslan's slaying and resurrection follows closely the biblical accounts of Jesus Christ's crucifixion and resurrection with the difference that Aslan dies for Edmund only, not for all as Christ did. To conduct a comparison, see John 19–20.

- **Special theme:** Much like biblical prophesy is God's way of foretelling something that will happen, in this book, the Pevensie children's arrival into Narnia is seen as a fulfillment of the ancient prophesy:

  When Adam's flesh and Adam's bone
  Sits at Cair Paravel in throne,
  The evil time will be over and done.

  The White Witch knows this prophecy and attempts to thwart it by eliminating the Pevensie children.

Good guys vs. bad guys

The Lion, the Witch and the Wardrobe has good Narnians who are loyal to Aslan and bad Narnians who side with the White Witch. Although some creatures, such as the trees, have mixed loyalties, most species side fully with the good or the bad:

✔ **Good Narnians:** Birds, centaurs, deer, dryads, dwarfs, fauns, nymphs, owls, unicorns

✔ **Bad Narnians:** Boggles, cruels, efreets, ettins, ghouls, hags, incubuses, minotaurs, ogres, orknies, people of the Toadstools, spectres, sprites, werewolves, wooses, wraiths

---

Prince Caspian

Prince Caspian chronicles the adventures of the Pevensies and Prince Caspian in their battle against the Telmarines.

✔ **Major theme:** The underlying theme in *Prince Caspian* is the restoration of forgotten truth to Narnia. Under generations of New Narnian Telmarine leadership, Narnia systematically quieted the talking animals and squelched belief in Aslan. Prince Caspian, the Pevensie children, and their army fight to defeat the New Narnians and restore old Narnia to her former glory.

✔ **Crisis of belief:** Lucy must decide whether to follow Aslan in a direction opposite to the common sense route that her siblings recommend they take. She initially fails but then vows to follow Aslan regardless of what others think and do. Nikabrik the Black Dwarf also faces a critical decision of whether to believe in Aslan and old Narnia or pursue a Machiavellian strategy of using sorcery to defeat Miraz. He makes the wrong decision and pays with his life.

✔ **Key spiritual journey:** Lucy trusts in Aslan even when doing so goes against what others think and what common sense indicates is right.

✔ **Key role of Aslan:** Deliverer (Romans 11:26).

✔ **Evil and sin portrayed:** Sin is depicted in *Prince Caspian* as unbelief, which shows itself in two different ways. First, the unbelievers — Miraz, Telmarines, and Nikabrik — who fight against the reality of Aslan and old

Narnia are the evil characters of the story. Second, unbelief rears its ugly head when Aslan's supporters doubt his leading. Peter and Susan are the most noteworthy of these unbelievers because they both know better than to doubt Aslan. (See Chapter 8 for more on unbelief in Narnia.)

✔ **Beacons of faith:** Trufflehunter the Badger, Edmund, and Doctor Cornelius.

✔ **Biblical parallels:** *Prince Caspian*'s restoration of old Narnia has some interesting parallels to the story of Nehemiah in the Old Testament. In the days of Nehemiah, the ancient Israelites had been living for generations under Babylonian rule and had forgotten their spiritual heritage and faith in God. However, Nehemiah and Ezra restore the truth to the Israelites and bring them back into a relationship with God once again. To compare, see Nehemiah 8–10.

Turkish Delight

Turkish Delight, the delight of Edmund Pevensie, is a jellied candy that originated in Turkey, but it has since become a popular seasonal treat in England around Christmastime. *Lokum,* as the candy is known in Turkey, dates back to the Ottoman Empire but was exported to the west by a British traveler in the 19th century. He's the one who called the confection "Turkish Delight."

You can make your very own batch of Turkish Delight using the following recipe:

✔ 5 tablespoons cornstarch

✔ 1/2 cup cold water

✔ 1/2 cup hot water

✔ 2 cups sugar

✔ 1/2 cup orange juice

✔ 1 teaspoon rosewater or lemon juice

✔ 2 cups chopped toasted almonds or pistachios

✔ Powdered sugar (enough to coat finished candy)

1. Mix cornstarch with cold water in a small bowl and set aside.

2. In a saucepan, mix hot water, sugar, and orange juice and heat to a boil. Stir in the cornstarch mixture. Let simmer for 15 minutes, stirring often.

3. Remove from heat and add rosewater or lemon juice. Stir in the nuts, and then pour the mixture into a shallow pan that's been buttered.

4. Let cool completely. Cut into 1-inch squares (a knife dipped in hot water is recommended to make cutting easier). Toss squares in powdered sugar to coat, and enjoy!

Don't forget to save some for hungry authors!

What's in a title?

C.S. Lewis wasn't thrilled about the title *Prince Caspian,* which his publisher selected. However, he did get a subtitle, *Return to Narnia,* added; it's the only subtitle used in the series.

The Voyage of the "Dawn Treader"

The Voyage of the "Dawn Treader" follows King Caspian and his shipmates as they travel to the End of the World in search of the seven missing lords of Narnia.

- **Major theme:** *The Voyage of the "Dawn Treader"* uses a motif similar to Homer's *Odyssey* to depict a spiritual journey of faith.

- **Crisis of belief:** Eustace Scrubb's crisis of belief on Dragon Island offers a vivid portrayal of a person coming face to face with his "wretched self" and deciding what to do about it. King Caspian also faces a crisis of belief at the World's End when he longs to continue on with Reepicheep rather than return to Narnia and fulfill his responsibilities as king.

- **Key spiritual journey:** Eustace changes from a selfish brat to a "redeemed" servant of Aslan. (See Chapter 9 for more on Eustace's transformation.)

- **Key role of Aslan:** Transformer (parallels Jesus's role as discussed in 2 Corinthians 5:17 and Psalm 51:5–12)

- **Evil and sin portrayed:** *The Voyage of the "Dawn Treader"* is unique among the Narnian Chronicles in that it features no major evil villains. Instead, sin is portrayed in everyday, real world terms, including Eustace's selfishness; the corruption of Gumpus, the governor of the Lone Islands; the social evils of slavery on the Lone Islands; Deathwater Island's greed; the Dufflepuds' foolishness; the Three Sleepers' quarreling; and Caspian's attempt to abdicate his responsibility.

- **Beacon of faith:** Reepicheep.

- **Biblical parallels:** Aslan's shedding of Eustace's dragon skin is a loose parallel to the shedding of scales from the eyes of the Apostle Paul in Acts 9:18.

Did Caspian take a GPS?

The following is the official travel route of the islands that the *Dawn Treader* stopped at during their voyage to the end of the world: Cair Paravel to four western islands, to the Lone Islands, to Dragon Island, to Burnt Island, to Deathwater Island, to the Island of the Voices, to Dark Island, to Ramandu's Island, and on to the World's End.

The Silver Chair

The Silver Chair tells of the quest of Eustace Scrubb, Jill Pole, and Puddleglum the Marshwiggle to free Prince Rilian from the evil Green Witch.

- ✔ **Major theme:** *The Silver Chair* shows how Aslan carries out his will in spite of the occasional disobedience of his believers. Eustace, Jill, and Puddleglum can only rescue Prince Rilian by following Aslan's specific instructions, but they're vulnerable to distraction and tend to forget those commands.

- ✔ **Crisis of belief:** Eustace, Jill, and Puddleglum face a crisis every time they're distracted by circumstances (which is often) and fail to follow Aslan's plan. They also face a second crisis when they go head to head against the Green Witch in Underland. However, as the Bible promises, remaining steadfast in faith allows one to overcome evil.

- ✔ **Key role of Aslan:** Protector (Psalm 91).

- ✔ **Evil and sin portrayed:** Like Queen Jadis, the Green Witch is a Satan-like character who offers a vivid representation of evil. Sin is also portrayed in this book as the disobedience of Eustace, Jill, and Puddleglum as they stray from Aslan's instructions.

- ✔ **Beacon of faith:** Puddleglum the Marshwiggle.

- ✔ **Biblical parallels:** The image of the Green Witch as a serpent parallels Genesis 3, in which Satan appears as a serpent in order to tempt Eve.

- ✔ **Special theme:** In the 1940s, Lewis wrote *The Abolition of Man* as a deliberate argument against modern "value-free" education that promoted relativism and denied absolutes. Lewis's depiction of Eustace's and Jill's school, called Experiment House, is a direct attack on modern education in line with *The Abolition of Man* as well as his sci-fi novel *That Hideous Strength*. He notes the "mixed up minds of the people who ran it," complete lack of discipline, ignorance of biblical truth, and willingness by the teachers to let the bullies "rule the roost."

In addition, the student bullies (known as "Them") at Experiment House are a clear reference to Lewis's own bad experiences at Malvern College (see Chapter 2). Just as Experiment House is ruled by Them, Malvern was ruled by the "Bloods." Lewis shows his familiarity with the ins and outs of the bad crowd with his comment, "It was the voice of Edith Jackle, not one of the Them herself but one of their hangers-on and tale-bearers."

The Horse and His Boy

The Horse and His Boy follows the adventures of a boy, Shasta, and a talking horse, Bree, as they attempt to save Narnia from invasion.

- **Major theme:** *The Horse and His Boy* explores how Aslan raises up unassuming Shasta to a princely destiny while simultaneously humbling the proud and arrogant Bree and Aravis.

- **Crisis of belief:** Shasta struggles with a low sense of self-worth, while Bree and Aravis enjoy over-inflated senses of self. Aslan works through the crises that occur in their lives to bring them to proper views of worth, in accordance with Romans 12:3–5:

  For I say, through the grace that was given me, to every man who is among you, not to think of himself more highly than he ought to think; but to think reasonably, as God has apportioned to each person a measure of faith. For even as we have many members in one body, and all the members don't have the same function, so we, who are many, are one body in Christ, and individually members one of another.

- **Role of Aslan:** Guide (parallels the Lord's role depicted in Psalm 25:9, Psalm 32:8, and Psalm 23).

- **Evil and sin portrayed:** Evil is portrayed as deep, self-absorbed arrogance in Prince Rabadash, the Calormene leaders, as well as Bree and Aravis. Rabadash's haughtiness is so extreme that he remains defiant even when facing Aslan. In contrast, Bree and Aravis are repentant when confronted by Aslan, although Bree still has a long way to go before he overcomes his vanity. (See Chapter 8 for more on this struggle.)

- **Beacon of faith:** Hwin.

- **Biblical parallels:** The story of Shasta has some loose parallels to the story of Joseph in Genesis 30–50. Both are forced to live away from their homes at early ages and live in far-off "pagan" lands. Both play pivotal roles in preventing disasters that affect their families and homelands (Joseph from drought and famine, Shasta from invasion), and both are restored to their true fathers. In addition, the story of Shasta being guided by Aslan across the mountain pass to Narnia is reminiscent of Psalm 23 ("The Lord is my shepherd . . .").

Silvery humor

The Silver Chair stands out from the other Narnian Chronicles thanks to the witty humor that seeps through the story. Here are some noteworthy examples of this humor:

- A near-deaf Trumpkin, when being introduced to Jill Pole and told her name, remarks, "What's that? The girls are all killed! I don't believe a word of it. What girls? Who killed 'em?"

- Because other Marshwiggles think he's too flighty, Puddleglum is convinced that the job of helping Eustace and Jill is ideally suited to him. He explains, "Now, a job like this — a journey up north just as winter's beginning, looking for a Prince that probably isn't there, by way of a ruined city that no one has ever seen — will be just the thing."

- Orruns the Faun, when summarizing his thoughts after talking about how much a centaur (which has two stomachs) eats, reminds, "That's why it's such a serious thing to ask a Centaur to stay the week-end. A very serious thing indeed."

The Magician's Nephew

The Magician's Nephew takes you back to the beginning of the Narnia saga, when children from our world first arrived in Narnia.

- **Major theme:** *The Magician's Nephew* is a Narnian version of the Book of Genesis in that it tells how Narnia was created by Aslan and how evil was introduced into the new world.

  Within this backdrop, the allure of power is a dominant theme in *The Magician's Nephew.* Queen Jadis has an insatiable lust for ruling whatever world she inhabits. Uncle Andrew wants to acquire secret magical powers at all cost. Digory tries to get his hands on the magical power of an enchanted apple that can save his sick mother.

- **Crisis of belief:** Digory Kirke faces two crises of belief in *The Magician's Nephew:*

  - He knows he shouldn't ring the bell in Charn but defiantly does so anyway.

  - He's tempted by Jadis to take an apple and use it to heal his sick mother. However, Digory overcomes this crisis and remains obedient to Aslan.

  Digory's crises of belief are more emotional and tied to the heart than perhaps any other storyline in *The Chronicles of Narnia.* Clearly, Lewis is imagining a "what if" scenario, recalling the sadness and helplessness he felt at 10 years old when his mother died. He's obviously using personal experience to express the agony of Digory's situation. (For more on Lewis's personal life and challenges, see Chapter 2.)

- **Role of Aslan:** Creator (parallels Christ's role discussed in Colossians 1:15–17).

- **Evil and sin portrayed:** Evil is personified by Queen Jadis and Uncle Andrew Ketterley.

- **Beacon of faith:** Frank the cabby.

- **Biblical parallels:** The story of Narnia's creation is an obvious parallel to Genesis 1–3. The tale of Digory's ringing the bell is a loose parallel to the original sin in Genesis 3, while Digory's refusal to take the apple to his mother is an alternative spin on Eve's eating of the apple.

The Last Battle

The Last Battle chronicles the final defeat of evil in Narnia and the start of the "real Narnia."

- **Major themes:** Deception, deliverance, and new beginnings dominate *The Last Battle*. The deception engineered by Shift the Ape leads to the events that destroy Narnia, but the faithful Narnians are delivered by Aslan and given a new beginning in the real Narnia.

- **Crisis of belief:** Every Narnian faces a major crisis of belief when Shift the Ape deceives them with a fake Aslan; they must decide whether to believe the words of the new Aslan or cling to what they knew Aslan to be before.

  Perhaps the rebellious Dwarfs face the most poignant crisis in *The Last Battle*. Stung by the false claims of Shift the Ape, they decide that they can trust in no one but themselves. As a result, their hearts became so hardened that even Aslan can't do anything to change them. The saga of the Dwarfs is explored further in Chapter 8.

- **Role of Aslan:** Judge (see Matthew 25:32 for Jesus as judge) and Joy Giver (parallels Christ's role in Matthew 25:34).

- **Evil and sin portrayed:** Evil is shown through Shift the Ape and the invading Calormenes and most vividly through the demonic presence of Tash. Temptation and sin are expressed through both the bad decisions made by the unbelieving dwarfs and King Tirian's rash decision making.

- **Beacon of faith:** Seven Friends of Narnia.

- **Biblical parallels:** *The Last Battle* is a Narnian depiction of the Christian view of the end of this world. The events that unfold in this book resemble what Jesus tells his followers will happen in Matthew 24–25.

Don't we all do that?

C.S. Lewis, on occasion, makes some witty observations on human behavior in *The Chronicles of Narnia.* For instance, in *The Voyage of the "Dawn Treader,"* the narrator comments on Eustace Scrubb's mother's dislike of the picture of the Dawn Treader ship, obviously given to her by either Digory Kirke or Polly Plummer. According to the narrator, "Aunt Alberta didn't like [the picture of the *Dawn Treader*] at all (that was why it was put away in a little back room upstairs), but she couldn't get rid of it because it had been a wedding present from someone she did not want to offend." So too, in *The Horse and His Boy,* the narrator comments on Shasta trying to figure out what do with the reins of a horse: "[Shasta] looked very carefully out of the corners of his eyes to see what the others were doing (as some of us have done at parties when we weren't quite sure which knife or fork we were meant to use)."

It's a Given: Presuppositions of Narnia

Before you enter Narnia, you need to understand certain "givens" in order to get the most from your literary adventure.

A world built on absolutes

Narnia is a world created on absolutes, which means there exists a definite right and a definite wrong. Morality in Narnia isn't based on what's popular or what's expedient — it's based on Aslan. Although the stories' characters sometimes encounter a gray area when it comes to identifying what exactly is right or wrong, truth is never depicted as being gray. (For more on this topic, turn back to Chapter 4.)

Perhaps nowhere is the clarity of truth more apparent than in *The Lion, the Witch and the Wardrobe.* In this story, the White Witch appeals to the Deep Magic — Narnia's ultimate standard — for judgment on Edmund's sin. She says, "The Emperor put into Narnia at the very beginning . . . [that] every traitor belongs to me as my lawful prey and that for every treachery I have a right to a kill." Rather than Aslan saying "to heck with that idea," he knows the Deep Magic is unchangeable. As a result, Aslan allows the White Witch to kill him in Edmund's place.

TRIVIA

Dedications

Except for *The Last Battle,* all the books in *The Chronicles of Narnia* are dedicated to children that Lewis knew.

- *The Lion, the Witch and the Wardrobe* is dedicated to Lucy Barfield, daughter of Lewis's close friend Owen Barfield.

- *Prince Caspian* is dedicated to Mary Clare Havard, daughter of Lewis's doctor and fellow Inkling Robert Havard. Mary was a very enthusiastic supporter of *The Lion, the Witch and the Wardrobe* when Lewis was deciding whether to publish it.

- *The Voyage of the "Dawn Treader"* is dedicated to Geoffrey Barfield, adopted son of Lewis's close friend Owen Barfield.

- *The Silver Chair* is dedicated to Nicholas Hardie, son of Lewis's fellow Inkling Colin Hardie.

- *The Horse and His Boy* is dedicated to David and Douglas Gresham, two boys who would eventually become Lewis's stepsons. At the time of the writing, however, they were just the sons of his American friend Joy Davidman Gresham.

- *The Magician's Nephew* is dedicated to "The Kilmer Family." Several of the Kilmer children wrote to Lewis about Narnia, and Lewis's letters to the Kilmers make up much of the book *C.S. Lewis Letters to Children.* The Kilmer family were descendents of Joyce and Aline Kilmer, early 20th-century poets.

- *The Last Battle* has no public dedication. (I personally think it's because I was yet to be born, and Lewis didn't know what my name would be.)

A natural hierarchy

At the creation of Narnia, Aslan sets apart pairs of animals from the rest of the pack and gives them the gifts of speech, intelligence, and dominion over the rest of the "Dumb Beasts" (normal animals). Talking Beasts are almost human, but they aren't meant to rule Narnia — that responsibility lies with the Sons of Adam and Daughters of Eve. Trufflehunter speaks of this truth in *Prince Caspian,* saying, "Narnia was never right except when a Son of Adam was King." Therefore, a hierarchy exists in Narnia as the natural order of things: Humans, Talking Beasts, then Dumb Beasts.

All creatures, both Talking and Dumb, are never to be mistreated. Dumb Beasts can be eaten for food, but eating a Talking Beast is akin to cannibalism. In *The Silver Chair,* the horrified reactions of Eustace and Puddleglum when they discover they're eating a Talking Stag demonstrate this reality.

When the Talking Beasts receive the gift of speech, Aslan warns that the gift will be taken away if they don't refrain from their former ways. Implicit in this warning is an understanding that Talking Beasts (and humans, too) have an inherent dignity and nobility that the Dumb Beasts do not.

Lewis's characterization of animals in Narnia reflects his real world beliefs. Although Lewis believes that animals should never be mistreated, he clearly sees an undeniable difference between humans and four-legged creatures. Humans aren't "mere animals;" they possess God-given dignity and nobility that sets them apart from all other species. Therefore, were Lewis around today, he likely would be quite outspoken, for example, against animal rights extremists who equate putting stray dogs to sleep with genocide.

Monarchy as the preferred form of government

Lewis considers democracy the best method of government for a fallen world, but in a world without sin, he believes a monarchy is the best form government (see Chapter 18). This belief, coupled with his love for medieval history, obviously influences his choice of political systems in Narnia.

Throughout *The Chronicles of Narnia,* two basic styles of governing appear:

- **A just monarchy serving with obedience to Aslan.** Freedom, peace, happiness, and faith are characteristics of life under this type of government. Examples of just monarchies include Frank I and Helen I, Narnia's Golden Age (Peter, Susan, Edmund, and Lucy), Caspian X, Rilian, Tirian, and the Archenland leaders Lune and Cor.

- **An unjust tyranny ruling as an enemy to Aslan.** Lack of freedom, slavery, persecution, a splintered society, and unbelief are characteristics of life under this type of system. Examples of unjust tyrannies include: Narnia under the White Witch and the early Telmarine rulers, Miraz, and the Calormenes.

Establishing Time in Narnia

Narnian time moves at a far quicker pace than the passage of time on Earth. For example, in the span of 49 years on Earth, thousands of years of Narnian history come and go. However, there's no logical relationship between a Narnian year and an Earth year — Lewis never intended one.

Professor Kirke speaks of the nonstandard nature of Narnian time in *The Lion, the Witch and the Wardrobe,* saying "I should not be at all surprised to find that that other world had a separate time of its own; so that however long you stayed there it would never take up any of *our* time." Edmund concurs in *Prince Caspian:* "Once you're out of Narnia, you have no idea how Narnian time is going. Why shouldn't hundreds of years have gone past in Narnia while only one year has passed for us in England?" But perhaps the best comment about the illogical nature of the time differences comes from Eustace in *The Last Battle:* "It's the usual muddle about times, Pole."

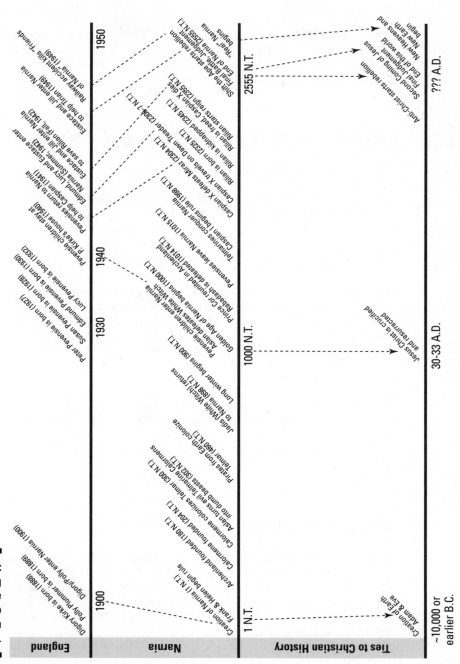

Figure 5-1:
Surveying
Narnia time
relative to
Christian
history.

Figure 5-1 details the chronology of major events in Narnian history. It shows the relationship between events in the fictional England of the Narnian Chronicles and events in Narnia. However, the timeline also shows the relationship between real world events in Christian history and the events that Lewis symbolizes in Narnia. Earth dates are denoted with BC and AD, while Narnian dates are indicated by NT (Narnia Time).

Tackling Characterization by Design

The Chronicles of Narnia are filled with scores of enchanted characters and creatures, which I describe further in Chapter 7. When it came to deciding the types of characters to include in the series and how to characterize them, Lewis took three noteworthy approaches.

A "kitchen sink" approach

As I read through *The Chronicles of Narnia,* a few of the creatures in Narnia seem out of place to me and appear unnecessary in the grand scheme of things. For example, from my perspective, the stories wouldn't lose anything valuable were you to remove Father Christmas in *The Lion, the Witch and the Wardrobe,* Bacchus and the dryads and naiads in *Prince Caspian,* and Father Time in *The Silver Chair* and *The Last Battle.* For me, these characters are simply distractions.

For Lewis, however, the hodgepodge of characters gave him immense pleasure, and he felt strongly about their inclusion. Because creatures from a variety of mythical traditions fit together naturally in his mind, he thought it perfectly appropriate to include them all in his children's stories. (As Chapter 6 explains, this "kitchen sink" approach caused the purist J.R.R. Tolkien endless frustration.)

Depth of characters

Some people have criticized Lewis for his shallow characterization in *The Chronicles of Narnia* when compared to, for example, J.R.R. Tolkien's *The Lord of the Rings.* But, as Chapter 6 details, it's important to remember that Lewis wrote characters for a fairy tale, not an adult novel. To Lewis, the fairy tale form and overall purpose actually forced him, as the author, to restrain the depth of his characters.

You never get to know characters like Peter or Susan Pevensie to a great degree. I believe that's because Lewis adds more texture and insight to the characters in the story that go through crises, such as Lucy Pevensie, Eustace Scrubb, and Shasta.

Some readers argue that Lewis's female characters have more depth than the male ones. If this claim is true, perhaps it's because Lewis was exposed to girls on a day-in, day-out basis when they stayed at the Kilns during World War II (see Chapter 4 for the full story).

Uninvolved parents

The English children in Narnia are characterized by a lack of "normal" family life, meaning parents who are involved in the everyday lives of their children. The Pevensie parents apparently are a good mom and dad, but the children are never with them. In *The Lion, the Witch and the Wardrobe,* the Pevensies stay with Professor Kirke during the London bombings of WWII. Then, in *Prince Caspian,* the children prepare to go off to boarding school, again traveling away from their parents. In *The Magician's Nephew,* Digory's father is off in India, and his dear mother is at home but deathly ill and bedridden. So too, Eustace's "modern" parents are completely uninvolved in his life and send him to Experiment House in *The Silver Chair.* Even in Narnia, a normal household is a rarity; Prince Caspian lives with his evil uncle and aunt after his father is killed, and Prince Rilian's mother is eventually killed by the Green Witch.

In *The Chronicles of Narnia,* Lewis seems to be creating a parentless world similar to that of his own childhood (see Chapter 4 for details). Like Digory, Lewis was quite close to his mother, but after she died, his relationship and interaction with his father was minimal and strained. Lewis lived detached from his father and spent the rest of his adolescent years at school.

Narrating the Chronicles

When creating a story, authors must decide the point of view in which to tell the tale. First person puts you (the reader) in the shoes of a specific character, allowing you to experience the story through that character's eyes. In contrast, third person is a sort of God's eye view in which the narrator knows everything that's going on and as a result, you (the reader) do, too. In *The Chronicles of Narnia,* Lewis wisely takes neither of these approaches. He tells the stories from a *limited* third-person point of view. The perspective is limited because the narrator doesn't know everything. For example, in *The Lion, the Witch and the Wardrobe,* he says, "There is no need to tell you (and no one ever heard) what Aslan was saying."

The narrator also is detached from the story itself, sometimes referring to the other Narnian tales. For example, in *Prince Caspian,* the narrator alludes to *The Lion, the Witch and the Wardrobe* when he says, "This was his own fault and you can read about it in the other book." He also teases the reader at one point in *The Voyage of the "Dawn Treader"* about a story that was never to be: "By the way, I have never yet heard of how these remote islands became attached to the crown of Narnia; if I do, and if the story is at all interesting, I may put it in some other book."

If you've seen the film *The Princess Bride,* think of the grandfather who reads the story to his grandson and thus narrates the film. The Narnian Chronicles have the same kind of narrator! He's engaged, impassioned, and excited about the story, but he always remains separated from the tale and treats it as a story he's sharing with you.

Uncovering Colloquialisms

Narnia's a timeless fantasy world, but it can't escape the fact that C.S. Lewis wrote *The Chronicles of Narnia* in 1950s England. As such, he uses a handful of colloquialisms and words not commonly used today. Many pop up in *The Magician's Nephew,* perhaps because Lewis made a deliberate decision to convey the vernacular of England in 1900. Here's a list of some unfamiliar words and phrases you encounter in the series.

- **"Before you could say Jack Robinson."** A way of expressing that something will be done right away. There are a couple theories on how this term originated. One idea from the early 19th century is that Jack Robinson was a well-known gentlemen who went against convention and often changed his mind. A second possibility is that it refers to Sir John Robinson, who was in charge of frequent beheadings at the Tower of London in the mid-17th century. Lewis also uses this term in *Mere Christianity.*

- **Brick.** A reliable, supportive person. Digory tells Polly in *The Magician's Nephew,* "You are a brick." In *The Horse and His Boy,* Cor (Shasta) says, "Father's an absolute brick."

- **Canter.** Pace. From the narration in *The Horse and His Boy:* "By now the whole party was moving off at a brisk canter."

- **Funk.** Shrink in fright. Cor in *The Horse and His Boy* says, "If you funk this, you'll funk every battle all your life."

- **Hansom.** Horse-drawn carriage. Referred to in *The Magician's Nephew.*

- **Hovel.** A shack. Referred to in *The Horse and His Boy.*

- **Jaw.** Cocky talk. Digory speaks of the words that appear on the golden gates in *The Magician's Nephew,* "I don't know what all that jaw in the last line is about."

✔ **Loquacity.** Talkativeness. Referred to in *The Horse and His Boy*.

✔ **Pax.** Peace. In *The Magician's Nephew*, Polly says of her spat with Digory, "We'll call it Pax."

✔ **Rum.** Out of the ordinary, bizarre. Frank the cabby says of the transformation of Strawberry into Fledge in *The Magician's Nephew*, "This is a rum go." In *The Last Battle*, Digory comments, "It'll be rum for Peter and the others."

✔ **Sal volatile.** Smelling salts. Aunt Letty uses these after her encounter with Jadis in *The Magician's Nephew*.

✔ **Yeomanry.** Former British cavalry force. Referred to in *The Magician's Nephew*.

The *For Dummies* "Best of" Awards: The best and wittiest of *The Chronicles of Narnia*

Move over Oscar, it's time to hand out my awards for the best and wittiest lines and characters in *The Chronicles of Narnia*. I dub these the first ever *For Dummies* "Best of" Awards. So put on your tux or evening gown and let the drum roll begin. . . .

Wittiest opening line. Humor can be found throughout *The Chronicles of Narnia,* but there's no wittier line than the opening line of *The Voyage of the "Dawn Treader:"* "There was a boy called Eustace Clarence Scrubb, and he almost deserved it."

Best theological line. Chapters 8 and 9 discuss many of the unforgettable quotes in the Narnian Chronicles that have amazing theological depth. Yet, I'm not sure if any can beat this line's simplicity. Summing up perfectly the role of Aslan in the lives of all Narnians, King Tirian says to Jill Pole in *The Last Battle:* "Courage, child: we are all between the paws of the true Aslan."

Most poetic line. In *The Magician's Nephew,* the narrator describes the new Narnian sun after its creation: "You could imagine that it laughed for joy as it came up."

Most creative description. In *The Horse and His Boy,* the narrator describes the noise made by Bree's and Hwin's hooves: "Not *Propputty-propputty* as it would be on a hard road, but *Thubbudy-thubbudy* on the dry sand."

Most imaginative line. In *The Silver Chair,* Golg the Earthman describes what gold and diamonds are like deep beneath the ground's surface: "I have heard of those little scratches in the crust that you Top-dwellers call mines. But that's where you get dead gold, dead silver, dead gems. Down in Bism we have them alive and growing. There I'll pick you bunches of rubies that you can eat and squeeze you a cup full of diamond-juice."

Most empathetic line. As you read *The Silver Chair,* your heart aches for Prince Rilian when he says, "All these years I have been the slave of my mother's slayer."

Best line to use at a party. When Puddleglum introduces himself in *The Silver Chair,* he quips, "Puddleglum's my name. But it doesn't matter if you forget it. I can always tell you again."

(continued)

(continued)

Best insult. In *The Last Battle,* Emeth calls himself a "dog" in a derogatory fashion. Some talking dogs overhear him and are insulted. But one of the dogs responds, "He doesn't mean any harm. After all, we call our puppies, Boys, when they don't behave properly."

Best sarcastic line. In *The Horse and His Boy,* Prince Cor speaks of his new life as a prince in Archenland. He tells the others that he's looking forward to it "even though Education and all sorts of horrible things are going to happen to me."

Best "glass is half full comment." In *The Silver Chair,* when Eustace, Jill, Rilian, and Puddleglum appear to be stuck underground forever, the Marshwiggle reasons, "And you must always remember there's one good thing about being trapped down [in Underland]: It'll save funeral expenses."

Most original name. The real name of Bree, the talking Narnian horse in *The Horse and His Boy,* is Breehy-hinny-brinny-hoohy-hah. That's one Narnian name you'd never want to use on your own pet!

Chapter 6

Allegory and Symbolism: Deciphering the Chronicles

*W*hen people read books, watch films, or listen to music, they can get carried away searching for hidden meaning. Sometimes the whole thing even starts to resemble a wacky conspiracy theory. Consider some of the more interesting ones — that the Hulk in *The Incredible Hulk* is actually a metaphor warning of the dangers of a worldwide Communist revolution or that the Hobbits in *The Lord of the Rings* represent a secret group of people bent on ridding the world of those "No shirt, no shoes, no service" signs.

These examples demonstrate the perspective you should avoid as you search for symbolism in *The Chronicles of Narnia* or any other work of literature or art: Just because someone claims that a work has a particular hidden meaning doesn't mean that the author actually intended it to be so. Instead, you should fully examine the author's intent and purpose. As I explain later in this chapter, you can certainly apply your own ideas to a story, but be sure to recognize that there's a difference between this "personal application" and the author's deliberate objective.

When most readers read *The Chronicles of Narnia,* they get the sense that Lewis is telling more than just a good story, that some of the themes and characters have underlying symbolism just waiting to be discovered. Some readers even suggest that the Narnian stories are an allegory of the Christian faith.

In this chapter, don your detective hat as you discover how to decipher the meaning behind the Narnian Chronicles. As you do so, you understand what author C.S. Lewis did and did not intend with the symbolism expressed in the series. This chapter also helps you also compare Narnia with J.R.R. Tolkien's Middle-earth and explore Lewis's and Tolkien's different approaches to penning *The Chronicles of Narnia* and *The Lord of the Rings,* respectively. After you read this chapter, you'll be fully equipped to explore the symbolism detailed in Chapters 7 through 9.

Is Narnia an Allegory?

Perhaps the single most common question about *The Chronicles of Narnia* asks whether Lewis wrote the series as an allegory. After all, even if your biblical knowledge is limited to a few Sunday school classes in third grade, you probably notice that Aslan has many similarities to Jesus Christ. If Lewis added that symbolism on purpose, does that mean that everything in Narnia represents something in the Bible?

C.S. Lewis makes clear that he didn't write the Narnian Chronicles as a biblical allegory. But you may be asking: How can this be true given the obvious symbolism used throughout the series? In order to understand Lewis's side of the story, you need to understand the difference between allegory and something he called *supposal.*

The gory details of allegory

An *allegory* is a literary device in which an author uses the form of a person, place, or animal to represent an abstract idea. For example, an eagle can represent the abstract concept of "freedom," a witch can represent "evil," or a photo of yours truly can express "amazing, profound wisdom."

Some of the most popular literature in history is allegorical. In Dante Alighieri's *The Divine Comedy,* for example, Dante represents humanity as he journeys through Hell, Purgatory, and Paradise. In John Bunyan's *The Pilgrim's Progress,* concepts like hope and mercy become real-life characters in his saga of a man (named Christian) searching for salvation. So too, Lewis's first book written after his Christian conversion was *The Pilgrim's Regress,* a Bunyan-like allegory that describes his road to the Christian faith.

In *The Allegory of Love,* Lewis writes that when you use allegory, "you can start with [facts] . . . and can then invent . . . visible things to express them." He adds, "What is good or happy has always been high like the heavens and bright like the sun. Evil and misery were deep and dark from the first."

A slightly broader definition of allegory applies when an author represents real people or places in a fictional context. George Orwell's *Animal Farm* is a well-known example of this allegorical type. As a way of addressing the issues surrounding the Russian Revolution, Marx, Lenin, Stalin, and other real historical figures are represented as pigs on a farm.

The Chronicles of Narnia is not in this genre. Lewis did *not* write the series as an allegory using his fantasy setting to represent abstract concepts or real people. In terms of literary style, the series bears no parallels to allegorical works like *The Divine Comedy, Animal Farm,* or even Lewis's own *The Pilgrim's Regress.*

In fact, Lewis explicitly warns readers against trying to make a one-for-one match between Narnia and in the real world. In a May 1954 letter to a fifth grade class in Maryland, he writes, "You are mistaken when you think everything in the books 'represents' something in this world. Things do that in *The Pilgrim's Progress* but I'm not writing in that way."

Supposedly, there's a supposal

Although Lewis makes it clear that *The Chronicles of Narnia* isn't an allegory, he doesn't deny that some symbolism was written into the series. But, to understand his approach, you need to recognize that Lewis differentiates allegory from something he calls *supposal.* In a December 1959 letter to a young girl named Sophia Storr, he explains the difference (emphasis mine):

> *I don't say. 'Let us represent Christ as Aslan.' I say, '**Supposing** there was a world like Narnia, and **supposing,** like ours, it needed redemption, let us imagine what sort of Incarnation and Passion and Resurrection Christ would have there.'*

Allegory and supposal aren't identical devices, according to Lewis, because they deal with what's real and what's unreal quite differently. In an allegory, the ideas, concepts, and even people being expressed are true, but the characters are make-believe. They always behave in a way reflective of the underlying concepts they're representing. A supposal is much different; the fictional character becomes "real" within the imaginary world, taking on a life of its own and adapting to the make-believe world as necessary. If, for example, you accept the supposal of Aslan as true, then Lewis says, "He would really have been a physical object in that world as He was in Palestine, and His death on the Stone Table would have been a physical event no less than his death on Calvary."

Aslan isn't an allegory of Jesus Christ. Instead, he's a supposal. Lewis emphasizes this point in a December 1958 letter to a lady named Mrs. Hook:

> *[Aslan] is an invention giving an imaginary answer to the question 'What might Christ become like if there really were a world like Narnia and He choose to be incarnate and die and rise again in that world as He actually has done in ours?' This is not allegory at all.*

Much of *The Chronicles of Narnia* is built on the concept of supposal. For example:

- ✔ Suppose Christ came into the world of Narnia as Aslan. What would he be like?
- ✔ Suppose Aslan created Narnia out of nothing and centuries later brought it to a conclusion. How would these stories play out?
- ✔ Suppose evil were introduced into Narnia. What would that be like?
- ✔ Suppose a person or talking animal could freely choose to obey or disobey Aslan. What would life in Narnia be like?

By using supposal, Lewis doesn't feel compelled to have a direct 1:1 correlation between the experiences of Aslan and the real life of Jesus Christ. In his letter to Sophia Storr, Lewis talks of this freedom: "When I started *The Lion, the Witch and the Wardrobe,* I don't think I foresaw what Aslan was going to do and suffer. I think He just insisted on behaving in His own way."

Using supposal as the vehicle for getting him there, Lewis views *The Chronicles of Narnia* as myth. He explains that an allegory is a story with a single meaning, but a myth is a story that can have many meanings for different readers in different generations. According to Lewis, an author puts into an allegory "only what he already knows," but in a myth, he puts "what he does not yet know and could not come by in any other way."

Comparing Narnia and Middle-earth

The fantasy worlds of Lewis's Narnia and J.R.R. Tolkien's Middle-earth are both so enchanting and absorbing that readers can easily become lost in them. They're crafted so masterfully that you may finish *The Chronicles of Narnia* or *The Lord of the Rings* and start searching your house for a magic portal or check the Web for a discount flight to Hobbiton. They both seem so much like real worlds you can visit.

Given the major influences that both Narnia and Middle-earth have had on literature over the past 50 years, it's perhaps not surprising that the originators of these worlds, Lewis and Tolkien, had a strong friendship and significantly influenced each other's work. (See Chapter 3 for more on their unique relationship.)

However, in spite of the ties that exist between their authors, don't get lulled into thinking that you can approach Narnia and Middle-earth in the same way. As I explain in the following sections, both are "subcreations" of this world, but these two worlds are quite distinct from each other, so much so that you're nearly comparing apples and oranges.

Both worlds are subcreations

Tolkien developed a concept he called *subcreation.* He believed God is the only one who can truly create *ex nihilo,* or create something from nothing. However, a fantasy author can take God's creations and use them as raw material for creating (or *subcreating*) an entirely new secondary world. When the author is successful, his subcreation has all the same stuff — such as the search for meaning and the struggle between good and evil — inside it as real life does. Middle-earth was Tolkien's subcreation.

Tolkien's idea of subcreation had a strong influence on Lewis, and Narnia became Lewis's subcreation. In *Transposition and Other Essays,* Lewis offers a glimpse into the thought that went into the world he subcreated. He writes:

> *We do not want merely to see beauty . . . We want something else which can hardly be put into words — to be united with the beauty we see, to pass into it, to receive it into ourselves, to bathe in it, to become part of it. That is why we have peopled air and earth and water with gods and goddesses, and nymphs and elves.*

Undoubtedly, one of Lewis's greatest joys in writing was subcreating the enchanted world of Narnia.

Both worlds feature eucatastrophes

Tolkien and Lewis both believed that at the heart of a real fairy tale is something Tolkien called *eucatastrophe,* which means, in essence, good catastrophe. According to Tolkien, a eucatastrophe is a sudden, miraculous, and unexpected turn in the story from the worst possible situation to the best. He believed that a eucatastrophe "contain[s] many marvels — peculiarly artistic, beautiful, and moving: 'mythical' in their perfect, self-contained significance."

As a Christian, Tolkien considered the birth of Jesus Christ *the* eucatastrophe in human history. Christ's birth, death, and resurrection rocked the world apart: Before these events, evil was winning, but Christ's atonement on the cross for the sins of the world perfectly defeated the eternal consequences of sin. In a similar way, each Christian's death becomes his or her personal eucatastrophe. Or, as the poet Robert Browning writes in *Prospice,* "For sudden the worst turns the best to the brave."

Tolkien features several eucatastrophes in *The Hobbit* and *The Lord of the Rings,* such as Bilbo's finding of the Ring, the destruction of the Ring on Mount Doom, and the final defeat of Sauron.

Lewis, too, incorporates the concept of the eucatastrophe throughout the Narnian Chronicles. In *The Lion, the Witch and the Wardrobe,* Aslan's resurrection and defeat of the White Witch come only when all hope is lost. In *Prince Caspian,* Caspian and his army are on the verge of extinction when Peter and Edmund and later Aslan and his army arrive; together, they defeat King Miraz and the Telmarines. In *The Voyage of the "Dawn Treader,"* Caspian and his crew face several mini-eucatastrophes in their odyssey to the remote end of the Eastern Sea. In *The Horse and His Boy,* the eucatastrophes are the defeat of the Calormenes and Shasta's discovery of his true royal self. *The Silver Chair* sees Prince Rilian eventually freed and restored to his proper place. In *The Magician's Nephew,* Queen Jadis is banished, and Digory's mother is healed. And finally, *The Last Battle* chronicles the final defeat of evil and the promise of eternal life in the real Narnia.

Allegory versus supposal versus applicability

Just as *The Chronicles of Narnia* is often mistakenly considered an allegory, many readers are similarly tempted to look for allegories in *The Lord of the Rings.* For example, some contend the Ring represents the atomic bomb, while others see Gandalf as a representation of Christ. But the problem with these interpretations is that, although there are some intriguing parallels, they break down when you look at the totality of the story. In fact, Gandalf, Frodo, and Aragorn all suggest Christ at certain points in the story.

Although neither can accurately be considered an allegory, Narnia and Middle-earth differ significantly in terms of their symbolism. On the one hand, Lewis embraced the idea of supposal (see the section "Supposedly, there's a supposal," earlier in this chapter). On the other hand, Tolkien argued for something he called *applicability,* the idea of giving a reader the freedom to extract meaning from an author's work rather than an author forcing a particular idea onto the reader. As he explains in the foreword to *The Lord of the Rings:*

An "allegoric" reaction

Lewis didn't write the Narnian Chronicles as an allegory, but he didn't have a problem with the use of allegory in literature. Not only were some of his favorite works allegories (*The Faerie Queene, The Divine Comedy,* and *The Pilgrim's* *Progress*), but also he penned the allegorical *The Pilgrim's Regress*. In contrast, Tolkien detested allegory as a writing device and avoided it like the plague.

> *I cordially dislike allegory in all its manifestations, and always have done so since I grew old and wary enough to detect its presence. I much prefer history, true or feigned, with its varied applicability to the thought and experience of the readers. I think that many confuse 'applicability' with 'allegory'; but the one resides in the freedom of the reader, and the other in the purposed domination of the author.*

Lewis openly expressed his intent to present Aslan as what God might be like if he appeared in Narnia. Tolkien, however, believed a writer should never be as explicit in his intent. As a result, Tolkien lumped Lewis's concept of supposal squarely into the allegorical camp, considering it just another a manifestation of allegory.

Fairy tale versus mythical history

Both *The Chronicles of Narnia* and *The Lord of the Rings* are often referred to either as myths or fairy tales. As a result, people sometimes mistakenly believe that Lewis and Tolkien purposefully wrote in the same style for the same audience. In fact, it's my belief that *The Chronicles of Narnia* is best thought of as a "fairy tale," while *The Lord of the Rings* may more accurately be depicted as a "complete mythology."

Lewis wrote *The Chronicles of Narnia* as a fairy tale "in the spirit of E. Nesbitt." Although Tolkien's Middle-earth came first, Lewis didn't set out to create a Middle-earth wannabe. He instead wanted to create a world perfect for a children's series. He spoke of his love of writing fairy tales in his essay "Sometimes Fairy Stories May Say Best What's to Be Said:"

> *I fell in love with the [fairy tale's] form itself: its brevity, its severe restraints on description, its flexible traditionalism, its inflexible hostility to all analysis, digression, reflections and 'gas.' I was now enamored of it. Its very limitations of vocabulary became an attraction; as the hardness of the stone pleases the*

sculptor or the difficulty of the sonnet delights the sonneteer. On that side (as Author) I wrote fairy tales because the Fairy Tale seemed the ideal Form for the stuff I had to say.

In contrast, Tolkien created an entire mythical world in Middle-earth; it's a world that perhaps has no equal in literature. Tolkien's Middle-earth comes complete with original languages, distinct cultures, extensive background histories, and details out the wazoo. As such, Tolkien wrote for an older audience than Lewis, one that could handle his heavier prose style and appreciate the depth of the mythology.

Because of these differences, *The Lord of the Rings* fans sometimes write off the Narnian Chronicles as overly simplistic. But in doing so, they misunderstand the nature of Lewis's master work. Although *The Chronicles of Narnia* and *The Lord of the Rings* are both fantasy stories, they're written in different styles for different audiences.

Chapter 7

Faces and Places in Narnia

In This Chapter

▶ Knowing "who's who" in the world of Narnia

▶ Noting characters' biblical parallels

▶ Discovering "where's where" inside Narnian geography

Drinian, Rilian, and Tirian. All are Narnian leaders, but which one is the son of Caspian? Does that quirky professor from *The Lion, the Witch and the Wardrobe* appear in any other stories? Are the evil Queen Jadis of Charn and the White Witch the same person? Are they even human?

Questions like these are common among *The Chronicles of Narnia* readers, and with good reason seeing as the world of Narnia is filled with an eclectic cast of characters and creatures. The books may be children's stories, but that doesn't mean they aren't jam-packed with details. What's more, Lewis filled *The Chronicles of Narnia* with symbolism (see Chapters 6, 8, and 9), so there's often more to characters than initially meets the eye.

In this chapter, you explore the "who's who" and "where's where" of Lewis's fantasy world. Treat this chapter as your handy-dandy reference guide, essential to helping you maximize your understanding of *The Chronicles of Narnia*.

Who's Who in Narnia

The Chronicles of Narnia is filled with a host of heroes, villains, talking animals, shady characters, and mythical creatures. Lewis didn't intend for these characters to be strict allegories of actual people or concepts, preferring instead, as Chapter 6 discusses in detail, to see them as *supposals*.

They may not be allegories, but Lewis does pack many symbolic ideas into his characters. In some cases, a character bears some resemblance to a real person or idea. For example, Edmund in *The Lion, the Witch and the Wardrobe* shares parallels with Judas from the Bible. So too, Reepicheep is in many ways a symbol of a chivalrous knight from the Middle Ages. In other cases, a character in the story represents the ways in which you and I can respond to God in real life. For instance, self-absorbed Eustace at the start of *The Voyage of the "Dawn Treader"* probably reminds you a bit of yourself, even if your self-ishness is subtler. Alternatively, the simple, steadfast faith of Trufflehunter in *Prince Caspian* is a reminder of the kind of child-like faith that Jesus Christ calls his followers to in Matthew 19:14.

This section explores the major characters of *The Chronicles of Narnia*.

Adventurous children

Each of stories in *The Chronicles of Narnia* features children as the primary characters. Lewis uses children as a way to draw the target reader — a child as well — into the story by giving him characters he can identify with.

However, they also represent the children of God discussed in the Bible. The children in the Narnian Chronicles aren't perfect; each is, to varying degrees, disobedient and sinful at times. Some, such as Edmund and Eustace, are far more treacherous before their encounters with Aslan. Yet, like children of God, those who need redemption are restored by Aslan after they repent. Also, just as some people in the real world fall away from faith, Susan demonstrates how this crisis of faith plays out in Narnia.

In all, eight children from England enter Narnia via a number of different magical entrances: a wardrobe, magic rings, a magic door, and a picture. They are:

- ✔ **Digory Kirke.** At age 12, Digory travels to the Wood Between the Worlds in *The Magician's Nephew* using magic rings from his wicked uncle, Andrew Ketterley. He eventually witnesses the creation of Narnia by Aslan. In *The Lion, the Witch and the Wardrobe*, Digory's known as "Professor Kirke," the owner of the great country house where the Pevensie children stay. By *The Voyage of the "Dawn Treader,"* Kirke has become poor and has moved into a small cottage. In *The Last Battle*, Digory is 61 years old when he goes to real Narnia.

    Digory's sin of ringing the bell in Charn is symbolic of "the original sin" by Adam and Eve (Genesis 3). Digory's selfishness ultimately causes evil to be introduced into the pristine world of Narnia, but he repents of his wrongdoing and is fully restored by Aslan.

- ✔ **Edmund Pevensie.** Edmund is the scoundrel in *The Lion, the Witch and the Wardrobe* because he betrays his siblings after being tempted by the White Witch with Turkish Delight and the promise of power. When

Edmund tries to return to Aslan and the side of the good Narnians, the White Witch demands his life for his traitorous actions. Aslan dies in his place at the Stone Table. After he's restored by Aslan, Edmund is named King Edmund the Just and becomes a strong leader. Edmund is 10 years old in *The Lion, the Witch and the Wardrobe* and 19 when he dies in the railway accident in *The Last Battle.*

Edmund's betrayal of the Pevensies bears some similarity to Judas's betrayal of Jesus. However, Edmund repents of his sin and is restored fully by Aslan, while the real Judas simply kills himself (see Matthew 27:5). Edmund is much more like Peter the disciple, who denied Jesus three times (Matthew 26:67–75) but repented, was restored by Jesus, and played a leading role in the early Christian Church (Acts 4). Also, because Aslan dies to save Edmund from punishment, Edmund is also a symbol of an "an everyman," representing each person of the human race that Jesus died for on the cross (Romans 5:11).

✔ **Eustace Scrubb.** Cousin of the Pevensies, Eustace is a spoiled and thoroughly self-centered kid at the start of *The Voyage of the "Dawn Treader."* After turning into a dragon during the voyage, however, his heart is changed. Aslan transforms Eustace back into a boy, and he becomes a leader in his own right during the events of *The Silver Chair* and *The Last Battle,* although he's still far from perfect.

Eustace is symbolic of a sinner who has been transformed by the grace of God. See Chapter 9 for details.

✔ **Jill Pole.** Along with Eustace, Jill is drawn into Narnia in *The Silver Chair* and *The Last Battle.* On her first trip, she's charged with remembering Aslan's four instructions for finding Prince Rilian. She gets distracted at times, but she and Eustace are ultimately successful. Jill's mountaintop experience with Aslan in *The Silver Chair* has some similarity to Moses's experience on the top of Mount Sinai in the Book of Exodus.

✔ **Lucy Pevensie.** At age 8, Lucy Pevensie is the first child to enter Narnia through the wardrobe in *The Lion, the Witch and the Wardrobe.* She's later named Queen Lucy the Valiant during the Golden Age of Narnia.

When it comes to her faith in Aslan, Lucy is the most steadfast of all the children. However, she faces times of disobedience, too. In *Prince Caspian,* she succumbs to peer pressure rather than follow Aslan. And in *The Voyage of the "Dawn Treader,"* she gives in to temptation when she reads the Magician's Book. Finally, Lucy also struggles with "nib-nosing," asking Aslan things that she has no business knowing. Overall, however, Lucy's symbolic of the simple faith that Christians are called to have in Christ.

✔ **Peter Pevensie.** Peter's the oldest of the Pevensie children who enter Narnia from the wardrobe in *The Lion, the Witch and the Wardrobe.* He eventually becomes the High King of Narnia during its Golden Age. Peter's 13 years old before his first trip and 22 when he goes to real Narnia in *The Last Battle*.

Peter's a strong, consistent leader who bears some loose resemblance to the apostle Peter, who led the early Christian Church. The primary reason for the link is that the apostle was, more or less, the *de facto* head of the early church, and, for part of the series, Peter's the highest authority in Narnia. As with the Apostle Peter, Peter Pevensie at times struggles with too much self-reliance and too little trust in Aslan. For example, he chooses the practical route to Aslan's How in *Prince Caspian* rather than listen to Lucy's claim of seeing Aslan leading them in the other direction. However, he realizes his mistake and eventually is able to see Aslan for himself.

✔ **Polly Plummer.** Polly is Digory Kirke's 11-year-old neighbor in *The Magician's Nephew*. She's the first person to enter the Wood Between the Worlds when she's tricked by Digory's uncle (Andrew Ketterling) into touching a magic ring. She and Digory explore the ruins of Charn and witness the creation of Narnia. In *The Last Battle,* Polly (now 60 years old) is one of the seven members of the Friends of Narnia. Referred to as "Miss Plummer," Polly apparently never marries; however, she's a close friend of the Pevensie family, who call her "Aunt Polly."

Polly struggles with stubbornness at times but has a "good head on her shoulders." She's balanced and a solid, loyal friend to Digory throughout their travels.

✔ **Susan Pevensie.** Susan is the second oldest of the Pevensie children and is 12 years old when she enters the wardrobe. She becomes Queen Susan the Gentle in Narnia. In *The Lion, the Witch and the Wardrobe,* Susan is a courageous leader, although by *Prince Caspian,* her faith in Aslan shows "some cracks" when she stubbornly refuses to believe the Great Lion appears to her sister Lucy. In *The Horse and His Boy,* Susan's folly of a possible marriage to Prince Rabadash of Calormen leads to the Narnians' need to escape Tashbaan. By *The Last Battle,* Susan has abandoned her faith in Aslan and Narnia altogether, dismissing them as "child stories."

Susan symbolizes a person who had a Christian faith early in life but left it behind. In fact, she's the one child from England who isn't part of the Friends of Narnia council at the end of *The Last Battle*. Lewis never resolves Susan's storyline and leaves the question of whether she ever "returns to her faith" up in the air.

Imperfect heroes

In *The Chronicles of Narnia*, Lewis creates several heroic characters, but he never depicts them as perfect people with no struggles or temptations. In fact, each of the major characters has unique struggles that he or she has to deal with. In this way, Lewis is echoing what the Apostle Paul says in Romans 3:23: "For all have sinned and fallen short of the glory of God." The following table lists some of the major strongholds of temptation that each character faces.

Character	Struggles with
Peter Pevensie	Self-reliance
Susan Pevensie	Worldliness
Edmund Pevensie	Power, appetite
Lucy Pevensie	Curiosity, peer pressure
Digory Kirke	Curiosity, pride
Polly Plummer	Stubbornness
Eustace Scrubb	Selfishness, pride
Jill Pole	Pride
Caspian	Selfishness, reluctance to lead
Reepicheep	Pride
Tirian	Rashness

Good rulers of Narnia

In addition to High King Peter, Queen Susan, King Edmund, and Queen Lucy, the following good rulers of Narnia are important characters in the series:

✔ **Caspian.** King Caspian X becomes the king of Narnia in *Prince Caspian* and continues his reign in *The Voyage of the "Dawn Treader."* By the time of *The Silver Chair,* Caspian has ruled for 53 years and is an elderly man who simply longs to find his kidnapped son, Prince Rilian. Caspian descends from a long line of Telmarine rulers; his father, King Caspian IX, was murdered by his evil uncle Miraz who then usurped the power of the throne.

King Caspian X is a good military leader and has a love for Aslan and old Narnia, but his selfish reluctance to lead is his weakness. Caspian's immaturity is a reminder of a similar struggle with apparent fickleness that John Mark had in days of the early Church (see Acts 15:36–39). However, like Caspian, John Mark overcame his struggles and went on to do important things for the Lord (namely, authoring the Book of Mark in the New Testament).

✔ **Frank I and Helen I.** Frank's a London cabby who, in *The Magician's Nephew,* is accidentally pulled into Narnia just as it's being created. Aslan makes Frank and his wife Helen the first king and queen of the newly created land, and they serve as good rulers. They never return to England.

Frank and Helen are symbolic of Adam and Eve from the Book of Genesis but without the disobedience. (Digory took care of the "original sin" in Charn before Frank and Helen entered the picture.)

✔ **Rilian.** Prince Rilian is the son of Caspian X and is a principal character in *The Silver Chair*. After his mother's killed by a serpent, Rilian seeks revenge for her death. His plan fails when he's cast under a spell by the Green Witch; she gives him the identity of the Black Knight and holds him in Underland for ten years. Rilian's eventually freed by Eustace Scrubb, Jill Pole, and Puddleglum the Marshwiggle and goes on to become a good King of Narnia.

✔ **Tirian.** King Tirian, the final king of Narnia (seven generations removed from Rilian), is depicted in *The Last Battle*. He's a valiant and heroic leader but is too rash at times, a trait that causes problems when he fights Shift the Ape and the Calormenes.

Tirian's slaying of a Calormene soldier bears some resemblance to Moses's anger-induced killing of an Egyptian in Exodus 2:11–12. In both cases, the rash actions of Tirian and Moses complicate matters for what Aslan (and God) have in store.

Narnians and friends

Narnia is filled with an eclectic cast of characters, some with major roles and some who are just briefly mentioned. This section explores the characters and creatures that are most noteworthy:

✔ **Aravis.** The daughter of Calormene leader Kidrash Tarkaan, Aravis runs away from home in *The Horse and His Boy* to avoid an arranged marriage. Aravis joins up with Shasta, who she initially looks down upon as an ignorant, unsophisticated boy. Aravis later marries Shasta (Prince Cor of Archenland) and becomes Queen of Archenland. *The Horse and His Boy* shows Aravis's gradual transformation from being smug and arrogant to displaying graciousness, honor, and humility.

✔ **Bacchus.** In Roman mythology, Bacchus is the god of wine. In *Prince Caspian*, Bacchus is described as a boy with a wild face who dances in celebration after the victory over King Miraz.

✔ **Bree.** Bree is a talking Narnian stallion whose adventures are chronicled in *The Horse and His Boy*. Bree was taken from Narnia at an early age and forced to serve as a war stallion in the Calormene army; he sees Shasta's desire to run away as his chance to return to his homeland. The arrogant and haughty Bree assumes the role of leader in the journey to Narnia, but when the going gets tough, he's outdone by two creatures he looks down upon: the common horse Hwin and the boy Shasta. See Chapter 8 for a discussion of Bree's struggle with pride.

✔ **Centaurs.** From ancient mythology, a centaur is a creature that's half man and half horse. In the words of Lewis, the horse part is "like huge English farm horses" and the man part resembles "stern but beautiful giants." Three centaurs are named in the Narnian Chronicles: Glenstorm, Cloudbirth, and Roonwit.

✔ **Coriakin.** Lord Coriakin is the kind overseer of the Dufflepuds, as depicted in *The Voyage of the "Dawn Treader."* He's also a fallen star, serving over the Duffers as some type of punishment for a sin that's never discussed.

✔ **Corin.** Prince Corin of Archenland is the twin brother of Shasta (Prince Cor) in *The Horse and His Boy*. Corin willingly gives up the Archenland throne to allow his older brother to take his rightful place. Corin is a tough fighter in battle and is given the nickname "Corin Thunder-Fists."

✔ **Doctor Cornelius.** Prince Caspian's tutor Doctor Cornelius tells him about old Narnia and helps the young prince escape from his uncle Miraz. Cornelius is part Dwarf, part Telmarine. He bears some loose resemblance to the prophet Samuel in the Old Testament, who names a young David to be King of Israel over King Saul, a ruler deemed illegitimate by God. Similarly, Cornelius lets Caspian know his true identity — the proper King of Narnia.

✔ **Drinian.** Lord Drinian is the worthy captain of the *Dawn Treader,* serving under King Caspian.

✔ **Dryads.** Derived from ancient mythology, dryads are tree-women (or tree nymphs) who inhabit the trees in Narnia. Their lives are completely dependent upon the health of their trees.

✔ **Dufflepuds (Duffers, Monopods).** The Dufflepuds are the invisible, silly, one-footed creatures that Caspian and his crew discover on their voyage in the Eastern Ocean. Led by Chief Monopod, the Dufflepuds are a bunch of yes-men who agree with anything the chief says. They believe they're ruled by a bad wizard, Lord Coriakin, only because they misunderstand him and mistakenly think he's bad. Lucy Pevensie uses the Magician's Spell to make the Dufflepuds visible once again.

The Dufflepuds are perhaps a parody on how foolish humans can be at times, from believing anything someone says to believing that they can "put one over" on God (see Chapter 8 for more).

✔ **Earthmen.** The Earthmen are creatures that live under the earth in *Prince Caspian.* They're enslaved by the Green Witch and forced to work for her. They range from small, gnome-like creatures to others that are so tall they could start for the Chicago Bulls. Their home is Bism, which lies far below the Witch's Underland.

- **Emeth.** In *The Last Battle,* Emeth is a Calormene who seeks truth in the false god Tash only to discover that he's been serving Aslan all along. Emeth is the one Calormene who ends up in the real Narnia after the end of the world. The name Emeth means "truth" in Hebrew.

  Emeth's story gives strong insight into Lewis's perspective on what happens to people who earnestly seek other faiths. See Chapter 8 for more discussion on this topic.

- **Farsight the eagle.** In *The Last Battle,* Farsight is a talking eagle that warns King Tirian of the fall of Cair Paravel and death of Roonwit the centaur.

- **Father Christmas.** Father Christmas is a large, bearded man who shows up briefly in *The Lion, the Witch and the Wardrobe* at the end of the Hundred Years of Winter. He gives Peter, Susan, and Lucy Pevensie gifts that they use later in the Narnian stories: Peter receives a sword and shield, Susan an archery set and ivory horn, and Lucy a small dagger and healing elixir.

- **Father Time.** Father Time is a sleeping, giant-like man seen in Underland by Eustace Scrubb, Jill Pole, Puddleglum the Marshwiggle, and Prince Rilian in *The Silver Chair.* In *The Last Battle,* Father Time's awakened at the end of the world. Aslan indicates that because he's awake, Father time must receive a new name, indicating that our concept of time is outmoded in eternity.

- **Fledge the horse (Strawberry).** As told in *The Magician's Nephew,* Fledge starts out as a working London cabby horse named Strawberry who's owned by Frank. However, after Frank and the horse are accidentally pulled into Narnia, Aslan gives Strawberry the gift of speech and the ability to fly. He's renamed Fledge and performs an important task for Aslan: flying Digory Kirke and Polly Plummer to the garden in the west.

- **Glimfeather the owl.** Glimfeather is the owl that helps Eustace Scrubb and Jill Pole as they start their quest for Prince Rilian in *The Silver Chair.* Glimfeather and another owl transport the two children from Cair Paravel to Puddleglum the Marshwiggle's home.

- **Hermit of the Southern March.** This old hermit cares for a wounded Aravis and the talking horses (Bree and Hwin) in *The Horse and His Boy* while Shasta journeys to warn Archenland of the Calormene invasion. The hermit also offers a play-by-play of the battle between the Calormenes and Narnia (with Archenland's support).

- **Hwin.** Hwin is Aravis's talking mare in *The Horse and His Boy.* The understated and gentle Hwin is a strong contrast to the arrogant, condescending Bree, yet Hwin proves herself as the stronger horse during the journey. Hwin is characteristic of the humility and strength that a Christian should possess.

- **Jewel the unicorn.** Jewel, a close friend of Tirian's, is a fierce, loyal unicorn in *The Last Battle*. He's part of Tirian's last stand against the Calormenes.

- **Lune.** King Lune rules over Archenland in *The Horse and His Boy* and is father to Shasta (Prince Cor).

- **Mr. and Mrs. Beaver.** Mr. and Mrs. Beaver are talking beavers that provide assistance to Peter, Susan, and Lucy Pevensie in *The Lion, the Witch and the Wardrobe*. They also introduce Aslan to the children. The Beavers are symbolic of humble, loyal, faithful believers.

- **Mr. Tumnus.** Mr. Tumnus is the faun (half man, half goat) that Lucy Pevensie encounters when she first enters Narnia in *The Lion, the Witch and the Wardrobe*. Tumnus is turned to stone by the White Witch but eventually becomes alive again. In *The Horse and His Boy,* he's part of the Narnian court and travels to Tashbaan with Edmund, Susan, and Lucy.

  The crisis of belief — whether or not to hand Lucy over to the White Witch — that Mr. Tumnus faces at the start of *The Lion, the Witch and the Wardrobe* symbolizes a decision that many people have to make in life: Do I choose the expedient way out or do I risk everything for what I know to be right?

- **Naiads.** Taken from ancient mythology, naiads are well-women (or water nymphs) that inhabit the water in Narnia.

- **Nain.** King Nain rules Archenland during the days of *Prince Caspian*.

- **Poggin the Dwarf.** In *The Last Battle,* Poggin is a Dwarf who sides with Tirian and fights alongside him in the final battle against the Calormene army. Poggin proves himself courageous, not only for his fighting but also for going against the other rebellious Dwarfs who don't side with King Tirian.

- **Puddleglum the Marshwiggle.** Puddleglum is a Marshwiggle, a Narnian creature that's very tall and thin and has webbed hands and feet like a frog. (As the narrator describes him, "He seemed to be all arms and legs.") Puddleglum serves as a guide to Eustace Scrubb and Jill Pole on their journey to rescue Prince Rilian in *The Silver Chair*.

  Besides Aslan, Puddleglum is arguably the most brilliantly conceived character in *The Chronicles of Narnia*. He's a loyal and brave Narnian, but he always looks at life through gloomy eyes. From a reader's perspective, Lewis ingeniously pulls off Puddleglum's pessimism as an endearing quality. Puddleglum proves extremely faithful to Aslan when under attack from the Green Witch in Underland. Jill Pole describes him perfectly, saying, "You sound as doleful as a funeral and I believe you're perfectly happy. And you talk as if you were afraid of everything when you're really brave — as a lion." Puddleglum, therefore, symbolizes a Christian who remains faithful even during the most difficult of circumstances.

- **Puzzle the donkey.** In *The Last Battle,* Puzzle's a simple donkey foolishly convinced by Shift the Ape to wear a lion's skin and impersonate Aslan.

- **Ramandu.** Ramandu is a retired star that Caspian and his crew encounter in *The Voyage of the "Dawn Treader."* Caspian eventually marries Ramandu's daughter.

  The story of the bird laying the live coal in Ramandu's mouth is strikingly similar to the story depicted in Isaiah 6:6.

- **Reepicheep the mouse.** Reepicheep is a chivalrous and valiant talking mouse that's faithful to Aslan and old Narnia. In *Prince Caspian,* Reepicheep is severely wounded, but he's healed by Lucy Pevensie and his tail is restored by Aslan. In *The Voyage of the "Dawn Treader,"* he's a member of Caspian's crew to the End of the World and goes onward alone to Aslan's country.

  Reepicheep isn't an allegory for any particular person in the Bible or otherwise. Even though he has some weaknesses such as occasional pride or vanity, often in the Narnian Chronicles, Reepicheep characterizes what a Christian disciple should be like. He has courage, honor, and loyalty. He knows his home isn't Narnia, but Aslan's country, the world beyond. Reepicheep also shows a certainty of faith as he goes over the wave of the Last Sea, emulating the assurance all Christians should possess when they die.

- **Sea People.** As depicted in *The Voyage of the "Dawn Treader,"* the Sea People are a mysterious race of creatures living under the sea near the World's End, in the Eastern Sea.

- **Seven Lords.** Seven Lords of Narnia were sent by Miraz to discover new lands in the Eastern Ocean, but they never returned from the journey. The search for these missing lords is the basis for *The Voyage of the "Dawn Treader."* Each of the lords is eventually accounted for — Lord Bern (living on the Lone Islands), Lord Octesian (died on Dragon Island), Lord Restimar (turned into gold on Deathwater Island), Lord Rhoop (rescued from Dark Island), and Lords Revilian, Argoz, and Mavramorn (the Three Sleepers on the Island of the Star).

- **Shasta (Prince Cor).** As told in *The Horse and His Boy,* Shasta is raised in Calormen by a poor fisherman named Arsheesh but runs away with talking horse Bree just before he's to be sold into slavery. He's joined by Aravis and her horse, Hwin. During his adventures, Shasta discovers he's actually Prince Cor, the twin brother of Prince Corin of Archenland and son of King Lune. He eventually marries Aravis and becomes King of Archenland.

  Shasta bears some loose resemblance to Joseph of the Old Testament. Like Shasta, Joseph left home at an early age against his will and lived in a far-off land. He eventually reunited with his father by God's leading and helped his father and family escape disaster.

Narnian Hall of Faith

Hebrews 11 has a listing of believers in God who stood out in living "by faith" regardless of the circumstances. This list, which includes people like Moses, Joshua, and David, has become popularly known as the "Hall of Faith." If Aslan had a similar Hall of Faith for Narnia, he'd surely include Narnians such as Puddleglum, Trufflehunter, Mr. and Mrs. Beaver, Mr. Tumnus, Reepicheep, Poggin, and Doctor Cornelius. Each is unwavering in faith and devotion to Aslan.

✔ **Trufflehunter the badger.** Trufflehunter is one of the leaders of the old Narnians in their fight against King Miraz in *Prince Caspian*. He stands apart from others in the story for his steadfast faithfulness to Aslan when circumstances appear bleak.

✔ **Trumpkin the Dwarf.** Trumpkin is a red Dwarf rescued by the Pevensie children in *Prince Caspian*. He's initially skeptical of the existence of Aslan and old Narnia but is convinced of the truth by the children. Trumpkin emerges as a loyal, faithful Narnian. During *The Voyage of the "Dawn Treader,"* he's Regent serving under Caspian, and by the days of *The Silver Chair*, he's a chancellor. Trumpkin's affectionately nicknamed "D.L.F." (Dear Little Friend).

Enemies of Narnia

Each of the Narnian Chronicles focuses on a different enemy that the good Narnians have to overcome. The major villains of Narnia and enemies of Aslan include the following characters:

✔ **Andrew Ketterley (Uncle Andrew).** Andrew Ketterley's the wicked uncle of Digory Kirke and an amateur magician (actually, he's just a "hack"). Too afraid to go himself, he suckers Polly Plummer into touching the magic ring that takes her to the Wood Between the Worlds; Uncle Andrew then forces Digory to go after her. He witnesses the creation of Narnia but hates Aslan and is afraid of the talking animals. Uncle Andrew is reminiscent of the amoral scientist that Lewis characterizes so well in his space trilogy books (see Chapter 12).

✔ **Green Witch (The Lady of the Green Kirtle, Queen of Underland).** The Green Witch is the villain of *The Silver Chair* who puts Prince Rilian under a spell and holds him in Underland for ten years. She initially appears as a spectacularly beautiful woman but shows her true nature, a serpent, at the end of the story. She's planning to invade Narnia with her army of Earthmen but is defeated at the last minute by an awakened Rilian, Eustace Scrubb, Jill Pole, and Puddleglum the Marshwiggle.

✔ **Gumpas.** In *The Voyage of the "Dawn Treader,"* Gumpas is the wicked governor of the Lone Islands who loses his post to Lord Bern.

✔ **Lords Glozelle and Sopespian.** In *Prince Caspian*, Lords Glozelle and Sopespian are Telmarine lords and military leaders who trick King Miraz into dueling High King Peter and end up murdering him. Although their actions serve old Narnia well, they remain enemies of Caspian and the Pevensies.

✔ **Maugrim (Fenris Ulf).** Maugrim is a large wolf and captain of the White Witch's secret police in *The Lion, the Witch and the Wardrobe*. Maugrim's known as Fenris Ulf in early American versions of the book. He's killed by Peter Pevensie during a fight.

✔ **Miraz.** King Miraz is the wicked uncle of Prince Caspian. He usurps the throne of Narnia by murdering Caspian's father, Caspian IX, and rules for 13 years until he's defeated by his own troops.

✔ **Nikabrik the Dwarf.** Nikabrik is the black Dwarf in *Prince Caspian* who teams with Caspian, Trumpkin, and Trufflehunter against King Miraz. Nikabrik's extremely pragmatic and skeptical of old Narnia and is willing to use any means necessary to achieve Miraz's defeat. In the end, he tries to use the White Witch's sorcery but is killed by Caspian and Peter Pevensie in the process.

Nikabrik is symbolic of the Machiavellian ("the end justifies the means") worldview of today's relativistic culture.

✔ **Pug.** In *The Voyage of the "Dawn Treader,"* Pug's the nasty slave trader on the Lone Islands who attempts to enslave Caspian, Edmund Pevensie, Lucy Pevensie, and Eustace Scrubb.

✔ **Rabadash.** Rabadash is a haughty prince of Calormen who proposes marriage to Queen Susan and later tries to invade Narnia in *The Horse and His Boy*. Because of his persistent defiance, Aslan turns him into a donkey temporarily.

✔ **Shift the Ape.** Shift the Ape is the great deceiver who lulls Narnia into an attack from the Calormenes in *The Last Battle*. He's closely modeled after the Antichrist, a person of great evil depicted in biblical prophesy (see, for example, 1 John 2:18–23, 2 John 5:7, and 2 Thessalonians 2:1–12). In biblical terms, the Antichrist will be a false prophet who uses deception to go against Christ and the people of God in the days leading up to the Second Coming of Jesus Christ. Shift follows a similar path, disguising

Puzzle (the donkey) as Aslan and trying to lead Narnians away from the real Aslan and expose them to invasion from the Calormenes.

✓ **Telmarines (New Narnians).** The Telmarines are a race of humans that originally were pirates from our world and who stumbled into Narnia through a cave. They inhabit the distant land of Telmar, far beyond the western mountains. Until Caspian X, Telmarines feared the sea because Aslan was said to come into Narnia from over the sea.

✓ **Tash.** Tash is a false god of the Calormenes. In *The Last Battle,* he appears in the Stable as a demonic bird-like creature with a vulture's head, four arms, and twenty razor-sharp fingers. Tash is symbolic of Satan as depicted in the Book of Revelation.

✓ **Tisroc.** Tisroc is the title for the king of Calormen. The name's invariably followed by the line "may he live forever."

✓ **White Witch (Queen Jadis, Queen of Charn).** The "Darth Vader" of Narnia, Queen Jadis is the evil witch who destroys the world of Charn in *The Magician's Nephew* and later casts a wintry spell over Narnia in *The Lion, the Witch and the Wardrobe.* Jadis kills Aslan at the Stone Table but is eventually killed by Aslan after his resurrection. Jadis isn't human; rather, she's half Jinn and half giantess. Her mother was Lilith, a female demon who originates from Babylonian and ancient Hebrew mythology (non-biblical tradition). The mythical Lilith is something of a vampire, seeking out children to murder and harming women who are giving birth.

Jadis is symbolic of Satan in a number of ways. First, her attempts to tempt Digory Kirke at the Tree of Protection resemble Eve's temptation by the serpent in the Garden of Eden. Second, her 100-year stranglehold over Narnia symbolizes the temporary power of Satan in the world. Third, her victory over Aslan before his resurrection symbolizes the fleeting victory that Satan had over Jesus Christ on the cross before He was resurrected.

Divinities

As Chapter 8 explores, Lewis portrays Narnia as a world created and overseen by a divinity that resembles the Christian Triune God. The two divinities clearly depicted in the Narnian Chronicles are as follows:

✓ **Aslan.** Aslan's the Great Lion, creator, and ruler over Narnia. He symbolizes what Jesus Christ would have been like if He had come to a world called Narnia (see Chapter 6). Chapter 8 addresses Aslan's symbolic relationship to Jesus Christ.

Because Narnia is a world of Talking Beasts, it's natural and logical for Aslan to be a Talking Beast as well. However, as to why Aslan is a lion, Lewis indicates three reasons for this decision in his essay "It All Began With a Picture":

- The lion is the "king of the beasts" (as I'm sure you know if you've ever seen the Disney film *The Lion King* or watched old *Wild Kingdom* reruns). The lion is a fierce animal, but it has a certain majesty that has always drawn people to it.

- Jesus Christ is referred to as "The Lion of Judah" in the Bible. Revelation 5:5 says, "See, the Lion of the tribe of Judah, the Root of David, has triumphed." Similarly, the Old Testament prophet Joel said, "The Lord also will roar from Zion," while the prophet Hosea adds, "They will follow the Lord; he will roar like a lion. When he roars, his children will come trembling from the west."

- As I mention in Chapter 4, when Lewis started writing *The Lion, the Witch and the Wardrobe,* he began having strange dreams about lions. When, as he claims, Aslan came bounding into his story, he recognized a connection between his dreams and his stories.

Aslan, which means "lion" in Turkish, is a word that Lewis came across while reading *Arabian Nights.*

✔ **Emperor-Over-the-Sea (Emperor-Beyond-the-Sea).** The Emperor-Over-the-Sea is the father of Aslan; this figure symbolizes God the Father in the Christian Triune God (Father, Son, and Holy Spirit). The Emperor is mentioned but never actually appears in the stories. Instead, Aslan carries out his work.

Making Repeat Appearances in Narnia

Several characters make multiple appearances in *The Chronicles of Narnia.* Figure 7-1 shows how each character fits into the series as a whole. (Where applicable, the relative ages of the character appear in parentheses.)

Figure 7-1:
Lewis's characters make appearances throughout his Narnian Chronicles.

Character	The Magician's Nephew	The Lion, the Witch and the Wardrobe	The Horse and His Boy	Prince Caspian	The Voyage of the "Dawn Treader"	The Silver Chair	The Last Battle
Peter Pevensie		Travels as a boy to Narnia; rules as High King of Narnia (13)	Rules as High King of Narnia (27)	Enters Narnia to help Caspian (14)			Goes to real Narnia after railway accident (22)
Susan Pevensie		Girl in England; Queen of Narnia (12)	Rules as Queen of Narnia (26)	Enters Narnia to help Caspian (13)			
Edmund Pevensie		Travels as a boy to Narnia; rules as King of Narnia (10)	Rules as King of Narnia (24)	Enters Narnia to help Caspian (11)	Enters Narnia through magic picture; joins Caspian		Goes to real Narnia after railway accident (19)
Lucy Pevensie		Girl in England; Queen of Narnia (8)	Rules as Queen of Narnia (22)	Enters Narnia to help Caspian (9)	Enters Narnia through magic picture; joins Caspian		Goes to real Narnia after railway accident (17)
Digory Kirke	Travels as a boy to Narnia with magic rings (12)	Known as Professor Kirke; owner of the grand house with the wardrobe (52)			Lives in a small cottage in England and works as a tutor		Goes to real Narnia after railway accident (61)
Polly Plummer	Travels as a girl to Narnia with magic rings (11)						Goes to real Narnia after railway accident (60)
Eustace Scrubb					Enters Narnia through magic picture; joins Caspian	Enters Narnia to help find Rilian	Enters Narnia to help Tirian; goes to real Narnia by entering the Stable
Jill Pole						Enters Narnia to help find Rilian	Enters Narnia to help Tirian; goes to real Narnia by entering the Stable
Caspian				A young prince who overthrows his evil uncle Miraz (13)	King of Narnia; takes a voyage to the Eastern Ocean (16)	Elderly King of Narnia (66)	Appears in real Narnia
Reepicheep				Fights against Miraz's army	Sails with Caspian and continues on to the End of the World		Appears in real Narnia
Mr. Tumnus		Introduced as an ordinary Faun	A trusted member of the inner circle of Narnia				Appears in real Narnia
Jadis	Known as Queen Jadis, destroyer of Charn; an evil presence in Narnia	Known as the White Witch					

To Narnia and Beyond

Geography is an important element in *The Chronicles of Narnia* because many of the stories' events occur based on the juxtaposition of one land and another. Geographical relationships are sometimes territorial, such as the bordering nations of Narnia and Archenland, and sometimes they're inter-worldly, such as people moving between our world and Narnia. This section explores the major lands of the Narnian Chronicles.

England

Except for *The Horse and His Boy,* all the Narnian Chronicles involve English children entering the world of Narnia. These inter-worldly travels begin and end at Digory Kirke's house in London, Professor Kirke's house in the country, Eustace Scrubb's house, a train station, and the Experiment House school attended by Eustace and Jill Pole.

Not counting the Telmarines, 11 people from England travel to Narnia. However, Prince Caspian is the *only* Narnian to visit England; he does so briefly at the end of *The Silver Chair* to help defend Eustace and Jill.

Like old Narnia, England is shown in *The Last Battle* as a Shadowlands of a world far greater. In fact, the Pevensie children see the real England connected to the real Narnia by the great mountains of Aslan.

Narnia

Narnia refers to both the enchanted world in *The Chronicles of Narnia* as well as to a specific country within that world. Aslan, the Great Lion, creates the world of Narnia in *The Magician's Nephew* and has dominion over it. Narnia is filled with a host of creatures, including talking animals, dwarfs, giants, dryads, naiads, centaurs, and fauns. Humans traditionally rule Narnia, except during the Hundred Years Winter when the White Witch casts a spell over the land.

The word "Narnia" sounds tailor-made for a fairy tale, but actually it originates from an ancient Roman colony on a hilltop in central Italy. The town called Narni is considered the geographical center of Italy.

The terms "old Narnia" and "new Narnia" carry special significance in the Narnian Chronicles. In *Prince Caspian*, old Narnia refers to the "Golden Age of Narnia" in which Peter, Susan, Edmund, and Lucy Pevensie rule over the land of talking beasts. By Caspian's day, the Telmarines prevent any mention of old Narnia and thus force the real Narnians — talking animals and trees — to go undercover. In fact, after the Telmarines invade Narnia, they fashion themselves "New Narnians."

At the end of *The Last Battle,* old Narnia refers to the shadow world that's destroyed by Aslan in the final war against evil. In its place, the "real Narnia" is revealed as a place for the faithful Narnians to enjoy with Aslan for all eternity.

Some of Narnia's major geographical features are

- **Aslan's How.** Aslan's How is a hollow mound that, by Prince Caspian's time, covers the Stone Table.

- **Cair Paravel.** Cair Paravel's the capital of Narnia and the traditional seat of power for the king and queen.

- **Caldron Pool.** Caldron Pool is the source of the Great River, which is located in the western part of Narnia. The pool is caused by the Great Waterfall. Caldron Pool is an important location in *The Last Battle;* Shift the Ape discovers the lion skin here at the start of the story, and, at its end, the children and Narnians enjoy the refreshment of the pool in real Narnia.

- **Dancing Lawn.** Dancing Lawn's the meeting place of the Great Council of Caspian in *Prince Caspian*.

- **Lantern Waste.** Located in far western Narnia, Lantern Waste is the area around an ever-lit lamppost on the edge of a dense forest. In *The Lion, the Witch and the Wardrobe,* the Pevensie children enter and exit Narnia near this point. The lamppost was planted in the ground at Narnia's creation after Queen Jadis threw a piece of a London lamppost at Aslan. The piece bounced off him and planted itself into the ground.

- **Stable Hill.** Stable Hill's the site of the climactic battle between the Narnians and the Calormenes in *The Last Battle,* and it's the location of the Stable, the site for the Last Judgment.

- **Stone Table.** The Stone Table's the site of Aslan's slaying in *The Lion, the Witch and the Wardrobe*. It's a large gray stone slab that rests on four upright stones. The Stone Table is the Narnian equivalent of the cross that Jesus Christ was crucified upon.

Other areas

In addition to England and the country of Narnia, the Narnian Chronicles discuss other geographical areas, including the following:

- **Archenland.** Archenland is a mountainous land to the south of Narnia. It's a traditional ally and friend of Narnia. Archenland takes center stage in *The Horse and His Boy* when Shasta is discovered to be Prince Cor of Archenland.

- **Aslan's country.** Aslan's country is the home of Aslan. It's symbolic for Heaven.

- **Calormen.** Calormen is an arid country that lies to the south of Narnia and Archenland, across the Great Desert. The capital of Calormen is Tashbaan. This country is the traditional enemy of Narnia; the Calormenes attempt an invasion of Archenland and Narnia in *The Horse and His Boy* and conquer the two countries in *The Last Battle*.

  Lewis derived the name Calormen from *calor,* the Latin word for "heat." His descriptions of the place make it sound like an ancient Persian empire or something out of *Arabian Nights*.

- **Charn.** Charn is the dying city that Digory Kirke and Polly Plummer enter in *The Magician's Nephew*. In Charn, Digory makes the grave mistake of ringing a bell that wakens Queen Jadis, causing a chain of events that introduce evil into Narnia.

- **City Ruinous.** This is the name for the ruins of a city inhabited by ancient giants, just outside of Harfang. Eustace Scrubb, Jill Pole, and Puddleglum the Marshwiggle go through City Ruinous on their quest for Prince Rilian in *The Silver Chair*.

- **Eastern Ocean.** The Eastern Ocean borders Narnia, Archenland, and Calormen and stretches all the way to the World's End, where Aslan's country is located. In *The Voyage of the "Dawn Treader,"* Prince Caspian crosses the Eastern Ocean in search of the seven lords. The Eastern Ocean is home to many islands discovered by Caspian and his crew, and at its far eastern edge is the sweet Silver Sea.

- **Ettinsmoor.** Ettinsmoor is a region of moorland that's north of Narnia and the home of giants. Eustace Scrubb, Jill Pole, and Puddleglum the Marshwiggle cross this area in search of Prince Rilian in *The Silver Chair*.

- **Harfang.** Harfang is a city of the Gentle Giants. In *The Silver Chair*, Eustace Scrubb, Jill Pole, and Puddleglum the Marshwiggle stay there during their search for Rilian. However, the city proves to be a dangerous place for them — they're almost eaten by the giants at the Autumn Feast, but they escape in the nick of time.

- **Telmar.** Telmar's a land beyond the Western Mountains that's founded by pirates from our world who accidentally enter Narnia.

- **Underland.** Underland is the underground land that the Green Witch rules over in *The Silver Chair*. It's home to the Earthmen.

- **Wood Between the Worlds.** This mysterious place lies between created worlds in *The Magician's Nephew*. Using the magic rings, Digory Kirke and Polly Plummer can go to the Wood Between the Worlds from England, Charn, and the newly created Narnia. Digory doesn't see it as a world by itself; instead, he says, "I think it's just a sort of an in-between place."

Naming Narnia: Design and coincidence

Many names in Narnia have special significance. Aslan, for example, means "lion" in Turkish, while Digory Kirke was so named as a nod to Lewis's old tutor, William Kirkpatrick. However, not all names were meant to necessarily carry any special significance. Lewis spoke specifically about the difficulty in devising names in his space trilogy, although the same could almost certainly be said for Narnia as well. In a letter to Sister Penelope in August of 1939, he speaks of the speculation over his name choices for some of the characters in *Out of the Silent Planet*. He writes that all "are . . . accidents, which I knew nothing of . . . It only shows how hard it is to invent something which wasn't there already."

Chapter 8

The Gospel According to Aslan

*W*hen C.S. Lewis sat down to write *The Chronicles of Narnia,* he didn't dream up a master theological plan and then set about writing fairy tales that fit into that framework. He simply aimed to tell a good tale. However, because his Christian faith was such an integral part of him as a man and as an author, the Christian gospel "came bounding into it." Aslan the lion, who is symbolic of Jesus Christ, entered the scene first, but other fundamental Christian truths naturally became part of Narnia and its characters. As a result, all the story's major questions are answered by Lewis's Christian faith: How did Narnia begin? How is sin introduced into the enchanted world? How can traitorous Edmund be restored? How do the children and Narnians live "by faith" in Aslan? How active is Aslan in the lives of his followers? How is Narnia going to end?

In both this chapter and Chapter 9, you explore Christianity through Narnia-colored glasses. In doing so, you see that the Narnian Chronicles are packed with Christian truth that's just waiting to be discovered.

Many of the fundamental Christian beliefs covered in this chapter are discussed in greater detail in *Christianity For Dummies* (Wiley), which I also wrote. Check out that book if you want to dive deeper into these topics.

Aslan's Sacrifice: The Heart of Christianity

In *The Lion, the Witch and the Wardrobe,* the battle of good versus evil plays out between Aslan and the White Witch, but it also rages inside the heart of Edmund. Edmund knows deep down that siding with the White Witch is wrong, but his pride, insatiable appetite for Turkish Delight, and desire for power win out. He betrays his brother and sisters and agrees to help the White Witch. Eventually, he realizes his horrible error and wants to leave the Witch and return to his siblings. However, the White Witch resists, protesting to Aslan, "[Edmund's] life is forfeit to me. His blood is my property." Her claim is based upon the Deep Magic that's at the heart of Narnia and "engraved on the scepter of the Emperor-Beyond-the-Sea."

Deep Magic played out

"Deep Magic" is a term used in the Narnian Chronicles to refer to laws imposed upon Narnia by the Emperor-Beyond-the-Sea. These laws are non-negotiable, and when they're broken, justice must be satisfied. "Deeper Magic" references Aslan's willingness to sacrifice himself to satisfy the demands of "Deep Magic."

The principle of Deep Magic is at the heart of Christianity in the belief that a perfect and holy God embedded his "holy character" into the fabric of this world. At the same time, he created free will, allowing each person to have a choice of whether to live in line with God's character or to rebel against it. (For more discussion of free will, see Chapter 15.) Christianity maintains that all people have sinned and fallen short of God's "Deep Magic" (Romans 3:23). Like Edmund's fate in the hands of the White Witch, the inevitable result of our sin is death — with Satan telling God that *our* blood is his property (Romans 6:23).

In many ways, Romans 6:23 demonstrates the tightly bound relationship between "Deep Magic" and "Deeper Magic" in the real world. This New Testament passage says: "For the wages of sin is death, but the free gift of God is eternal life in Christ Jesus our Lord." The first part of this passage expresses "Deep Magic," and the second part of the passage conveys the sense of "Deeper Magic."

According to Christianity, given our undeniable sin, all would be lost if not for God; God loved you and I so much that he willingly stepped in and took the punishment that was due us. Or, as Romans 5:8 says, "But God commends his own love toward us, in that while we were yet sinners, Christ died for us." Aslan makes the same sacrifice for Edmund when he chooses to lay down his life for the boy. For his part, Edmund needs only to submit to Aslan in return. Nothing more is required.

Aslan's Gethsemane

The events of the night before Aslan's slaying at the Stone Table resemble Jesus's evening in the Garden of Gethsemane on the eve of his crucifixion (see Matthew 26:36–46). Jesus took the disciples closest to him into the garden while he prayed about the events to come. He looked visibly troubled and sorrowful to the disciples.

Aslan's also deeply saddened and needs the companionship of Lucy and Susan, telling them, "I am sad and lonely. Lay your hands on my mane so that I can feel you are there and let us walk like that." Similarly, Jesus wanted his disciples to be a support to him and was hurt when they feel asleep during his time of need.

In the sickening scene at the Stone Table, the White Witch isn't content with killing Aslan; she wants to humiliate him as well. So after he's bound on the Table, she muzzles him and shaves his mane — which would seem to be the most disgraceful punishment for a lion. In similar disgrace, the Roman guards put a crown of thorns on Jesus's head and knelt in front of him, mocking him as a king. The religious leaders also got into the act, taunting Jesus as he was being crucified, saying, "He can save others, but he can't save himself" (Matthew 27:42).

Keep in mind, however, that Aslan initiates his sacrifice and is never forced into it. In the same way, Jesus Christ engineered the circumstances that put him on the cross. He wasn't condemned by the Jewish leaders and killed by the Romans so much as he *allowed* them to condemn and execute him. Only in truly grasping the voluntary nature of Christ's death does the extent of his infinite love for humanity become real to Christians.

Victory on the Stone Table

During Aslan's humiliation and slaying at the hands of the White Witch, Lucy looks at his face and sees that he's "braver, and more beautiful, and more patient than ever." The same reaction likely came from onlookers of Jesus's crucifixion, especially when they heard perhaps the most beautiful, graceful words imaginable from Jesus's lips: "Father, forgive them, for they don't know what they are doing" (Luke 23:34).

After Aslan dies, the Stone Table is broken into two pieces "by a great crack that ran down it from end to end." Here, Lewis echoes what happened to the curtain of the Jewish temple in Jerusalem at the moment Jesus died: The "veil of the temple was torn in two from the top to the bottom. The earth quaked and the rocks were split." (Matthew 27:51).

The White Witch is convinced of her coup d'état over Aslan and the Emperor-Beyond-the-Sea. So too, with Jesus's death, Satan would have thought he'd foiled God's plan to save the world. Yet, in the same way that there's a Deeper Magic that the Witch doesn't know about, Satan almost certainly didn't realize that if "a willing victim who had committed no treachery was killed in a traitor's stead," death and sin would be defeated. That's what happens in Narnia given that Aslan's resurrected the night following his death, and that's what happened in real life when Jesus was resurrected three days after his death (John 20).

Lucy's and Susan's reactions to a resurrected Aslan sounds very much like the reactions of Jesus's disciples when they see him the first time. Lucy exclaims, "Aren't you dead then, dear Aslan? . . . You're not — not — a (ghost)?" Aslan replies, "Do I look it?" and then gives them a hug and kiss. Similarly, when Jesus first appears to a frightened group of disciples, he says: "Why are you troubled? Why do doubts arise in your hearts? See my hands and my feet, that it is truly me. Touch me and see, for a spirit doesn't have flesh and bones, as you see that I have" (Luke 24:38–39).

Aslan's victory at the Stone Table is the turning point not only for *The Lion, the Witch and the Wardrobe* but for the entire Narnia series. The White Witch is defeated, and the cure for the disease of sin begins to spread. In the same way, the victory of Jesus Christ on the cross is the crux of Christianity as well as the turning point for all human history.

Finding Jesus Christ in a Roaring Lion

By the time C.S. Lewis wrote *The Chronicles of Narnia,* he'd been a Christian for nearly 20 years, so his Christian beliefs and underlying theology were quite mature and developed. He'd represented Christ in his earlier fiction — as the "Man" in *The Pilgrim's Regress* and Maledil in the space trilogy — but Aslan is far more developed as a character (easily Lewis's most compelling portrayal of Christ) and is the very foundation of the Narnian Chronicles. As such, Aslan's a valuable window into Lewis's understanding of Jesus Christ.

On the impact of Aslan's character, former Lewis student Dom Bede Griffiths adds in *The Canadian C.S. Lewis Journal:* "[Aslan] has all of the hidden power and majesty and awesomeness which Lewis associated with God, but also all the glory and the tenderness and even the humor which he believed belonged to him, so that children could run up to him and throw their arms around him and kiss him . . . It is 'mere Christianity.'"

As you examine Aslan's role in the Narnian Chronicles, pay special attention to the qualities I outline in this section. Because of their parallels, understanding Aslan will help you better understand Jesus Christ.

More than just a man

When Lucy first hears of Aslan from Mr. and Mrs. Beaver in *The Lion, the Witch and the Wardrobe*, she asks tentatively, "Is — is he a man?" "Certainly not," is Mr. Beaver's emphatic reply. "I tell you he is the King of the wood and the son of the great Emperor-Beyond-the-Sea. Don't you know who is the King of Beasts? Aslan is a lion — *the* Lion, the great Lion."

Jesus Christ, too, is far more than just a man or an angelic being that came to earth. No, he is none other than God himself. "I and the Father are one," Jesus said boldly in John 10:30. And elsewhere, he spoke that he always existed: "Before Abraham came into being, I am" (John 8:58). ("I am" is a reference to God's holy name used in the Old Testament — "I AM WHO I AM;" see Exodus 3:14.)

Over the years in Narnia, some try to dismiss Aslan as being something other than the son of the great Emperor-Beyond-the-Sea. Likewise, one of the popular beliefs concerning Jesus Christ today is that he was a simply good moral teacher who lived 2,000 years ago, but he couldn't possibly have been God in the flesh. In *Mere Christianity,* however, Lewis emphasizes that a good teacher is the one thing that Jesus Christ could *not* have been. Given everything he claimed, Jesus was either a liar, a crazy man, or else truly the Son of God. (See Chapter 20 in this book for Lewis's full explanation.)

Son of God

The basic idea of the Christian "Triune" God (or Trinity) is that one God exists with three distinct identities: God the Father, God the Son, and God the Holy Spirit. Although they're unified, each of the members of the Trinity has a unique role and personality. See Chapter 16 for a more complete discussion of the Trinity.

The "God" of Narnia resembles, more or less, the Christian Trinity. Two members of the Trinity are obviously present in Narnia: The Emperor-Beyond-the-Sea is God the Father, and Aslan is God the Son. As for the third member, Lewis never clearly displays the Holy Spirit's role inside Narnia. Some have suggested that Father Christmas in *The Lion, the Witch and the Wardrobe* plays this role because he gives gifts to Peter, Susan, and Lucy. Yet, that idea seems dubious (since the gifts are given before Aslan's sacrificial death) and inconsistent (not every "believer" receives a gift). The albatross that leads the *Dawn Treader* away from Dark Island in *The Voyage of the "Dawn Treader"* certainly serves the function of the Holy Spirit. Yet, even here, Lewis implies that the albatross is actually Aslan.

The most obvious allusion to a Narnian Trinity is in *The Horse and His Boy* in an exchange between Aslan and Shasta. When Shasta asks Aslan who he is, Aslan (referred to here as "the Voice") repeats "Myself" three times, in three different ways, reflecting the different roles of Father, Son, and Holy Spirit:

> *"Myself," said the Voice, very deep and low so that the earth shook: and again "Myself," loud and clear and gay: and then the third time "Myself," whispered so softly you could hardly hear it, and yet it seemed to come from all round you as if the leaves rustled with it.*

(Also, note the parallel between "Myself" and Jesus Christ's use of "I AM", which is discussed in the "More than just a man" section above.)

Practically speaking, the God of Narnia seems to resemble *two-oneness* (Aslan and the Emperor-Beyond-the-Sea) rather than *three-oneness* — with Aslan assuming some of the roles that Christians traditionally view as those of the Holy Spirit.

By and large, however, Aslan functions in a manner indicative of Jesus Christ as the Son of God. Jesus came to the earth as a man to sacrifice his own life for the sins of the world. "I am the great Bridge Builder," says Aslan to Lucy in *The Voyage of the "Dawn Treader."* So too, Jesus Christ is also the only one who can build a bridge between God and his people. To paraphrase Hebrews 9:15, Christ is the great Bridge Builder, enabling people who believe in him to receive an eternal inheritance now that he has died as a ransom and set them free from sins committed against the "Deep Magic."

Aslan also carries out the will of the Emperor-Beyond-the-Sea just as Jesus Christ carries out the will of his Father. What's more, just as Aslan created the world (see the "Played a key role in creation" section below), so too Jesus always existed and participated in the world's creation.

Not a tame savior

As you read through *The Chronicles of Narnia,* you discover quickly that Aslan isn't a pushover. He's constantly described as "not a tame lion," and Lewis depicts him as both "good" and "ferocious." Several characters speak of this paradox:

- Mr. Beaver tells Lucy in *The Lion, the Witch and the Wardrobe:* "Safe? . . . Who said anything about safe? 'Course he isn't safe. But he's good. He's the King, I tell you."

- When Aslan leaves Coriakin and Lucy in *The Voyage of the "Dawn Treader,"* Coriakin says, "It's always like that, you can't keep him; it's not as if he were a *tame* lion."

- Aslan speaks of his ferocity to Jill at the start of *The Silver Chair:* "I have swallowed up girls and boys, women and men, kings and emperors, cities and realms."

- Lucy notes Aslan's dangerous potential in *The Lion, the Witch and the Wardrobe* when she says, "Terrible paws if he didn't know how to velvet them."

- At one point in *The Horse and His Boy,* Shasta faces Aslan and, according to the narrator, "A new and different sort of trembling came over [Shasta]. Yet he felt glad too."

- In *The Horse and His Boy,* Aravis proclaims to the Great Lion when she meets him, "You're so beautiful. You may eat me if you like. I'd sooner be eaten by you than fed by anyone else."

- The narrator in *The Lion, the Witch and the Wardrobe* comments on Aslan's duality: "People who have not been in Narnia sometimes think that a thing cannot be good and terrible at the same time."

Like Aslan, Jesus Christ isn't a "tame" savior. During his earthly ministry, he preached "turn the other cheek," loved the sick and downtrodden, never led a revolt, and voluntarily went to his death on the cross without resistance. Each of these actions certainly is an example of Christ's goodness, holiness, and amazing love for people, but one's mistaken to assume that Christ is only about goodness. In his years on earth, Christ was anything but a wimp when it came with dealing with the Pharisees, the religious leaders of the day. Time and time again, he challenged them to get off their self-righteous behinds, so to speak, and start loving the God they claimed to be serving. Matthew 23 reveals Christ's ferocity, motivated not by venom but by a broken heart.

Aslan in the Willows

Kenneth Grahame's book *The Wind in the Willows* was highly influential to Lewis, and that influence is especially notable in Lewis's portrayal of Aslan. The Great Lion shares some traits with Grahame's character Pan, namely the ability to instill both love and fear in others. Note the paradox of these reactions in the following exchange: "When Rat and Mole approach Pan, the Mole asks Rat whether he is afraid. "'Afraid?' murmured the Rat, his eyes shining with unutterable love. 'Afraid? Of Him? O, never, never. And yet, and yet, O Mole, I am afraid.'"

The Book of Revelation gives Christians a dramatically powerful glimpse of what Jesus will be like in the future when he, like Aslan, takes care of business:

> *I saw the heaven opened, and behold, a white horse, and he who sat on it is called Faithful and True. In righteousness he judges and makes war. His eyes are a flame of fire, and on his head are many crowns. He has names written and a name written which no one knows but he himself. He is clothed in a garment sprinkled with blood. His name is called "The Word of God." The armies which are in heaven followed him on white horses, clothed in white, pure, fine linen. Out of his mouth proceeds a sharp, double-edged sword, that with it he should strike the nations. He will rule them with an iron rod. He treads the winepress of the fierceness of the wrath of God, the Almighty. He has on his garment and on his thigh a name written, "KING OF KINGS, AND LORD OF LORDS."* (Revelation 19:11–16)

As you read this passage, picture Aslan leading the Narnian armies against the White Witch in *The Lion, the Witch and the Wardrobe* and Miraz's army in *Prince Caspian*.

In depicting Aslan as a roaring lion, Lewis reveals his belief in Jesus Christ as a mind-blowing contrast of absolute goodness and absolute ferocity. Christ loved the sinners of the world so much that he was willing to die for them, but when he returns to the earth a second time, he will fiercely stomp out evil once and for all, just like Aslan does in *The Last Battle*.

There are two ways to interpret Lewis's description of Aslan as "not a tame lion." See the section "Isn't at our beck and call," later in this chapter, for further explanation of how neither Aslan nor Jesus is a "tame savior."

Ever compassionate

Aslan may not be a tame lion, but he has a deep love for the humans and Talking Animals of Narnia. In *The Magician's Nephew,* when Digory is scared about his mother's grave condition, Aslan comes alongside him and shares his grief. In fact, Digory struggles with his decision not to take a curing apple to his mother behind Aslan's back, but "whenever he remembered the shining tears in Aslan's eyes he became sure." Aslan expresses his love and compassion for "his children" in other ways as well; for example, in *The Horse and His Boy,* he touches Shasta's forehead with his tongue as a visible expression of his love.

In the Narnian Chronicles, Lewis uses Aslan to depict the compassionate love that God has for all humankind. A great example of this love is found in the prodigal son parable in Luke 15. You probably know the story: A son selfishly demands his inheritance before his father is even dead, throws the money away in a far-off country, ends up in desperate straits, and realizes he has no choice but return home. In Luke 15:20, Jesus says that the father sees him from off and "has compassion for his son." "Compassion" is a fairly commonplace word in modern English and therefore has lost much of the impact of the Greek word used in the original scriptures, which is more intense. Applied to Luke 15:20, when the father saw his son, "his innards were all cut up in compassion for the younger son." This parable, in effect, says that God's love is so deep for his children that his "intestines are all cut up" in his concern. This same compassion appeared throughout Jesus's ministry, such as when he healed the sick, forgave the sinners, fed the hungry, and spent time with society's riffraff instead of hobnobbing with the movers and shakers.

Fun-loving

Although he has plenty of serious and somber moments, Aslan's a fun-loving character throughout *The Chronicles of Narnia.* Soon after Narnia's created in *The Magician's Nephew,* he emphasizes the fact that life is meant to be enjoyed: "Laugh and fear not, creatures . . . For jokes as well as justice come in with speech." He plays with the children on a number of occasions, and after his resurrection, he tells Lucy and Susan, "I feel my strength coming back to me. Oh, children, catch me if you can!" (Lucy remarks that she never could decide whether playing with Aslan was "more like playing with a thunderstorm or playing with a kitten.") In *Prince Caspian,* Aslan invites children to get on his back and go for a ride, and in *The Last Battle,* he's among the crowd as they race "further up, further in."

Many people don't see Jesus Christ as fitting into this fun-loving mold. In fact, I think many would compare him to a Marshwiggle, always with a solemn view of life. But if you read "between the lines" of the Gospels, you see that nothing could be farther from the truth. Jesus was a man of joy (Hebrews 1:9). In fact, during his time on earth, he must have had an infectious joy that made him fun to be with — look at the crowds that followed him constantly! What's more, those who were attracted most to Christ were the fun-loving sinner types; the stodgy, no-fun religious curmudgeons couldn't stand him.

Identifies with others

Aslan may be the Great Lion, but he identifies with other, normal lions. In fact, in *The Lion, the Witch and the Wardrobe,* fellow lions love that Aslan refers to them collectively as "us lions;" they express their excitement, saying, "Did you hear what he said? Us lions. That means him and me. Us lions. That's what I like about Aslan. No side, no stand-off-ishness. Us lions. That meant him and me."

Jesus is God in the flesh, but, like Aslan, he also identifies with *us humans.* Hebrews 2:14–18 speaks directly to this point (emphasis added):

> [Jesus] himself **shared in our humanity**, that through death he might defeat the one who had the power of death, that is, the devil, and might deliver all of them who through fear of death were all their lifetime subject to bondage. Therefore **he had to be made like his brothers**, that he might become a merciful and faithful high priest in things pertaining to God, to make atonement for the sins of the people. For in that he himself has suffered when he was tempted, he is able to help those who are tempted.

Literally exists

Within the world of Narnia, Aslan is a *real* lion. He's not a myth — he really exists. However, over the years, belief in Aslan as a real creature fades. In *The Horse and His Boy,* for example, Bree likes the idea of Aslan but writes off his reality. Therefore, when Aslan confronts Bree, he tells the horse, "Touch me. Smell me. Here are my paws, here is my tail, these are my whiskers. I am a true Beast."

Christians believe that Jesus is also a real person who was born some 2,000 years ago, was crucified, was resurrected, and ascended into Heaven to be with his Father. In the same way that Aslan responds to Bree, Jesus tells Thomas, a skeptic following Christ's crucifixion, "Reach here your finger, and see my hands. Reach here your hand, and put it into my side. Don't be unbelieving, but believing" (John 20:27). Christianity rests on the fact that Christ exists today as a literal person and not as a mythical creature.

Having the limitlessness of God

The children who enter Narnia notice that the bigger they grow, the bigger Aslan becomes. Lewis uses this relationship to express how Christians' views of God grow and change. God can look small when you don't know him or when you first enter into a relationship with him. But, as you grow in your faith and discover more and more about him, the bigger he becomes in your eyes. God doesn't change, but your perspective does; your capacity to discern his greatness grows as well as your understanding of how meager you measure up in comparison.

Played a key role in creation

In *The Magician's Nephew,* Digory, Polly, and the gang arrive in Narnia before anything is created. In the ensuing moments, they witness Aslan creating the world of Narnia. Jesus, similarly, is creator of the world; according to Colossians 1:16–17, "For by him all things were created, in the heavens and on the earth, things visible and things invisible, whether thrones or dominions or principalities or powers; all things have been created through him, and for him. He is before all things, and in him all things are held together."

Aslan as a Pointer to Jesus Christ

As Chapter 7 indicates, Aslan's presence in Narnia is a great "what if" — *What if* there was a world like Narnia that needed redemption? *What if* Jesus Christ came into that world like he did ours? What would Christ have been like there? As the Great Lion and son of the Emperor-Beyond-the-Sea, Aslan is Lewis's answer to these questions.

Although Aslan is Lewis's supposal of Jesus in Narnia, he isn't meant to replace Christ in the stories' fictional England. Instead, Lewis works from the idea that the Christian Son of God assumes the appearance of Jesus Christ in our world and the appearance of Aslan in Narnia. In *The Silver Chair,* Eustace alludes to the fact that Aslan is not limited to Narnia, saying, "They call him Aslan in that place." Aslan confirms his reach when he says, "There is a way into my country from all the worlds."

Aslan is intended as a pointer to Jesus Christ, for the English children returning to England as well as for the readers of the books. "For you the door into Aslan's country is from your own world," Aslan says. He tells Lucy at the end of *The Voyage of the "Dawn Treader"* that in England he has "another name. You must learn to know me by that name. This was the very reason why you were brought to Narnia, that by knowing me here for a little, you may know me better there."

Perhaps the most revealing evidence of Aslan as the Narnian incarnation of Christ is the significant change in Aslan at the end of *The Last Battle,* when the children are in real Narnia. The narrator says that as Aslan spoke to them, "He no longer looked to them like a lion." Clearly, Lewis imagines that in this new world, the children look at Aslan and see Jesus Christ.

How God Interacts with the World

C.S. Lewis's characterization of Aslan reveals the author's take on God as a being as well as his beliefs about how God interacts with the world. This section draws from the Narnian Chronicles to explore several of Lewis's beliefs about God's real-world interaction.

Varies his visibility

Aslan's always in charge of Narnia but, by design, varies his visibility in the country over the course of Narnian history. He's visible and hands-on during Narnia's creation, but he's largely quiet during the thousand years that follow. Then, in *The Lion, the Witch and the Wardrobe,* rumors swirl that "Aslan is on the move." The children are told that Aslan is "the King but not often here, you understand." He returns to Narnia for all to see when he suffers a sacrificial death at the Stone Table and eventually defeats the White Witch. After the "Golden Age of Narnia," Aslan again lays low while the Telmarines conquer Narnia and squelch the teaching of Aslan. Yet, during Prince Caspian's day, Aslan returns to a hands-on role in the defeat of Miraz.

During the adventures of *The Voyage of the "Dawn Treader," The Silver Chair, The Horse and His Boy,* and most of *The Last Battle,* Aslan is visible only occasionally to guide his followers, and he never takes up arms against an enemy. In fact, by the time of *The Last Battle,* Shift the Ape uses Aslan's quietness to his advantage: "He never does turn up, you know. Not now-a-days." However, at the climax of *The Last Battle,* Aslan returns to Narnia one last time, brings an end to the world, and establishes "real Narnia."

In the real world, God varied his visible presence over the ages. Reminiscent of Aslan, the Book of Genesis talks about God "walking with Adam" in the Garden of Eden before Adam and Eve's disobedience. During the Old Testament period, he had a hands-on role in the affairs of ancient Israel and communicated verbally to prophets such as Isaiah and Jeremiah. However, God was the most visible when he came to earth as Jesus Christ. But, this visible presence was temporary; after his death and resurrection, he went to his Father, where he'll stay until his Second Coming on earth. Thus, for the past 2,000 years, God's role is more reminiscent of Aslan's subtlety in *The Voyage of the "Dawn Treader"* and much of *The Silver Chair* than his more visible presence in *The Lion, the Witch and the Wardrobe* or *The Magician's Nephew.*

In *The Voyage of the "Dawn Treader,"* Caspian comes closest to describing the way in which Christians communicate and interact with God today. He remarks, "Aslan has spoken to me. No — I don't mean he was actually here.

He wouldn't fit into the cabin, for one thing. But that gold lion's head on the wall came to life and spoke to me." Although you may not have an encounter with a talking lion's head, you can sense the same unmistakable presence of Jesus Christ when you pray to him in earnest. He may not "fit into your cabin," so to speak, but he's actually there.

Largely works through his followers

Aslan plays an active role in certain events of Narnian history, but he largely works through the children and Narnians and depends on them to carry out his will:

- ✔ Peter, Susan, and Lucy play pivotal roles in the defeat of the White Witch and her army in *The Lion, the Witch and the Wardrobe.*

- ✔ Caspian's cry for help doesn't bring Aslan to the rescue but instead draws the Pevensie children back into Narnia to help him in *Prince Caspian.*

- ✔ Eustace and Jill carry out Aslan's mission to save Prince Rilian in *The Silver Chair.*

- ✔ Eustace and Jill return to Narnia to help King Tirian in his battle against Shift the Ape and the invading Calormenes in *The Last Battle.*

- ✔ Aslan guides Shasta on his mission to warn Archenland of the coming invasion by Prince Rabadash, but he never gets involved in the actual battle. He lets the Archenland and Narnian armies handle that task in *The Horse and His Boy.*

Similarly, God took a hands-on approach to the world at specific times in history. By and large, however, since the ascension of Jesus Christ to heaven and the coming of the Holy Spirit (see Acts 1–2), God has tended to work through his followers (the Church, the worldwide "Body of Christ") to carry out his will in this world. But make no mistake: Just as Aslan is highly involved in the events of Narnia, so too does God guide and enable Christians along their ways.

Engineers circumstances

According to Proverbs 16:9, "In his heart a man plans his course, but the Lord determines his steps." Supporting this truth, Acts 17:26 indicates the active role that God had in circumstances of the early church: "God determined the times set for them and the exact places where they should live." Finally, Paul adds an exclamation point to the idea, saying, "And we know that all things work together for good to them that love God" (Romans 8:28).

Heartily agreeing with these passages, Lewis portrays Aslan as a lion who engineers circumstances. You can see this truth throughout *The Chronicles of Narnia*. For example, Aslan preordains the meeting with the Pevensie children at the Stone Table, knowing full well what ultimately happens there. In *The Silver Chair*, when Eustace falls over the ledge, Aslan is on hand to blow him into Narnia. *The Silver Chair* also shows how perfect God's design can be; not only does Aslan use Scrubb and Jill to save Rilian, but he also engineers their arrival back to Experiment House to rescue Eustace and Jill from bullies, complete with Caspian to help save the day. Aslan's talk with Shasta in *The Horse and His Boy* best sums up God's active role in the world:

> *I was the lion who forced you to join with Aravis. I was the cat who comforted you among the houses of the dead. I was the lion who drove the jackals from you while you slept. I was the lion who gave the Horses the new strength of fear for the last mile so that you should reach King Lune in time. I was the lion who you do not remember who pushed the boat in which you lay, a child near death, so that it came to shore where a man sat, wakeful at midnight, to receive you.*

Because God is actively involved in the world, there's no such thing as luck. The Hermit in *The Horse and His Boy* speaks to this point, saying, "I have now lived a hundred and nine winters in this world and have never yet met any such thing as Luck." Shasta echoes the Hermit later that night, saying, "I must have come through the pass in the night. What luck that I hit it! — at least it wasn't luck at all really, it was *Him*. And now I am in Narnia."

Isn't at our beck and call

Aslan loves the children and Talking Animals of Narnia, but he isn't a magician waiting to do tricks at their beck and call. For example, in *The Silver Chair*, when Eustace and Jill talk about whether they can just ask Aslan to be transported to Narnia and away from Experiment House, Eustace has the right perspective: "It would look as if we thought we could make him do things. But really, we can only ask him."

In addition, Aslan doesn't do bargains, a fact that Digory picks up on in *The Magician's Nephew*. The narrator tells that Digory "had had for a second some wild idea of saying 'I'll try to help you if you'll promise to help my Mother,' but he realized in time that the Lion was not at all the sort of person one could try to make bargains with."

Similarly, God isn't sitting up in heaven waiting to perform magic tricks or make deals. Lewis struggled with this misconception in his early years; at age

10, he saw God as duty-bound to answer his prayers to heal his mom. As a result, his mother's death was a huge shock to him and left his faith reeling for years.

The fact that Aslan isn't a tame lion also reflects the truth of God's independence. You can't harness God and get him to perform for you like a lion in a circus. He's far too wild for that!

Doesn't do encores

Aslan isn't one to do a "reunion tour" to relive past glory. Lucy laments in *Prince Caspian,* "And I thought you'd come roaring in and frighten all the enemies away — like last time." Aslan responds, "Things never happen the same way twice." In the same way, God doesn't do encores; after he does something, he moves on and doesn't look back. However, like Lucy, human nature constantly fools us into thinking he just might bring back the glory days.

Always serves as the initiator

Throughout *The Chronicles of Narnia,* Aslan is always the initiator, the one making the first move. In *The Silver Chair,* when Jill Pole wonders whether hers and Eustace's calls prompted Aslan to action, Aslan corrects her: "You would not have called to me unless I had been calling to you." In this passage, Aslan mirrors 1 John 4:19: "We love because he first loved us."

Along the same line, in *The Voyage of the "Dawn Treader,"* Eustace asks Edmund whether he knows Aslan. Edmund replies, "Well — he knows me." In this passage, Lewis echoes the Apostle Paul in Galatians 4:9: "Now that you know God — or rather are known by God. . . ."

Stretches and disciplines

Aslan loves and has compassion for "his children," but that doesn't mean he's easy on them or handles them with kid gloves. In fact, he stretches, challenges, and outright disciplines the children and Narnians. Nowhere is this more evident than in *The Horse and His Boy.* Consider two examples:

- **God stretches.** Racing across the desert towards Archenland, Bree and Hwin are convinced that they're running their fastest. Yet, Aslan sees that their efforts aren't good enough and knows that if he doesn't act, the Calormenes will beat Bree and Hwin to Anvard. So, Aslan chases the two horses, and lo and behold, Bree discovers that he hadn't been running as fast as he thought. On a similar note, Ephesians 4:14–15 reminds

Christians that they're going to be stretched as well. Instead of remaining infants "tossed back and forth by the waves," Christians will "in all things grow up into" Jesus Christ.

✔ **God disciplines.** At one point in the story, Aslan actually jabs Aravis with his right paw. On first take, the action is out of character for Aslan and seems like a curious twist in the story. Yet, the narrator is quick to say that the ten scratches left Aravis sore but weren't deep or dangerous. You find out towards the end of the story that Aslan scratched Aravis because he believed she "needed to know what it felt like" (her selfishness at the start of the story leads to a servant getting whipped when Aravis runs away from Calormen). By having Aslan punish Aravis for her selfishness, Lewis merely echoes Hebrews 12:6: "The Lord disciplines those he loves, and he punishes everyone he accepts as a child." Aslan knows that Aravis needs discipline in order to get over some of the self-centeredness that has always been a part of her life. It works!

Using Narnia to Examine How Humans React to God

Biblical Christianity holds that when all is said and done, people must choose whether or not to submit to God. It's a zero-sum game: There are no in-betweens. Therefore, we can hem and haw and use stall tactics, but in the end, our choice is either to love God and surrender our lives to him or hate God and cling to our own lives.

In Narnia, reactions to Aslan clearly indicate which of these two choices the characters have made. When the Pevensie children first hear about Aslan from Mr. and Mrs. Beaver, their reactions come from their hearts: "Each of the children felt something jump in his inside. Edmund felt a sensation of mysterious horror. Peter felt suddenly brave and adventurous." In *The Magician's Nephew,* the song Aslan "sings" during creation "made you want to rush at other people and either hug them or fight them." Uncle Andrew's and Jadis's reactions to Aslan fall into the second camp — hating God. They hate seeing Aslan in the newly created Narnia; Uncle Andrew's "mouth was open too, but not open with joy . . . He was not liking the Voice."

Yet, regardless of whether a creature loves or hates Aslan, everyone fears him:

✔ In *The Lion, the Witch and the Wardrobe,* Mrs. Beaver says, "If there's anyone who can appear before Aslan without their knees knocking, they're either braver than most or else just silly."

✔ After Aslan finishes telling the White Witch that he's taking Edmund's place at the Stone Table, she doesn't strut her stuff with glee, but rather she "picked up her skirts and fairly ran for her life."

✔ Frank the Cabby's reaction to Aslan in *The Magician's Nephew* is, "Glory be! I'd ha' been a better man all my life if I'd known there were things like this."

✔ In *The Magician's Nephew,* the children have a mixture of fear and attraction when they see Aslan. The narrator says "They were terribly afraid [Aslan] would turn and look at them, yet in some queer way they wished [he] would."

✔ In *The Last Battle,* when he enters real Narnia, Puzzle the donkey is scared about what happens next, saying "What I'll do if I really have to meet Aslan I'm sure I don't know."

Similarly, for Christians, a healthy fear of the Lord is the beginning of knowledge (Proverbs 1:7) and wisdom (Proverbs 16:6). But the wicked flee from the holiness of God (Proverbs 28:1 and Revelation 6:15–17).

Just as reactions to Aslan reveal much about how different characters relate to God, characters who are tainted with sin can't seem to look into Aslan's eyes. There's just something about his holiness and greatness that instinctively makes them want to turn away. The evil White Witch avoids looking directly into Aslan's eyes during their meeting at the Stone Table. In Digory's first encounter with Aslan, he "dared not look into the great eyes," yet something amazing happens to Digory after he avoids temptation and is restored by Aslan: "This time he found he could look straight into the Lion's eyes. He had forgotten his troubles and felt absolutely content."

Finally, when people understand who Aslan is, they see his greatness and glory. At the end of *The Silver Chair,* Eustace and Jill see Aslan as "so bright and real and strong that everything else began at once to look pale and shadowy compared with him."

Dealing with Sin, Evil, and All Things Yucky

Narnia and our world rest upon the same stuff: right, wrong, and a free choice between the two. The central plot of each Narnian story incorporates these principles by dealing with temptation and sin, the effects of sin, and the portrayal of evil in different characters.

Sin is any deliberate action, attitude, or thought that goes against what's known to be right. Sin includes

✔ Physical sins that you act out.

✔ Spiritual sins that are hidden within your heart.

> ✔ "No-no's," the things you shouldn't do but do anyway.
>
> ✔ "Should have's," the things you should do but don't.

In addition, like when Jadis eats the apple, sin can be something you do that isn't inherently wrong but becomes wrong when it's done "at the wrong time or in the wrong way."

Temptation is the attraction of choosing wrong over what you know to be right. By itself, temptation isn't a sin, but giving into temptation results in sin. *Evil* is another word for sin, but you can also think of it as a quality acquired by people who sin over and over again in defiance of God.

Viewing sin through Narnian eyes

In the Narnian Chronicles, Lewis gives a vivid picture of what sin is and how it manifests itself in the lives of the characters.

Sin is deliberate disobedience

Lewis portrays sin as "deliberate disobedience." When Edmund makes the decision to side with the White Witch in *The Lion, the Witch and the Wardrobe,* he knows exactly what he's doing. Edmund "managed to believe, or to pretend he believed, that she wouldn't do anything very bad to them . . . deep down inside him he really knew that the White Witch was bad and cruel." In *Prince Caspian,* Susan knows better "deep down inside" when she refuses to believe that Lucy has seen Aslan. But Susan's desire to get out of the woods is stronger than her desire to obey Aslan. Lucy, however, gives perhaps the best example of deliberate disobedience in *The Voyage of the "Dawn Treader."* In spite of her conscience telling her not to, she decides to say a spell from the Magician's Book anyway: "I will say the spell. I don't care. I will." The narrator adds that Lucy says "'I don't care' because she had a strong feeling that she mustn't."

Sin can be rationalized, but never excused

When I am convicted about a sin I am planning or have already committed, my natural reaction is to attempt to justify and rationalize my actions. This self-defense mechanism shows up in Narnia as well. For example, before Lucy sins by reading the "mind reading" spell from the Magician's Book, she justifies her upcoming action by saying that because she didn't say the "beautifying" spell, she should certainly be allowed to say this one. Likewise, in *The Magician's Nephew,* Digory rationalizes the sin of taking a magic apple back to his mother. You can see the wheels spinning in his mind when he says, "The notice on the gate [not to steal the apples] might not have been exactly an order; it might have been only a piece of advice — and who cares about advice?"

Sin is "me-first"

In *The Great Divorce* (see Chapter 11), Lewis presents a common quality of all the inhabitants of Hell: They're self-absorbed and unwilling to get out of themselves. This me-first mentality exists in Narnia as well. Before turning into a dragon in *The Voyage of the "Dawn Treader,"* Eustace experiences the self-absorbed nature of sin. He can't get out of himself, even when the wrongness of his feelings and actions is so obvious. In writing in his journal, Eustace whines, "Caspian and Edmund are simply brutal to me. The night we lost our mast . . ., though I was *not at all* well, they forced me to come on deck and work like a slave." In *The Magician's Nephew,* Uncle Andrew has the same attitude when he can't get the rings from Digory or Polly to exit Narnia; "But what about *me*? . . . No one thinks of *me*," laments Andrew.

This me-first attitude is even stronger when people are tempted. When Jadis tries to entice Digory into taking an apple back to his mother, she says, "What has the Lion ever done for you that you should be his slave?" Self-absorption also causes people to blame others for their own sins; in *The Lion, the Witch and the Wardrobe,* for example, Edmund "thought more and more how he hated Peter — just as if all this had been Peter's fault."

Sin is "mine, mine, mine"

The sinful nature in you and I wants ownership over something or someone else, just like a toddler crying out "mine, mine, mine" for a toy. In *The Screwtape Letters,* Screwtape talks about how the idea of ownership plays right into Satan's hands: "The sense of ownership in general is always to be encouraged."

In *The Magician's Nephew,* Queen Jadis reflects the evil nature of ownership when she speaks of Charn: "I was the Queen. They were all *my* people. What else were they there for but to do my will?" Similarly, in his rage over Susan's refusal to marry him in *The Horse and His Boy,* Prince Rabadash of Calormen cries out, "I must have the barbarian queen."

Facing the consequences of sin

Sin has its consequences, and the many results of sin are made evident in Narnia. Sin leads to

✓ **A dead-end.** One of the great ironies of the Gospels is that Judas betrayed Jesus in exchange for thirty pieces of silver. Yet when he realized the horror of what he'd done, the silver lost any value, and he threw it away. This dead-end nature of sin is reflected in the Judas-like character of Edmund. He betrays his siblings for Turkish Delight, but instead of receiving his desired dessert, he gets a hunk of dry bread from the White Witch. (I bet the stuff was yucky low-carb bread, too!)

✔ **Despair.** Etched over the gates of the garden where Digory picks the apple in *The Magician's Nephew* are the words:

Come in by the gold gates or not at all,
Take of my fruit for others or forbear,
For those who steal or those climb my wall
Shall find their heart's desire and find despair.

Jadis may think she's getting her heart's desire when she eats the apple, but she really only finds despair. In fact, she ends up loathing the tasty fruit forever. As Aslan says, "Length of days with an evil heart is only length of misery."

✔ **A hardened heart.** The Apostle Paul says in Romans 1 that continued unrepentant sin will lead to a hardened heart. When Uncle Andrew is in the newly created Narnia, his horror over Aslan and the Talking Animals reflects this spiritual bankruptcy. Aslan even says, "But I cannot [talk] to this old sinner, and I cannot comfort him either; he has made himself unable to hear my voice. If I spoke to him, he would hear only growlings and roarings."

✔ **Stains.** Sin even has a physical impact in Narnia. When Jadis eats the apple in *The Magician's Nephew,* the juice creates a horrible stain around her mouth. In addition, her face in *The Lion, the Witch and the Wardrobe* "was deadly white, white as salt." Likewise, some sins in the real world can manifest themselves physically.

✔ **Lasting consequences.** When a child or Talking Animal disobeys Aslan and is repentant, Aslan always forgives them. But at the same time, sin has lasting consequences that the character has to deal with. For example, Lucy confesses her sin to Aslan over the "mind reading" spell that she shouldn't have said. Aslan is quick to forgive her, but she still has to deal with effects of her action. By reading the spell, Lucy spoils a friendship she previously held dear; "I don't think I'd ever be able to forget what I heard her say," laments Lucy.

The faces of evil

In a letter to an American named Mr. Kinter, Lewis wrote, "We are born knowing the White Witch, aren't we?" Indeed, people of all shapes, sizes, countries, and religions have an instinctive understanding of right and wrong. And so in reading *The Chronicles of Narnia,* we see wrong personified in characters like the White Witch Jadis, the Green Witch, Uncle Andrew, King Miraz, and Shift the Ape.

Evil is portrayed in the White Witch Jadis and the Green Witch as a mixture of incredible beauty on the outside, but with coldness, sternness, and hatred lurking underneath. In so doing, Lewis gets at a key component to sin — it looks great from the outside, but the inside is nothing but a bunch of nasty stuff.

The evil characters invariably see themselves as innately superior to others. Before the adventures in *The Magician's Nephew* begin, Uncle Andrew boasts, "Men like me, who possess hidden wisdom, are freed from common rules." Jadis echoes these sentiments, telling Digory, "What would be wrong for you or for any of the common people is not wrong in a great Queen such as I."

Not surprisingly then, non-evil people are to be used by evil ones — or to use Screwtape's words from *The Screwtape Letters*, treated as "cattle that can finally become food." Sounding much like Weston in the space trilogy, Uncle Andrew says, "I am the great scholar, the magician, the adept who is *doing* the experiment. Of course I need subjects to do it *on*." Similarly, Queen Jadis ignores Polly in Charn because she wants to make use of Digory. But in England, Jadis ignored both of them because she wanted to use Uncle Andrew. The narrator in *The Magician's Nephew* describes Uncle Andrew and Jadis: "They are not interested in things or people unless they can use them; they are terribly practical."

Fooling Ourselves: Three Ways We Do It

Within *The Chronicles of Narnia*, Lewis provides compelling insight into the ways in which people fool and deceive themselves from accepting Christian truth.

Dwarfs: Jaded and skeptical

In *The Last Battle*, the Dwarfs' jaded skepticism offers a revealing look into human nature. The Dwarfs are taken in by the false Aslan that Shift the Ape dresses up to fool the Narnians. Later, when King Tirian approaches the Dwarfs to join his fight against Shift and the Calormenes, the Dwarfs want nothing to do with him or his battle. Griffle the Black Dwarf sums up their feelings by declaring, "I don't know how all you chaps feel, but I feel I've heard as much about Aslan as I want to for the rest of my life." He continues, "We're going to look after ourselves from now on and touch our caps to nobody . . . Dwarfs are for the Dwarfs."

More than anyone in *The Chronicles of Narnia*, the Dwarfs personify the cynicism and skepticism of postmodern culture. Many today are doubtful of any claims of truth and scoff when they hear of scandals in the church or see so-called "Christians" living like pagans every day but Sunday. Griffle speaks for these people when he says, "You must think we're blooming soft in the head, that you must. We've been taken in once and now you expect us to be taken in again the next minute. We've no more use for stories about Aslan, see!"

Cynicism usually springs from being hurt, deceived, or disappointed — sometimes by Christians or at least people who call themselves Christians. The effects of this treatment can be heartbreaking. To use today's vernacular, pain sucks — but it's not a viable excuse to turn away from God. Instead, how you react to pain or disillusionment is all that matters. The disillusioned Dwarfs have a choice — to seek the truth, even when the path to it is challenging, or to shut down completely and rely wholly on themselves. Sadly, they choose the latter option.

Try as he might, even Aslan can't do anything to change their minds. First he tries to frighten them with a long growl, but they dismiss it, believing it's someone on the other side of the Stable just trying to scare them. "They won't take *us* in again!" they exclaim. So Aslan tries to bless them by preparing an incredible feast of the fanciest foods and wine imaginable. But, in their disbelief, the Dwarfs can't taste the meal as it really is and dismiss it as animal feed. In the end, they declare in defiance, "We haven't let anyone take us in. The Dwarfs are for the Dwarfs."

Just as Aslan tries to convince the Dwarfs of his existence, God often acts in the world to get people to turn to him. He sometimes uses hardship and difficult circumstances to sober people up and shake them from their comfort zones so that they realize their need to look to him. So too, he showers them with love and blessings to get them to look toward the source of those blessings.

In what are perhaps Aslan's most lamentable lines in the entire Narnia series, he says of the Dwarfs: "They will not let us help them. They have chosen cunning instead of belief. Their prison is only in their minds, yet they are in that prison; and so afraid of being taken in that they can not be taken out." With this characterization of the Dwarfs, Lewis warns people in postmodern society to heed the self-defeating choice of the Dwarfs.

Dufflepuds: Foolish

In *The Voyage of the "Dawn Treader,"* the children, Caspian, and his *Dawn Treader* crew have a rather entertaining encounter with the Dufflepuds (also called Monopods or Duffers). The Dufflepuds are invisible, one-footed creatures living on the Island of the Voices that Lucy makes visible after she says a spell from the Magician's Book. The Dufflepuds are humorous, but their function is serious: They provide insight into the tendency that humans have towards foolishness, particularly towards our relationship with God.

The Dufflepuds' scatterbrained view of Coriakin (the lord over the island and the Dufflepuds) reflects, in many ways, humans' view of God. Coriakin remarks, "One minute they talk as if I ran everything and overheard everything and was extremely dangerous. The next moment they think they can take me in by tricks that a baby would see through — bless them!"

Humans have a tendency to believe, consciously or unconsciously, that we can somehow beat God, ignoring the fact that he's the one, not us, enabling victories. An example of this point in Narnia comes after Lucy speaks the spell that makes the Monopods visible again. Clueless as to the role that Coriakin plays in the transformation, the Chief Monopod says, "We've beaten him this time."

Bree: Prideful and vain

In *The Horse and His Boy,* Bree is a Narnian stallion that was taken from his homeland as a young colt to serve in the Calormene army. Bree starts the story looking like he'll be a hero, but he ends up as one of the most pitiful characters in *The Chronicles of Narnia.* Bree is a case study in how pride and vanity can completely fool someone. A celebrated war horse, Bree talks in a "superior tone" and looks down upon both Shasta and the more ordinary talking horse Hwin. Yet, when the going gets tough, he's outdone by both Hwin, who sets the pace in their race toward Archenland, and Shasta, who shows bravery by retracing his course through danger to recover Aravis.

Yet, instead of taking his humble pie and learning from it, Bree clings to his pride and feels sorry for himself because he thinks he's lost everything. The Hermit of the Southern March, however, corrects him: "You've lost nothing but your self-conceit . . . If you are really so humbled as you sounded a minute ago, you must learn to listen to sense. You're not quite the great horse you've come to think, from living among the dumb horses." The Hermit then alludes to Romans 12:3 ("Don't think of yourself more highly than you ought") when he tells Bree, "But as long as you know you're nobody very special, you'll be a very decent sort of Horse."

Bree, however, is slow to learn. When he and Hwin get their chance later in the story to go to Narnia, Bree wants to wait until his tattered tail is grown out again to "make a good impression." He's also overly concerned about whether it's proper for Talking Horses to roll around on the ground, which he loves to do. Hwin simply rolls her eyes over the war stallion's silliness.

Although Bree's humbled by the events that transpire in *The Horse and His Boy* and has a face-to-face encounter with Aslan, even at the story's end, he clings, to some extent, to his pride and vanity. Lewis shows how self-defeating this choice is for Bree. After all, his dream during his time in Calormen was to return to Narnia. And yet, because of his vanity, the narrator says that when Bree went into Narnia, "He looked more like a horse going to a funeral than a long-lost captive returning to home and freedom."

Belief versus Unbelief in Narnia

Lewis believes that in an increasingly secularized society, the debate between naturalism and supernaturalism is one of the primary philosophical battle-grounds. The issue is a key topic in three of his major apologetic works: *Mere Christianity, The Abolition of Man,* and *Miracles.* The tension between super-naturalism and naturalism shows up time and again in *The Chronicles of Narnia.* Within Narnia, supernaturalism is expressed as believing in Aslan, the sons of Adam and daughters of Eve, and a world beyond Narnia. Naturalism is portrayed as unbelief in all these things, essentially that Narnia is all there ever was, is, or ever will be.

Lewis sprinkles unbelief and skepticism throughout the seven-book series. In *The Lion, the Witch and the Wardrobe,* you see a book in Mr. Tumnus's home called *Is Man a Myth?* In *The Horse and His Boy,* Bree says smugly of Aslan, "It would be quite absurd to suppose he is a real lion." In the same book, Prince Rabadash comments on the recent thawing of Narnia's Long Winter, "I am rather of the opinion that it has come about by the alteration of the stars and the operation of natural causes."

Nowhere is the battle between belief and unbelief more obvious than in *Prince Caspian.* The underlying theme for the entire story is the choice that each person or creature makes: to believe in Aslan and old Narnia or to dismiss these stories as fairy tales. King Miraz tells Caspian that belief in old Narnia is "all nonsense, for babies," but Doctor Cornelius counters that the stories that Caspian has heard of old Narnia are all true and that Narnia "is not the land of men. It is the country of Aslan."

Before his encounter with the Pevensie children, Trumpkin the Dwarf is a skeptic. He says to Caspian, "Do you believe all of those old stories? . . . But who believes in Aslan nowadays?" Caspian isn't so sure: "Sometimes I did wonder if there really was such a person as Aslan: but then sometimes I wondered if there were really people like you. Yet there you are."

Nikabrik the Black Dwarf and Trufflehunter the Badger offer the greatest contrast in perspectives. Nikabrik is the most vocal and hostile skeptic in the book. "I think the Horn . . . and your great King Peter — and your Lion Aslan — are all eggs in moonshine," dismisses Nikabrik. He writes off Aslan's resurrection by saying, "You'll notice that we hear precious little about anything he did afterwards. He fades out of the story. How do you explain that, if he really came to life? Isn't it much more likely that he didn't and that the stories say nothing more about him because there was nothing more to say?"

In contrast, Trufflehunter remains faithful to Aslan regardless of what anyone says. When Nikabrik argues that the call to High King Peter, Queen Susan, King Edmund, and Queen Lucy has failed because they either haven't heard, can't come, or are enemies, Trufflehunter has a different perspective. He adds, "Or they are on the way."

In *Miracles,* Lewis writes that "we all have Naturalism in our bones . . . its assumptions rush back upon the mind the moment diligence is relaxed." This idea crops up in *The Silver Chair* when the Green Witch tries to convince Scrubb, Jill, and Puddleglum that the Overworld (Narnia) is just a dream. "There never was any world but mine," she says. "There is no Narnia, no Overworld, no sky, no sun, no Aslan." Fighting the spell that the Green Witch is trying to place on them, Puddleglum explains why he doesn't believe that Underland is *all* there is:

> *The made-up things seem a good deal more important than the real ones. Suppose this black pit of a kingdom of yours is the only world. Well, it strikes me as a pretty poor one . . . Four babies playing a game can make a play-world which licks your real world hollow. That's why I'm going to stand by the play world.*

Future Glory: Looking Through a Heavenly Spyglass

In the first six books of *The Chronicles of Narnia* (that's all but *The Last Battle*), you get glimpses of something beyond death for Narnians, of Aslan's country awaiting his followers. Reepicheep's solo journey to the utter east is the most memorable example, although even by the end of *The Voyage of the "Dawn Treader,"* you never really know what happens to him. In his final installment of the Narnian Chronicles, Lewis focuses on issues of death and life after death. What's more, he doesn't just have a quick, obligatory "they live happily ever after" wrap-up at the end of *The Last Battle*. Instead, he spends considerable time after the climactic battle telling you exactly *why* and *how* they truly lived happily ever after.

Experiencing death as a gateway

Like it or not, death is the gateway to Heaven (and Hell), both in real life and in Narnia. Lewis adds in *C.S Lewis, Letters to Children:* "The only way for us to [get to] Aslan's country is through death, as far as I know; perhaps some very good people get just a tiny glimpse before then." Even though death is the Great Unknown for those of us still living, Lewis provides a window into what it must be like for a Christian to actually experience it. The Friends of Narnia

(Eustace, Jill, Peter, Edmund, Lucy, Lord Digory, and Aunt Polly) are all sent to the real Narnia by way of a railway accident that kills them. Edmund describes what it was like for him on the station curb when the accident occurred: "There was a frightful roar and something hit me with a bang, but it didn't hurt. And I felt not so much scared as — well, excited." Lord Digory, who was on the train, says things were much the same for him, but with a difference because he's older — he "stopped feeling old."

In *The Screwtape Letters*, Lewis paints a similar picture when the Patient is killed by a bombing raid during World War II. According to the devil Screwtape, the Patient's experience was "sheer, instantaneous liberation." Screwtape then laments over how good death is for the Patient:

> *One moment it seemed to be all our world; the scream of the bombs, the fall of houses, the heart cold with horrors . . . the next moment all this was gone, gone like a bad dream, never again to be of any account . . . Did you mark how naturally — as if he'd been born for it — the earth-born vermin entered the new life? How all his doubts become, in the twinkling of an eye, ridiculous? I know what the creature was saying to itself! 'Yes. Of course. It was always like this . . . How could I ever have doubted it?'*

Submitting to final judgment

Within *The Chronicles of Narnia*, Lewis never gives specifics on the eternal fate of unbelievers. They're away somewhere, presumably in Hell, but they're not part of real Narnia. (The narrator says "The children never saw them again. I don't know what become of them.")

However, Lewis does describe what Christians call the "final judgment," which will take place at the end of the Second Coming of Jesus Christ (Revelation 20:11–15). In a story reminiscent of Jesus's parable of the sheep and the goats in Matthew 25:31–46, the creatures that pass through the Stable door at the end of *The Last Battle* all have to face Aslan. They then go to his right or left depending on their faith, or lack thereof.

Finding out what Heaven and its inhabitants are like

In *The Chronicles of Narnia*, Lewis provides some of the most descriptive, captivating images of Heaven in all modern literature. His vision of Heaven doesn't involve harps, puffy clouds, and wimpy angels because he knows that those stereotypical images have no biblical basis. Instead, Lewis's depiction of Heaven is reflective of his knowledge of who God is and what kind of place he wants his children to inhabit for eternity.

A place of unlimited adventure and unlimited security

In this world, adventure and security are opposites; you can't embrace one without abandoning the other. As a result, many people gravitate toward one of these two extremes. Some people live for the rush of adrenaline that accompanies closing a major business deal or climbing a 14,000-footer in Colorado. Others simply thrive when they feel safe and secure in their quiet suburban houses and get enough adventure from ordering Chinese take-out on a Friday night.

Lewis's real Narnia is a world that offers "secure adventure" (or is it "adventurous security"?). For example, when Eustace and Lucy jump into the Caldron Pool and head straight for the Great Waterfall, Eustace says, "This is absolutely crazy." Lucy replies, "Isn't it wonderful? Have you noticed one can't feel afraid, even if one wants to? Try it." The two are actually able to swim up the waterfall, and if you can imagine swimming up Niagara Falls or Angel Falls, you can guess at how terrifying that is. But as Eustace and Lucy experience in real Narnia, "It was only gloriously exciting."

Even Aslan's cry "further up, further in" implies the mixing of adventure and security. He's calling for everyone to move further up in the mountains to experience wonder as they head deeper into Aslan's country and closer to his comforting and protective arms.

What's more, the adventure and security never stop growing. "The further up and the further in you go, the bigger everything gets," says Mr. Tumnus. This snowball effect is the gist of what Aslan tells Caspian in *Prince Caspian:* "Every year you grow, you will find me bigger."

A place of reunion

Reunions are a real drag when you don't enjoy being with the people you're seeing. However, when you're reunited with someone you love, there's hardly anything better than rekindling that relationship. Heaven is a place where Christians are reunited — forever — with spouses, parents, children, friends, and other loved ones. In real Narnia, King Tirian is reunited with his father, King Erlian. The Pevensie children rush toward their mother and father — who were killed in the railway accident — in "new England" (not to be confused with America's New England, although some New Englanders may contend that they indeed live in Heaven).

Besides family, however, Narnia's faithful are all present and accounted for in real Narnia, enjoying each other's company and reveling in old stories together. In the final chapters of *The Last Battle,* Lewis mentions many of the Narnian "faithful" by name, including Reepicheep, Puddleglum, Rilian, Rilian's mother, Ramandu, Caspian, Trumpkin, Trufflehunter, Glenstorm the Centaur, King Cor of Archenland, Queen Aravis, Prince Corin, Bree, Hwin, Mr. and Mrs. Beaver, and Mr. Tumnus.

Taking a symbolic view of reality

C.S. Lewis was highly influenced by such classical philosophers as Plato and Aristotle. These influences surface within *The Chronicles of Narnia* in the Platonic idea of symbolism, the idea that our physical world is a copy of an invisible world. Lewis writes in *The Allegory of Love,* "The world which we mistake for reality is the flat outline of that which elsewhere veritably is all the round of its unimaginable dimensions."

Plato's concept of symbolism is what led Lewis to the term *Shadowlands,* which he uses to describe Earth: Earth is but a shadow of what Heaven will be like. Lewis's perspective on this reality plays out in *The Last Battle.* When Peter, Edmund, Lucy, and the Narnians enter the real Narnia, they marvel at its beauty. Lucy tries to describe how this new place is different from the old Narnia, but she doesn't have the words. Lord Digory sums it up by saying it's "more like the real thing." He then adds, "[Narnia] was only a shadow or a copy of the real Narnia which has always been here and always will be here: just as our world, England and all, is only a shadow or copy of something in Aslan's real world."

"More real" than earth

When some people think of Heaven, they see it as a blissful place that's somehow less real or less tangible than the soil of good ol' planet earth. Yet, one of Lewis's most firmly held beliefs about Heaven is that the earth is but the Shadowlands for a far more real and tangible world to come (see the sidebar "Taking a symbolic view of reality"). When a Narnian comments that real Narnia is "like Narnia," Digory corrects him by stating that it's *more* like the real thing." Lord Digory expresses Lewis's ideas on earth and heaven when he contrasts old Narnia and real Narnia:

> [Old Narnia] was only a shadow or a copy of the real Narnia, which has always been here and always will be here: just as our world, England and all, is only a shadow or copy of something in Aslan's real world . . . All of the old Narnia that mattered, all the dear creatures, have been drawn into the real Narnia through the Door. And of course it is different; as different as a real thing is from a shadow or as waking life is from a dream . . . It's all in Plato, all in Plato. Bless, what do they teach them at these schools!

A place where good things never end

When you "get lost" in *The Chronicles of Narnia, The Lord of the Rings,* or any other fantastic book, you likely look upon the final page with dread because you know that as soon as you read it, your adventure ends forever. For a contemporary book or film, you can always hope for a sequel, but for the Narnian Chronicles or the Ring series, there's no hope: Lewis and Tolkien have long since passed away! Narnia and Middle-earth will never again come to life at the hands of their creators (okay, "subcreators" is more accurate, if you read

Chapter 6). Yet, imagine for a moment the unbridled joy if you were to discover a storehouse of Narnian adventures that Lewis wrote but never published. What's more, suppose you were to find more books than you could possibly read in your lifetime. Then, to top it off, imagine that each story is better than one before. That's Heaven, according to Lewis.

All good things on earth have an ending, but not in "real life" (Heaven). Consider the remarkable contrast between the start of *Prince Caspian* and the end of *The Last Battle*. When *Prince Caspian* begins, the Pevensie children are at the train station dreading their return to boarding school. The narrator says that "everyone felt that the holidays were really over and everyone felt their term-time feelings beginning again, and they were all rather gloomy and no-one could think of anything to say." At the end of *The Last Battle,* however, this symbolism is turned completely around when Aslan tells the children, "The term is over: the holidays have begun. The dream is ended: this is the morning."

Filled with creatures designed for eternity

When the children and Talking Animals arrive in real Narnia, they're all amazed to find it's what they were made for. Jewel the unicorn exclaims, "I have come home at last! This is my real country! I belong here. This is the land I have been looking for all my life, though I never knew it till now." The following sacred qualities apply to those living in real Narnia:

- ✔ **Everyone's in the prime of their lives.** On arriving in real Narnia, Digory's gray beard turns golden blond. In fact, Jill remarks that Digory and Polly, both forty years older than she on earth, now look so much younger than back in England: "I don't believe you two really are much older than we are here." So too, King Erlian, Tirian's father, looks to his son as "young and merry as he could just remember him from very early days."

- ✔ **Everyone's in tip-top physical shape.** Physically, whatever ails humans on earth is made new in real Narnia. For example, Edmund's knee was sore, but it feels perfect in real Narnia.

- ✔ **Everyone's free from the constraints of time.** Time as we know it is different in real Narnia. Lewis depicts this reality in *The Last Battle* by having Father Time awaken and assume a new name.

- ✔ **Everyone's free from the bondage of sin.** Sin doesn't exist in Heaven, but people aren't automatically turned into robots either. What's different in Heaven is the way people look at sin. Aslan speaks to this point when he tells Caspian at the end of *The Silver Chair,* "You cannot want wrong things any more, now that you have died, my son." In other words, people in Heaven don't sin because they see sin for what it really is — that sin is, for example, the Green Witch as a horrid serpent, not her beauty queen façade.

Welcoming the unexpected: Surprised by Emeth

Perhaps the most provocative part of *The Last Battle* is the presence of Emeth the Calormene in real Narnia. After all, Emeth worshipped Tash, the false god of the Calormenes. So why does Aslan allow him into his kingdom?

Backing up a little, biblical Christianity is built on the understanding that Jesus is the one and only means for people to receive salvation and redemption from God. After all, he's the one and only person who can bridge the gap between God and man (John 14:6, 1 Timothy 2:5–6, Acts 4:12).

However, the Bible is largely silent on how God deals with people who've never heard the gospel of Jesus Christ. Some Christians believe that salvation rests on explicit knowledge of Jesus Christ, while others maintain that God, in his mercy, makes some allowances for people who've never heard the gospel. Given the story of Emeth, it's clear that Lewis believes God redeems earnestly seeking "pagans" like Emeth. Writing in *Mere Christianity,* Lewis explains this position:

> *The truth is God has not told us what His arrangements about the other people are. We do know that no man can be saved except through Christ; we do not know that only those who know Him can be saved through Him. But in the meantime, if you are worried about people on the outside, the most unreasonable thing you can do is to remain on the outside yourself.*

For his part, Emeth is as surprised as everyone else and certainly didn't expect to be in Aslan's country. When he first sees Aslan, Emeth thinks he's nothing more than an appetizer for the Great Lion. He's obviously stunned when Aslan welcomes him, saying "Child, all the service thou hast done to Tash, I account as service done to me." Aslan explains himself further:

> *Therefore if any man swear by Tash and keep his oath for the oath's sake, it is by me that he has truly sworn, though he know it not, and it is I who reward him. And if any man do a cruelty in my name, then though he says the name Aslan, it is Tash whom he serves and by Tash his deed is accepted . . . For all find what they truly seek.*

The story of Emeth is based on the passage from Proverbs 8:17: "If you ever surely seek me, you shall ever surely find me." Lewis explains his position best in *C.S Lewis, Letters to Children:* "Anyone who devotes his whole life to seeking Heaven will be like Reepicheep and anyone who wants some worldly thing so badly that he is ready to use wicked means to get it will likely behave like Nick-i-brick." In the end, Emeth resembles Reepicheep far more than Nikabrik.

Chapter 9

Faith and Discipleship in Narnia

. . . .

In This Chapter

▶ Recognizing the power of a transformed life

▶ Finding the Christian life in Narnia

▶ Discovering the power of the "little guys"

▶ Seeing Joy, Narnia-style

▶ Receiving highest praise in Narnia

. . . .

C.S. Lewis trekked a rocky spiritual journey in his first 33 years. He went down many dead-end paths searching for answers to the major questions of life. In the end, he discovered what he was looking for — truth, meaning, and Joy — in Jesus Christ. Because Lewis was an academic type, you may think that when he resolved these issues intellectually, he moved on with his everyday life as usual with the sense of satisfaction that he'd figured everything out. Yet, after Lewis began to really understand the implications of his newfound faith, "business as usual" was the one thing that Lewis couldn't go back to. He realized that one's belief in Jesus Christ has a ripple effect. If Christ's message is true, your faith isn't just something you take out of your closet for one hour on Sunday; instead, it's a 24/7 deal because true faith means you surrender your entire life to Jesus Christ.

Lewis presents the all-encompassing nature of the Christian faith in *The Chronicles of Narnia*. There are no "Sunday Narnians" — living for Aslan on one day, and for themselves and the White Witch the rest of the week. In the good versus evil world of Narnia, everyone understands that following Aslan is more than a *lifestyle;* it's a *life choice.*

In this chapter, you explore faith and discipleship, Narnia-style. You discover how the stories of Edmund and Eustace reveal that true faith results in a transformed life. You also see how various truths of Christian discipleship are revealed through *The Chronicles of Narnia.*

Edmund and Eustace: The Power of a Transformed Life

More than any other characters in the Narnian Chronicles, Edmund and Eustace show what becoming a Christian is really all about. After all, let's face it: Peter, Lucy, and Polly aren't perfect children, but they don't have many struggles with sin; they start out as pretty good kids and get even better as they mature. Susan may start the series off strong, but she drops off the map by *The Last Battle* so no one ever really knows whether she makes it to "real Narnia." And both Digory and Jill have their good and bad moments, but their changes aren't overly dramatic.

In contrast, as much as we'd probably like to deny it, Edmund and Eustace are far more like us than anyone else in the Narnian Chronicles. Their struggles with sin aren't petty, and their experiences painfully expose the sinful nature that exists inside each of us. Both boys start their journeys in Narnia motivated by pride and self-interest — Edmund sides with the White Witch over his siblings and Aslan, and Eustace is fully absorbed by his needs and desires. Yet, despite their sinful beginnings, each has a genuine life-changing encounter with Aslan and is transformed into a new person as a result.

Edmund: Traitor turned king

At the start of *The Lion, the Witch and the Wardrobe*, Edmund is a nasty boy. He's deceitful, spiteful, and easy prey for the White Witch. Desiring power and delicious Turkish Delight, he abandons and betrays his siblings.

In time, Edmund realizes his dreadful mistake and is rescued from the White Witch's clutches. When he returns to Aslan's camp, Edmund has a one-on-one conversation with the lion. No one knows what's said between them, but the result is one of repentance, restoration, and transformation.

Repentance

Readers can only imagine Edmund's words to Aslan when they go on a walk together after Edmund's return. Edmund is clearly repentant of his actions, and shortly thereafter, he apologizes to his brother and sisters for endangering them.

Restoration

In the prodigal son parable (see Luke 15:20–24), the father showers love on his repentant son and restores his son to himself, his family, and his entire village.

Similarly, when the meeting between Aslan and Edmund is over, Aslan presents a fully restored Edmund to Peter, Susan, and Lucy. "Here is your brother," says Aslan, "and — there is no need to talk to him about what is past."

Transformation

Edmund is more than just a kid who's only sorry he gets caught. Clearly, he's not the same person after the encounter as he was before. The one-time traitor is transformed into a virtuous and honorable king, known as King Edmund the Just during the Golden Age of Narnia.

In *The Lion, the Witch and the Wardrobe,* a newly restored Edmund plays an important role in the defeat of the White Witch's army. In fact, after the battle, Peter says, "It was all Edmund's doing . . . We'd have been beaten if it hadn't been for him." Throughout the rest of *The Chronicles of Narnia,* Edmund shows time and time again that that his transformation is genuine. In *Prince Caspian,* he's the only one to faithfully side with Lucy on her sighting of Aslan. In *The Horse and His Boy,* Edmund believes mercy should be shown to Rabadash; he argues, "Even a traitor may mend. I have known one that did." Finally, in *The Last Battle,* Edmund's an integral member of the Friends of Narnia, remaining faithful to Aslan to the end.

Eustace: Self-absorbed twit turned faithful servant

Like Edmund, Eustace Scrubb is an example of the power of a transformed life. As *The Voyage of the "Dawn Treader"* begins, Eustace is as rotten a kid as you can imagine — always whining, insulting, and driving everyone aboard the ship crazy. He's so self-absorbed that he feels it's criminal to force him to help out in a crisis when he isn't feeling well, and he feels completely justified (rather than gracious) when others sacrifice themselves for him. But when Eustace sneaks away from camp on Dragon Island to avoid doing work, everything changes. He awakens to find himself turned into a scaly, fire-breathing dragon. As events unfold on the island, Scrubb goes through a process of repentance, restoration, and transformation.

Repentance

When Eustace realizes he's a dragon, he begins to see life in a new light. Rather than seeking revenge on Caspian and Edmund, he longs simply to be friends. Scrubb realizes how selfish he's always been and how awful he's treated others. As if to sum up his repentant spirit, Eustace the dragon "lifted up [his] voice and wept."

Restoration

After Eustace suffers as a dragon for several days, Aslan pays him a visit one night. He says that Eustace can enter a pool of water only after he sheds his dragon skin. Eustace scratches his body and sheds a layer of scales. He peels off another layer of skin, followed by another. But when yet another layer of dragon skin appears, Scrubb believes he may never be able to fully shed the dragon skin. Finally, Aslan says to Eustace, "You will have to let *me* undress you." Aslan's rips are so deep and raw that Eustace is convinced that the claws go straight into his heart. But these deep tears do the trick: The scales removed are so much "thicker, and darker, and more knobby looking than the others had been." Aslan throws Eustace into the water, stinging him terribly for a second or two. Eustace tells Edmund later, "After that it became perfectly delicious and as soon as I started swimming and splashing I found that all the pain had gone from my arm. And then I saw why. I'd turned into a boy again." Only Aslan can restore Eustace to his true condition.

Transformation

Eustace's encounter with Aslan is the real deal. When he returns to the *Dawn Treader,* everyone on board notices the change in him. Then, as *The Silver Chair* begins, Jill Pole also sees the difference: "It's not only me. Everyone's been saying so." During the adventure to rescue Price Rilian and later in *The Last Battle* to help King Tirian, Eustace proves himself a faithful servant of Aslan. He remarks much later about his pre-Aslan days, "I was a different chap then. I was — gosh! what a little tick I was."

However, the narrator reminds that this kind of transformation is a *process,* not a one-time complete turnaround: "It would be nice, and fairly nearly true, to say that 'from that time forth Eustace was a different boy.' To be strictly accurate, he began to be a different boy. He had relapses. There were still many days when he could be very tiresome. But most of those I shall not notice. The cure had begun."

Recognizing that Aslan does the work

The stories of Edmund and Eustace (see the preceding sections) have a similar pattern: Repentance by the offender leads to restoration by Aslan, which leads to transformation of the offender. This three-stage process is identical to Christ's redemption of people who come to him.

Notice, however, that Aslan is the one who actually does the restoring. Eustace, for example, is capable of peeling off layers of dragon skin on his own, but he can't get to all of them or through the deepest layers. Eustace needs Aslan to fully remove his dragon-ness and then cleanse and restore him. Similarly, people can conquer some sins and problems in their lives through sheer willpower, but they can't cleanse themselves fully and can't ever earn salvation just by being good. Instead, this restoration can take place only when people surrender their lives to Jesus Christ (1 John 1:9).

Aslan tells Eustace, "You will have to let me undress you" in much the same way that Jesus tells Nicodemus in John 3:7, "You must be born again." The message here is that, in effect, you need to shed your sin coating, be undressed by Jesus, and then be reborn as a clean child of God.

Revealing new spiritual genetics

Edmund and Eustace are proof of the "new spiritual genetics" that you receive when you believe in Christ. Because true belief is more than just an intellectual exercise, it affects your entire life. In fact, the Apostle Paul says that you're actually a "new creation" (2 Corinthians 5:17, Ephesians 4:23) and that you now have the Holy Spirit living inside of you (Colossians 1:27, John 14:16–17). As a result, you no longer live for yourself but rather for Jesus Christ. Or, as the Apostle Paul writes, "I have been crucified with Christ and I no longer live, but Christ lives in me" (Galatians 2:20).

And, although Christians are new creations, they aren't perfect. They still have a sinful nature that remains with them as long as they walk on this earth. And yet, a Christian on Earth is transformed, albeit slowly, into the new person he becomes fully in Heaven. Philippians 1:6 says that, "He who began a good work in you will carry it on to completion until the day of Christ Jesus." Or, as Lewis says of Eustace: The cure has begun.

Living as a Christian: Lessons from Narnia

The term *disciple* is commonly used within the Church to describe a "follower of Christ," a Christian who has accepted Jesus as savior and surrendered his or her life to him. *The Chronicles of Narnia* provides several lessons on what it means to live as a Christian disciple. I discuss these lessons in the following sections.

Living by faith, not by sight

"We live by faith, not by sight," says the Apostle Paul in 2 Corinthians 5:7. Throughout the Narnian Chronicles, the children and Narnians are called to live by faith in Aslan, not necessarily by what happens before their eyes.

In *Prince Caspian,* the Pevensie children are called to go by faith as they proceed with Trumpkin to Aslan's How. Lucy sees Aslan, who's there to help guide the group, but failing to truly seek Aslan, Peter, Susan, and Trumpkin doubt Lucy and proceed on a different route. When Aslan appears to Lucy again, she realizes that she has to go with him "whether anyone else does or not." As the group reluctantly follows Lucy, they each see Aslan in their own time. In each case, trust comes first, then sight. Because Edmund trusts most (after Lucy), he sees first. Peter sees Aslan next, and Susan and the Dwarf are last.

In *The Silver Chair,* Jill, Eustace, and Puddleglum are called to "live by faith" when the Black Knight (Rilian) calls out "by Aslan himself" to free him from the chair. The trio is uncertain what to do next: Aslan tells Jill at the start that those words are the final of the four Signs she's supposed to follow, but untying the Black Prince in the midst of his rage seems like certain suicide. In the following exchange, Puddleglum gets to the heart of what living by faith is all about:

> *"Oh, if only we knew!" said Jill.*
>
> *"I think we do know," said Puddleglum.*
>
> *"Do you mean you think everything will come right if we do untie him?" said Scrubb.*
>
> *"I don't know about that," said Puddleglum. "You see, Aslan, didn't tell Pole what would happen. He only told her what to do. That fellow will be the death of us once he's up, I shouldn't wonder. But that doesn't let us off following the Sign."*

By its very nature, living by faith is risky. You may have to go against gut instinct and even common sense in order to do what you believe Christ is calling you to do. The Pevensies don't know that following Aslan's direction leads them to Aslan's How until they start down his path. So too, Eustace, Jill, and Puddleglum obey Aslan even when doing so looks foolish, like certain death. In *The Last Battle,* Jewel the Unicorn underscores the message of steadfast faith regardless of cost when he says, "Nothing now remains for us seven but to go back to Stable Hill, proclaim the truth, and take the adventure that Aslan sends us."

Bookends to a life of faith

The Pevensie children's time in Narnia is illustrative of a life of faith. When they first enter Narnia in *The Lion, the Witch and the Wardrobe,* Mr. Beaver calls them into the woods saying, "Further in, come further in." That symbolic start of their "life of faith" is later bookended by "Further up, further in," which Aslan calls out to Peter, Edmund, and Lucy in the real Narnia.

Trusting God and doing the next thing

Scottish pastor and early 20th-century author Oswald Chambers lived by a simple motto: "Trust God and do the next thing." In other words, a Christian is called to trust in God and then act upon that trust, not to sit around and just think about it.

In *Prince Caspian,* when Lucy needs to wake up the others and tell them that she's seen Aslan again, she says, "I mustn't think about it, I must just do it." Later in the story, just before the battle against Miraz, Peter sounds much like Chambers, saying, "We don't know when [Aslan] will act. In his time, no doubt, not ours. In the meantime he would like us to do what we can on our own."

Lewis, however, makes a point of saying that so long as you keep on trusting and doing, you can still follow God even if you screw up along the way. In *The Silver Chair,* Jill and Eustace are saddened by their failure to look for the Signs in their quest for Rilian. Puddleglum, however, tells them that Aslan worked his will in spite of their disobedience along the way: "There's one thing you've got to remember. We're back on the right lines. We were to go under the Ruined City, and we *are* under it. We're following the instructions again."

Living to the hilt

Missionary Jim Elliot wrote, "Wherever you are, be all there. Live to the hilt every situation you believe to be the will of God." With these instructions, Elliot sums up the essence of what Christian discipleship is all about. In *The Silver Chair,* Prince Rilian displays this attitude when he expects a life-or-death battle in Underland. He tells Eustace, Jill, and Puddleglum, "When once a man is launched on such an adventure as this, he must bid farewell to hopes and fears, otherwise death or deliverance will both come too late to save his honor and his reason." He reaffirms later, "Whether we live or die Aslan will be our good lord."

Reepicheep also serves as an excellent example of a disciple "living to the hilt." In *The Voyage of the "Dawn Treader,"* when speaking of going to the utter east to Aslan's country, he says:

> *My own plans are made. While I can, I sail east in the Dawn Treader. When she fails me, I paddle east in my coracle. When she sinks, I shall swim east with my four paws. And when I can swim no longer, if I have not reached Aslan's country, or shot over the edge of the world in some vast cataract, I shall sink with my nose to the sunrise and Peepiceek will be head of the talking mice in Narnia.*

Becoming humble and "self-forgetful"

"Let us fix our eyes on Jesus, the author and perfecter of our faith," says Hebrews 12:2. When you follow that command, your attention falls more and more on Christ and less and less on yourself; you become more humble and forget about your own wants and needs. You naturally begin to live out Christ's command to "take up your cross and follow me" (Mark 8:34). In *The Chronicles of Narnia,* Lewis shows examples of this transformation when folks focus their full attentions on Aslan:

- ✔ In *The Magician's Nephew,* Aslan praises Digory by saying, "Well done" when Digory resists the temptation of secretly taking the magic apple back to his mother. Yet, the narrator points out that Digory "was in no danger of feeling conceited for he didn't think about it at all now that he was face to face to Aslan."

- ✔ In *The Lion, the Witch and the Wardrobe,* Edmund's heart starts to change, and his selfishness slowly starts to go away as a result. In particular, when he sees creatures turned to stone by the White Witch, the narrator says Edmund "for the first time in this story felt sorry for someone besides himself."

- ✔ At the end of *Prince Caspian,* Caspian shows the humility and proper sense of self that Christ desires in the faithful. Aslan asks Caspian whether he feels ready and adequate to serve as King of Narnia. Instead of faking confidence, Caspian replies in humility, "I — I don't think I do, Sir. I'm only a kid." Aslan is pleased by this response, replying, "Good. If you had felt yourself sufficient, it would have been a proof that you were not."

Christian humility is very important to Lewis because he believes pride and self-absorption to be the key qualities of an inhabitant of Hell. See Chapter 11 for how this position plays out in *The Great Divorce.*

Finding strength through Christ

Paralleling Philippians 4:13 ("I can do everything through him who gives me strength"), Aslan gives the children and Narnians strength during the times that they most need it. In *Prince Caspian,* Lucy buries her head in Aslan's mane, and "There must have been magic in his mane. She could feel lion-strength going into her." Similarly, before Digory leaves to fetch the apple in *The Magician's Nephew,* Aslan gives him a Lion's kiss. According to the narrator, "Digory felt that new strength and courage had gone into him."

Receiving help in times of need

Aslan doesn't simply give the children assignments and let them fend for themselves. He's faithful in helping them during their times of need. In *The Voyage of the "Dawn Treader,"* Caspian and his crew are desperate during their passage around Dark Island. As circumstances appear bleak and hope seems lost, Lucy calls out to Aslan for help and he responds. The darkness remains, but she begins to feel a "little — very, very little — better." The "whole ship was lit up as if by searchlight," and finally, an albatross came and led the ship toward safety. Lucy even hears the bird say to her alone "Courage, dear heart." She's comforted by the certainty that the voice is none other than Aslan himself, known by "a delicious smell breathed in her face."

Aslan helps Lucy when she asks for it, but sometimes Christians can overlook the asking part. In *The Magician's Nephew,* Lewis speaks to the point of being real with God and asking him for your needs. When Digory, Jill, and Fledge go off to fetch the apple, Digory complains that he's hungry after their long journey. The brief exchange that takes place between the three underscores the importance of simply asking God for help:

> "Well, I do *think someone might have arranged about our meals,"* said Digory.
>
> "I'm sure Aslan would have, if you'd asked him," said Fledge.
>
> "Wouldn't he know without being asked?" said Polly.
>
> "I've no doubt he would," said the Horse . . . "But I've a sort of idea he likes to be asked."

When we realize the security we have in Jesus Christ and his ability to provide for our needs, then we can echo Tirian in *The Last Battle:* "Courage, child: we are all between the paws of the true Aslan."

Common Stumbling Blocks on the Christian Walk

Although *The Chronicles of Narnia* contains many examples of children and Narnians "living out their faith" in Aslan, Lewis creates a realistic picture of faith by including several stumbling blocks that can spring up along the ways of the faithful. These diversions are discussed in the sections that follow.

Following common sense

Common sense is one of the great enemies of Christian discipleship. It kills any attempts to walk by faith because it demands certainty before taking a first step.

On occasion, common sense becomes a stumbling block to following Aslan in Narnia. In *Prince Caspian,* Lucy pleads with her siblings to believe her certainty of seeing Aslan, "I didn't *think* I saw him. I saw him." Yet, in spite of that plea, Peter opts for common sense, uttering, "Lucy may be right, but I can't help it."

When she's outvoted by Peter, Susan, and Trumpkin, Lucy settles for the common sense route, too, and goes along with the crowd rather than forging her own way. Aslan doesn't let Lucy off the hook when he sees her again, however. When she tries to blame the others, the narrator observes that "there came the faintest suggestion of a growl." Aslan wants Lucy to live by faith, even if it means going against the grain.

The Silver Chair shows another instance where common sense gets in the way of living by faith. When the Black Prince speaks the last Sign of Aslan's (see the "Living by faith, not by sight" section earlier in the chapter), Eustace and Jill search for a common sense explanation. "It's the Sign," said Puddleglum. "It was the *words* of the Sign," said Scrubb more cautiously. The narrator then expresses what's on the minds of the three: "What had been the use of learning the Signs if they weren't going to obey them? Yet could Aslan have really meant them to unbind anyone — even a lunatic — who asked it in his name? Could it be a mere accident?"

Succumbing to doubt

Doubt is a stumbling block on the Christian walk of a disciple because it's easy to believe when things are going well, but when tested or confronted, strong faith can grow brittle and crack into a thousand pieces. That's what happens to Eustace and Jill in *The Silver Chair* when the Black Knight tries to dismiss the idea that the words UNDER ME were meant for them, as another Sign from Aslan. The Black Knight's words of doubt were "like cold water down the back of Scrubb and Jill: for it seemed to them to them very likely that the words had nothing to do with their quest at all, and that they had been taken in by a mere accident."

Yet, Puddleglum proves his discipleship when he answers back, "There are no accidents. Our guide is Aslan; and he was there when the giant king caused the letters to be cut, and he knew already all things that would come of them; including *this.*"

Forgetting the "big picture"

In the hustle and bustle of everyday life, it's easy to become focused on the here and now and forget what's really important. In *Prince Caspian,* for example, the Pevensies spend time at the beginning of the story at the railway station longing to return to Narnia. But after they're drawn back, they become so concerned with the practical issues of their hike that they miss out on the thrill of their journey and the sense of purpose that they should feel.

In *The Silver Chair,* Jill also has a hard time staying on track with the Four Signs. She memorizes them initially, but as time goes on, she starts to forget about the signs and starts to get their order mixed up. "That was because she had given up saying the Signs over every night," comments the narrator. Eustace admits, "The truth is we were so jolly keen on getting to [Harfang] that we weren't bothering about anything else." Rather than being focused on the quest and their end goal, the three are distracted by the individual steps and taken in by their small adventures along the way.

Being nosy

It seems pretty minor when compared to the other stumbling blocks outlined in this section, but another area of disobedience among the children and Narnians is nosiness or curiosity about issues that they have no business knowing.

In *The Voyage of the "Dawn Treader,"* Lucy asks Aslan whether Eustace will ever return to Narnia. Aslan replies, "Child, do you really need to know that?" Likewise, in *The Horse and His Boy,* Aslan tells Shasta, "I tell no-one any story but his own."

In addition, "what if's" shouldn't be a concern of ours either. Aslan tells Lucy in *Prince Caspian,* "To know what would have happened . . . nobody is ever told that." Then, in *The Voyage of the "Dawn Treader,"* Aslan reminds her once again, "Did I not explain to you once before that no one is ever told what *would have happened?*"

The Hermit of the Southern March puts everything in the proper perspective when he tells Aravis, Bree, and Hwin, "There is something about all this that I do not understand: but if ever we need to know it, you may be sure that we shall." As a disciple, one can apply the Hermit's advice to the real world by realizing that everyone is on a "need to know" basis — if you need to know, God's gonna tell you. Otherwise, don't worry about it.

God Uses the "Little Guys"

Throughout history, God tended to use the "little guy" to do great things for him. For example, Gideon was called by God to lead the Israelite army even though his family was part of the weakest clan in Israel and he the smallest of his family (see Judges 6). So too, Christ's disciples were uneducated, "bush league" fisherman, not learned Ivy League theologians.

In *The Chronicles of Narnia,* C.S. Lewis makes a point of giving the "little guys" important roles:

- The people from our world who go into Narnia to lead and rescue Narnians are all *children,* not adults.

- In *The Lion, the Witch and the Wardrobe,* small mice chew through the cords that bind Aslan after he's slain at the Stone Table. The mice also feed King Tirian in *The Last Battle* when he's tied to a tree.

- In *The Magician's Nephew,* Aslan chooses Frank, a humble London cab driver, as the first King of Narnia. Frank responds only as a little guy would: "Begging your pardon, sir, and thanking you very much I'm sure . . . but I ain't no sort of chap for a job like that. I never 'ad much eddycation, you see."

God works through the "little guys" because they have the right perspective — they know they can't rely on their own strength and self-reliance to get the job done. Instead, they know they must rely on Jesus Christ to help them. As a result, they can more easily echo the words of the Apostle Paul, "For when I am weak, then I am strong" (2 Corinthians 12:10).

Glimpses of Joy in Narnia

One of the major factors in Lewis's conversion to Christianity was that he discovered Jesus Christ was both the source and the object of the deep yearning Lewis called Joy (see Chapter 2 for more on Joy).

In *The Chronicles of Narnia,* Lewis makes allusions to his understanding of what Joy is like. In *The Lion, the Witch and the Wardrobe,* he describes the moment in which the Pevensie children first hear the name of Aslan:

> *Each one of the children felt something jump in his inside . . . Susan felt as if some delicious smell or some delightful strain of music had just floated by her. And Lucy got the feeling you have when you wake up in the morning and realize that it is the beginning of the holidays or the beginning of summer.*

In *The Voyage of the "Dawn Treader,"* when thumbing through the Magician's Book, Lucy comes across a spell that, if spoken, refreshes one's spirit. She's immediately captivated by the story-like spell; in fact, she's so absorbed that she could keep reading it for years. When she finishes reading, she longs to feel that Joy again but finds she can't turn the pages back. Lucy's contentment with simply remembering the story is lessened because she quickly forgets what exactly the story is about. The narrator points out, "And she never could remember; and ever since that day what Lucy meant by a good story is a story which reminded her of the forgotten story in the Magician's Book." Lewis believes Joy is much like Lucy's experience: life-changing and all-absorbing but not something you can recreate or get your hands around.

Similarly, at the end of the story, Reepicheep, Lucy, Edmund, and Eustace get a glimpse of Heaven — Joy — when they're near the End of the World. When they're in their small boat, a breeze comes. The narrator describes the scene:

> *It lasted only a second or so but what it brought them in that second none of those three children will ever forget. It brought both a smell and a sound, a musical sound. Edmund and Eustace would never talk about it afterward. Lucy could only say "It would break your heart." "Why," said I, "was it so sad?" "Sad!! No," said Lucy.*

None of children question the fact that they're peeking into Aslan's country during that moment. The pang deep in their hearts was what Lewis knew to be Joy.

"Well Done," the Best Phrase Imaginable

Perhaps the ultimate desire of every earnest Christian is to someday hear Jesus Christ tell them personally, "Well done, good and faithful servant" (Matthew 25:21). Aslan, too, utters these words at specific times in Narnia:

- In *Prince Caspian,* Edmund's praised "Well done" when he's quick to believe in Aslan's appearance to Lucy.

- In *The Magician's Nephew,* Digory's told "Well done, son of Adam" after he obtains the apple and withstands the temptation of Jadis.

- In *The Last Battle,* King Tirian's praised "Well done, last of the Kings of Narnia who stood firm at the darkest hour."

Edmund, Digory, and Tirian each make some lousy decisions along the way and are far from perfect. Yet, by his mercy and grace, Aslan forgives them, restores them, and enables them to accomplish great things in spite of their past scars.

Part III

Tell Me More Stories: Lewis's Other Novels and Fantasies

The 5th Wave · By Rich Tennant

"I found 'The Screwtape Letters' quite profound. However, I initially thought it was going to be someone's first person account of installing an outdoor shower."

In this part . . .

C.S. Lewis may be best known for his children's literature, but he's got quite a stack of fictional works for adults as well. But, I should warn you — you're gonna have a "helluva" time in the first two chapters of this part as I lead you through Lewis's spiritual ride into Hell in *The Screwtape Letters* and *The Great Divorce.* After that, I fire up the rocket ship so you can sail into outer space with his space trilogy. Finally, you explore the first major book Lewis published after becoming a Christian and his take on a tale of mythic proportions.

Chapter 10

The Screwtape Letters: A View from the Land Down Under

Ever wonder what your life looks like from the land down under? No, I'm not talking about Australia. I mean the land *way* down under — that's right, Hell. Over the course of their lives, most people give at least some thought to how God views them, but rarely does anyone look at the world from Satan's point of view. The idea reminds me of looking cross-eyed in a carnival mirror — it's a skewed perspective.

Whether or not C.S. Lewis was looking at the world cross-eyed when he dreamed up the idea for *The Screwtape Letters* is a closely guarded secret. But that question — What does human life look like from the skewed eyes of Hell? — is the premise of this master work.

In this chapter, you discover how this book came to be and explore its major themes. *The Screwtape Letters* is a goldmine of information about Lewis's beliefs concerning who Satan is, what Hell is like, and how Satan tempts humans, so I discuss these ideas as well.

Background: As One Devil to Another

The idea of *The Screwtape Letters* has its roots in a radio speech by Adolph Hitler that Lewis heard in July of 1940. Lewis was struck by the speech's impact on him, and in writing to his brother Warnie, he confessed that he found it impossible not to waver slightly in his thinking in the midst of the speech. Lewis added, "Statements which I know to be untrue all but convince me . . . for the moment, if only the man says them unflinchingly."

The next day, as he was sitting through a Communion service, Lewis reflected on how Satan's temptations are much like Hitler's persuasive power. In other words, Satan can twist reality and the truth into something you know to be false, yet you still get suckered into believing it. And so Lewis began to consider how this premise could be turned into a book. Originally calling the work *As One Devil to Another,* Lewis's idea was to create a series of letters from a senior devil to a junior devil discussing the art of tempting humans. One of his key ideas for this project was to look at the world from Satan's point of view. Therefore, the book is full of opposites: Bad is good, good is bad, God is *The Enemy,* and Hell becomes *Our Father's House.*

The exact timeline isn't known, but Lewis probably wrote and finished up *The Screwtape Letters* before the end of 1940. However, before they were to be published collectively as a book, the letters originally appeared as weekly installments in *The Guardian* (an Anglican Church publication) from May to November 1941.

Not every reader "got" the premise to these letters, a fact which Lewis found quite humorous. In *C.S. Lewis: A Biography,* Green and Hooper recount a humorous episode in which a country pastor canceled his subscription to *The Guardian* on the grounds that "much of the advise given in these letters seemed to him not only erroneous but positively diabolical."

These letters were compiled and then published under the name *The Screwtape Letters* the following year. The book met with considerable critical and popular praise and has gone on to become one of Lewis's most memorable, innovative works.

Exploring the Screwy (err, Screwtape) Letters

The Screwtape Letters follows the work of a senior devil named Screwtape as he instructs a junior devil named Wormwood in the art of temptation. Both are in the civil service of Hell, charged with tempting humans. The format of the book is a collection of 31 letters from Screwtape to his nephew Wormwood, with each letter sharing tips and techniques on how Wormwood can derail the Christian faith of his "patient," a 20-something British man living during World War II.

Over the course of the letters, you discover much about the patient's life. For example, he lives with his mother in war-time Britain and becomes a Christian by Letter 2. He initially enjoys spending time with friends who aren't Christians, but eventually he falls in love and becomes engaged to a Christian girl. By the final letter, he's killed when a German bomb detonates on a building he's in.

In an ingenious twist by Lewis, unlike the book's readers, Screwtape and Wormwood don't care much at all about the events of the patient's life. In fact, you could think of the events in his life as being the "MacGuffin" in the book. *MacGuffin* is a movie term popularized by Alfred Hitchcock that refers to an object that the entire plot of a story is built around, but the object isn't actually important to the story itself. In the same way, the focus of *The Screwtape Letters* is the spiritual battle that takes place; the events of the patient's life are only important insofar as they impact his spiritual life.

For example, because the story's set in the dark days of World War II, you'd think that the devil Screwtape would be excited about the killing going on because of the war. But he's is hardly concerned with that at all, except for how it impacts the spiritual state of the patient. As Screwtape writes to Wormwood in Letter 24, "I am not in the least interested in knowing how many people in England have been killed by bombs . . . That they were going to die sometime, I knew already. Please keep your mind on your work." Screwtape thinks of events and matters concerning humans as simply, to borrow his words from Letter 19, "raw material" that can move people closer either to God or to Satan.

What's in a name?

Lewis claimed that the names used in *The Screwtape Letters* didn't have any hidden meanings and that he only aimed at making them sound nasty or sinister or diabolical. He writes, "I fancy that Scrooge, screw, thumbscrew, tapeworm, and red tape all do some work in my hero's name, and that slob, slobber, slubber, and gob have all gone into slubgob."

Here's just a sampling of the sinister names that appear in the book:

- Screwtape: A retired devil in Hell's civil service; official title is Abysmal Sublimity Under Secretary

- Wormwood: Junior devil assigned to tempt the patient

- Slubgob: Principal of the Tempters' Training College in Hell

- Glubose: Tempter assigned to the patient's mother

- Triptweeze: Colleague of Screwtape

- Toadpipe: Assistant to Screwtape; takes over writing Letter 22

- Slumtrimpet: Tempter assigned to the patient's fiancée

When you read *The Screwtape Letters,* don't skip over the preface. Lewis warns in the preface that you shouldn't believe everything Screwtape says. Just as Satan lies, Screwtape manipulates, bends, and twists reality into the image of what he wants it to be.

Each of Screwtape's letters tends to focus on one or two major topics. Table 10-1 lists these topics according to the letter in which they're discussed and, when applicable, notes the patient's major life events that trigger the discussion of each topic.

Table 10-1	Major Topics Discussed in *The Screwtape Letters*	
Letter	**Screwtape's Ideas About**	**Corresponding Events in Life of Patient**
1	Human reason as an obstacle to Satan	
2	Human freedom, disappointment	Becoming a Christian
3	Irritations of living with others, prayer	
4	Prayer, emotions	
5	War, death	
6	Uncertainty, hatred, being conscious of virtues	
7	Existence of Satan, tendencies towards extremes and lukewarmness, the world as an end in itself	
8	Life as a roller coaster, view of humans from the perspective of Satan and God, having a persistent faith	
9	Sensual temptations, pleasure, temptations during the low points of a person's life	
10	Being fake with others, living in two worlds	Making friends with "worldly" people
11	Humor and jokes	

Letter	Screwtape's Ideas About	Corresponding Events in Life of Patient
12	Drifting away from God, why backsliding Christians avoid God	Backsliding in his faith
13	Surrendering your life to Christ, acting out your convictions	Rededicating his life to Jesus Christ
14	Humility	
15	Past, present, and future, fear of the future	
16	Un-Christian churches	
17	Hidden expressions of gluttony	
18	Being in love, marriage, and sex	
19	Being in love, what God's up to with love	
20	Sex, fashion	
21	Time, ownership	
22	God's idea of pleasure, noise as the goal of Satan	Falling in love with a Christian girl
23	"Historical" Jesus, social justice-oriented Christianity	
24	Spiritual pride, Christianity as a special club	Putting on "airs" around his girlfriend's family
25	Horror of the "Same Old Thing"	
26	Selfish unselfishness vs. real charity	
27	Prayer, history as a basis for truth	
28	Perseverance in faith, death avoidance, the meaning of a normal life	
29	Courage and cowardice, the lure of Plan B	
30	What is "Real"?	
31	Death of a Christian eternity	Dying in a war-time bombing

Discovering the Real Satan through a Fictional Screwtape

According to biblical Christianity, Satan (also known as the Devil) is the arch-enemy of God and the one ultimately behind all evil in the world. The Bible indicates that Satan is a fallen angel who rebelled against God and took a third of the angels in heaven with him. Satan and his cohorts (known as *demons*) seek to prevent, distort, or destroy people's relationships with God. In *The Screwtape Letters,* Lewis offers a unique and revealing portrait of Satan and why he does what he does.

The following sections explore Lewis's key beliefs concerning who Satan is, specifically the ideas that

- Satan really exists.
- Satan is a liar and a self-deceived "ass."
- Satan is the enemy of God but is not his equal.
- Satan is a pragmatist.

Arguing for the existence of Satan

Lewis believes in Satan as a real creature, although unlike many Christians, he doesn't see this issue as a required belief for historical Christianity. As he writes in an updated preface to the 1961 paperback edition, "My religion would not be in ruins if this opinion were shown to be false."

Lewis believes that you can fall into two traps when you think about Satan and his demons. You either

- **Ignore or deny their existence:** This first trap is the one that's most popular today. Essentially, you look upon any reference to Satan in the Bible purely as a metaphor for evil.
- **Focus on them too much:** Falling into this second trap means that you focus on Satan and his demons so much that they become an unhealthy preoccupation.

Lewis writes in the book's preface that Satan and his demons are happy with either of these mistakes and "hail a materialist or a magician with the same delight." When you ignore Satan, you fail to realize his power. But when you focus on him too much, you begin to remove accountability for your own actions — "the Devil made me do it," after all.

Lewis sees the denial of the existence of the spiritual world, angels, and devils as an important objective in Satan's plans. He comments in *God in the Dock,* "Of course, [Satan and his devils] don't want you to believe in the Devil. If devils exist, their first aim is to give you an anesthetic, to put you off your guard. Only if that fails, do you become aware of them." Lewis illustrates this practice in *The Screwtape Letters;* in Letter 7, Screwtape tells Wormwood how to make his existence seem silly to the man he's tempting:

> *The fact that 'devils' are predominately comic figures in modern imagination will help you. If any faint suspicion of your existence begins to arise in his mind, suggest to him a picture of something in red tights, and persuade him that since he cannot believe in that . . . he therefore cannot believe in you.*

From Lewis's perspective, one shouldn't be surprised that Christians recognize the existence of Satan and see him clearly operating in the world and non-Christians seem so unaware and unaffected by him. Lewis writes in *God in the Dock,* "The more a man was in the Devil's power, the less he would be aware of it . . . It is when you start arming against Hitler that you first realize your country is full of Nazi agents."

Viewing Satan as a liar and pitiful creature

At heart, Lewis believes Satan to be a liar, someone you should never be duped into believing for even a moment. He warns the readers of *The Screwtape Letters* that not everything that Screwtape says should be assumed to be true. He echoes this theme in his book *A Preface to Paradise Lost,* where he calls Satan a "personified self-contradiction" and labels his world "a world of lies and propaganda."

But Lewis also believes Satan to be more than just manipulative and conniving. He sees Satan as a pitiful creature, someone not in full touch with reality. In the preface to *The Screwtape Letters,* Lewis writes, "There is wishful thinking in Hell as well as on Earth." And in *A Preface to Paradise Lost,* Lewis makes a stronger statement by observing, "What we see in Satan is the horrible co-existence of a subtle and incessant intellectual activity with an incapacity to understand anything . . . in order to avoid seeing one thing he has, almost voluntarily, incapacitated himself from seeing at all."

To illustrate his perception of Satan, in Letter 19, for example, Lewis shows how Screwtape can't accept the reality that God really loves humans. Screwtape considers that an impossibility and is ever looking for an ulterior motive:

All His talk about Love must be a disguise for something else — He must have some real motive for creating them and taking so much trouble about them . . . What does He stand to make out of them? This is the insoluble question . . . We know that He cannot really love: nobody can: it doesn't make sense. If we could only find out what He is really up to!

Ironically, Satan and his demons think of themselves as the only true realists. Consequently, they delude themselves into thinking that victory over God is actually possible. Screwtape closes his final letter to Wormwood by emphasizing the delusion: "All that sustains me is the conviction that our Realism, our rejection (in the face of all temptations) of all silly nonsense and claptrap, *must* win in the end."

Ultimately, Lewis believes that Christianity commits every Christian to believing that the Devil is not only a liar, but also, as he writes in *A Preface to Paradise Lost,* a self-deceived "ass."

Considering Satan and God: Enemies but not equals

Despite believing Satan to be a pitiful creature, Lewis sees Satan as a powerful force to be reckoned with. In his book *The Weight of Glory,* Lewis compares Satan to "a good chess player [who] is always trying to maneuver you into a position where you save your castle only by losing your bishop." At the same time, Satan should never be considered an equal force directly opposite of God. Lewis writes in the updated preface that as a fallen angel, "Satan, the leader or dictator of the devils, is the opposite not of God but of Michael." (Michael is an archangel discussed in the scriptures.) The Bible confirms what Lewis is saying, talking about Satan as a limited creature, not one that can rival God (see Job 1:12, Luke 4:6, and 2 Thessalonians 2:7–8).

Just as they're unequal in terms of their power and influence, so too are Satan and God fundamentally different in their views of humans. In Letter 8 of *The Screwtape Letters,* Lewis provides insight into this truth. God wants to fill the universe with "little replicas of Himself." He does so not to control the "replicas" but to have creatures that are freely aligned to His will. Satan, on the other hand, wants to draw "all other beings into himself." While God gives out freely, Satan sucks in. Naturally then, Satan sees people as "cattle who can finally become food," while God views humans as "servants who can finally become sons." Not surprisingly, the manner in which they conduct themselves with humans matches their objectives: God "woos" and Satan "ravishes."

Screwtape and *The Truman Show*'s Christoff: Separated at birth?

While there's discussion of one day making *The Screwtape Letters* into a motion picture, an already released film, *The Truman Show* (1998), offers several intriguing parallels with Lewis's writing. In fact, on close viewing, you may wonder whether Screwtape and the character named Christoff are identical twins separated at birth. *The Truman Show*, starring Jim Carrey, is the story of Truman Burbank, a man who has been living in a non-stop television show since birth — he just doesn't know it. The "universe" that Truman lives in, called Seahaven, is filled with actors and is run by a visionary named Screwtape . . . err . . . Christoff.

As the film begins, Truman grows restless with his 30-something life in Seahaven and has an ever-increasing desire to travel and see the world. Similarly, Screwtape sees the same instinctive unsettledness in the humans he tempts: "The truth is that the Enemy [God], having oddly destined these mere animals to life in His own eternal world, has guarded them pretty effectively from the danger of feeling at home anywhere else" (Letter 28).

To offset this desire to leave Seahaven, Christoff and the actors continuously manipulate Truman, trying to make him content to stay put. In Letter 28, Screwtape agrees with this strategy when he tells his nephew to have the patient "build up a firm attachment to the earth." To dampen Truman's wanderlust, his wife stresses the financial risks of traveling and the need to plan months ahead for such a trip. "Precautions have a tendency to increase fear," concurs Screwtape. When that doesn't work, Truman's best friend tries to convince him that such thoughts are perfectly natural but will soon pass. He says, "Who hasn't wanted to travel around? Who hasn't wanted to be somebody?" Likewise, Screwtape advises Wormwood in Letter 9, "The mere word *phase* will likely do the trick."

Both *The Screwtape Letters* and *The Truman Show* present the idea that people quickly become complacent with the world they're in. For nearly all his life, Truman never seriously questioned the reality of his world because, as Christoff says, "We accept the reality of the world with which we are presented." Echoing the same tune, Screwtape tells Wormwood, "Your business is to fix his attention on [immediate experiences]. Teach him to call it 'real life' and don't him ask what he means by 'real' . . . Never having been a human . . . you don't realize how enslaved they are to the pressure of the ordinary" (Letter 1).

Both Christoff and Screwtape have an almost motherly instinct to protect their "patients." They do so not out of genuine concern, but because, as long as the patients are safe, Christoff and Screwtape are free to manipulate them. In Christoff's control room, for example, one of the workers wears a t-shirt that says "Love him, protect him." Perhaps Screwtape wears a similar shirt when he writes in Letter 28, "You should be guarding him like the apple of your eye."

By the end of *The Truman Show,* it's clear that Christoff "loves" Truman only as long as he can own him and use him. In the same way, Screwtape writes: "To us a human is primarily food; our aim is the absorption of its will into ours, the increase of our own area of selfhood at its expense" (Letter 8).

Truman eventually discovers that the world he's lived his entire life in is a fraud. And at the film's end, he escapes the artificial world of Seahaven. The moment Truman exits the door of the Seahaven set is the climax of the film, and the scene closely parallels the description Screwtape gives Wormwood at the moment his patient dies and goes to heaven. In Letter 31, he writes, "He got through so easily! . . . Sheer, instantaneous liberation."

Revealing the motives of Satan and his demons

In Lewis's view, demons aren't very interested in pursuing evil for evil's sake. He thinks of Satan and his demons as very practical creatures with two motives, both of which are always on the mind of Screwtape:

- **Demons fear punishment from Satan and other demons.** Hell contains its own "houses of corrections," just as totalitarian governments contain torture camps. Throughout *The Screwtape Letters,* an undercurrent of backstabbing and infighting flows between Screwtape and Wormwood. Each demon attempts to steer clear of punishment while informing on the other. In Letter 22, for example, Screwtape chastises his nephew:

  You may be interested to learn that the little misunderstanding with the Secret Police which you tried to raise about some unguarded expressions in one of my letters has been tidied over . . . You shall pay for that as well as for your other blunders. Meanwhile I enclose a little booklet, just issued, on the new House of Correction for Incompetent Tempters. It is profusely illustrated and you will not find a dull page in it.

- **Demons have a carnivorous hunger to eat, in a spiritual sense, the souls of humans and of one another.** With an obvious hunger for Wormwood, Screwtape writes in Letter 31, "I have always desired you, as you (pitiful fool) desired me . . . Love you? Why, yes. As dainty a morsel as ever I grew fat on." And finally, as he signs off on the last correspondence to his nephew, Screwtape pens, "Your increasingly and ravenously affectionate uncle, Screwtape."

The Nature of Hell, According to Screwtape

As you read *The Screwtape Letters,* you get a clear vision of what Hell is like from Lewis's perspective. He fully believes that Hell is an actual place, but he isn't certain of how suffering manifests itself there. Lewis never dismisses the idea of physical torture in Hell, but he doesn't see clear evidence in the Bible to support or refute it. Instead, in writing to his friend Arthur Greeves, Lewis speaks of Hell as a place of mental torture visited when a person is "left with nothing at all but one's own envy, prurience, resentment, loneliness, and self conceit . . . But when there is nothing for you but your own mind, . . . it will be as actual as . . . a coffin is actual to a man buried alive." This perspective carries over to *The Screwtape Letters;* you begin to see Hell as a place that's filled with selfish people, where only the strong survive and where bureaucracy reigns.

Hell is filled with self-absorbed creatures

As he illustrates in *The Screwtape Letters,* Lewis believes Hell to be filled with creatures absorbed totally in their own self-interests. Every creature has a chip on his shoulder. Any kindness or charity (from Screwtape to Wormwood or between anyone else) always has an ulterior motive. Lewis stresses this same idea in *The Problem of Pain,* saying "The characteristic of lost souls is their rejection of everything that is not simply themselves." In fact, in *The Great Divorce,* Hell's inhabitants seem to be unable to go beyond themselves, prompting a heavenly creature to ask a creature from Hell, "Could you, only for a moment, fix your mind on something not yourself?" (See Chapter 11 for more on *The Great Divorce.*) This self-absorbed nature has a tremendous effect on their view of the world; in *The Problem of Pain,* Lewis writes of "the demand of the loveless and self-imprisoned that they should be allowed to blackmail the universe: that till they consent to be happy (on their own terms) no one else shall taste joy: that theirs should be the final power; that Hell should be able to veto Heaven."

Ultimately, the creatures of Hell are imprisoned by their obsessions to make the universe revolve around their whims and fancies. And, as time goes on, this self-made prison eats away at the creature itself. In *The Great Divorce,* Lewis explains, "A damned soul is nearly nothing: it is shrunk, shut up in itself." What's more, as you read *The Screwtape Letters,* you may agree that Screwtape himself is a devil who loses his spiritual nature and is reduced more and more to something resembling a carnivorous worm.

Hell is Darwinian

Although Lewis completely disagrees with Charles Darwin on the origins of the universe, you can bet he'd say that Darwin got it right when it comes to the nature of Hell. In Lewis's view, Hell is Darwinian. It's governed by "survival of the fittest" — only the strongest beings survive by feeding on the weak.

The Darwinian nature of Hell can be seen throughout *The Screwtape Letters.* In the preface, Lewis writes that "'Dog eat dog' is the principle of the whole organization. Everyone wishes everyone else's discrediting, demotion, and ruin." Screwtape and Wormwood, for example, are usually polite on the surface of their communication, but they're always stabbing each other in the back, trying to get the other in trouble with the Secret Police. As time goes on, you can see that the "survival of the fittest" nature of Hell goes even further. Much like a lion preparing to eat its prey, Screwtape sounds like a cannibal when he writes to Wormwood. In Letter 30, he demands, "Bring us back food, or be food yourself."

Lewis's Hell is filled with creatures who see reality as a "zero-sum game" — in order for a creature to succeed, another creature must lose. In Letter 18,

Screwtape writes, "The whole philosophy of Hell rests on recognition of the axiom that one thing is not another thing, and specially, that one self is not another self . . . 'To be' means 'to be in competition.'" He seconds this thought in Letter 19: "All selves are by their very nature in competition."

As it turns out, this Darwinian view of the universe is one of Screwtape's (and Satan's) hang-ups with God: Satan is determined to believe that God can't really love humans. But he can't figure out what God is up to. At the end of the book, when the patient dies and goes to Heaven, all Screwtape has left to cling to is this belief that humans are unloved by God. In spite of the evidence to the contrary, he concludes "All that sustains me is the conviction that our Realism, our rejection (in the face of all temptations) of all silly nonsense and claptrap, *must* win in the end."

Hell is bureaucratic

More than just thinking of it as a chamber of torture, Lewis believes in the true, insidious nature of Hell. The sinister nature of evil is perhaps best personified not as a gang of thugs but as bureaucrats dressed in the finest designer suits. Writing in the updated preface, Lewis says:

> *I live in the Managerial Age, in a world of "Admin." The greatest evil is not now done in those sordid "dens of crime" that Dickens loved to paint. It is not done even in concentration camps and labour camps. In those we see its final result. But it is conceived and ordered (moved, seconded, carried, and minuted) in clean, carpeted, warmed, and well-lighted offices, by quiet men with white collars and cut fingernails and smooth-shaven cheeks who do not need to raise their voice. Hence, naturally enough, my symbol for Hell is something like the bureaucracy of a police state or the offices of a thoroughly nasty business concern.*

I think that Lewis would identify strongly with the portrayal of evil in the film *The Matrix* (1999), in which the villain Agents are crisply attired in black suits. When you read *The Screwtape Letters,* you probably can imagine Screwtape looking much like Agent Smith did in the film — neat and clean on the outside with insidious evil lurking just underneath.

We're Screwed: Understanding the Crafty Art of Temptation

In *The Screwtape Letters,* Lewis provides insight into the techniques that Christians believe Satan uses to tempt humans and the traps that he ensnares people in. The book reveals five actions that Satan takes advantage of:

> ✔ Denying the spiritual nature of the universe
>
> ✔ Making the current world the end goal for people
>
> ✔ Distracting people from "the big picture"
>
> ✔ Using fashion as a trap
>
> ✔ Using change as a trap

I discuss each of these temptations in the sections that follow.

Satan disguises the spiritual world

Lewis believes that Satan is most effective when he gets people to deny the reality of spiritual world. In this light, Screwtape advises Wormwood to get the patient to focus on the physical, material world around him. The idea is that the more real the physical world is, the less real the spiritual world becomes. Screwtape writes, "Your business is to fix his attention on the stream [of immediate sense experiences]. Teach him to call it 'real life' and don't let him ask what he means by 'real.'"

In Letter 1, Screwtape recalls the story of a man he once tempted who was close to considering Christianity. Screwtape tells Wormwood that, "a healthy dose of 'real life' . . . was enough to show him that all 'that sort of thing' just couldn't be true." Screwtape describes how effective this technique can be: "[Humans] find it all but impossible to believe in the unfamiliar while the familiar is before their eyes." Wormwood applies this strategy to the patient, with Screwtape commenting in Letter 30, "You will notice that we have got them completely fogged about the meaning of the word 'real' . . . Here 'real' means the bare physical facts . . . [I]n all experiences which can make them happier or better only the physical facts are 'real' while the spiritual elements are 'subjective.'"

Satan holds out the world as the prize

Not only does Satan want people to deny the reality of the spiritual realm, but he also wants people to invest their hearts and minds in this current world. For example, in Matthew 4, Satan tempts Jesus in this way. After taking Jesus to a high mountain that overlooks a huge land area, Satan says, "All this I will give you if you bow down and worship me." In the same way, Screwtape continually reminds Wormwood to get the patient's focus off God and Heaven and back onto the temporal world.

By redirecting the focus of Christians from God to the here and now, Screwtape can render their Christian faith harmless. He wants Christians to focus on a cause, such as poverty or some political issue, rather than on Jesus Christ. In Letter 25, Screwtape writes, "Keep them in the state of mind I call 'Christianity And' . . . If they must be Christians let them at least be Christians with a difference." Screwtape reinforces this point in Letter 23, saying, "Make men treat Christianity as a means; preferably, of course, as a means to their own advancement, but failing that, as a means to anything." He tells Wormwood to guide his patient to "'believe [Christianity], not because it is true, but for some other reason.' That's the game."

Satan doesn't want people to think clearly

According to Lewis, Satan doesn't have the power to control or change your thoughts. But he does do everything he can to keep you from thinking clearly. In Letter 24, for example, Screwtape urges Wormwood to focus his efforts on the patient's emotions; "He must be made to feel," says Screwtape. Noting the danger of people thinking too much, Screwtape says, "[Your patient had] better not put into words" what he is thinking about, and he later adds, "Never allow him to raise the question. . . ."

Lewis believes that if people look at reality with a clear and level mind, Satan will always lose. That's why Satan must do everything in his power to distract you. Screwtape writes in Letter 1, "The trouble about argument is that it moves the whole struggle on to the Enemy's own ground . . . By the very act of arguing, you awake the patient's reason; and once it is awake, who can foresee the result?"

Satan distracts with fashion

Lewis views *fashion* as another tool that Satan uses to distract people from the Christian faith. The kind of fashion that Lewis speaks of is more than what comes down the runway at fashion shows; it's whatever's hip and popular. In *The Screwtape Letters,* Screwtape tries to use "the latest" in all human activities, including the following, to distract patients from Christianity:

- **Fashionable bodies:** By continually changing around people's concepts of a woman's beauty, Satan ensures that people are never content with who they are or who they're married to. Screwtape writes of the fashionable bodies of the 1940s, "The age of jazz has succeeded the age of the waltz, and we now teach men to like women whose bodies are scarcely distinguishable from those of boys."
- **Fashionable friends:** Screwtape instructs Wormwood to get the patient interested in friends who are up on the popular philosophies of the day. He believes that people who are consumed with "being hip" will always dismiss God as being either old-fashioned or just plain irrelevant.

Writing in Letter 10, Screwtape says, "I gather that the middle-aged married couple who called at [the patient's] office are just the sort of people we want him to know — rich, smart, superficially intellectual, and brightly skeptical about everything in the world. I gather they are even vaguely pacifist, not on moral grounds but from an ingrained habit of belittling anything that concerns the great mass of their fellow men and from a dash of purely fashionable and literary communism." In the same way, Lewis believes fashion — the popular views of society — will always look down upon traditional orthodox Christianity.

✔ **A fashionable Jesus:** If a person is interested in Jesus, then Screwtape is hell-bent on distracting him from the real historical Jesus and instead substituting a Jesus who is more hip and in tune with modern times. In Letter 23, Screwtape says, "In the last generation we promoted the construction of such a 'historical Jesus' on liberal and humanitarian lines; we are now putting forward a new 'historical Jesus' on Marxian . . . and revolutionary lines. The advantages of these constructions, which we intend to change every thirty years or so, are [crystal clear] . . . We . . . distract men's minds from who He is, and what He did."

✔ **A fashionable faith:** Satan can't prevent people from believing in Christianity, but he can tempt humans to water down their faith with fashion. Screwtape says in Letter 25, "Substitute for the faith itself some Fashion with a Christian coloring." In other words, Satan waters down Christianity by using faith as the means to another end, such as politics, world hunger, or the abortion issue.

Lewis expounds on the idea of distracting with fashion in *The Great Divorce,* in which a person from Heaven admits to his friend from Hell how fashion influenced his thinking. He confesses, "Let us be frank. We simply found ourselves in contact with a certain current of ideas and plunged into it because it seemed modern and successful."

In several of his writings, Lewis explains how modern society falls for the dead ends of fashion every time. He writes in the essay "De Descriptione Temporum:" "How has it come about that we use the highly emotive word 'stagnation' . . . for what other ages would have called 'permanence'? Why does the word 'primitive' suggest clumsiness, inefficiency, barbarity? When our ancestors talked of the primitive church . . . they meant nothing [derogatory]." He adds in *The Discarded Image,* "In modernism, i.e., evolutionary thought, man stands at the top of a stair whose foot is lost in obscurity; in [medieval thought] . . . he stands at the bottom of a stair whose top is invisible with light."

Satan uses monotony as a weapon

While promoting change through fashion, in Lewis's view, Satan also uses the routines of everyday life as a weapon. In Letter 23, Screwtape refers to the general everyday routine as "the horror of the Same Old Thing." When people are tempted into believing that they're enslaved by the normal routines of life, then Satan believes he has won the day. Screwtape writes, "The horror of the Same Old Thing is one of the most valuable passions we have produced in the human heart — an endless source of heresies in religion, folly in counsel, infidelity in marriage, and inconstancy in friendship."

Screwtape Is Toast: A Look at the Sequel

Because of the commercial and critical success of *The Screwtape Letters,* many urged Lewis to write a sequel. But he balked at the idea because he disliked writing this book more than anything else he had written. In fact, Lewis wrote in the updated preface that he was "resolved never to write another letter." However, when invited by the *Saturday Evening Post* to write a follow-up many years later, he penned "Screwtape Proposes a Toast." This essay is a toast made by Screwtape at the "annual dinner of the Tempter's Training College for young Devils." The *Post* published the essay in December of 1959, but modern editions of *The Screwtape Letters* usually include the essay in the book.

"Screwtape Proposes a Toast" is quite unlike the letters of the original book. First, Lewis avoids the familiar style of a letter of correspondence; true to its content, the so-called sequel is meant to be read as an address that would be spoken aloud to a group of young tempters. Second, the subject matter is of a higher level than the more practical and down-to-earth issues discussed in the letters to Wormwood. Rather than techniques of tempting a single individual, Screwtape speaks of sidetracking the human race as a whole.

Lewis uses the essay to deal with a trend that he sees emerging in government, education, and especially society at large: people's desires to be equal, to conform, and to be like everyone else around them. Screwtape sees an opportunity for Satan's intervention in this feeling of wanting to say, "I'm as good as you are." He can use the desire to drown out individualism and ultimately "turn a human being away from almost every road which might finally lead him to heaven."

Screwtape sees the impact that this I'm-as-good-as-you-are mentality has on the education of humans. "The basic principle of the new education," says Screwtape, "is to be that dunces and idlers must not be made to feel inferior to intelligent and industrious pupils. That would be 'undemocratic.'" As a result, developing a student's self-esteem becomes more important than trying to educate him or her. Screwtape believes that this trend turns teachers into "nurses" and eventually dumbs down people to such an extent that education is meaningless.

As a result of the dumbing-down of students, Screwtape sees the world becoming filled more and more with lukewarm and watered down people, folks who have no convictions or individuality. Truly evil people, such as Henry VIII or Hitler, become something of a rare breed. The senior devil complains that lukewarm people are less tasty to feast on than the great sinners of the past. However, overall, he thinks that the change is for the better, because great sinners are made "out of the very same material" as great Christians. Screwtape also admires the impact that the lone great sinner can have on a world of lukewarm people: As "the majority lose all individuality, the great sinners become far more effective agents for us. Every dictator . . . almost every film-star . . . can now draw tens of thousands of the human sheep with him . . . Catch the bellwether and his whole flock comes after him."

Chapter 11

The Great Divorce: Hitching a Ride on a Cosmic Road Trip

1 love traveling. Yet, leaving home is a challenge for me at this point in my life. I'd like to take my family on a road trip across the United States, but the plan's a no-go: My van's transmission would surely break down halfway through Kansas. A dash to Europe? I'd love to, but with three children, even a great airfare special is too much when it's multiplied by five for the fam. Seeing these limitations, I consider setting my sights on a destination closer to home. But, my excitement wanes after realizing that I'd have to find someone to care for my family's pets while we were away. In the end, I give up because it's too much trouble.

I may have a hard time traveling out of my home town, but the citizens of Hell don't have the same problem in C.S. Lewis's *The Great Divorce;* people in Hell are offered an all-expenses-paid trip to Heaven. As you read this work of Lewis's, you too are transported into a world beyond the here and now. And as a result you experience a vivid picture of what the true nature of Heaven and Hell may be like.

In this chapter, you explore why Lewis wrote *The Great Divorce,* examine how Lewis saw Heaven and Hell, and discover why Hell is a location where people choose to go, not a jail they're sent to by God.

Background: Getting Familiar with The Great Divorce

The Great Divorce is a fantasy that follows a group of passengers who board a bus in Hell and visit Heaven. The passengers discover how different Heaven looks and feels compared to Hell; many of them also interact with loved ones or acquaintances who are residents of Heaven. The story's narrator is a passenger on the bus, and all the events that take place are seen through his eyes. Scottish pastor and author George MacDonald, who was a lifelong hero of Lewis's, serves as the narrator's heavenly guide for much of the excursion into Heaven. (See Chapters 3 and 21 for more on MacDonald.)

As you discover at the end of the book, the narrator is none other than Lewis himself. The premise of the story is that the entire bus ride saga is actually a dream Lewis has after he's knocked unconscious by falling books in his library.

Although C.S. Lewis sat down to write *The Great Divorce* in 1943, he envisioned the book's basic idea ten years earlier. In 1933, Lewis first read works by 17th-century Anglican writer Jeremy Taylor and early church fathers who speculated on the idea of the *refrigerium*. I know, "refrigerium" sounds like a cross between a refrigerator and an aquarium, but actually it's a theological concept. The gist of refrigerium is that although punishment in Hell is never-ending, God allows intermittent periods of rest. A refrigerium, therefore, is something like a holiday from Hell. The concept of a refrigerium has no biblical basis, but Lewis was intrigued by this idea and began to brainstorm about a book that explores what would happen if a group of people from Hell visited Heaven on holiday.

As you read *The Great Divorce,* you notice that it has an episodic feel to it. The conversations that take place are self-contained and take place one after the other, usually in separate chapters. The reason for the structure is that, like *The Screwtape Letters,* this work was originally published in 14 weekly installments in *The Guardian* periodical between November 1944 and April 1945. Noting the serial quality of the book and its impact on the content in a letter to a student, Lewis writes, "The dialogues succeed one another arbitrarily and might have come in any other order and might have gone on a longer or shorter time."

More than a wallflower

Lewis dedicated *The Great Divorce* to Barbara Wall, who typed several books for him, including *That Hideous Strength, Miracles,* and *The Great Divorce.*

Upping the Dante

One influence in the idea for *The Great Divorce* was Dante's classic work *Purgatorio*. In that story, Beatrice (the guide, much like George MacDonald in *The Great Divorce*) and Dante (the narrator) know one another and meet up again in the Earthly Paradise. In Chapter 12 of *The Great Divorce,* however, Lewis offers a new twist on Dante's story. In Lewis's tale, a husband who is a resident of Hell is reacquainted with his heavenly wife. Unlike Dante's version, Lewis was intrigued by what could happen in such an encounter "when one side won't play."

The full text of *Purgatorio* is available online at `www.ccel.org/d/dante/purgatorio/purg.htm`.

Lewis originally wanted to call the book *Who Goes Home?,* which is a yell traditionally shouted by a guard in the British Parliament building when he is preparing to close the doors. However, before publication, Lewis found that there was already a book in print with that title. So, the title was changed to *The Great Divorce: A Dream* and was later shortened to simply *The Great Divorce.*

Lewis doesn't try to paint realistic portraits of Heaven and Hell in *The Great Divorce.* He knowingly offers fantasy versions. In the preface to the book, he cautions that the actual description and conditions of Heaven and Hell are purely imaginative; in his words, "They are not even a guess or speculation at what may actually await us." Instead, as the fictional George MacDonald says at the end of *The Great Divorce,* the purpose of the book is to see more clearly the choices we make on earth.

Divorcing Heaven and Hell

The title *The Great Divorce* may lead you to expect a story about the latest Hollywood breakup or royal split. But, the divorce in the title actually refers to the chasm that exists between those people who surrender to God and those who refuse to do so and follow their own paths instead.

This word choice is meant as a direct rebuttal to William Blake's 18th-century poem entitled *The Marriage of Heaven and Hell.* Suggesting such a marriage is possible, Blake believes it unnecessary to separate one from the other, that the two places are but ends of the same string. Lewis observes that people naturally want to believe Blake. They have a head-in-the-sand optimism hoping that — with enough skill, patience, and time — they can avoid deciding between God's way (Heaven) and their own way (Hell). Lewis sees that belief as a "disastrous error." "Evil can be undone," Lewis writes, "but it cannot *develop* into good."

Lewis maintains that the universe was created in an all-or-nothing reality — that God's gift of free will means that people either choose to obey the Lord or they choose to obey themselves. In *The Great Divorce,* the guide MacDonald points out the reality of "either/or" to the narrator: "Son, son, it must be one way or the other." In the end, MacDonald concludes that "there are two kinds of people in the world: those who say to God 'Thy will be done' or to whom God says 'Thy will be done.'"

As a result, Hell and Heaven are on opposite ends of the decision spectrum and are completely divorced from each other. You can't straddle the fence. According to Lewis, if you wish to hang on to something from Hell or earth, you won't see Heaven. And, if you submit to God, then you can't keep "even the smallest and most intimate souvenirs of Hell."

Attempting to Jibe Universalism with Christian Beliefs

One of the most intriguing plot twists in *The Great Divorce* is that the passengers from Hell have a genuine opportunity to stay in Heaven — if they really want to — or they can choose to return to Hell. To you and I, such a decision would be a no-brainer, like the choice between cappuccino (yeah!) and tea (yuck!). The irony of Lewis's story, however, is that all but one passenger choose to return to Hell.

This "second chance" to get into Heaven after death opens the door to *universalism,* the idea that everyone submits to God, either before or after death, and goes to live with their Maker in Heaven. The real-life George MacDonald, for one, held this belief. Lewis, on the other hand, neither believed in universalism nor did he see the concept as fitting in with the truths of biblical Christianity. As Lewis notes in *The Pilgrim's Regress,* "You must not try to fix the point after which a return [to God] is impossible, but you can see that there will be such a point somewhere."

However, in *The Great Divorce,* Lewis attempts to marry MacDonald's universalism with historical Christian beliefs. He does so in a creative way by bringing in the Roman Catholic idea of *purgatory,* an intermediate stop on the road to Heaven that Catholics believe Christians inhabit in order to atone for their sins. Throwing all of these concepts together, Lewis makes Hell and purgatory the same place. For people who refuse to obey the Lord, Hell is a permanent home. But for those who turn away from their selfish ways and surrender to God, Hell serves as just a temporary stopping place, a purgatory, on the road to Heaven. Therefore, in Lewis's fantasy world of *The Great Divorce,* Hell is a place that God uses to bring people to Him.

Seeing no biblical grounds for the concept, most Protestants (and Catholics, too) are quick to dismiss the notion of a person having a second chance at Heaven after death. Catholics further disagree with Lewis's premise that Hell and purgatory are the same place. But, no matter your spiritual background, be sure to read *The Great Divorce* in the way Lewis intends — as a fantasy that helps you see yourself more clearly. As long as you are alive, you have the second chance that Lewis is writing about. That's exactly Lewis's point.

In addition, you can uncover many Christian truths in *The Great Divorce,* but the work also contains a lot of details added by Lewis simply to tell a great story. For unambiguous Christian doctrine, look to his apologetic works, such as *Mere Christianity.*

The Nature of Heaven and Hell

In *The Great Divorce,* Lewis never attempts to paint a realistic view of Heaven and Hell. But at the same time, as you read the book, you can get a glimpse of what Lewis understood Heaven and Hell to be like.

Before I dive into the details, though, I need to explain two fundamental and overriding beliefs that Lewis has about the spiritual world beyond earth.

- **Heaven and Hell are real places.** "Heaven is reality itself," writes Lewis, thus dismissing the idea that the spiritual worlds of Heaven and Hell are somehow less real and tangible than the earth you walk on today. In talking to a passenger from Hell, a resident of Heaven points out, "We know nothing of religion here: we think only of Christ. We know nothing of speculation. Come and see. I will bring you to Eternal Fact, the Father of all other facthood."

- **Heaven and Hell are polar opposites.** As I discuss in the section "Divorcing Heaven and Hell" earlier in this chapter, the truth of "either/or" means that everything Hellish is completely foreign to Heaven and no quality of Heaven will ever be found in Hell.

  Understanding this "either/or" principle can help you make sense of the differences in geography of Heaven and Hell as well as the physical and spiritual qualities of their respective inhabitants.

These fundamental beliefs create the backdrop for Lewis's contrasts of the natures of Heaven and Hell, which I present in the following sections.

Peering down at Hell and its inhabitants

As you discover in Chapter 10, Lewis gives insight into the nature of Hell in *The Screwtape Letters*. In *The Great Divorce,* Lewis follows up this devilish discussion with even more thoughts on Hell and the people that inhabit it. This section takes a look at how Hell and its creatures are portrayed in this book.

What's Hell like?

When most people consider Hell, they probably think of it much as a couch potato considers an exercise club: a place of around-the-clock physical torture and pain. The Bible indicates that Hell is a place of torture, although Christians disagree on whether this pain is physical, spiritual, or a combination of both. Lewis opts to make *The Great Divorce*'s Hell a place of mental anguish, not physical torture. According to Lewis, Hell is

- ✔ **A drab place to live.** "It's just like any other town," complains a resident of Hell. "They lead you to expect fire and devils and all sorts of interesting people on grids," but instead, Lewis's Hell is a "grey town," a place that's always rainy and on the cusp between daylight and nightfall. (Hmmm, based on that description, one may wonder whether Lewis traveled to Seattle before he penned *The Great Divorce.*)

- ✔ **Perfect for hermits.** Hell is a place that begs the question, "Why can't we all just get along?" People live alone, not in communities, simply because they can't stand each other. In fact, when a person moves into a new place, he invariably begins arguing with his neighbor within a day of his arrival. Then, after a few days of living there, he becomes so ticked off that he moves and builds a new house on the edge of the town. As this cycle continues, Hell expands exponentially, giving new meaning to the concept of urban sprawl.

- ✔ **Full of rugged individualists.** On earth, you and I can talk a lot about being independent, but every aspect of our society is based on *interdependency.* For example, I need a house, so I pay a carpenter to build one for me. The carpenter is glad to offer his services because he needs cash for food and iPods. Both of us, in turn, pay a farmer for his corn (so we can eat) and Steve Jobs for his MP3 player (so we can relax).

  But people in Lewis's version of Hell don't have this same interdependency: They can get something just by imagining it, although the imagined goods are of inferior quality. As a result, because people aren't dependent on each other to meet their needs, they have no motivation to build a community.

- ✔ **Based on "survival of the fittest."** Reflecting the same attitude as *The Screwtape Letters* (jump back to Chapter 10 for an explanation of that work), Hell in *The Great Divorce* is a place in which only the best-equipped people survive. For example, when standing in line for the bus ride to Heaven, a lady steps out of line to argue with a man who cheated her. And when she does so, the narrator remarks that "others immediately closed up and flung her out." In addition, without God to help temper matters, people in Hell have less self control than they ever had on earth. They do what's best for them, regardless of the cost to the next guy.

✔ **A state of mind.** In an exchange with MacDonald, the narrator discovers that Hell is a "state of mind." Don't misunderstand Lewis when he proposes this concept: He doesn't mean that Hell is imaginary or make-believe. Rather, Hell is a sort of self-imposed mental prison that a person chooses for himself (see the section "What a Bunch of Morons: Why Some People Choose Hell" later in this chapter). MacDonald adds, "And every state of mind, left to itself, every shutting up of the creature within the dungeon of its own mind — is, in the end, Hell."

✔ **Irrelevant.** In the end, Hell is basically a non-issue in the universe. MacDonald tells the narrator, "The whole difficulty of understanding Hell is that [it] is so nearly Nothing." Lewis depicts the physical nature of Hell as a "crack in the soil" of Heaven. As the narrator's guide, MacDonald observes, "All Hell is smaller than one pebble of your earthly world: but it is smaller than one atom of this world, the Real World." He adds that even if a butterfly were to swallow all of Hell, Hell would not be significant enough "to do it any harm or to have any taste."

What kind of person lives here?

Given the picture of Hell described in the previous section, what sort of creatures would inhabit such a place? According to *The Great Divorce*, the people you find in Hell are

✔ **"So last year."** Physically, the creatures of Hell in *The Great Divorce* look stale compared to their previous earthly appearances. You may think of them as you would a depressed 50-something actress who unsuccessfully tries to hide her age with countless rounds of plastic surgery. Everyone looks, in some way, "distorted and faded." They end up "full not of possibilities, but of impossibilities."

✔ **Ghosts.** When seen in the light of Heaven, the residents of Hell are transparent, or as Lewis vividly depicts, "man-shaped stains on the brightness of [the] air." The narrator says that "one could attend to them or ignore them at will as you do with the dirt on the window pane." Not surprisingly, one of the female passengers on the bus is horrified by the prospect that people have been staring *through* her.

Lewis uses the people's vapor-like natures to explain phenomena of ghosts and haunted houses on earth. In the story, every creature has the opportunity to go to Heaven on refrigerium (a sort of holiday away from Hell), but most prefer to go to earth and haunt their old stomping grounds instead.

- **Preoccupied with themselves.** Inhabitants of Hell are selfish, even when they have no need to be. The narrator comments that his fellow passengers "fought like hens to board the bus though there was plenty of room for us all." (Sounds a lot like the school bus I used to ride in grade school.) They argue and bicker about everything and always put the blame on someone else. For example, one passenger talks about seeing Napoleon in Hell muttering to himself all the time, "It was Soult's fault. It was Ney's fault. It was Josephine's fault. It was the fault of the Russians. It was the fault of the English."

- **Insistent on doing things their own ways.** Judging from Lewis's depiction, the national anthem of Hell must be the old Frank Sinatra song, "I Did It My Way." As I discuss further in the section "Selfish Pride: Hell's Most Common Trait," every person in Hell wants his or her own way, even if it means being damned in Hell as a result. MacDonald tells the narrator that, in spite of their damned home, Hell's inhabitants have a sense of satisfaction that they can at least say "they've been true to themselves." Reflecting on this truth, MacDonald later quotes Milton: "Better to reign in hell than serve in Heaven."

- **Irrelevant.** The passengers from Hell are non-entities and "unsubstantial." They're distinct from one another, but only as "smokes differ." Grass doesn't bend when they walk on it; dew drops don't break up when they step on them. But these ghosts aren't just tiny, they're even less than that. MacDonald tells the narrator, "For a damned soul is nearly nothing: it is shrunk, shut up in itself." What's more, as time goes on, residents of Hell gradually become more and more dehumanized. When seeing a grouchy lady, MacDonald speculates, "The question is whether she is a grumbler, or only a grumble."

Gazing up to Heaven and its creatures

Because Hell is the direct opposite of Heaven, you would expect that Heaven is everything that Hell is not. Hell is called "nearly Nothing," so Heaven is dubbed "reality itself." Hell may be dreary and grey, but Heaven is bright, vibrant, and invigorating.

On earth as it is in Heaven

In *The Great Divorce,* Lewis suggests that, in the end, earth is not a distinct place recognized by people in either Heaven and Hell. He brings up the idea that for the saved, all their earthly pasts will have been Heaven. And the same with the damned: All their lives on earth will have been Hell. MacDonald adds, "The Blessed will say, 'We have never lived anywhere except in Heaven,' and the Lost, 'We were always in Hell.' And both will speak truly."

Keeping the focus on the characters, Lewis avoids being too descriptive about the geography or characteristics of Heaven itself. However, he does offer insight into what the people living in Heaven may be like. Specifically, he sees inhabitants of Heaven as

✔ **Both spiritual and solid.** Lewis refers to people in Heaven as "spirits," but they're not vapor-like ghosts in the way that creatures of Hell are. Instead, the inhabitants of Heaven are beings that you can touch and feel. In fact, the narrator calls them the "solid people." They have bodies that seem to be identical to the real life body that Jesus Christ received after his resurrection; the Gospels describe how Christ's body was similar to a human body but somehow different and not limited in the same way that our temporary, earthly bodies are.

✔ **Majestic and ageless.** The bus passengers from Hell may be fading, but the people in Heaven appear ageless to the narrator. Later in the story, he also refers to them as the "Bright People." Given their overall weakness, the ghosts of Hell are frightened and intimidated by the more awesome nature of the Bright People. In fact, two of the ghosts scream and run back to the bus for safety, while the others huddle closer together.

✔ **Carrying no baggage.** The people of Heaven are a psychiatrist's nightmare: They're problem-free and carry no emotional baggage. Sporting an emotional non-stick coating, they

  • Experience forgiveness without shame.

  • Can't get hurt by someone else.

  • Have given up all selfish consideration for "their rights."

  • Don't have any false pretenses as to why they're in Heaven — they know they did nothing specific to earn God's grace.

  • Realize that the suffering they experienced on earth was turned into glory in Heaven. (MacDonald calls it "the opposite of a mirage." When they thought they saw salt deserts on earth, in reality, "the pools were full of water.")

✔ **Having no selfish tendencies.** Heaven's citizens don't have a sense of selfishness or self-consciousness. They are individuals but are nonetheless freed from any of the prisons of "self." People in Hell can be characterized by an inability to get out of themselves, but the creatures of Heaven are exactly opposite: They're perfectly willing and able to leave themselves behind. For example, the narrator notes that they can appreciate something they've created or built just as if it were done by someone else — "without pride or modesty."

✔ **Loving as God does.** In *The Great Divorce,* Lewis contrasts the love Heaven's citizens have with the love experienced on earth. On earth, love is often based on need. For instance, a heavenly woman confesses to her husband that on earth, "in the main I loved you for my own sake:

because I needed you." Yet, in Heaven, love is *agape,* or all-giving. As Lewis describes it, when you don't have the need to feel love, only then can you fully love others.

✔ **VIPs.** On earth, we tend to idolize anyone famous — movie stars, musical artists, authors, and the movers and shakers of the political and business worlds. But Lewis's Heaven has no concept of celebrity. (Sorry, *People* magazine and E! Channel — you're plumb out of luck.) Instead, everyone is equally famous. As Lewis puts it, "They are all known, remembered, and recognized" by God.

✔ **Free of disguises.** Clothing is optional in Lewis's Heaven; some of the solid people are naked and some are clothed. But don't get any wrong ideas — the ones not wearing clothes aren't "nude" in an earthly sense. The narrator observes that the naked people are no "less adorned" than the clothed people and all that they reveal is their glorious spirit. So too, the clothed people don't disguise themselves by being attired. Clothes somehow become part of the person wearing them, not something that covers up who they really are. In other words, the spirit shines through the clothes and body.

Selfish Pride: Hell's Most Common Trait

The Great Divorce focuses on various persons from Hell that the narrator encounters as he tours Heaven with their group. Although each person (or, more accurately, ghost) has a unique personality and experience in Heaven, you can begin to see a common trait among each of these residents of Hell: an inability to "get out of" himself or herself. They're so consumed with their own concerns, needs, and desires that they're unwilling to leave those things behind. Because Lewis believes pride to be the root of all sin, he describes pride as the "least common denominator" among the citizens of Hell in *The Great Divorce.* In other words, Lewis believes that every sin that people commit is the result of the fact that they're more concerned with themselves than with God or others around them.

The Dirty Dozen: Twelve Types of People Found in Hell

Pride and selfishness take various shapes and forms. Sometimes they're obvious, but sometimes these sins are much more subtle. In *The Great Divorce,* Lewis shows many different types of people that can be found in Hell. But when you look "behind the scenes" of each person's story, you see that they're all motivated by a common selfishness. In this section, I highlight twelve of these ghosts that the narrator encounters during his trip.

What's striking about each of these vignettes is that none of the people depicted are stereotypical villains like Adolph Hitler or Darth Vader. Instead, they're normal people, much like those you probably work with and live around. And yes, they're also people much like you and me.

Note: In *The Great Divorce,* Lewis usually refers to the people from Hell as "ghosts." In this section, I freely interchange the term "ghost" with the identity a person had on earth (such as man, woman, or youth). But, in each case, I'm referring to the person in his or her ghostly, Hellish state.

The man obsessed with his rights

I've never asked for anything that wasn't mine by rights.

—The Big Ghost

The Big Man (later called the Big Ghost) is one of the first ghosts the narrator encounters while waiting to board the bus in Hell. The Big Ghost describes himself as "a plain man" who is only concerned with having his "rights same as everyone else." While living on earth, the Big Ghost was your typical all-around nice guy. I suspect he probably helped out his neighbors, voted in every election, and paid his taxes on time. However, as you see his experiences in Heaven unfold, you realize that his obsession with his rights — what he thinks he deserves — leads to his downfall.

When the bus arrives in Heaven, the Big Ghost comes across a resident named Len. Len is a man the Big Ghost knew on earth. To put things mildly, Len wasn't a squeaky clean guy on earth; in fact, he murdered someone that the Big Ghost knew. The Big Ghost is dumbfounded as to how he could have possibly wound up in Hell while a murderer like Len lives in Heaven. "I gone straight all my life," said the Big Ghost. "I don't say I was a religious man and I don't say I had no faults, far from it. But I done my best all my life, see?"

Len, however, makes it clear that he isn't in Heaven on account of his rights. In fact, Len confesses that if admittance to Heaven was based on "rights," then he certainly wouldn't be there.

In this part of the story, Lewis demonstrates what is often called the "scandal of the Cross." The outrageous truth of Christianity is that salvation isn't related to how good a person is or how much he or she has earned it. Instead, eternal life in Heaven is dependent only on believing in what God does for you through the work of Jesus Christ on the cross. People like the Big Ghost can't accept the fact that their good deeds can't earn them a spot in Heaven. On first take, you may sympathize with the Big Ghost's shock. After all, why should a nice guy go to Hell while a murderer lives on in heavenly bliss? Yet, if you look closer, you see that the dreaded "p" word — pride — underlies his complaints.

In an act of prideful self-reliance, the Big Ghost decides to pull himself up by his bootstraps and reach Heaven on his own. Seeing that he doesn't want God's help, Len responds, "Ask for the Bleeding Charity. Everything is here for the asking and nothing can be bought."

The Big Ghost continues to hold up his basic decency as proof for why he should be welcomed into Heaven. Finally, Len echoes the Apostle Paul's words in Romans: "All have sinned and fallen short of the glory of God." He tells the Big Ghost that he's deceiving himself: "You weren't a decent man and you didn't do your best." In other words, Len and the Big Ghost were *both* sinners; Len's sins were simply easier for everyone to see than the Big Ghost's, which were more subtle, buried deep in his heart.

In a revealing moment, Lewis writes about the underlying problem with selfish pride. When the Big Ghost says he expected their roles to be reversed, Len says "Very likely we soon shall be, *if* you'll stop thinking about it." What Lewis means by this provocative statement is that if people stop thinking about their rights and simply surrender themselves to God, then God will give them exactly what they want. Yet, the Big Ghost, in the end, never can escape his thoughts. In fact, the Big Ghost refuses to go with Len into Heaven and takes a certain pleasure in his refusal: "I'd rather be damned than go along with you. I came here to get my rights, see?"

The unappreciated youth

> [The tousle-headed youth] felt quite certain that he was going where, at last, . . . he would find 'Recognition' and 'Appreciation.'
>
> —The narrator

When the narrator finds a seat in the bus, a "tousle-headed" young man sits down beside him. After he talks with the narrator for just a few minutes, you quickly surmise that the youth has a "me-against-the-world" attitude. He tells the narrator that he's suffered endless indignities. His parents never appreciated him. The schools he attended never understood his genius. His girlfriend turned out to be possessive and bourgeois. And, to top it off, after he killed himself, "ill luck" sent him to grey town.

The young man's pride and arrogance lead him to blame others for his problems; he never accepts any responsibility whatsoever for his predicaments. His solo quest for recognition and appreciation became his passion on Earth and his entire reason for wanting to go to Heaven.

The youth's craving for appreciation and recognition is ultimately self-defeating. If he were to simply stop searching for these things, get out of himself, and fix his eyes on Jesus (Hebrews 12:2), then he'd receive exactly what he's looking for. Later in the story, Lewis underscores this point when he says of people in Heaven, "They are all famous. They are all known, remembered, recognized by the only Mind that can give a perfect judgment."

The materialist

> I'm not going on this trip for my health. As far as that goes I don't think it would suit me up there. But if I can come back with some real commodities . . . I'd start a little business . . . I'd make a nice little profit.
>
> —Ikey, the bowler-hatted Ghost

Another ghost that the narrator encounters in the bus en route to Heaven is an intelligent looking man wearing a bowler hat. Big Ghost refers to him as "Ikey." Ikey's going to Heaven purely for economic opportunity. He wants to bring back goods from Heaven and sell them for a profit in Hell.

After the bus trip is over, the narrator comes across Ikey while walking in Heaven. He sees the Ghost futilely trying to fill his pockets with apples to take back to Hell. But his efforts are — dare I say it — fruitless. The heavenly apples are much too solid and heavy for him to collect. Ikey's lofty expectations for a sizable loot keep shrinking: from a bunch of apples, to a couple, to one big apple, and finally to a single tiny apple. Much like carrying a huge iron cannonball, Ikey struggles every step of the way as he lugs his apple back to the bus.

As the bowler-hatted Ghost heads for the bus, a nearby waterfall (called the Water-Giant) tries to talk some sense into him. It says that, in spite of his best efforts, he can't really take the apple back to Hell because there's not enough room in Hell for it. The Water-Giant then invites the Ghost to "stay here and learn to eat such apples." Ikey, however, ignores the voice and continues on in his futile effort.

In this vignette, Lewis depicts a man who is so bent on achieving his self-made plans that it never occurs to him to consider any alternative. He never looks around to discover the infinite riches that are available to him if only he'd stay.

Jesus Christ speaks of the bowler-hatted man in Mark 8:36 when he asks, "For what shall it profit a man, if he shall gain the whole world, and lose his own soul?"

The speculative theologian

For me there is no such thing as a final answer.

—Episcopal Ghost

The last ghost that the narrator talks to during the bus trip to Heaven is described as a "fat clean-shaven man" with a "cultured voice." Later referred to as the Episcopal Ghost, he's Lewis's caricature of a liberal theologian who goes to Hell.

The Episcopal Ghost initially sounds like he's interested in spiritual issues, but you soon find out that he isn't concerned at all with seeking God. In fact, he's so close-minded that he denies Heaven's literal reality even when he's standing in it.

The Episcopal Ghost much prefers his own progressive ideas to God's reality. During his life on earth and in Hell, he's always into the latest modern, fashionable thought. On the bus, he dismisses as "superstitious" the other passengers' talk of approaching nightfall. The Ghost informs the others that the latest discoveries in "educated circles" say that dawn that is actually coming to grey town. Later, he tells of his involvement in a Theological Society in Hell (yes, you heard me right) and his latest paper giving a new theory on the "tragedy" of the crucifixion of Jesus Christ.

When the Episcopal Ghost gets to Heaven, he has an encounter with an old colleague named Dick. Dick tells the Ghost that he's not being intellectually honest in his theology. Looking back at his time on earth before he came to a Christian faith, Dick says, "Our opinions were not honestly come by. We simply found ourselves in contact with a certain current of ideas and plunged into it because it seemed modern and successful."

Dick invites the Ghost three separate times in three different ways to join him in Heaven, but on each occasion, the Ghost deflects or outright rejects coming face-to-face with God's truth:

✔ When Dick asks him, "Will you, even now, repent and believe?," the Ghost deflects, "I'm not sure I've got the exact point you are trying to make."

✔ Dick offers him a chance to experience truth and to quench his thirst for knowledge, but the Ghost rejects the "ready-made truth" offered to him in Heaven.

✔ Dick asks the Ghost to "become that child again: even now." In this plea, he echoes Jesus Christ in Matthew 18:3: "Most certainly I tell you, unless you turn, and become as little children, you will in no way enter into the Kingdom of Heaven." However, the Episcopal Ghost spits back a biblical reference of his own to defend himself. Twisting the Apostle Paul's words in 1 Corinthians 13:11, the Ghost responds, "Ahh, but when I became a man I put away childish things."

The Ghost does consider Dick's offer to stay in Heaven but will only stay if he's given assurances that he'll be useful and given a chance to display his talents. Dick, of course, offers no assurances because no one is "needed" in Heaven in the way the Episcopal Ghost desires.

The Ghost is interested in speculation, not the facts. Dick tries to reason with him by explaining, "We know nothing of religion here: we think only of Christ. We know nothing of speculation. Come and see. I will bring you to Eternal Fact, the Father of all other facthood." But in the end, the Episcopal Ghost is too preoccupied with *his* ideas and *his* need for usefulness that he returns to Hell with smug satisfaction.

The glass-is-half-empty guy

Same old lie. People have been telling me that sort of thing all my life.

—The Hard-Bitten Ghost

In Heaven, the narrator comes across a tall, lean, "hard-bitten" Ghost who is disillusioned, disbelieving, and skeptical about everything he encounters. You could describe him as the kind of guy who sees the glass as half empty, although perhaps it's more accurate to say he sees the glass as *completely* empty.

In his conversation with the narrator, you see that this Ghost's jaded attitude has completely taken over his mind. During his time on earth, he traveled considerably and visited exotic places around the world. But, to him, everything was a waste of time. The Ghost says, "They're all advertisement stunts. All run by the same people." He even sees Hell as a "flop," a letdown compared to the hype. When speaking of the promise of staying in Heaven, the Hard-Bitten Ghost dismisses the promise as nothing but "propaganda" and "an advertisement stunt." Furthermore, he believes everyone is out to take advantage of him if he lets his guard down. He says, "All this stuff up here is run by the same people as the Town. They're just laughing at us."

The jaded attitude of Hard-Bitted Ghost closely resembles the unbelieving dwarfs depicted in *The Last Battle* (see Chapter 8). Their familiar mantra — "We haven't let anyone take us in. The Dwarfs are for the Dwarfs." — sounds like something from the mouth of the Hard-Bitted Ghost.

Like the Dwarfs in Narnia, the Hard-Bitted Ghost has a choice: He can seek the truth and risk himself in the process, or he can rely fully on himself. Sadly, the Ghost chooses the latter and never even considers the promises of Heaven.

The self-conscious woman

Could you, only for a moment, fix your mind on something not yourself?

—Spirit to the well-dressed woman

The narrator encounters a well-dressed woman whose life is completely dominated by self-consciousness. She's obsessed with how she looks to others and what others think of her. When the narrator comes across this Ghost, he sees that bright Spirits are trying to comfort her and invite her to join them in Heaven. But she wants nothing more than to be left alone. The Spirits offer her infinite happiness, but she seems incapable of receiving it in her self-absorbed state. She's too self-conscious that she'll be seen in her ghastly, ghost-like appearance.

When a Spirit continues encouraging her, the woman almost takes the risk and goes with it. But that moment vanishes, and she sinks back into herself and refuses, unwilling to expose herself to the shame of starting out as a ghost in Heaven. The Spirit then pleads with her, "Could you, only for a moment, fix your mind on something not yourself?"

On first take, the well-dressed female Ghost seems a direct opposite of the arrogant, prideful Bree in *The Horse and His Boy* (see Chapter 8). After all, Bree struggles with feeling too *good* about himself and his abilities. Yet, at the core, both characters struggle with the same self-absorbed view of the world and an inability to fix their minds on someone other than themselves.

However, if the self-conscious Ghost surrenders her pride and allows herself to be vulnerable to God, then God promises that she'll experience the acceptance and contentment she longs for. As the Apostle Paul promises in Romans 8:15, "For you didn't receive a spirit of bondage that makes you a slave again to fear, but you received the Spirit of sonship, by him we cry, 'Abba, Father.'"

The adventurer

If [Sir Archibald] would only have admitted that he'd mistaken the means for the end. . . .

—MacDonald on Sir Archibald

As described earlier in this chapter, the narrator of *The Great Divorce* meets up with George MacDonald, who assumes the role of Teacher during their journey into Heaven. In their conversations, MacDonald tells the narrator of a creature from Hell he once met named Sir Archibald. Sir Archibald was an adventurer who lived for experiencing and writing about "survival" activities.

Yet, when Sir Archibald visited Heaven, he found it useless. Everyone had "survived" already; as a result, nobody cared much about the issues that he was preoccupied with. MacDonald notes, "His occupation was clean gone."

Once again, Lewis shows how pride and self-centeredness get the better of a Ghost. MacDonald the Teacher reflects: "If he would only have admitted that he'd mistaken the means for the end and had a good laugh at himself he could have begun all over again like a little child and entered into joy. But he would not do that. He cared nothing about joy. In the end he went away."

The grumbler

I ought to be alive to-day and they simply starved me in that dreadful nursing home and no one ever came near me and. . . .

—The grumbling Ghost

The narrator and his Teacher are interrupted during their walk through Heaven by a grumbling Ghost who's talking a mile a minute. In a non-stop diatribe, she grumbles, moans, and complains about every aspect of her former life on earth. Eventually, the "shrill monotonous whine" dies away as she moves out of hearing distance.

The narrator is perplexed as to why this lady was sent to Hell. Questioning the Teacher, he sees the lady as silly, but not evil. She's someone who just has a bad habit of whining, reasons the narrator. The Teacher says that, if the narrator is correct, then there's hope for the grumbling Ghost yet. But, he adds that the key question is whether "she is a grumbler, or only a grumble."

In this vignette, Lewis underscores the dehumanizing nature of sin when it enslaves a person over a lifetime. If left unchecked, the grumbling Ghost will degenerate into nothing more than a grumbling heap of ashes. (Lewis also deals with the degenerative nature of sin in *The Screwtape Letters,* which is discussed in Chapter 10.)

The domineering spouse

I'm so miserable. I must have someone to — to do things to.

—The domineering wife of Robert

The narrator and his Teacher overhear a conversation between a domineering female Ghost and a bright Woman named Hilda. The narrator never learns the Ghost's name but discovers her husband is named Robert. The female Ghost is trying to figure out a way to see her Robert, who is somewhere else in Heaven.

The female Ghost is utterly controlling and domineering. Her conversation with Hilda reveals the vastly one-sided nature of her marriage to Robert. Her dialogue reeks of self-centeredness: "It was I who made a man of him! . . . It was I who had to drive him every step of the way . . . It was I who had to draw him out of himself . . . I was working my fingers to the bone for him: and without the slightest appreciation . . . I cured him of that." Although the Ghost drove her husband into depression and a nervous breakdown in his final days on earth, she says that her "conscience is clear;" she did her duty.

The Ghost is traveling to Heaven simply because she wants Robert back. Not because she loves him — she wants a project. She tells Hilda that she "must have someone to — to do things to." The Ghost says that she can't do anything to anyone back in Hell, and it's driving her mad. Besides, concludes the domineering Ghost, "Why should he have everything his own way?"

The possessive mother

He is mine, do you understand? Mine, mine, mine, for ever and ever.

—Pam, the possessive mother Ghost

The narrator and the Teacher come across another example of twisted love in an encounter with an extremely possessive mother. The Ghost named Pam is talking with her brother, Reginald, who lives in Heaven. Pam's complaining about the fact that she can't see her son Michael.

Seeing that Pam's priorities are out of whack, Reginald tells her that she can see Michael, but she needs to be "thickened up a bit" to do so. By thickening, Reginald means that she needs to get her relationship with God in order first: Pam needs to want God for his own sake, rather than simply as a means to see Michael. Yet, instead of demanding Pam give her total allegiance to God, Reginald says that God will be pleased even with her baby steps, that "It's only the little germ of desire for God that we need to start the process."

Pam, however, believes that her mother-son relationship overrides any kind of relationship she should have with God. Ironically, as the conversation continues, it becomes obvious that Pam's idea of love for Michael apart from God is not real love at all. The Teacher comments, "What she calls her love for her son had turned into a poor, prickly astringent sort of thing." Eventually, you discover that selfishness is at the root of her longings to see Michael. "Michael is mine," she says. "He is mine, do you understand? Mine, mine, mine, for ever and ever." (See Chapter 18 for more on how human love turns into a false god when it's apart from God.)

The slave to sin

It would be better to be dead than to live with this creature.

—Lizard-bearing Ghost

The narrator and his Teacher come across a Ghost who carries a little, red lizard on his shoulder. The Ghost is visibly angry, telling the lizard to shut up. Frustrated by the behavior of the creature, the Ghost is ready to forget about his trip to Heaven and return to the bus.

However, before this happens, an angel arrives on the scene and offers the Ghost a solution. The angel says that he can silence the lizard by killing it. The Ghost so despises the lizard that he agrees. But when the angel tries to kill the lizard, the Ghost protests, claiming that the angel is burning him. "I never said it wouldn't hurt you," says the angel later on. "I said it wouldn't kill you."

The Ghost looks for any way around completely killing the lizard. When the lizard sleeps, the Ghost becomes confident that he'll be able to keep things under control. "I think the gradual process would be far better than killing it." But, the angel counters, "The gradual process is of no use at all."

The angel can't kill the lizard without the Ghost's permission, so the angel asks for it. Finally, after considerable debate, the Ghost realizes that he would be better dead than to live with the creature. So, he submits and the angel kills and removes the lizard.

When the angel completes this action, something remarkable happens. Symbolizing a Christian conversion, the Ghost is transformed into a man — "an immense man" — and the lizard is transformed into a horse. The Ghost is "born again," so to speak.

Remarkably, of all the passengers from Hell in *The Great Divorce,* this Ghost is the only one that takes up the offer to stay in Heaven for good. By surrendering his lizard to the angel, he's able to free himself from his slavery to sin and be transformed.

Of all of the Ghosts that the narrator encounters, the Ghost with the lizard is the most symbolic in nature. The lizard represents lust that the Ghost must surrender completely to the Lord so that God can kill it and prevent it from dominating the Ghost's life. But when the Ghost agrees to put himself at risk, he's transformed into a new creature. To top it off, God even turns his lust into a horse, something pure and holy and useful in Heaven.

The man in a "Tragedian" mask

For a second [Frank] had almost let the chain go, then, as if it were his life-line, he clutched it once more.

—The narrator

Towards the end of their journey, the narrator and his Teacher come across a strange-looking pair of Ghosts: a tall, shaky, and thin Tragedian (an actor) and a tiny dwarf-like Ghost named Frank. The dwarf holds a chain attached to a collar on the Tragedian. The narrator realizes that they are one person, "or rather that both were the remains of what had once been a person."

Nearby is a female Spirit, called "the Lady" by the narrator, who was Frank's wife back on earth. The Lady comes to the duo and begins to speak directly to Frank, completely ignoring the tall Ghost. Her first words are an earnest apology for any wrongdoing in the past. But, instead of responding himself, Frank has the Tragedian respond to the Lady.

The Lady desires reconciliation and a future together in Heaven, but Frank struggles with the idea of forgiving her and getting rid of his façade. The narrator observes, "For a second he had almost let the chain go, then, as if it were his life-line, he clutched it once more."

The Lady cries out to Frank to release the chain — that she wants him, not the Tragedian. He gets close to letting go, but doesn't. The narrator remarks, "I do not know that I ever saw anything more terrible than the struggle of that Dwarf Ghost against joy." In the end, the Dwarf Ghost grows tinier and tinier until he eventually vanishes, leaving only the Tragedian.

In this vignette, Lewis shows the inevitable result of Frank's selfishness. His unwillingness to be real with his wife, his lack of forgiveness, and his selfish ideas of love ultimately destroy him.

What a Bunch of Morons: Why Some People Choose Hell

One of the inescapable conclusions that Lewis draws in *The Great Divorce* is that people who go to Hell do so voluntarily. Yes, instead of being banished by God to the naughty place, they actually choose to go there, even after they consider the alternative. As I mention earlier in the chapter, Lewis believes that when all is said and done, people can be divided into two groups: "those who say to God 'Thy will be done' or to whom God says 'Thy will be done.'"

This idea of Hell as self-chosen can be seen throughout Lewis's writings. In *The Dark Tower and Other Stories,* he writes, "A man can't be taken to Hell, or *sent* to Hell: you can only get there on your own steam." He adds in *The Problem of Pain,* "I willingly believe that the damned are, in one sense, successful rebels to the end; that the doors of Hell are locked on the *inside.*" Lewis adds a final thought on who does the locking of Hell's doors in *The Pilgrim's Regress:* "The door out of Hell is firmly locked . . . on the inside; whether it is also locked on the outside need not, therefore, be considered."

The Great Divorce also illustrates the idea that the ghosts of Hell aren't there because they didn't have sufficient opportunity to accept God's love and joy. Lewis echoes Proverbs 8:17 ("those who truly seek me, will surely find me") when he says that "no soul that seriously and constantly desires joy will ever miss it. Those who seek find, those who knock it is opened." Therefore, as he notes in *The Pilgrim's Regress,* "It is meaningless to talk of forcing a man to do freely what a man has freely made impossible for himself."

Chapter 12

Spacing Out with the Space Trilogy

Although C.S. Lewis is best known for *The Chronicles of Narnia* and his Christian apologetics, a trilogy of space fantasy books that he wrote in the late 1930s and early 1940s have become classics in their own right: *Out of the Silent Planet, Perelandra,* and *That Hideous Strength.* The trio is popularly known as the space trilogy.

The space trilogy is often dubbed "science fiction," a moniker that may or may not be quite accurate. Even if you call the series sci-fi, it certainly doesn't have that genre's stereotypical plot devices. The hero of *Out of the Silent Planet* and *Perelandra* is neither a scientist nor an astronaut; he's a professor — a specialist in philology and medieval literature. That's right, dead books in dead languages. In addition, the extraterrestrials in the series aren't the Earth-invading, bug-eyed monsters you expect in sci-fi thrillers either. They aren't evil, they speak articulately, and their messages are crucially important for humanity and for the universe.

In this chapter, you explore Lewis's space trilogy. Along the way, you get to know the beings that populate this universe. You also discover an alternative reality — what may have happened if Eve hadn't given in to temptation. Finally, you discover some of the underlying themes of the series, including evil, language, and progress.

Background: A Christian Look at Science and Space Travel

At an early age, C.S. Lewis developed an intense fascination with other planets. In *Surprised by Joy,* he writes, "The idea of other planets exercised upon me then a peculiar, heady attraction, which was quite different from any other of my literary interests." Yet, Lewis didn't find the intense longing he called Joy (see Chapter 2) in this fascination. In his words, "This was something coarser and stronger . . . The interest was ravenous, like a lust." Like several of his other works, Lewis wrote the space trilogy as a kind of therapy, a way to overcome his obsession, "My own planetary romances have been not so much the gratification of that fierce curiosity as its exorcism."

After Lewis became a Christian, he encountered a book called *Voyage to Arcturus* by David Lindsey. It wasn't well written and had diabolical plot lines, but Lewis was highly influenced by it nonetheless. Through Lindsey's book, Lewis began to see how the sci-fi genre could be used to convey not just planetary adventures but spiritual ones as well.

Another motivation he had in writing *Out of the Silent Planet,* the first book in the trilogy, was his reaction to views that he saw springing up around him (he calls them *Westonian* after a character in the story). In writing to his friend Roger Green in December of 1938, Lewis speaks of this motivation:

> What immediately spurred me to write was Olaf Stapledon's Last and First Men *and an essay by J.B.S. Haldane's* Possible Worlds *both of [which] seem to take the idea of such travel seriously and to have the desperately immoral outlook [which] I try to pillory in Weston. I like the whole interplanetary idea as a mythology and simply wished to conquer for my own (Christian) [point] of view what has hitherto been used by the opposite side.*

Lewis sheds more light on his point of view in a July 1939 letter to Sister Penelope, an Anglican nun and theologian who was a close friend and correspondent:

> What set me about writing the book was the discovery that a pupil of mine took all that dream of interplanetary colonization quite seriously, and the realization that thousands of people, in one form or another depend on some hope of perpetuating and improving the human species for the whole meaning of the universe — that a 'scientific hope' of defeating death is a real rival to Christianity.

The space trilogy reflects the frightening world that Lewis saw all around him. The technological advances of the 1930s made war even more hideous than it had been, and relativism and nihilism made science even more threatening. Lewis was similarly dismayed at the directions science had taken during his lifetime. He vehemently disapproved of vivisection (experimenting on living animals), so he made his villain Weston not only a physicist but also a vivisector and a eugenicist (one who experiments with human breeding). Weston's ideal world, in which mentally disabled people are handed over to state laboratories for experimentation, anticipates policies of Hitler during this era, as does the rhetoric of progress in *That Hideous Strength*.

In the late 1930s and early 1940s, the academic world was also changing. New subjects such as sociology and economics were gaining prominence. The "young Turks" in these emerging disciplines grew impatient with the "old guard" and the classics. Weston expresses this arrogance, considering the philologist Ransom's work entirely useless: "I do not call classics and history and such trash education."

In real life, Lewis was deeply suspicious of these new disciplines. As a result, the evil organization in *That Hideous Strength* is run by a gang of wicked psychologists, sociologists, and economists. And the public relations section of the company is a thoroughly German-style propaganda machine, while the private police force is plainly modeled on Nazi S.S. troops.

Critics have tried to paint the space trilogy and Lewis himself as "anti-science." Yet during his lifetime, Lewis denounced that charge, saying that he was attacking something he called *scientism*. In an essay, he clarifies his defense by describing scientism as "the belief that the supreme moral end is the perpetuation of our own species, and that this is to be pursued even if, in the process of being fitted for survival, our species has to be stripped of all those things for which we value it — of pity, of happiness, and of freedom." If the forces in favor of scientism were to win out, this victory would have frightening implications for what human beings may turn into somewhere down the road.

Lewis's poem "Evolutionary Hymn" gives a bleak picture of how our descendents may look at the world:

> *Ask not if it's god or devil,*
> *Brethren, lest your words imply*
> *Static norms of good and evil*
> *(As in Plato) throned on high;*
> *Such scholastic, inelastic,*
> *Abstract yardsticks we imply.*

A dose of Middle-earth in the space trilogy

In *That Hideous Strength,* Merlin's magic comes from J.R.R. Tolkien's fictional land of men and elves, Numénor. The elves in *The Lord of the Rings* speak of Numénor as a lost kingdom from the distant past. Tolkien himself considered the story of Numénor's fall as his own re-telling of the myth of Atlantis. To find more about Numénor, see Tolkien's *The Silmarillion.*

Notable Characters and Creatures

The space trilogy contains several notable characters, creatures, and places. Use this section as your reference to identify and understand who they are and in which books they appear.

Major characters in the trilogy

The following are characters who play significant roles throughout the series:

- ✔ **Elwin Ransom:** The main character and hero of *Out of the Silent Planet* and *Perelandra* and an important force for good in *That Hideous Strength*.

  Ransom's name is perhaps the most significant in the trilogy. In *Perelandra,* he becomes a "ransom" for the Lady. Additionally, an *eldil* remarks on the similarity of his first name, "His name is Elwin, friend of the *eldila.*" Later, in *That Hideous Strength,* Ransom takes the name of Mr. Fisher-King as a tribute to a saintly aunt of that name. (The Fisher King is a figure from Arthurian legend who had a wound that wouldn't heal. Ransom too has a wound that doesn't heal after his battle with Weston in *Perelandra.*)

  Ransom is considered a fictional portrait of J.R.R. Tolkien. (See Chapter 3 for more on the friendship between Tolkien and Lewis.)

- ✔ **Edward Weston:** A scientist from Cambridge who is the chief villain in *Out of the Silent Planet* and *Perelandra.* In *Perelandra,* he becomes Satan's tool for tempting the Lady and eventually is possessed by Satan himself (being called the "Un-Man" at that point). Weston's killed by Ransom on Perelandra.

  The name Weston may have some connection to the fact that in Homer's *Odyssey* the land of the dead is reached by sailing west. Another possibility is that his name has something to do with Oswald Spengler's widely read and deeply pessimistic book, *The Decline of the West,* published prior to Lewis's work on the space trilogy. As a point of contrast, in *The Chronicles of Narnia,* the East symbolizes goodness — Aslan's country is in the utter east.

- ✔ **Dick Devine:** A major villain in *Out of the Silent Planet* and *That Hideous Strength.* Later known as Lord Feverstone, Devine's an entrepreneur and Fellow of Bracton College and is powerful within N.I.C.E. (National Institute of Coordinated Experiments). Devine's name is ironic because he's as far from "divine" as anyone can be.

- ✔ **Maleldil:** Creator and Sustainer of the universe; he's symbolic of Jesus Christ. In the space trilogy, Maleldil assumed human form on Earth as Jesus Christ. Christ's sacrificial death brought salvation not only to humans but for all the universe's creatures. (Perelandra and Malacandra's great hymn to Maleldil is a triumphant vindication of the planet Earth.) Because of Maleldil's assumption of human form, Earth is "the center of all worlds." By blending Himself with mortal dust, Maleldil imbues all creation with Himself.

Representing God the Father, Maleldil's father is called the "Old One" and is reminiscent of Narnia's silent but ever-present Emperor-Beyond-the-Sea.

The name Maleldil means "The Lord:" *Mal* is a definite article like "the," and *eldil* can be defined as "lord or ruler."

✔ *Eldila:* Holy spiritual beings, like angels, who aren't bound by time and space. They can speak without being physically present, and they can take on many forms. Like angels, *eldila* can be either good or evil. Good *eldila* come in different orders: Some are messengers, others visit Earth to guard it, and some are even patrons of their own planets. The evil *eldila* of Earth also seem to have various ranks; the entities that terrify Lewis in *Perelandra* on his way to Ransom's cottage are apparently lesser beings than those that possess Weston in *Perelandra* and the Head in *That Hideous Strength.*

Eldila most often look like a flame hovering in the air or as "concentric wheels moving within one another." This symbolism is similar to that used in the first chapter of Ezekiel, in which angels appear as wheels within wheels. In *Out of the Silent Planet,* a *hross* says of *eldila,* "Light is instead of blood for them."

Eldila often cause fear when they appear, which is similar to angelic appearances in the Bible. When, for example, an angel appeared announcing the birth of Christ, the shepherds were scared stiff. Beholding the seraphim, all Old Testament prophet Isaiah could say was "Woe is me! I am lost." Similarly, *eldila,* even benevolent ones, are terrifying. When Ransom perceives that Meldilorn is full of *eldila,* he's profoundly uneasy. In *Perelandra,* when Lewis first experiences the presence of an *eldil,* he wants to be far, far, away.

✔ **Oyarsa:** The title of the *eldila* who governs a planet. Speaking of the Oyarsa of Malacandra, a *sorn* tells Ransom, "Oyarsa does not die . . . and he does not breed. He is the one of his kind who was put into Malacandra to rule when Malacandra was made. His body is not like ours, nor yours, it is hard to see and the light goes through it . . . he is the greatest of the *eldila.*"

Because of its fallen state, Earth is the only planet without an Oyarsa. Satan, the original Oyarsa of Earth, is now called the Dark Oyarsa of Thulcandra.

Out of the Silent Planet

Out of the Silent Planet contains several creatures from Malacandra:

- ✔ *Hrossa:* Large, black creatures with skin like seals. They're good at making music and hunting. (The singular is *hross*.)

- ✔ *Sorns (or séroni):* Tall, skinny creatures with legs covered in feathers. Devoted to science, they're the most intellectual race on Malacandra.

- ✔ *Pfifltriggi:* Small, frog-like creatures with long arms who are fond of making things.

- ✔ **Hnau:** A term that refers to the three intelligent species of Malacandra: *hrossa, sorns,* and *pfifltriggi.*

- ✔ **Hyoi:** A *hross* who makes friends with Ransom but is ultimately killed by Weston and Devine.

- ✔ **Augray:** A *sorn* who serves as Ransom's host.

Perelandra

In *Perelandra*, C.S. Lewis introduces three new characters that prove important to the overall story:

- ✔ **Lewis:** The story's narrator. The character Lewis seems to be C.S. Lewis himself.

- ✔ **The Lady:** Plays an Eve-like role in the story; also known as The Queen and Tinidril.

- ✔ **The King:** Plays an Adam-like role in the story; also known as Tor.

Malacandra's inescapable hierarchy

Just as *The Chronicles of Narnia* has an implicit hierarchy of humans, talking animals, and dumb animals, so too does Malacandra. Therefore, when the *sorns* discover that Earth has no Oyarsa, they attribute human evils to a lack of order. They reason, "Beasts must be ruled by *hnau,* and *hnau* by *eldila,* and *eldila* by Maleldil."

The solar system (Fields of Arbol)

If you aren't fluent in Old Solar, you can use this chart to help you untangle the space trilogy cosmos. *Arbol,* by the way, is the Old Solar word for the Sun.

Planet	Old Solar name	Attribute
Mercury	Viritrilbia	Language
Venus	Perelandra	Charity

Earth (also called Tellus)	Thulcandra (Silent Planet)	Bentness
Moon	Sulva	Bentness
Mars	Malacandra	Courage
Jupiter	Glund	Majesty
Saturn	Lurga	Time

That Hideous Strength

That Hideous Strength introduces several noteworthy organizations and people, including the following:

- **N.I.C.E.:** The evil National Institute for Coordinated Experiments.

- **St. Anne's:** The headquarters of the Company of Logres, a set of friends Ransom gathers around him to combat the evil at N.I.C.E.

- **Jane Studdock:** The heroine who's married to Mark Studdock. Her name is a play on her personality because she thinks of herself as a "plain Jane."

- **Mark Studdock:** A sociologist who becomes entangled with N.I.C.E. at Belbury.

- **Camilla Denniston:** Lives, along her husband Arthur (a colleague of Mark's), with Ransom at St. Anne's. Camilla's name is reminiscent of Vergil's Camilla, a heroic warrior-maiden.

- **MacPhee:** A skeptical Ulster Scot at St. Anne's. He refuses to believe in anything supernatural, but his name actually means "son of the Dark Fairy." (MacPhee's mentioned in passing in *Perelandra.*)

- **Curry:** Sub-Warden and ringleader of the power-hungry "Progressive Element" at Bracton College.

- **The Head:** Director of N.I.C.E.; the Head is actually the severed head of a murderer, being kept alive by tubes and machinery.

- **Miss Hardcastle:** Head of the N.I.C.E. Institutional Police; also known as the Fairy.

Eldila and the Olympian gods

While in Meldilorn, Ransom's attention is drawn by what looks a carved map of the universe. On the map, each of the planets has an *eldil:* Mercury's holds a trumpet, and Venus's is distinctly female. These details aren't extraneous — in *That Hideous Strength,* it's revealed that the *eldila* of the planets have earthly and inferior forms, the pagan gods of Greece and Rome.

The ancients believed that the immortals lived along the Milky Way, so it's no coincidence that we call the planets by the names of Roman gods. Lewis makes good use of this connection by making each planet's *eldil* a Christian incarnation of the pagan god it's named for. Thus Venus, for example, originally the goddess of sexual love, becomes a patron of marriage and of charity in its deepest sense. By the same token, the bloodthirsty war-god Mars is a mere shadow of the guardian of planets, Malacandra.

Exploring Sin, Temptation, and Alternative Realities

The presence of evil in the world serves as an underlying theme of the space trilogy. Lewis not only creates a picture of what sin is like on Earth but also explores the idea of what happens when pristine and pure planets are exposed to sin and temptation. This section explores the issue of evil in the space trilogy.

Revealing the nature of sin

In *Out of the Silent Planet,* Ransom views a map of the universe that depicts planet Earth as mutilated. According to the book, "The ball was there, but where the flame-like figure should have been, a deep depression of irregular shape had been cut as if to erase it." Oyarsa reveals to Ransom that the Oyarsa of Thulcandra (Earth) somehow became "bent" (wicked). War in Heaven ensued, and the Bent One was driven back to Earth, which was shut off from communication with other planets. This story is a Malacandran rendering of Satan's rebellion against God.

The Incarnation and Crucifixion of Christ are also hinted at in this interview when Oyarsa tells Ransom he's sure Maleldil wouldn't abandon Earth. Oyarsa explains, "There are stories among us that He has taken strange counsel and dared terrible things, wrestling with the Bent One on Thulcandra."

Notice the usage of "bent" in both contexts. The Old Solar word for evil is "bent," which reflects Lewis's understanding of the true nature of sin. The New Testament Greek verb *hamartano,* regularly translated as "to sin," literally means something more like "to fall short" or "to miss the mark." So, Lewis recognizes that many acts of sin aren't necessarily bad in and of themselves. Instead, they become sinful when they miss God's mark and are insufficiently good or obedient.

In *Out of the Silent Planet,* Augray underscores the prideful nature of sin as well. When he hears about the sin taking place back on Thulcandra, his explanation is that "every one of them wants to be a little Oyarsa himself."

Coming to a pristine planet near you

In *Out of the Silent Planet,* Ransom arrives on Malacandra and discovers that because of its fallen state, Earth, which is nicknamed "the silent planet," is the only planet not in direct communication with its maker. In contrast to Earth's sinful beings, the other planets' inhabitants are innocent and don't understand evil.

In the real world, Christians believe that sin and evil entered the scene when Adam and Eve sinned in the Garden of Eden. In *Out of the Silent Planet,* Lewis imagines what would happen if evil from Earth were introduced into the pure world of Malacandra. The result is that Malacandra's indirectly affected by the Earth's sin.

This theme of the introduction of evil continues in *Perelandra.* Whereas Malacandra is an old world damaged by Earth's sin, Perelandra is a brand-new world: All its history lies in the future. Therefore, *Perelandra* is able to pose the following questions: What if Eve had never given in to the serpent's persuasion? What would a world be like if evil had never won?

Imagining an alternative reality to the Garden of Eden

At the heart of *Perelandra* is Lewis's alternative reality, imagining a world in which its Eve is able to resist temptation when confronted by a tempter. However, in this situation, Ransom is called upon by Maleldil to play a critical role in achieving this victory.

If the earthly Eve was given any knowledge that might have saved her, she apparently ignored it. Perelandra's Lady, however, delights in learning. For Lewis, ignorance and innocence are different things. Innocence isn't a bad thing, but ignorance is potentially perilous. In his 1939 sermon "Learning in Wartime," Lewis emphasizes this point: "To be ignorant and simple now — not to be able to meet our enemies on their own ground — would be to throw down our weapons." As soon as Perelandra's threatened by Weston, knowledge becomes the principal weapon against the forces of evil. Until Ransom's arrival, the Lady knows very little, though all of it good and true. With Ransom and aided by Maleldil, she discovers the nature of time, Earth's terrible history, and the evanescence of mortal races. This knowledge gives her the wisdom to choose well, and learning doesn't damage her innocence.

Weston enters the scene and tries to manipulate the Lady by declaring that he has come to believe in something he calls the Life-Force, which is both God and Satan. This belief is reminiscent of Manichaeanism, a philosophy popular in the early 20th century which touted the idea that God and Satan had equal power and that neither could predominate. (Lewis also discusses Manichaeanism in *The Pilgrim's Regress.*) Weston says openly that he himself is the dark side of the Life-Force, and for once, he speaks the truth.

Weston tries to persuade the Lady to yearn for the forbidden land and envy Earth women, who (he says) are wiser, more beautiful, and more beloved than she. The Lady isn't convinced: The Tempter is appealing to her vanity, but she has none. The serpent in the Garden of Eden tells Eve that knowledge will make her like God: "You will be like gods, knowing good and evil." (Genesis 3:5). Like the serpent, Weston tells the Lady that knowledge and growth come from disobedience. The Lady, however, is a more complex person than Eve. She can't be tempted by this old line because she knows that, for her world, she's already a goddess (at least potentially). Weston's most dangerous arguments are ones that strike at her wish to be good, her love for the King, and her innocent and virtuous delight in her own beauty.

A crux is reached when she's enticed to adorn herself with clothing and to accept the present of a mirror. Ransom urges the Lady to resist but isn't winning the debate. He understands that the tempter can't be stopped with mere words.

Ransom is afraid because he knows that by physically attacking the creature Weston has become, he'll probably lose his life. Maleldil's voice tells him: "It is not for nothing you are called Ransom." Later, the stakes rise much higher when Maleldil says, "My name is also Ransom."

The battle is every bit as awful as Ransom has dreaded, and he suffers, among other injuries, a terrible, incurable wound in his heel. It's significant that ultimately, before he can kill the creature, he must make another difficult decision. Temptation is universal, even for a planet's savior. Jesus, in the Garden of Gethsemane, prays even at the ninth hour that the cup be taken from him. (Chapter 18 provides Lewis's perspective on the Garden of Gethsemane prayer.) Even though Ransom's assailed by an influx of feelings of despair and meaninglessness, he forces himself to attack Weston one final time.

Christianity in the space trilogy

In addition to the underlying Christian symbolism, Christianity — by name — is never very far from the surface in the space trilogy. When the pious Ransom flirts with idea of suicide on Malacandra in *Out of the Silent Planet,* he hopes for forgiveness. In *Perelandra,* Ransom prays for Weston's soul. Then, just before hurling a stone at Weston in their great battle, he utters: "In the name of the Father and of the Son and of the Holy Ghost, here goes — I mean Amen."

In *That Hideous Strength,* when the time comes to confront Merlin, who may or may not be friendly, Ransom refuses to send MacPhee and instead chooses the older Dr. Dimble, who is a believer. If Merlin proves hostile, he advises Dimble, "You must rely on your Christianity. Say your prayers and keep your will fixed in the will of Maleldil." Jane Studdock, too, is exhorted to accept Maleldil as her guide. Even the skeptical MacPhee's last words to Ransom are "God bless you."

Ransom's incurably wounded heel resonates on several levels. The Arthurian Fisher King Anfortas, who was connected to the Holy Grail, had a wound that couldn't be healed. And even further back than Anfortas is Philoctetes, who lived in incurable agony but without whose bow Troy couldn't have been defeated. Like Philoctetes, Ransom is wounded by the bite of a serpent, but while Philoctetes possessed the key to a city's destruction, Ransom's wounding results in the salvation of a world.

Ransom's courage has its reward; thanks to his aid, the Lady, now called Queen Tinidril, makes a wise choice: She doesn't yield to temptation. Whereas the actions of Eve brought disaster upon Adam and on all his descendents, the actions of Tinidril give Tor, the King, his kingdom. The patron *eldil* of Perelandra blesses the two and puts the whole planet into their keeping — they're revealed as the planet's Oyarsa. Because of the Lady's wise choice, Perelandra becomes a paradise that will never be lost.

Exploring Language in the Space Trilogy

Language, always a fascinating field of study for the academic Lewis, is a key to understanding the whole of the space trilogy. It's no accident that Ransom's a philologist; his mastery of Old Solar saves Malacandra, Perelandra, and, eventually, Earth. Also, good and evil characters make themselves known by their speech, such as Weston's appearance to the Lady in *Perelandra.*

Believing that Heaven is on the side of simple truths and clarity, Lewis cares a great deal about good prose, even going so far as to criticize St. Paul's flaws as a writer; in *Reflections on the Psalms,* Lewis writes, "I cannot be the only reader who has wondered why God, having given him so many gifts, withheld from him (what would to us seem so necessary for the first Christian theologian) that of lucidity and orderly exposition." Music and poetry belong to Heaven as well (in the trilogy, the unfallen *hrossa* are singers and poets). Hell, on the other hand, delights in obscurity, deception, and meaningless babble. Noise and chaos, selective deafness, and euphemism all belong on the side of the Devil.

In this section, you explore the ways in which communication and language are used for evil and good in the space trilogy.

Language as a tool for evil

In the space trilogy, Earth languages reflect the fallen state of the planet. For example, in *Perelandra,* when Ransom finds his experiences hard to describe, Lewis comments, "Of course, I realize it's all rather too vague for you to put into words." Ransom responds, "On the contrary, it is words that are vague . . . it's too *definite* for language."

Yet, Earth languages are more than just inadequate: They're also well suited for Satan's purposes. Lewis expresses this thought in *The Screwtape Letters* when Screwtape writes, "We have contrived that their very language should be all smudge and blur."

To Lewis, jargon and bombast are not only aesthetically offensive, but they're actually tools of evil. At best, they impede communication, and at worst, they take the place of communication entirely. In *That Hideous Strength,* communication is used for evil in two ways:

- ✔ **Propaganda.** Mark Studdock composes propagandistic editorials to justify the riots that N.I.C.E. causes in the surrounding countryside. Interestingly, Lewis has Mark do more than merely twist the truth: He's also committing a sin against language itself, writing dishonesties in a dishonest way. The glee that he takes in reading them is a sure sign of his deplorable spiritual state: "The more often he read the articles, the better he liked them."

- ✔ **Confusion.** "Confuse the wicked, O Lord, confound their speech," wrote the Psalmist. Lewis does just that to his wicked characters in *That Hideous Strength.* Wither, the Deputy Director of N.I.C.E., is capable of using speech merely for the sake of avoiding communication. He can talk for hours without saying anything at all; in addition, he contradicts himself, often in the same sentence. Wither repeatedly tells other characters that failures to obey and failures to disobey (by showing flexibility and independent initiative) are both liable to punishment. This truth is so cloaked in equivocation, re-phrasings, ill-linked dependent clauses, and prudent retrenchments that the message is almost unintelligible. This kind of speech is a particularly diabolical form of deceit because it takes genuine information of a damning sort and cloaks it in so much noise that the message is drowned out.

In the book's climactic scene, Wither and his staff finally lose all power to speak intelligibly: "We all — er — most steeply rebut the defensible, though, I trust, lavatory Aspasia which gleams to have selected our redeemed inspector this deceiving." The gift they abuse is finally taken away.

Taking on heavenly speech

Lewis reveals his understanding of the qualities that language takes on when it is in line with God. Three such qualities are

- ✔ **Simplicity and clarity.** Old Solar, the language of Heaven, reveals a great deal about Lewis's thoughts on communication and language. He likes prose to be simple and clear; speech need not, after all, be elaborate to be both beautiful and poetic. The vocabulary of Old Solar is relatively limited (but then, so is that of Homeric Greek). However, Old Solar can express great profundities; look, for example, at the grand hymn at the end of *Perelandra* or at the *hrossa's* dirge for Hyoi in *Out of the Silent Planet*. What Old Solar *can't* express is vagueness, pomposity, and meaningless abstractions, all of which are evil. Thus, in *Out of the Silent Planet*, when Ransom acts as an interpreter for Weston, the truth comes out:

  Weston continued, 'Life is greater than any system of morality; her claims are absolute . . .' 'He says,' began Ransom, 'that living creatures are stronger than the question of whether an act is bent or good — no, that cannot be right — he says it is better to be alive and bent than to be dead — no — he says, he says — I cannot say what he says, Oyarsa, in your language.'

- ✔ **Wittiness.** All his life, Lewis was aware of the connection between brilliant speech and brilliant thought. He expresses this belief in the space trilogy. In particular, one of the most pleasing scenes in *That Hideous Strength* is when the Oyarsa of Viritrilbia (Mercury), who's the patron of language, descends upon St. Anne's and the company of Logres suddenly becomes wonderfully witty and clever. They delight in "plays on thoughts, paradoxes, fancies, anecdotes, theories laughingly advanced yet (on consideration) well worth taking seriously."

✔ **Creativity.** Speech need not be simple to be heavenly; another character-istic of heavenly speech is that it betrays the divine exuberance of the mind working at its creative best. For example, Lewis writes that Mother Dimble had never heard "such eloquence, such melody . . . such toppling structures of double meaning, such skyrockets of metaphor and allusion." Whereas speech at Belbury is dry, flaccid, and obscure, Viritrilbia gives language energy, wit, and poetry.

Progressivism: That Hideous Change

In *That Hideous Strength,* progress is an underlying theme evident in the people and events surrounding Bracton College. Lewis, an academic for most of his life, was intimately familiar with college politics and their potential for harm. He was also a teacher of undergraduates and therefore never had an opportunity to forget how intimidating institutional life can be for newcom-ers. Young people are both easily frightened and easily impressed. Insecurity and vanity make people willing to make all kinds of compromises for the sake of fellowship, even the worst kind of fellowship. Mark Studdock is no fool, but he's young, new to Bracton College, and open to evil influences. Additionally, he has been progressively educated:

> *It must be remembered that in Mark's mind hardly one rag of noble thought, either Christian or pagan, had a secure lodging. His education had been neither scientific nor classical — merely "Modern." The severities of both abstraction and high human tradition had passed him by . . .*

Bracton's faculty is a mixed bag but is dominated by "Curry and his gang," who think of themselves as "the Progressive Element." The gang, all scholars in new fields like economics and sociology, disdain history, architecture, literature, religion, and ordinary human decency. Hence, they're willing to sell Bragdon Wood, the ancient heart of their college, to N.I.C.E., which plans to tear it up.

Confronted with change, Mark is especially vulnerable to the desire to be a member of the Progressive Element at Bracton. After all, they're the powerful people who hired him. But his vulnerability rests not only on the fact that his career depends on their approval but also on his longing to be a member of a set that is rich, glamorous, and powerful. Lewis's thoughts on these issues are also apparent in his 1944 sermon, "The Inner Ring;" it's a serious medita-tion on the problems that come when we give way to the temptation to enjoy the "delicious sense of secret intimacy" that the wrong kind of fellowship offers so beguilingly (see the "Fellowships: For good or evil" sidebar for more). Changes at Bracton only make the temptation stronger for Mark.

Flip to Chapters 10 and 11 for discussions on how progress, change, and fash-ion can be bad things.

Fellowships: For good or evil

That Hideous Strength centers on four fellowships: two on the side of God and two on the side of Satan:

✔ The first fellowship is Jane and Mark Studdock's marriage, which has great potential for good.

✔ The second fellowship is the company of Logres, a highly assorted but harmonious and faithful band of people and animals who are all summoned by Maleldil and followers of Ransom (who at this point is going by the name of Mr. Fisher-King).

✔ The third fellowship is Mark's college, Bracton, which is an evil parody of what a college ought to be. Mark's social life there does much damage to his marriage.

✔ The fourth fellowship is N.I.C.E., an utterly diabolical privatized scientific research institution that's full of backbiting and treachery.

Chapter 13

There and Back Again: A Pilgrim's Tale

Several years ago, I rode my bicycle from California to Massachusetts. That's 3,400 miles in 29 days. The trip was grueling, but from the start, one deep longing kept me pedaling mile after mile — the thrill of dipping my front tire in the Atlantic Ocean as a symbolic end to the journey.

Somewhere along the way, however, something in me snapped . . . maybe it was the endless heat, the day-long mountain climbs, or the nasty headwinds across the plains. Whatever it was, my dreamy completion of the ride morphed into something darker. Instead of simply dipping my tire in the Atlantic, nothing gave me greater pleasure than the thought of arriving on the beach, getting off my bike, stomping on it again and again, and heaving the two-wheeled torture device into the ocean. Fortunately, when the end of the trip came, I was restrained — albeit by several people in white suits — from carrying out this darker dream. (Had I been forced to cycle immediately back to California and retrace my route, however, I suspect my dark side would have prevailed and my bike would have been fish food.)

C.S. Lewis didn't bike cross-country, but he did take a spiritual journey that had more detours, pit stops, and potty breaks than my bike trip! In the end, he chronicled his "there and back again" experiences in the allegorical book *The Pilgrim's Regress*. In this chapter, you explore *The Pilgrim's Regress* and discover how to appreciate one of Lewis's more challenging reads without resorting to stomping on your copy and throwing it out to sea.

Background: Lewis's Two-Week Brain Dump

When Lewis converted to Christianity in 1931 (see Chapter 3), he felt compelled to write about his spiritual journey. His attempts were unsuccessful because he wasn't sure of the best literary approach to take in order to capture the various issues that he dealt with along the way. Then, in September of 1932, Lewis went on a two-week vacation to Ireland to visit his close friend Arthur Greeves. Maybe Greeves inspired him, or maybe Lewis was so bored that he had nothing else to do but write. Whatever the reason, in a sudden rush of inspiration, Lewis penned *The Pilgrim's Regress* during his holiday. "It spurted out so suddenly," recalled Lewis to Greeves in a letter written soon after his visit.

Initial criticism

Greeves played an important part in the writing process for *The Pilgrim's Regress*. Not only did Lewis stay at his friend's home while writing the book, but also in those pre-Inklings days, Lewis bounced many ideas off Greeves as he edited the work. That's not to say that Greeves really saw eye-to-eye with Lewis on how the book should be written. In fact, Arthur had three main complaints:

- ✔ Too many Greek and Latin quotes
- ✔ Not simple enough
- ✔ Not written in the style he'd expected

Lewis was reluctant to bend much to Greeves's criticisms. For example, until his publisher forced him to do so, Lewis refused to remove the Greek and Latin quotes because he considered them important to the story. He didn't want to "dumb down" the book, either. Writing to Greeves on December 17, 1932, Lewis notes, "The *intellectual side* of my conversion was *not* simple and I can describe only what I know!" As for Greeves's style complaint, Lewis believed that his more popular style of writing worked better than the classical style that Greeves expected. However, in a humorous note in December of 1932, Lewis wrote to his friend that there are many sentences in the book that are "bad by *any* theory of style."

Lewis dedicated *The Pilgrim's Regress* to Greeves. In fact, he quipped to his friend before its publication: "So if the book is a ghastly failure I shall always say 'Ah it's this Arthur business.'"

The public's reaction

The Pilgrim's Regress was published in May of 1933. Lewis's publisher pushed for an illustrated version, but Lewis argued against it, thinking the additional cost to readers' wallets would be more than anyone would be willing to pay. However, perhaps his book could have used some visual assistance in those early days, because it initially sold just over 600 copies of the 1,000 printed. Lewis was "greeved" (sorry, I couldn't resist!) by the lack of success, but he was less devastated than when his poetry works (see Chapter 2) tanked in years prior. Maybe his reaction wasn't as strong because he'd spent relatively little time on the book. Or perhaps Lewis was beginning to realize that, as a Christian, he was called to faithfulness to God, not worldly success.

Lewis may have been brilliant, but he wouldn't have made it on Madison Avenue. His original "catchy" title for the book was: *The Pilgrim's Regress, or Pseudo-Bunyan's Periplus: An Allegory Apology for Christianity, Reason, and Romanticism.* Fortunately, his publisher had the common sense to drop the "*or Pseudo-Bunyan's Periplus*" phrase. (If you're curious, "periplus" means circumnavigation.)

Although Lewis was Anglican, a Roman Catholic publisher became interested in publishing *The Pilgrim's Regress* in 1935. As pleased as Lewis may have been with the renewed interest, he was irked to discover that the text written for the inside cover of this publisher's version stated that the story "begins in Puritania (Mr. Lewis was brought up in Ulster)." An obviously frustrated Lewis wrote to Arthur Greeves in December of 1935 that this comment implied "that the book is an attack on my own country and my own religion."

"A Kind of a Bunyan Up To Date"

In the book, C.S. Lewis presents the story of his conversion to Christianity in the form of an allegory. As the name *The Pilgrim's Regress* suggests, it's written in the spirit of John Bunyan's classic work, *The Pilgrim's Progress.* As Lewis expressed in a proposal to his publisher, this book is "a kind of a Bunyan up to date." Although the allegory is loosely based on Lewis's personal journey, not every part of the story is meant to be autobiographical.

An *allegory* is a literary device that an author can use to represent an abstract idea or real person in the form of a fictional person, place, or animal. (Flip to Chapter 6 for full coverage of this and other literary devices employed by Lewis.) So, in the book, characters named Wisdom and Virtue represent, quite obviously, the qualities bearing the same names. The allegorical style that Lewis uses in *The Pilgrim's Regress* was commonly used by medieval writers such as Bunyan.

The Pilgrim's Regress focuses on a man, named John, who lives an empty life in a land called Puritania. After seeing a vision of a beautiful island, an intense longing fills him and makes John immediately want to try and find it. "I know now what I want, " says John. (The search for the Island symbolizes Lewis's lifelong quest for Joy, which is explained in Chapter 2.) His odyssey leads him to many different detours and destinations, but he encounters false joy in one place after another. Physical sins, spiritual sins, and various philosophical movements all become dead ends and never fulfill him.

Along the way, John comes across Reason, Mr. Wisdom, and Mother Kirk (that's reason, wisdom, and biblical Christianity), and he finally discovers the Island when he quits trying to save himself. As the journey ends, John returns to his parents' cottage in Puritania, where he's able to live with the Joy he's found.

Lewis's philosophical path to Christianity isn't the typical road for a person living in this day and age. He waded through a series belief systems before finding truth in Christianity. Lewis moved:

1. From *popular realism,* a movement common in the late 1800s and early 1900s that was a reaction against Romanticism of the past. Proponents focused on "what's real" in the here and now. Influencers were such people as Freud, Marx, and Darwin.

2. To *philosophical idealism,* which was a reaction against realism. This philosophy argues that matter doesn't exist on its own but is purely a product of one's mind.

3. To *Pantheism,* a worldview that claims "God" is part of the universe and can be found in everything.

4. To *Theism,* the general belief that a distinct God exists and is separate from his creation.

5. To *Christianity,* which claims that the God that exists came to the earth as a man in Jesus Christ.

John encounters these broad worldviews in *The Pilgrim's Regress,* but he also finds many related philosophies and persons along the way. In particular, he argues against or satires modernism, materialism, Freud and psychoanalysis, Anglo Catholicism (a movement within the Anglican Church), and even T.S. Elliot.

If you've read some of Lewis's later works, such as *Mere Christianity,* you may notice that the tone of *The Pilgrim's Regress* is noticeably sharper, much like a young, energetic boxer ready to throw punches. Lewis developed a much more conciliatory style as he grew in his faith.

Regress: Does the Pilgrim Backslide?

The term "regress" in the title *The Pilgrim's Regress* leads some readers to believe that the book is about a Christian backsliding after his conversion. Actually, Lewis is making the point that when you become a Christian, you aren't simply shuffled off to heaven by a host of angels. You have to go back to the real world after you make a decision for Jesus Christ.

John's regress, therefore, is his retracing of the steps he took after discovering the Island. But this time, things are different for him. Not only does he have a Guide (symbolizing the Holy Spirit), but also he can see the false destinations for what they really are. John's "eyes are altered," and he sees "nothing now but realities," proving, as the Guide tells him, "The country will look very different on the return journey."

When you think of John's regress, consider a contemporary example of regress from the 1998 film *The Truman Show*. In this film, Truman, the main character played by Jim Carrey, unknowingly lives his entire life in Seahaven, an artificial town that's actually one giant television studio. The film ends with Truman discovering the truth and exiting Seahaven through a door to the real world. Now, suppose Truman were to return to Seahaven. He would see his hometown for what it really was (a television studio) and recognize the town inhabitants as actors, nothing more. In the same way, John's regress back through the same lands he journeyed before is much like Truman returning to Seahaven. When John travels through the lands in which he once was tempted, he sees right through the fakeness, hollowness, and smoke and mirrors.

Overcoming Stumbling Blocks As You Read the Book

Some Lewis books, such as *Miracles* or *The Abolition of Man*, are challenging for many readers because they dive headfirst into dense philosophical issues. *The Pilgrim's Regress*, in contrast, is written in a readable style that's fairly easy to understand. Nonetheless, many modern readers encounter four major stumbling blocks as they work their ways through this book:

- ✔ Its classic allegorical form
- ✔ References to outdated philosophical movements
- ✔ The journey's complexity
- ✔ Confusion over what Mother Kirk symbolizes

Before getting frustrated and abandoning the book altogether, read the following sections, which are intended to help you work through the problem issues you're likely to encounter as you read *The Pilgrim's Regress*.

Swallowing a heavy dose of allegory

Some allegories are subtle undercurrents of the narrative. For these books, you can take note of the allegory or else completely ignore it. Other allegories, however, more or less hit you over the head with their symbolism. Both *The Pilgrim's Regress* and its medieval model *The Pilgrim's Progress* fall into the latter camp. The "heavy" allegorical style of *The Pilgrim's Regress* is one of those things that people either love or hate. If you enjoy the obvious symbolism of characters with names like Wisdom or Mr. Enlightenment and places called Thrill and the Valley of Humiliation, then you'll do just fine. If these things distract you from getting into the story, then you'll want to do your best to downplay the names as you read and focus your attention on the storyline.

Some of the characters in the story, such as Contemplation, Wisdom, and Virtue, represent abstract ideas that aren't always easy to distinguish from one another. In these cases, you may want to have a dictionary handy (the older the better) to help you decipher the subtle differences in meaning.

That's so last century

Unlike nearly all of Lewis's other works, *The Pilgrim's Regress* can seem dated. Many of the specific philosophies that Lewis argues against, such as neo-Hegelian Idealism or Neo-Classicism, were all the rage during the early 20th century but have long since fallen out of favor. In addition, his contemporaries in the 1930s would have instantly recognized several people he alludes to, such as Benedict Spinoza, George Bernard Shaw, D.H. Lawrence, and Edith Sitwell. But many of these references fly over the heads of today's average readers.

When you encounter philosophies or people that you're unfamiliar with, use the section "Making Sense of the People and Places" later in this chapter as a guide. Some editions of *The Pilgrim's Regress* contain headlines at the top of each page; the headline, which is a running one-line commentary pointing out the page's symbolism, may help you make sense of a particular person or movement mentioned in the text. If all else fails, punt and skip to the next stop along John's journey.

Getting travel fatigue

John's trip to the Island isn't a straight, five-stop trek directly to his destination. Instead, his quest is more of a zigzag trip here and there; he makes stops along the way and takes a multitude of detours and diversions. And, then, just when you think he's done, John finds out he has to go back again to Puritania! As a reader, you may feel some travel fatigue thanks to so many stops, especially if you don't understand how each stop fits into the bigger picture.

If you start to get "pilgrim's lag," simply focus on each stop without trying to make sense of how it all fits together. What's more, use the maps that many editions of *The Pilgrim's Regress* supply on the front or back covers to help you follow the logistics of John's journey.

Sorting through the mother of all confusions

Perhaps the allegorical reference that causes the most trouble for readers is Mother Kirk. Mother Kirk symbolizes the Church, more specifically biblical, historical Christianity as a whole. Many early readers, however, mistakenly assumed that Lewis was referring to the Roman Catholic Church, and thus John's return to Mother Kirk was taken as an indication that Lewis was embracing Catholicism.

This message definitely wasn't Lewis's intent. He explains in a letter to Dom Bede Griffiths in January of 1936 that his overemphasis on Mother Kirk was purely for literary reasons, not theological ones: "I did not want to keep introducing the Lord Himself, and 'Christianity' is not a plausible name for a character. Hence the name, and some of the functions, of my Mother Kirk — adopted clumsily for convenience." Lewis realized after the fact that this allegory led to confusion over his view of the role of the worldwide Church.

When you encounter Mother Kirk as you read *The Pilgrim's Regress,* try replacing her name with "biblical Christianity" or, if that's too vague, think of the worldwide Christian Church, not a specific branch of Christianity.

Tips for the weary reader

If you struggle through *The Pilgrim's Regress,* keep in mind the following tips to get the most out of the book.

✔ **Use the headlines, but only as needed.** In later editions of *The Pilgrim's Regress,* Lewis added headlines to the top of the pages to help readers understand the symbolism in the story. For example, "John decides that Aesthetic Experience is the thing to pursue." The headlines can be quite useful to keep you on track, but be careful with them — they can be a major distraction to getting into the flow of the story.

In fact, reading *The Pilgrim's Regress* with headlines reminds me of watching a film with subtitles that constantly tell you what you should be noticing in the story. They may be helpful in dissecting the movie's meaning, but they don't necessarily produce a fulfilling film-going experience.

✔ **Pay special attention to the dialogue.** Even if you get lost in some of the details of John's journey, pay close attention to the dialogue. The conversations between John and the people he encounters along the way contain the heart of Lewis's message.

✔ **Mine for gold.** If you persevere through *The Pilgrim's Regress,* you'll be glad you did. In spite of the story's obstacles, nuggets of gold are just waiting to be discovered. For example, the story of the brown girls multiplying serves as a powerful metaphor to how sin gives birth to more and more sin. And the scene in which John must dive into the water rather than jump in order to reach the Island provides a perfect allegory for the Christian conversion process.

Making Sense of the People and Places

As you read through *The Pilgrim's Regress,* keep in mind the following allegorical meanings behind the book's people and places. This glossary of sorts will help you better understand John's journey:

✔ **Black hole:** Hell.

✔ **Brown girl:** The object of John's sexual lust.

According to Roger Green, Lewis's friend and biographer, the idea for brown girl may have come from a dream that Lewis had years before writing *The Pilgrim's Regress.*

✔ **Claptrap:** Fashionable, pretentious nonsense.

✔ **Clevers:** Avant-garde artists, such as Edith Sitwell and D.H. Lawrence.

✔ **Eschropolis:** "Red light" city of filth, indecency, and obscenity.

- **Grand Canyon:** The chasm that exists between humans and God due to sin.

- **Guide:** The Holy Spirit.

- **Hegeliana:** A reference to philosopher Georg Wilhelm Friedrich Hegel, who championed an idealistic philosophy.

- **Island:** The cause and object of Joy for John.

- **Landlord:** God.

- **Lilith:** The personification of a longing to be desired after rather than be beautiful; an allusion to a female spirit in Babylonian and Jewish mythology (and interestingly, as described in Chapter 7, the fictional ancestor of the White Witch in *The Chronicles of Narnia*).

- **Luxeria:** Lust.

- **Manichees:** Followers of the ancient belief that good and evil are separate but equal powers in the world.

- **Marxomanni:** Marxists.

- **Media Halfways:** Escapism.

- **Mr. Broad:** Modern or "liberal" Christian theology that denies a literal resurrection of Jesus Christ, denies a real Satan or Hell, dismisses the historicity of the Bible, and claims that all people will receive salvation.

- **Mr. Enlightenment:** 19th-century Rationalism.

- **Mr. Mammon:** Worldly riches.

- **Mr. Sensible:** Sophisticated worldliness.

- **Mother Kirk:** Biblical, historical Christianity.

- **Neo-Angular:** High Anglicans; based on T.S. Elliot.

- **Northerners:** Dogmatic people who are ruled by ideologies such as Marxism and humanism.

- **Puritania:** John's homeland; a reference to the Puritans; symbolizes organized but empty religion. The people of Puritania are "Sunday Christians," decent people who simply put on the act of being religious but actually care little about the Lord.

- **Sigismund:** Psychoanalysis; a reference to Sigmund Freud.

- **Shepherd:** God.

- **Shepherd People:** Jews.

- **Southerners:** People who are ruled by emotion, such as spiritualists, members of liberal churches, and poet D.H. Lawrence.

- **Spartiates:** Ancient Spartans known for their strict discipline and toughness.

- **Spirit of the Age:** The feeling or outlook of a specific period of time.

  In Lewis's day, *zeitgeist* was a popular term that referred to the "spirit of the age."

- **Steward:** Hypocritical religious leader and teacher.

- **Stoics:** An ancient philosophy that maintains that meaning is found by submitting yourself to "destiny." Stoics are concerned with neither suffering nor pleasure.

- **Superbia:** Pride.

- **Vertue:** Virtue.

- **Victoriana:** Symbolizes English poet Edith Sitwell, well known the early 20th century.

  In a letter to correspondent Herbert Palmer in November of 1945, Lewis writes of Edith Sitwell, "She was (or I thought she was) doing a sort of half mocking revival of the Victorian scene. I've repented about her since."

- **Zeitgeistheim:** See *Spirit of the Age*.

Chapter 14

Facing Off with an Ancient Myth: Till We Have Faces

In This Chapter

▶ Finding inspiration in a classical myth

▶ Revealing the destructive side of love

▶ Uncovering the truth in myths

Many C.S. Lewis fans turn eagerly to his last novel, *Till We Have Faces,* and turn back in disappointment. This isn't the childlike and imaginative world of Narnia; this isn't the Fields of Arbol (Lewis's name for our solar system in the space trilogy); this isn't even the edgy world of Screwtape, where demons rub shoulders with their "patients." In fact, if you didn't already know that C.S. Lewis actually wrote this novel, you may not guess that he's the author.

The setting of *Till We Have Faces* is strange: It's somewhere north (or is it east?) of ancient Greece, and the time is before the birth of Christ but otherwise unknown. And how about the strange names: the kingdom of Glome, its chief goddess Ungit, the main character Orual (pronounced, by the way, *or-you-all*)? Just when you're convinced that this is a pleasant historical novel, suddenly you meet the "the god of the wind: Westwind himself" and then the god of the Grey Mountain. And much of the second part of the novel seems to take place entirely inside Orual's head.

You're not alone if you wonder what this book is about. Is it just a piece of historical fiction set in the ancient world? Or is there more to it? In *The Chronicles of Narnia* and the space trilogy, you can see obvious Christian underpinnings, but is there any Christian subtext to this novel? In this chapter, you explore answers to these questions raised by Lewis's most unique fictional work.

Background: Rewriting an Old Myth

The story of Cupid and Psyche goes back to ancient Rome, more specifically, to the second century AD and a Latin writer named Apuleius (AD 120–190). In his most famous work (called either *Metamorphoses,* meaning "Changes," or *The Golden Ass*), a man called Lucius finds himself turned into an ass and undergoes all sorts of risqué and embarrassing adventures. At one point he's stabled inside a robbers' cave and overhears an old woman tell a kidnapped bride a "pretty story" about Cupid, the Roman god of Love, and a human princess named Psyche.

Lewis first read Apuleius's story of Cupid and Psyche when he was a young man, and it cast a spell on him for more than 35 years. In the early 1920s, he tried to write his own version — as a ballad, a play, a narrative poem, and even in poetic couplets — but it wasn't until the 1950s that Lewis was able to turn his ideas into a novel.

The book's idea came in the midst of his first ever bout of writer's block. One night in 1955, Lewis was sitting with Joy Davidman Gresham (see Chapter 2), whom he would marry the next year and to whom the novel is dedicated. They were kicking around some ideas for a story, and suddenly a new tale of Cupid and Psyche was born. Lewis wrote the first chapter the very next day.

Even though he felt it was his greatest critical failure, *Till We Have Faces* was one of Lewis's favorite works, along with *Perelandra* and *The Abolition of Man*.

A Cinderella Story through the Ugly Sister's Eyes

In the story of *Till We Have Faces,* Trom, king of Glome, has three daughters:

- **Orual,** the eldest, is so ugly that she wears a veil to cover her face.
- **Redival,** the middle daughter, is reasonably beautiful.
- **Psyche,** the youngest, has unsurpassed beauty and an unworldly, even saintly nature.

To relieve a disastrous drought upon the land, the beautiful Psyche is to be given in marriage to the Brute, the god of the Grey Mountain and son of a local mother-goddess (Ungit). Psyche is taken to the mountain and tied to a tree to await the Brute. Some days later, Orual discovers Psyche still alive, living in a valley of the mountain, married (she says) to a husband whom she's forbidden to look upon. Orual persuades her sister to gaze upon her husband's face, and Psyche does so, with disastrous consequences. Orual goes on to become queen of Glome, and at the end of her life records her story in a narrative that she calls her "indictment of the gods."

Lewis is more interested in Orual than Psyche. In one sense, *Till We Have Faces* is the story of Cinderella told from the point of view of one of the ugly stepsisters who's given a chance to plead her case.

An unreliable but sympathetic narrator

For the most part, readers are sympathetic to Orual. I say "for the most part" because, although narrators are usually given the benefit of the doubt, Orual's obsession with Psyche makes readers more and more uneasy as the story progresses. Note the prevalence of "I" in Orual's fantasy from early in the story:

> *I wanted to be a wife so that **I** could have been her real mother. **I** wanted to be a boy so that she could fall in love with **me**. **I** wanted her to be **my** full sister instead of **my** half-sister. **I** wanted her to be a slave so that **I** could set her free and make her rich.*

This line of thought may remind you of an insecure, self-absorbed person who just wants someone to love her. Strengthening the reality of Orual's obsession, consider her thoughts as she waits for Psyche to unmask her lover:

> *And after that — very, very soon after it, **I** hoped — there would be Psyche creeping through the darkness and sending a sort of whispered call ("Maia, Maia") across the stream. And **I** would be half-way over it in an instant. This time it would be **I** who helped her at the ford. She would be all weeping and dismayed as **I** folded her in **my** arms and comforted her; for now she would know who were true friends, and would love **me** again.*

From the eyes of a woman

With *Till We Have Faces,* Lewis successfully writes a first-person narrative told by a woman. Although his work has other prominent female characters — the Green Lady in *Perelandra* and Lucy in *The Chronicles of Narnia* — none are as strong and as vivid as Orual.

The novel is dedicated to Joy Davidman, who would soon become Lewis's wife (see Chapter 2). The close presence of a woman in his life and the experience of beginning a serious relationship may well have helped Lewis get into the mind of a woman and create the dynamics of Orual and her family.

When it comes to fiction, Lewis usually doesn't write in the first person; he prefers the more detached and reliable attitude of the third-person narrator. But here he cleverly has Orual tell her own story because she's a flawed human being who has been deceiving herself for years. The trick of this point of view for readers is to recognize and identify Orual's self-delusions.

Readers can identify with Orual's human inability to see her faults clearly until divine revelation shows her what she's done to those around her. Yet for all her faults, Arnom the priest writes her epitaph: "This book was written by Queen Orual of Glome, who was the most wise, just, valiant, fortunate and merciful of all the princes known in our part of the world."

A loving but destructive heroine

Love is one of the main themes of *Till We Have Faces*. Orual truly loves her younger sister, but her love is possessive and ultimately destructive. Psyche says as much after Orual resorts to emotional blackmail to get Psyche to break her promise to her husband:

> *You are indeed teaching me about kinds of love I did not know. It is like looking into a deep pit. I am not sure whether I like your kind better than hatred.*

At the end of the story, Orual meets Ansit, the widow of Bardia, Orual's greatest friend and confidant. Orual discovers that, in serving her, Bardia worked himself to death and neglected his family. Ansit describes how the queen dominated her husband:

> *Oh, Queen Orual, I begin to think you know nothing of love. Or no; I'll not say that. Yours is Queen's love, not commoners'. Perhaps you who spring from the gods love like the gods. Like the Shadowbrute. They say that loving and devouring are all one, don't they?*

Typecasting the Work: Part Historical Fiction, Part Fantasy

Historical fiction has been a popular genre of literature ever since Sir Walter Scott wrote the "Waverly" novels in the early 1800s. With *Till We Have Faces*, Lewis paints a picture of a partly civilized kingdom, called Glome, just coming into contact with the superior and more sophisticated culture of the Greeks some time around 300 BC. The three princesses have as a tutor a Greek slave (the Fox), who represents the classical Greeks with all their learning and scientific rationality. Orual is inordinately proud of her palace library with its 18 books in ancient Greek, and Orual's last wish is that her narrative be taken to Greece, presumably so that experts in knowledge and wisdom may hear her story.

Recycling names

At one point in Lewis's writing process, Psyche was to have only one older sister, named Caspian, and a handsome twin brother, named Jardis, who was "prettier than a boy would choose to be." Narnia fans will notice the similarity in names — *Caspian* is king of Narnia, while *Jardis* is very close to *Jadis,* the name of the White Witch.

Lewis never really says where Glome is. Scholars have suggested it's in the Balkans to the north of Greece, in the steppes of modern-day Ukraine, or in the mountains of Armenia. Modern historical fictions often give detailed maps and pages of appendixes and charts, but Lewis isn't so helpful. Not only is the location unclear, but the time is uncertain as well. Lewis provides a hint by placing a book by Aristotle (died in 322 BC) in the palace library, but very little ancient history makes its way into the story (for instance there's no mention of Alexander the Great or the rise of Rome).

The other side of the novel, the part that isn't a historical fiction, leans toward fantasy. Gods walk openly in the story: Psyche is rescued by the god of the Westwind, and her husband, the Brute, turns out to be the god of the Grey Mountain, who installs Psyche in a splendid palace that only she can see. In a stunning vision at the end of the novel, Orual pleads her case before the gods. As we shall see, Lewis is letting imagination and fantasy carry the story.

Unmasking the Novel's Title

The title *Till We Have Faces* wasn't Lewis's original choice for the book. As with so many of his other books, his first title idea was vetoed by his publisher. Lewis wanted to call the novel *Bareface,* the point being that only when we remove the masks we show to the world and reveal our real and bare faces can we talk to the divine and to one another. This perspective is relevant to the novel because so much depends on the veil that masks Orual's face — does it conceal exquisite ugliness or exquisite beauty? Speaking to this, Orual says:

> *The wildest stories got about as to what that veil hid . . . Some said . . . that it was frightful beyond all endurance; a pig's, bear's, cat's, or elephant's face. The best story was that I had no face at all; if you stripped off my veil you'd find emptiness. But another sort . . . said that I wore a veil because I was of*

a beauty so dazzling that if I let it be seen all the men in the world would run mad; or else that Ungit was jealous of my beauty and had promised to blast me if I went bareface.

The publisher rejected Lewis's title *Bareface,* however, because of concern that people would think the book was a Western. Ultimately, Lewis gave in and suggested *Till We Have Faces,* which comes from a very crucial passage in the second part of the novel:

I saw well why the gods do not speak to us openly, nor let us answer. Till that word can be dug out of us, why should they hear the babble that we think we mean? How can they meet us face to face till we have faces?

Read the last line out loud with emphasis on "we" — "till *we* have faces." To put the question another way, how can we have personal relationships with the divine if we don't have personalities?

We often ask God for a clear sign or a direct communication — tell us what to do, tell us what you want. But Lewis's novel illustrates through the heroine Orual that our own selves get in the way of that communication; we each interpret the world in our own ways, and until we clear the rubbish and overgrowth in our own lives, we truly can't understand a clear message from God. I especially like Lewis's phrase, "the babble that we think we mean." Communication is all about words, and we need faces and mouths to form and speak words.

Changing the Original Folktale

Ever since he first heard the story of Cupid and Psyche in the 1920s, Lewis believed that "Apuleius had got it all wrong." Therefore, when Jack sat down to write his own version, he purposefully made it different from the original. Table 14-1 summarizes the major differences between the two works.

Table 14-1	Contrasting Apuleius's "Cupid and Psyche" and Lewis's *Till We Have Faces*	
Point of Contrast	*"Cupid and Psyche"*	*Till We Have Faces*
Work as a whole	Folktale (interlude in a picaresque novel)	Serious novel with many levels
Point of view	Third-person narrative told by an old woman to a kidnapped bride	First-person narrative told by Orual
Characterization of Orual	Wicked stepsister to Psyche; acts out of jealousy	Loving stepsister to Psyche; acts out of possessive love

Point of Contrast	"Cupid and Psyche"	Till We Have Faces
Characterization of Psyche	Typical damsel in distress; not overly bright	Insightful; understands things that ordinary mortals don't
Characterization of the gods	Essentially comic; figures of fun	Deadly serious
Presence of Psyche	Center of attention throughout	Vanishes about halfway through the novel and reappears only in Orual's vision at the end
Fate of the sisters	Enticed to leap to their deaths off a cliff	Orual becomes queen; Redival marries the neighboring ruler
Role of Cupid	Major character and center of attention	Mysterious and invisible; readers hear his voice only when Psyche's palace collapses and she's sent away
Existence of Psyche's palace	Visible to Psyche's sisters	Seen only by Psyche, although Orual gets a glimpse in the dawn

If you're interested in Apuleius's version of the story of Cupid and Psyche, you can read *The Golden Ass* online at `eserver.org/books/apuleius/default.html`.

A Truthful Myth?

The subtitle of *Till We Have Faces* is *A Myth Retold*. In today's world, "myth" usually refers to something make believe, akin to a fairy tale. But, for people who study mythology, the popular conception is untrue. Myths may not always be factually true, but they raise great questions about important matters. Myths have power. They attempt to explain the universe and have an aura of magic and majesty about them. Above all, myths are about discovering truth — they attempt to lead you, the reader or the hearer, to the truth by way of symbols or metaphors.

As I explain in Chapter 3, Lewis's fascination with myth was one of the key factors in his Christian conversation. He discovered that the great Christian myth of Jesus was actually true — that God really *did* come to earth as a man and died so that those who believed in him could receive salvation.

In *Till We Have Faces,* the Fox (the slave) is a personification of Greek culture and rationality. As such, he resembles the logical side of Lewis. He writes: "'Not that this ever really happened,' the Fox said in haste. 'It's only lies of poets, lies of poets, child. Not in accordance with nature.'"

But, the Fox doesn't have all the truth, and in Orual's vision he admits that "the real gods [are] more alive and not mere thoughts nor words." Like Plato, Lewis believes that there are places where reason alone can't go, and *Till We Have Faces,* because it's about an encounter with the gods, is a story of one such place. Therefore, as you read it, react not by asking how it works but rather by surrendering your imagination to Lewis. In other words, just roll with it.

This mythical aspect of the book is what makes *Till We Have Faces* strange and uncomfortable for casual readers. For much of the story, you drift along with the facts unfolding much like an historical fiction novel. You become engrossed in the characters and affairs of Glome, Orual and her sisters, the too-rational character of the Fox, the neighboring kingdoms, and Orual's rise to power and fame. But then the gods burst into the story, the mysterious palace becomes real and visible (even if just for a moment), and Orual goes through a spiritual crisis that leads to a final judgment by the gods. Lewis's myth explores the relationship between humans and the divine, the limited nature of human understanding, and the ultimate love and forgiveness of the divine.

In describing Aslan in *The Chronicles of Narnia,* Lewis uses the concept of supposal (see Chapter 6). He explains supposal as such: "Supposing there was a world like Narnia, and supposing, like ours, it needed redemption, let us imagine what sort of Incarnation and Passion and Resurrection Christ would have there." Lewis applies this concept of supposal to the ancient myth he's retelling in *Till We Have Faces:* Suppose that before the time of Christ, the divine touched our world. This novel is Lewis's "myth" to document that encounter. He speaks of some of the novel's underlying meaning in a letter to two schoolchildren in 1957:

> *They're just human souls. Psyche has a vocation and becomes a saint. Orual lives the practical life and is, after many sins, saved. As for Redival — well, we'll all hope for the best for everyone.*

Part IV

Getting Real: Discovering Lewis's Nonfiction

The 5th Wave — By Rich Tennant

WHILE CS LEWIS PONDERS THE NATURE OF HELL, HIS DOG PONDERS THE NATURE OF HEAVEN.

TRASH

In this part . . .

Enough with such make-believe worlds as Narnia and Perelandra. In this part, it's time to *get real!* C.S. Lewis is considered by many to be the most influential Christian apologist since the Reformation. He had a knack for being able to explain and defend Christianity in a way that was a breath of fresh air for normal folks and left his challengers gasping for oxygen. In this part, you discover his major nonfiction books, including *Mere Christianity, The Problem of Pain,* and *The Abolition of Man.* Even though Lewis wrote these books over half a century ago, the discussions and arguments they contain remain astonishingly fresh and even prophetic in this postmodern, digital world.

Chapter 15

The Nagging Problem of Pain

From cradle to grave, people are barraged with pain, both physical and emotional. Babies get grouchy from diaper rash. Toddlers get boo-boos on their knees. Teenagers are bullied by other kids. Adults experience broken marriages and mid-life crises. Senior citizens suffer from arthritis and Alzheimer's. Reflecting on his life's disappointments, Westley, the hero of the 1987 film *The Princess Bride,* speaks for many when he says, "Life is pain. Anyone who says differently is selling something."

Before his conversion to Christianity, C.S. Lewis had the same jaded outlook on life as Westley expresses in this line. Several of Lewis's poems in his first published work, *Spirits in Bondage,* center on this problem of human pain and suffering. If any God is out there in the universe, Lewis believed, then he must be an unjust and spiteful Being who simply wants to terrorize people and make their lives miserable. "For all our hopes in endless ruin lie," writes Lewis in *De Profundis.* "The good is dead. Let us curse God most High." Expressing the despair of being utterly alone in the universe to deal with this plight, he adds in *Ode For New Years Day:* "None hears the heart's complaining. For Nature will not pity, nor the red God lend an ear."

Lewis understood both before and after his conversion that one of the most potent cases against the truth claims of Christianity is this nagging problem of pain. Indeed, it seems like a killer argument: How can evil and suffering exist in a universe supposedly controlled by an all-powerful, all-loving God? Given his own experience with doubt, Lewis knew that this question is one of the most important issues that Christians and non-Christians alike struggle with. *The Problem of Pain* emerged as the vehicle in which he set out to tackle this great issue.

In this chapter, you dive into the first great apologetics work written by Lewis and discover why Lewis argues that Christianity not only explains why pain must exist, but also tells why pain is actually a necessary thing in a fallen world.

Background: Exploring The Problem of Pain

The Problem of Pain was originally published as part of the Christian Challenge series, a collection of popular theology books produced by publisher Geoffrey Bles. The intent of the series was to introduce and explain the Christian faith to non-believers. Ashley Sampson, the editor of the series, first came across Lewis while reading *The Pilgrim's Regress* and loved his work. Sampson was certain that Lewis was the best author to write a book on the Christian perspective of pain and suffering.

In the preface to *The Problem of Pain,* Lewis confesses that his gut reaction when approached by Sampson was to write the book anonymously. He felt like an inadequate authority on the subject, both because he was a layman and because he believed he didn't live up to all that he would be writing about in the book. (Lewis even opens up in the book itself, saying "I am a great coward . . . If I knew any way of escape [from pain] I would crawl through the sewers to find it.") In the end, Sampson convinced Lewis to use his real name because an anonymous work didn't fit the nature of the book series.

Lewis started the manuscript for *The Problem of Pain* in the summer of 1939 and finished in the spring of 1940. During this time, he shared the manuscript with the Inklings and, in fact, ended up dedicating the book to this circle of friends. (See Chapter 3 for more on the Inklings.) In a letter to his brother in December 1939, Lewis notes one meeting in particular in which he and J.R.R. Tolkien met alone because the other Inklings were away. At this meeting, Tolkien read a chapter from *The Hobbit,* and Lewis read a chapter from *The Problem of Pain.*

When an author writes about a particular subject, he can sometimes become overly sensitive or even paranoid about facing that issue in real life. (Count me in that lot: You'd never find me writing *Treating Spider Bites For Dummies!*) Lewis, however, was careful not to over-theologize such connections. In a letter to his brother Warnie, he writes, "If you are writing a book about pain and then get some actual pain as I did from my rib . . . [it] remains quite unconnected and irrelevant, just as any other bit of actual life does when you are reading or writing."

I don't make house calls

The title of *The Problem of Pain* proved to be, shall I say, problematic to some booksellers. One advertisement for the book listed the author as C.S. Lewis, M.D. In *C.S. Lewis: A Biography,* authors Green and Hooper tell the story of the book being listed in a catalog as a medical handbook, a misunderstanding that Lewis chuckled about.

Released in late 1940, *The Problem of Pain* was well-received both by critics and the general public. Not only did it become a bestseller, but it also proved to be the book that launched Lewis as a popular Christian apologist.

Why Life Is Pain

If C.S. Lewis had lived long enough to have seen *The Princess Bride,* I wonder what he would have thought about Westley's remark that "Life is pain." For when you think about life on earth, far too much of it *is* painful. Sure, you and I can do a good job avoiding pain for years or even decades, but sooner or later, it lands on your doorstep and won't go away. Not surprisingly, then, the brutal reality of suffering and hardship can leave you questioning why God, if he is who he says he is, would allow such pain to take place. Lewis's chief objective in *The Problem of Pain* is to address this question and explain how Christianity resolves the apparent contradiction.

REMEMBER

In approaching this difficult subject, Lewis believes that if you start with the issue of suffering and pain, you can never make sense of it. Instead, pain can only be understood by backing up and looking at it within the context of all of Christian truth. With this understanding, Lewis guides the reader in a logical, step-by-step approach to the issue.

After the introduction, he works to establish the reality of God being all-powerful and all-loving. God chose to create humans with free will, but the reality of free will is the opportunity for bad as well as good. Lewis talks about how the Fall of Man (Adam and Eve's first sin) introduced pain into the world, and that event of human wickedness caused all hell to break loose, so to speak. As a result, pain is inflicted upon innocent and guilty people and upon helpless animals, and Hell is the ultimate result. But, for the Christian, pain can be used by God to achieve good.

In this section, I walk you through the points Lewis makes to build his case for why God allows pain to occur.

God is all-powerful, but he can't mess with free will

As *The Problem of Pain* begins, Lewis affirms one of the core beliefs of Christianity — that God is all-powerful and in control of all things. On first take, a God who is ruler over Heaven and earth sounds like he could jolly well do anything he pleases, including prevent pain from occurring in everyone's lives. But Lewis says that there are some things that even an all-powerful God finds impossible in the universe that he created.

Before you think Lewis is contradicting himself, note that he's simply making the distinction between two types of impossibilities:

- **Conditionally impossible:** If something is conditionally impossible, it's not possible to do *as long as* a condition occurs or *unless* something causes the present circumstances to change. For example, *as long as* I sit on my couch watching the Super Bowl, it's impossible for me to raid the refrigerator. It's equally impossible for me to play quarterback in the Super Bowl *unless* I get zapped by God off that couch and receive a Peyton Manning–sized dose of athletic ability. God can control all "as long as" and "unless" conditions; thus, nothing is conditionally impossible with God — not even my prayer to become a starting NFL quarterback! (However, whether God agrees with my bright idea is quite another matter altogether.)

- **Intrinsically impossible:** If something is intrinsically impossible, no change of conditions will ever make it work. For example, because the two cities are an ocean apart, I can't be in London and Boston at the same time. No change of conditions will ever change that fact; it would be nonsense to say otherwise. This same logical truth applies to God: No amount of power can make God do what is intrinsically impossible. Or as Lewis would say, God can't do nonsense.

Lewis applies this logic to the question of why God simply can't wave a magic wand and eliminate pain from the universe. God chose to create a world in which free will is a core part of its makeup. In so doing, he took away his own ability to control everything in the created universe. With free will, you and I and every other person on the planet have a choice between good and evil. We also inherit a world equipped for freedom thanks to independent laws of nature, such as gravity. We may take these natural laws for granted, but they allow us to operate independently in this free world.

But we humans want to have our cake and eat it too. We like the idea of free will and the freedoms that go along with it, but we want to bend the rules to exclude pain. As I reflect on this truth, I'm reminded of something my three boys used to do when I played them in a game of football. When things were going their way, the game was played according to the rules. But the moment something bad happened, they wanted to adjust the rules to their advantage. When they stepped out of bounds en route to a touchdown, for example, the boundary was simply extended. When they failed to make a first down, they expected a new set of downs to try again. All in good fun, I gave into them more often than not, but notice the end result: We may have had fun playing together, but we weren't playing genuine football. Our game changed the moment we bent the rules.

Just as the rules of football make a real game possible, the laws of nature are the "ground rules" that make human life possible, in spite of the suffering that occurs when those rules are violated. If God blocked all side effects of free will, he'd be destroying free will itself. Anything else is intrinsically impossible.

Eighteenth-century scholar Gottfried Leibniz put forth the idea that because we have a perfect God, this world is the best of all possible worlds. Skeptics including Voltaire found Leibniz's claim ridiculous given the suffering that exists all around. However, Lewis suggests that perhaps Leibniz and Voltaire both got it wrong. Instead, if free will is involved, maybe this is not the best but the *only* possible world God could have created. Says Lewis in *The Problem of Pain*, "If you try to exclude the possibility of suffering which the order of nature and the existence of free wills involve, you find that you have excluded life itself."

God is always loving, but not always kind

After establishing that an all-powerful God can (and frankly, must) coexist with pain in this world, Lewis turns to the issue of how a God who is good and loving can allow suffering and other bad stuff to go on under his nose without stopping it. In *The Problem of Pain,* Lewis says that people only have a problem with this truth when they misunderstand what love really is and the nature of the relationship between God and humans.

Seeing the difference between kindness and love

Lewis believes that one of the major causes of confusion over pain is that people have a distorted idea of what a "good, kind God" is. *Goodness* means something different to us than to God. To him, it's about love, not mere kindness. Yet, when people think of a loving God, they don't like to think of the God of perfect holiness discussed in the Bible. Instead, the much more agreeable image that comes into people's minds is a sort of jolly, out-of-touch grandfather.

A skewed perspective

When I reflect on the differences in how God and humans define goodness, I think of the perspective I have today about what makes good writing compared to my attitude back in college. Back then, I considered myself to be a decent writer, and I'd confidently turn in an essay or research paper thinking that I'd nailed it. Recently, however, I cleaned out my attic and came across some of those old college papers. Although I had a rousing time reading them, I was embarrassed by how amateurish they sounded. True, some portions may have flowed and shown some insight, but I couldn't get over the clumsy mistakes I was oblivious to at the time. Looking back with the experience I've gained as an author, I realize my concept of good writing was seriously flawed back in college. In the same way, our concept of goodness often looks as silly to God as my student papers do to me today.

Consider an example close to home that illustrates the difference between kindness and genuine love. Over the years, I've occasionally babysat other people's kids. I love them as one loves all children, but I don't treat them the same as I do my own three boys. I'm good to both, mind you, but when another parent's child acts up, I usually try to smile, make him happy, and generally smooth things over until my time is done. My goal is simply to make it through the night, not to get to the root of any behavioral problems. In contrast, my attitude and response is the exact opposite when it comes to my own boys' actions. Because my love for them runs far deeper than my love for someone else's child, I know I can't pacify my sons' bad behavior, no matter how inconvenient and painful the disciplining may be to me. Coming down hard on my children tears me up inside, but my love overshadows any desire for their temporary happiness.

In this example, love is clearly distinct from kindness. Kindness is bent on enjoying the moment or preventing suffering now; long-term consequences don't factor in. Lewis says in *The Problem of Pain,* "It is for people whom we care nothing about that we demand happiness on any terms." If we believe 1 John 4:8, which says "God is love," then Lewis points out the obvious: "He is, by definition, something more than mere kindness."

The Bible describes God as loving, kind, good, and even concerned for our safety (for example, Psalm 46:1). However, be careful of the meaning you attach to those words; they're not always as touchy-feely as you may think. Consequently, when push comes to shove, humans often wish less love from God, not more. Not because God's love isn't genuine but simply because the demand is less. Or, you and I say to God in our best Greta Garbo impersonation, "I just vant to be left alone."

Realizing God created people for his pleasure

Perhaps convinced the world has gone to the dogs, Lewis describes the relationship between God and people as being much like the relationship between a man and his dog. My family, for example, bought an English Sheepdog about two years ago, named her Cassie, and trained her (well, tried to anyway). Our motivation in getting Cassie was two-fold:

- ✔ We wanted to love a dog and care for it. The fact that she would also love us was secondary.

- ✔ We wanted a dog to serve us. The fact that we'd also serve the dog was beside the point.

On first take, our family's experience with Cassie may sound like a one-sided relationship. But the relationship between Cassie and my family is actually a balanced one. We love her, but we can't do much unless Cassie, in her own way, loves us back. In addition, Cassie can serve us, but she can't do a very good job unless we, in our own way, also serve Cassie.

Lewis takes his dog analogy a step further. A dog owner also interferes with a dog's natural habits so that the dog can be more loveable than it would be on its own. In my family's case, we wash Cassie, trim her hair regularly, housetrain her, and teach her not to steal our neighbor dog's toys. In doing so, we enable Cassie to be loved completely because she's not dirty, messy, or misbehaving. Now, a stray dog that has never had an owner may look on and question our "goodness," concluding that Cassie's being mistreated. But Cassie would have no such doubts and would tell the stray dog that she's entered, in Lewis's words, "by Grace, [into] a whole world of affection, loyalties, interests, and comforts entirely beyond [her] animal destiny."

Lewis was no five-point Calvinist

"Five-point Calvinism" is a common term used to describe the five key teachings of Protestant Reformation leader John Calvin and his followers. In *The Problem of Pain,* Lewis takes issue with the first of those five points: the idea that humanity is totally depraved. Based on both logic and experience, Lewis sees two problems with this idea. First, if people are truly and wholly corrupted, then logically, how would anyone know himself to be totally depraved in the first place? Second, in the real world, a lot of good, moral, worthy deeds are performed by people who don't believe in God. To dismiss these as depraved acts isn't being realistic. Therefore, from Lewis's standpoint, people may not be as basically good as secular society often believes, but they're not totally depraved either.

The relationship between God and people relies on the concept of a loving God. Christianity says that the love talked about in the well-known verse John 3:16 — "For God so loved the world" — is really true. But, you have to realize what this verse really means. As Lewis puts it, "You asked for a loving God: you have one." Only when you water down the meaning of love do you see a problem with a loving God who allows pain.

My dog Cassie only misunderstands my family's love when she thinks that the world revolves around her. I can't speak for the rest of my family, but I certainly don't exist for the sake of Cassie! Similarly, God doesn't revolve around me or you, catering to our every whim and desire. Clearly, then, you and I weren't made to love God, but rather for God to love us.

Perhaps the idea that we were created for God's pleasure sounds as if God is just being selfish, that we're nothing more than God's toys. But if you believe that, your view of reality is skewed. In *The Problem of Pain,* Lewis notes that in all history, there's a single test that we can point to as revealing the true nature of God's love — Jesus Christ coming to earth as a man to voluntarily die for the sins of the world. In this lone example, God passes the unselfishness test with flying colors.

In the end, when it comes to being happy, my dog Cassie has three options: She can visit a magic genie and become a human, she can live within my family's guidelines, or she can be miserable. In the same way, Lewis says that people only have three options in terms of accepting God's love: Be God, be like God and respond as he intends, or be miserable. The choice is ours.

Pain is inevitable when you understand reality

After making the case that the presence of pain in the world is not inconsistent with an all-powerful and all-loving God (see the previous sections for details), Lewis's *The Problem of Pain* takes a closer look at why pain does, in fact, happen in our world.

Lewis starts off by making it clear that people need to understand wickedness before Christianity can make sense to them. Without a sense that evil really exists and that all people, to varying degrees, participate in it, God comes across looking like an ogre. Yet, when people begin to understand how bad they are, God's wrath begins to look unavoidable. To this point, Lewis writes, "I have been trying to make the reader believe that we actually are, at present, creatures whose character must be, in some respects, a horror to God, as it is, when we really see it, a horror to ourselves."

It's mine!

As sinful creatures, people use their free wills and claim their lives as their own. In *The Problem of Pain,* Lewis points out that this selfishness surfaces even with people who try to give their days to God. He writes, "We try, when we wake, to lay the new day at God's feet; before we have finished shaving, it becomes *our* day and God's share in it is felt as a tribute which we must pay out of 'our own' pocket, a deduction from the time which ought, we feel, to be 'our own.'" Lewis makes this same point about ownership of time in *The Screwtape Letters* (see Chapter 10), when senior devil Screwtape writes, "The word 'Mine' in its fully possessive sense cannot be uttered by a human being about anything. In the long run either [Satan] or [God] will say 'Mine' of each thing that exists . . . [Humans] will find out in the end, never fear, to whom their time, their souls, and their bodies really belong — certainly not to *them,* whatever happens."

Consequences of going your own way

Because of free will, each person has to decide whether to choose God's way or his own way. In what Lewis calls the "central fall of every person," we inevitably choose ourselves; our selfishness and pride cause us to go our way instead of God's. The book of Genesis records many consequences of people going their own ways, but Lewis speculates on other likely results:

- ✔ A person's body becomes subject to biological laws and suffers their natural consequences. Before the Fall, the human body may have been controlled by his will, not so much by the laws of nature, so matters like hunger and sleep could have been matters of his own discretion and not something he was held slave to.

- ✔ Biological and environmental factors muddy the waters of a person's desires, which prior to the Fall were likely controlled solely by his will.

- ✔ The notion of the subconscious is produced, making a person's will controllable by something he isn't aware of. Before the Fall, a person's will may have been controlled exclusively by his conscious thoughts.

In the end, Lewis maintains that humans lose their "original specific nature" because of sin.

Denying reality

Because the reality of being accountable to God for one's sin is hard to take, people can fall into several traps that deny the consequences of sin and disobedience. In *The Problem of Pain,* Lewis points out the following four:

✔ **The refusal trap:** The first pitfall is refusing to acknowledge that sin exists in the first place or that God should care about that sin. Lewis expresses this perspective, saying, "The worst we have done to God is to leave him alone — why can't he return the compliment?"

✔ **The time trap:** The second trap is believing that time itself somehow cancels out sin. In other words, we think that if we drag our feet long enough, we can simply wear out God. Yet, as Lewis reminds, only the blood of Christ saves you and I, not time.

✔ **The safety in numbers trap:** The third pitfall is thinking that we have an excuse for sin because everybody does it. God, however, treats everyone individually and holds each person responsible for his or her own sins. There's no safety in numbers.

✔ **The kindness trap:** Related to the issue of confusing kindness and love (see the section "Seeing the difference between kindness and love" earlier in this chapter), the final trap is reducing "all virtues to kindness" and believing a *loving* God won't really punish sin.

Accepting the inevitability of earthly pain

When human life is looked at in light of all the evil we do, Lewis believes "the real problem is not why some humble, pious, believing people suffer, but why some do *not.*" In other words, with all people taking their freedom to rebel against God, it seems as if there should be *more* suffering in the world than there actually is. In a letter written to former pupil Dom Bede Griffiths, Lewis confesses that Heaven looks pretty good to him because earthly pain can never entirely be avoided:

> *I do not doubt that whatever misery He permits will be for our ultimate good unless, by rebellious will, we convert it to evil. But what state of affairs in this world can we view with satisfaction? If we are unhappy, then we are unhappy. If we are happy, then we remember that the crown is not promised without the cross and tremble. In fact, one comes to realize, what one always admitted theoretically, that there is nothing here that will do us good: the sooner we are safely out of this world the better.*

Lewis closes out his thoughts to Griffiths with a line from Shakespeare's *Henry IV:* "Would it were evening, Hal, and all well." In other words, Lewis would much prefer to escape all earthly pain and suffering and have everything simply be okay.

Pain is God's megaphone

In a letter to a friend in 1952, Lewis writes of pain, "I believe all pain is contrary to God's will . . . A mother spanking a child would be in the same position; she would rather cause it this pain than let it go on pulling the cat's tail, but she would like it better if no situation which demands a smack had arisen." While Lewis indicates in this letter a link between pain and sin in our lives, he believes that in some cases, suffering isn't always meant as a punishment.

Lewis believes God reluctantly uses pain to speak to people because we ignore him when he tries less extreme measures. Lewis writes, "God whispers to us in our pleasures, speaks in our conscience, but shouts in our pains: it is His megaphone to rouse a deaf world." Lewis also believes that God's use of pain to speak to us has two opposite effects on people: One group rebels against his use of pain and turns against him forever, and the other group of people discovers their sins and true standings before God.

God uses pain to communicate three distinct messages, each of which are discussed in the following sections.

Although God may use pain as a giant megaphone to get our attention, Lewis reminds readers not to think of pain as a good thing in and of itself. "I am not arguing that pain is not painful," he clarifies. "Pain hurts. That is what the word means." Instead, Lewis is simply trying to explain that the Apostle Paul's claim that we are made "perfect through suffering" isn't sheer lunacy. At the same time, Lewis freely admits, "To provide it palatable is beyond my design."

Pain reveals that everything isn't "fine"

A fiercely independent streak living inside people makes it hard for them to really turn to God when things are going well in life. I think back, for example, to a time in my life when times were great. My career was on the fast track, and I didn't think life could get any better. During this time of my life, I was also growing in my relationship with God. But, in hindsight, I realize that my cavalier attitude that "life was fine" put a limit on the amount God could really teach me. Years later, when I gave up the security of my career for a vastly uncertain future in full-time writing, I went through many trials and uncertainties. However, God was able to use those difficult circumstances to keep me focused on him, and I didn't look to this world for my security.

According to the 2003 film *The Italian Job,* when you tell someone "I'm doing fine," you're likely covering up what's really going on inside of you. In the film, "fine" actually means "freaked-out, insecure, neurotic, and emotional." I think that's very much how pain works; it takes our smugness and "I'm fine" sound bites and transforms us into people who are actually freaked out, insecure, neurotic, and emotional. But in so doing, pain opens up the opportunity to realize where our true hopes lie. Pain, according to Lewis, "plants the flag of truth within the fortress of a rebel soul."

Rather than giving us long-term security in this world, God prefers to give us moments of happiness instead. Reflecting on this truth, Lewis writes in *The Problem of Pain,* "We are never safe, but we have plenty of fun, and some ecstasy. It is not hard to see why. The security we crave would teach us to rest our hearts in this world and oppose an obstacle to our return to God . . . Our Father refreshes us on the journey with some pleasant inns, but will not encourage us to mistake them for home."

Wherever you are, be all there

My family uses a quote by missionary Jim Elliot as a sort of family motto for schoolwork and chores around the house: "Wherever you are, be all there. Live to the hilt every situation you believe to be the will of God." As I raise my boys, I hold them to that high standard, although I'm pleased with the small baby steps they take towards that goal. When they sin, I never tire of forgiving them, but I never condone even the slightest little sins. In *The Problem of Pain,* Lewis says this is exactly the kind of way that God thinks of people, too: "Of all powers he forgives the most, but he condones least: he is pleased with little, but demands all."

Pain shatters the concept of self-sufficiency

According to *The Problem of Pain,* pain serves as a reminder that we're not self-sufficient, that we can't just go solo and make it on our own without God. Writing to correspondent Warfield Firor in 1949, Lewis speaks to this point: "All his terrible resources (but it is we who force him to use them) will be brought against us to detach us from [this world] — insecurity, war, poverty, pain, unpopularity, loneliness. We must be taught that this tent is not home."

Jesus says in Matthew 7:14, "Narrow is the road that leads to life, and only a few find it." Lewis wonders whether a line should be added to complete the thought: "And that's why most of you have to be bustled and badgered into it like sheep — and the sheep-dogs have to have pretty sharp teeth, too."

God knows people simply fool themselves into thinking they're self-sufficient. "Yet we will not seek it in him," says Lewis, "as long as he leaves us any other resort where it can even plausibly be looked for." In our minds, we'd much prefer to think of God as a parachute or a fire extinguisher — something to use only in case of emergency. Yet when pain hits us firsthand, we're shaken from this delusion. In *The Problem of Pain,* Lewis observes:

> *At first I am overwhelmed, and all of my little happinesses look like broken toys. Then, slowly and reluctantly, bit by bit, I try to bring myself into the frame of mind that I should be in at all times. I remind myself that all these toys were never intended to possess my heart, that my true good is in another world and my only real treasure is Christ.*

The sad thing is that when the threat of pain is removed, life tends to become business as usual again. Lewis concludes, "And that is why tribulations cannot cease until God either sees us remade or sees that our remaking is now hopeless."

Pain teaches us to self-surrender

Not only does God use pain to zap people of over-confidence and brashness, but he also uses suffering to enable them to surrender their lives to him. The act of surrender is something that you actually have to go through; it's not just a mental affirmation. In other words, until you actually go through an experience that requires you to give everything to God, your surrender to him is incomplete. The act itself is what turns your surrender into something real. In this way, pain makes clear for *us,* not God, our faith and relationship with God. Lewis speaks to this in *A Grief Observed:* "God has not been trying an experiment on my faith or love in order to find out their quality. He knew it already. It was I who didn't."

Upon hearing the need to self-surrender, people often make the mistake of thinking that they'll be miserable if they truly follow God. Lewis believes reality is quite the opposite. He puts it best in *The Screwtape Letters* when senior devil Screwtape says, "When [God] talks of losing their selves, he only means abandoning the clamor of self-will; once they have done that, he really gives them back all their personality, and boasts (I am afraid, sincerely) that when they are wholly his they will be more themselves than ever." (For more coverage of *The Screwtape Letters,* flip to Chapter 10.)

When people surrender themselves to God after experiencing pain, God is able to work inside of them and mold and shape them into the kinds of people he wants them to be. The results can be amazing. In a letter to correspondent Leo Baker, Lewis observes, "Nothing confirms the Christian view of this world so much as the treasures of patience and unselfishness one sees elicited from quite commonplace people when the trial really comes."

Pain is also God's tool

As any fireman can tell you, fire is a fierce and terrible beast to contend with. But although fire has the power to destroy, it also can be harnessed by people and used for good purposes. The fireman who fights house fires during the week has no problem going to a picnic on the weekend and using a camp fire to roast hot dogs and make s'mores.

In the same way, God harnesses pain so he can use it as a tool to accomplish his will. To understand how and why God does this, Lewis distinguishes between *simple good* (something good originating from God) and *simple evil* (something bad acted out by sinful creatures). When I do simple good (such as helping my sick neighbor by cooking a meal for him), God's will is carried out by default. However, when I perform simple evil (such as robbing my sick neighbor's safe because he can't get up to stop me), God can hijack that evil act and still use it for his purposes. Whether I realize it or not, God can turn my sin into something Lewis calls *complex good,* a form of good produced through pain and repentance. Figure 15-1 illustrates the way God intercepts simple evil and turns it into good.

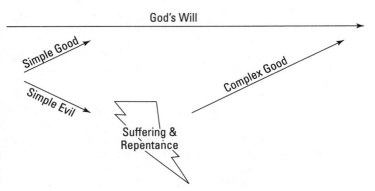

Figure 15-1:
God can
use pain
as a tool.

In *The Problem of Pain,* Lewis underscores that God's will is going to be carried out in this world; the only question is what your role will be in the process. Will you work directly with him by performing simple good, or will he use you as a tool to produce complex good? Judas and John, for example, were both used by God for specific purposes during Jesus Christ's crucifixion: Judas enabled the crucifixion by turning Jesus over to the authorities, and John helped care for Jesus's mother Mary during the ordeal. Lewis concludes, "For you will certainly carry our God's purpose, however you act, but it makes a difference to you whether you serve like Judas or John."

Pain is the cleanest mop-up operation

Because human disobedience has consequences that are impossible to sweep under the rug or ignore, pain becomes the "cleanest" way to deal with evil. To make this point, Lewis contrasts pain with the other two side effects of evil: error and sin.

Think of error as *intellectual evil.* A mental mistake you make produces errors and more errors because every action you perform after that first error is also wrong. Any software programmer can tell you that a simple bug in one part of a program can have a ripple effect, producing bugs that can take down an entire system. Similarly, any math student can testify to how a simple multiplication snafu in the first step of a five-step problem ruins the whole thing. The only way to fix both the buggy software and the incorrect math sum is to retrace your steps and correct the original error.

Sin is the act of *deliberate disobedience* resulting from giving into temptation. Just as an error generates more errors, a sinful act produces more sin because it helps develop sinful habits and weakens your conscience. The only way to undo the initial sin is to repent of the sin and then steer clear of temptation in the future.

In contrast to error and sin, "Pain is only sterilized or disinfected evil," writes Lewis in *The Problem of Pain*. In other words, pain is the remnant of evil after the sin part is stripped away. Pain is quite distinct from error and sin in that it never needs to be undone. When pain is over, it's gone forever. In fact, the ending of pain usually produces the exact opposite reaction — joy. In addition, although uncorrected errors and unrepented sins are like ticking time bombs waiting to explode, pains never multiply. Lewis concludes, "evil which God chiefly uses to produce the 'complex good' is . . . deprived of that proliferous tendency which is the worst characteristic of evil in general."

Table 15-1 highlights the similarities and differences among the three side effects of evil: error, sin, and pain.

Table 15-1	**Comparing the Effects of Sin**		
Effect of Sin	*What is it?*	*What is the result?*	*Does it need to be undone?*
Error	Intellectual evil	More errors result an error	Yes
Sin	Deliberate disobedience	More sin results from a sin	Yes
Pain	Sterilized evil	Joy or relief results from the ending of pain	No

When Real-Life Pain Confronted the Master Apologist

In *The Problem of Pain*, C.S. Lewis does a masterful job providing intellectual muscle to the Christian explanations of why God allows pain and suffering in the world. Given the strength of his arguments and his obvious intellect, you may expect Lewis to have been rather heady or stoic when pain struck him personally. But Lewis was never a stoic; he was definitely a man of the head *and* the heart. In some cases, he found a balance between the two, but in other cases, he did not. This section looks at three major reactions Lewis had when confronted with loss and pain.

Finding increased faith

When his dear friend and fellow Inkling, Charles Williams, died in 1945, Lewis was saddened but ultimately found that the experience bolstered his faith. Commiserating with Anne Ridler about the death of their mutual friend, Lewis said:

> *One feels curiously un-depressed, do you find? It has increased enormously one's faith in the next life and I can't help feeling him all over the place. I can't put it into words: I never knew the death of a good man could itself do so much good. I don't mean there isn't pain, pain in plenty: but not dull, sullen, sickening, drab, resentful pain.*

Feeling deserted by God

The death of a friend, even a close one, couldn't rattle the foundations of Lewis's faith like the premature death of his wife, Joy, after just four years of marriage. (See Chapter 2 for more on this story.) Lewis realized then that the emotional effects that result from this kind of suffering are far harder to resolve than the intellectual issues raised. As he writes in *A Grief Observed,* "I've got nothing that I hadn't bargained for. Of course it is different when the thing happens to oneself, not to others, and in reality, not in imagination."

After Joy's death, Lewis went through a time of deep despair during which he felt completely deserted by God. To cope, he put his questions, frustrations, and exclamations to God into a journal that was eventually published as *A Grief Observed.* Before his death, the book was published under the pseudonym N.W. Clerk (it was released under his actual name later). If *The Problem of Pain* is the voice of Lewis as the brilliant apologist, then *A Grief Observed* is the voice of Lewis as the broken-hearted widower. In it, he pours out the pain, suffering, and loneliness he experiences. He writes, "Go to him when your need is desperate, when all other help is vain, and what do you find? A door slammed in your face, and a sound of bolting and double bolting on the inside. After that, silence."

The logic-based arguments that Lewis put forth in *The Problem of Pain* concerning God's love and kindness seemed hollow for him during this period of his life. He writes, "The conclusion I dread is not 'So there's no God after all,' but, 'So this is what God's really like. Deceive yourself no longer.'" In *The Problem of Pain,* Lewis develops a strong case as to why God's goodness allows pain to occur (see "God is always loving, but not always kind"). But logic doesn't easily penetrate a broken heart. In *A Grief Observed,* Lewis seems determined to throw these reasoned arguments out the window and speak from his heart when he writes, "If God's goodness is inconsistent with hurting us, then either God is not good or there is no God."

Making peace with God

The film *Shadowlands* ends with Lewis in the midst of a crisis of faith. And although it's probably a true statement that Lewis never really got over Joy's death, it's quite clear that he made peace with God. In fact, it appears that he came to an even deeper faith as a result. Interestingly, his last published work before his death was *Letters to Malcolm: Chiefly on Prayer,* a book which affirms the hope and faith that Christians have in an all-powerful and all-loving God.

Within *Letters to Malcolm,* Lewis offers a clue about the peace he found between the intellectual arguments in *The Problem of Pain* and the emotional torments of *A Grief Observed.* He identifies with the suffering of Jesus Christ and thus realizes that he's not left stranded all alone to wallow in his pain. As Hebrews 2:18 says, we have a Savior who can sympathize with you and I because he experienced the same temptations and pains that we have to bear in our lives. Lewis drew comfort in the understanding that he could never suffer more isolation, doubt, and heartache than Jesus Christ suffered in the Garden of Gethsemane the night before he was crucified. Lewis reflects in *Letters to Malcolm,* "I think it is only in a shared darkness that . . . I can really meet . . . with our Master. We are not on an untrodden path. Rather, on the main-road."

As I consider the writings and life of C.S. Lewis, I've come to the conclusion that he would, in fact, have agreed with Westley's quip from *The Princess Bride:* "Life is pain. Anyone who says differently is selling something." But he'd have tacked on a much more hopeful ending to it. I picture Lewis responding to Westley by combining his apologist reasoning with his real-life experience. In doing so, perhaps he'd say something like this: "Life is pain, but you don't have to experience this heartache alone. Instead, Jesus Christ shared a life of pain with you so that one day you will be able to shed this present suffering forever and experience true, lasting peace and joy with him."

Chapter 16

Mere Christianity: Explaining Faith to the Average Joe

In the preface to *Mere Christianity,* C.S. Lewis likens Christianity to a great house. You enter by a hall, off of which are many doors leading to rooms where you can actually live. The rooms, of course, represent the branches and denominations within the Christian Church. Much like a central air system, God breathes his presence and life into the various rooms. To Lewis, the pervasiveness of God is the essence of Christianity. "At the center of each [room]," writes Lewis, "there is a something, or a Someone, who against all divergences of belief, all differences of temperament, all memories of mutual persecution, speaks with the same voice."

In *Mere Christianity,* Lewis sets his sights on presenting the house as a whole, discussing what he believes to be its undeniable truths. He ignores the various walls that separate the rooms; in fact, all Lewis says about the rooms is that if you're in one, you should "be kind to those who have chosen different doors and to those who are still in the hall. If they are wrong they need your prayers all the more; and if they are your enemies, then you are under orders to pray for them. That is one of the rules common to the whole house."

In this chapter, you explore what is perhaps Lewis's most influential Christian apologetic work, *Mere Christianity.* You discover how he came to write the book, and you examine some of his key focal points, including how we can know God exists, the radical claims of Jesus Christ, how God changes people who come to him, what it means to be a Christian, and the doctrine of the Trinity.

Background: Starting with Fireside Chats

During the 1930s, President Franklin D. Roosevelt was one of the first politicians to really "get" the power and influence of radio. He used this communications medium to share his political messages with the American people and calm fears resulting from the Great Depression. His popular talks, affectionately known as "fireside chats," became legendary.

C.S. Lewis gave his own fireside chats during World War II, and their overall impact was significant, like those of Roosevelt. As I outline in Chapter 2, Lewis's brief radio career started when J.W. Welch, religion director at the British Broadcasting Corporation (BBC), read *The Problem of Pain* and became convinced that Lewis was the perfect person to bring religious dialogue to the airwaves. Lewis was somewhat reluctant to take on the project, but he agreed, knowing that radio could be an effective way to reach people who would otherwise never read his books.

Lewis signed up for a month-long series of 15-minute talks to air in August of 1941. The series was entitled "Right or Wrong: A Clue to the Meaning of the Universe." You may think an academic "brainiac" such as Lewis would be a poor choice for explaining Christianity to regular folks and assume that he'd talk way over the heads of the average listener. But Lewis proved himself a natural. He presented heady topics with a witty and charming style that the British public soaked up. The first series of talks was so popular that before it ended, the BBC signed Lewis up for a second series, "What Christians Believe," which aired January through February of 1942. A third and fourth series, "Christian Behavior" and "Beyond Personality," aired in the autumn of 1942 and spring of 1944, respectively.

Lewis's broadcast talks were published as three separate books from 1943 to 1945. *Broadcast Talks* (titled *The Case for Christianity* in the United States) came first followed by *Christian Behavior* and finally *Beyond Personality*. In transferring his talks to paper, Lewis strove to remain faithful to the nature and style of the talks. Although he edited the talks to reflect his deepened understanding of the faith, he believed the books remained "familiar in tone." The three books were combined into a single volume in 1952, entitled *Mere Christianity*. That volume is divided into four mini-books, reflecting its compilation nature:

- Book I explores how we can know that God exists.

- Book II focuses on Christianity's unique claims, centering on Jesus Christ's claim to be God himself.

- Book III examines how Christians should act in light of the truth of Christianity.

- Book IV explores the Christian doctrine of the Trinity and its relationship to believers.

You won't find 'em on eBay

Modern fans of C.S. Lewis can only hear sec-ondhand how terrific Lewis's BBC radio talks were. Sadly, no recordings of the talks he made from 1941 to 1944 exist. In the late 1950s, he made a recording of his book *The Four Loves,* but according to people who heard both the BBC series' and *The Four Loves* recording, the latter lacks the wit and charm of his live BBC sessions. (If you're just dying to experience Lewis's work in his own words, *The Four Loves* recording is currently on the market.)

Mere Christianity as the Hub of Lewis's Literary Wheel

Suppose you were arranging actual copies of Lewis's books by topic. (Okay, I'm not sure why you would actually do this, but play along with me for a moment.) You'd probably put *Mere Christianity* smack dab in the middle and place all the other books in a circle around it. Not only does the centerpiece of your little arrangement serve as a "brain dump," so to speak, for Lewis's Christian beliefs, but the major themes and minor discussions found in *Mere Christianity* also ripple throughout his other works.

Lewis begins the book by constructing an argument for the existence of God based on every person's ingrained belief in an absolute right and an absolute wrong; Lewis calls this belief the "Law of Human Nature." This idea is simi-larly presented as Deep Magic in *The Lion, the Witch and the Wardrobe.* (For full coverage of *The Chronicles of Narnia,* flip to Part II.) Lewis continues the discussion of absolutes in *The Abolition of Man* (see Chapter 17) when he talks about what happens when attempts are made to remove from society the belief in an absolute right and wrong.

Another topic in *Mere Christianity* that appears in Lewis's other works is free will. In *Mere Christianity,* Lewis writes, "If a thing is free to be good it is also free to be bad. And free will is what has made evil possible." In many ways, this statement is a premise to *The Problem of Pain* (see Chapter 15), which explains that free will is at the center of the existence of evil and suffering in the world.

In discussing sin in *Mere Christianity,* Lewis paints pride as the greatest sin of all. "Pride leads to every other vice," says Lewis, "It is the complete anti-God state of mind." This philosophy reappears in two of his fictional works: *The Screwtape Letters* (see Chapter 10) and *The Great Divorce* (see Chapter 11). In *The Screwtape Letters,* Screwtape looks for many ways to use pride to tempt

Wormwood's patient into sin. So too, in *The Great Divorce,* self-absorbed pride is the common denominator among all the people from Hell.

In *Mere Christianity*'s coverage of marriage, Lewis considers the idea of "being in love" at the beginning of marriage and sees a "quieter love" develop as marriage matures. Lewis dives deeper into issues surrounding marital love in his book *The Four Loves* (see Chapter 18) and even in *A Grief Observed.* He explores the topic even further in letters written to his friend Sheldon Vanauken upon the death of Vanauken's wife. You can read these letters in Vanauken's book, *A Severe Mercy* (Harper).

In *Mere Christianity,* Lewis even foreshadows Aslan's famous cry in the final moments of *The Last Battle:* "Further up, further in." When discussing the new creatures that God desires to make his children into, Lewis writes in *Mere Christianity,* "God is forcing him on, or up, to a higher level."

Stepping through an Argument for Christianity

Some of Lewis's apologetics works, such as *Miracles* or *The Abolition of Man,* can be challenging reads for many people. But given the book's broadcast origins and approachable subject matter, *Mere Christianity* is Lewis's most user-friendly defense of the Christian faith's core beliefs. (Rumor has it that he really wanted to name the book *Christianity For Dummies,* but in a humble gesture, Lewis decided to save that title for another aspiring author — ahem, me — to use half a century later.)

Like his other apologetics books, *Mere Christianity* is structured in a logical step-by-step fashion. Each thought builds on the one before it, and new thoughts come only after prior thoughts have been considered from every angle. This approach to presenting the topic undoubtedly goes back to the logic skills Lewis developed under his school tutor William Kirkpatrick (see Chapter 2). Kirkpatrick taught Lewis never to accept an idea at face value. As a result, Lewis learned to consider every possible objection and only committed to a position after answering these questions to his satisfaction.

In *Mere Christianity,* Lewis deals with several questions that must be answered when examining Christianity. These include

1. Is there a God?

2. If so, is he the Christian God?

3. If he is, what should you believe?

4. How does this belief impact your life?

5. How do you live this kind of belief out in the real world?

Right or Wrong, You'll Find God

Tackling the question "Does God exist?" can involve many different approaches. A scientist may look to the universe and the physical world for proof. An historian may look to the historical reliability and authenticity of the Biblical scriptures as evidence. In *Mere Christianity,* Lewis approaches the question from a logical angle and doesn't deal with "external" evidence at all. Rather than looking for proof in the world around you, he suggests that perhaps the best evidence for God is something buried deep inside of you: your conscience, that little voice inside your head that knows right from wrong.

To help you understand Lewis's argument for God's existence, I recommend flipping over to Chapter 17 for an exploration of Lewis's argument on the reality of moral law in *The Abolition of Man.*

Arguing for the reality of moral law

In his classic song *Nebraska,* Bruce Springsteen tells the true story of two teenagers who go on a killing spree in the 1950s and leave 11 people dead. The last line in the song reveals something that most people, Christian or not, understand intuitively: "Well, sir, I guess there's just a meanness in this world." For Lewis, the fact that everybody knows that "there's just a meanness in this world" is the starting point in his defense of the existence of God.

Throughout history, people have understood that certain things are just "right:" being faithful to your spouse, helping a neighbor, or rooting for the Boston Red Sox. On the other hand, certain things are just "wrong:" murdering an innocent person, vandalizing an elderly neighbor's car, and cheering for the New York Yankees. Lewis calls this sense of right and wrong the *Law of Human Nature.* You can also call it moral law, absolute morality, or, as *The Abolition of Man* dubs it, the *Tao.* Laws of nature (think gravity, the speed of light, the inevitable agony when you stub your toe) dictate how things *must* act in the universe, but the Law of Human Nature governs how you *ought* to act, not always how you do act.

In *Mere Christianity,* Lewis deals with each of the major counterarguments that people give to deny the reality of the moral law. These counterarguments are covered in the sections that follow.

Moral law is independent of cultural differences

A first counterargument to the Law of Human Nature is that right and wrong are simply cultural norms, dependent on circumstances of time and place. Although Lewis agrees that there are differences in acceptable cultural behaviors, he disagrees that any important differences exist in the underlying moral law governing such behavior. Take marriage, for example. Modern cultures allow for one spouse, but men in some earlier cultures were permitted to have multiple wives. These are different acceptable cultural behaviors. However, *all* cultures have placed restraints on marriage so that you can't simply take another person's spouse if the urge strikes you. That's the underlying moral law governing marriage-related behavior. For example, the ancient Babylonians and the 17th-century Puritans had about as much in common as Red Sox and Yankee fans, but both societies believed adultery was morally wrong.

Anyone who takes time to study different civilizations and religions inevitably is amazed at how similar the moral codes are to each other and to modern Western norms. In fact, Lewis addresses this subject in detail in the appendix of *The Abolition of Man,* a must-read for anyone who believes Christians made up their own moral law.

Moral law is not just personal taste

A second counterargument to moral law is that the concept of right and wrong is based on personal opinion or experience. Or, to put it in popular terms, "to each his own." Lewis believes that although the counterargument sounds strong, it doesn't pan out in the real world. Consider the following examples in which "to each his own" can't be lived out:

 ✔ You're in school and have one final test you need a good grade on to graduate. You study your brains out and are convinced you aced the test when you hand it in to your teacher. Yet, when you receive your test back, you see a big red "F" on it. You realize after talking to your teacher that you failed not because your answers were wrong but because your teacher simply didn't like you and wanted you to get a failing grade. She adds with a smirk that her actions are her right based on her personal opinion of what you deserve.

 You're outraged, but your outrage goes beyond the fact that she probably broke some administrative rule on the books somewhere. Instead, you implicitly know that your teacher is *wrong* to give you a failing grade simply because she doesn't like you personally.

 ✔ You're in the grocery store in the ten-items-or-less aisle, but the person in front of you has a full shopping cart. If it's an elderly lady with obviously poor eyesight who turns around and says, "Dear me, I didn't realize I was in the wrong line," you probably relax and understand that she made a mistake. But if the person in front of you is a jerk who sneers and rolls his eyes at you, claiming his rights when you mention he's in the wrong line, you're probably outraged.

You may be equally inconvenienced by the nearsighted lady and the sneering jerk, but you hold up the jerk as being *wrong* because he ought to have behaved differently and has no excuse for acting as he did.

Your moral outrage in both of these situations is based on the fact that you believe your claim of being right is true and their claims are flat out wrong. But if right and wrong are merely matters of personal opinion, then their opinions are as valid as yours. However, if your ideas about what's true and right are closer to the truth than their ideas, then Lewis argues that there must be some "Real Morality for them to be true about." He sums up this concept by looking at it in terms of World War II and Nazi behavior.

> *What was the sense in saying the Nazis were in the wrong unless Right is a real thing which they at bottom knew as well as we did and ought to have practiced? If they had had no notion of what we mean by right, then, though we might still have had to fight them, we could no more have blamed them for that than for the color of their hair.*

Moral law is more than mere instinct

A third counterargument is that moral law is only a churchy term for *instinct,* the impulse one feels to behave in a certain way. Imagine, for example, that you see a man being beaten by a group of thugs. Lewis contends that most people feel two impulses in such a situation: an impulse to help the man ("the herd instinct") and an impulse to do nothing and stay out of danger ("the instinct for self preservation"). While these two instincts are at war, a person looks to his conscience to "follow the impulse to help, and suppress the impulse to run away." The first two reaction options are instincts, but your conscience, which judges the two instincts, cannot also be an instinct. That little voice inside you must be separate from the instincts that it helps you govern.

Lewis explains his point with a second example: A sheet of music telling you which notes to play on a piano cannot also be one of the notes on the piano. "The moral law tells us the tune we have to play," says Lewis. "Our instincts are merely the keys."

Lewis contends that instincts aren't really good or bad in themselves. In fact, thinking they are can be very dangerous. If you set up one impulse as the "thing you ought to follow at all costs," what happens when, in order to follow it, you have to act in a way you otherwise would consider wrong? Lewis cites patriotism and a mother's love as examples of how instincts are proven neither wholly good nor wholly bad. At times, your impulse to be patriotic must be suppressed lest it lead to acts of violence against an innocent country.

Likewise, a mother's love could potentially lead to unfair discrimination against other children. In that light, the Law of Human Nature is our conscience that ultimately governs these instincts.

Moral law is more than mere education

The final objection to the reality of the Law of Human Nature that Lewis addresses in *Mere Christianity* is the argument that morality is just something that's drilled into people through education. Lewis admits that children are taught rules of behavior, such as rules of driving (What side of road?), cultural greetings (Do I shake hands? Give 'em five? Hug? Kiss?), and hair styles (Crew-cut? Afro? Flat top?) by parents and teachers. These conventions or rules may change based on the setting or culture, but an underlying law of right and wrong affects all behavioral teachings. As Lewis points out, the fact that people make judgments about various moral teachings is, in itself, proof that there's an underlying standard that everyone is aware of and can therefore judge against.

Lewis contends that if no society's or individual's morality were truer or better than another's, then there'd be no sense in preferring civilized morality over savage morality, such as that expressed in the Rwandan genocide in the 1990s or the Nazi concentration camps during World War II. Yet, Lewis says, "Of course, we all do believe that some moralities are better than others." Lewis isn't comparing one "code of conduct" with another. Instead, he's arguing that you can't identify a "better" code without judging it by how close it measures up to something else, to an underlying standard that exists. This standard is the Law of Human Nature.

Problem children, the lot of us

In *Mere Christianity,* Lewis spends a lot of time on the reality of the existence of right and wrong because he knows there's no point in offering people solutions if they don't recognize their problems. For example, just try to get my son to eat his veggies at dinnertime. He's too young to understand that eating noodles and butter for breakfast, lunch, and dinner isn't exactly healthy. Or, consider the challenge of treating a child with diabetes. Too young to understand the disease, the child considers the reality of an insulin shot three times a day a horror, not a solution. Similarly, the Christian gospel is called the "good news," but its goodness is felt only by someone who understands that he or she needs forgiveness in the first place. Coming face to face with that need, Lewis writes:

> It is after you have realized that there is a Moral Law, and a Power behind that Law, and that you have broken that law and put yourself wrong with that Power — it is after all this and not a moment sooner, that Christianity begins to talk. When you know you are sick, you will listen to the doctor.

Peeking behind the moral law

As people, we understand that we ought to act in a particular way, and we feel the urge to act in such a way (or at least to tell others to act this way!). And when we don't act in the way we think is "right," we feel uncomfortable. Given that this moral law is distinct from individuals and entire societies, how did it get there in the first place?

Lewis argues that the materialist view (the belief that nature is all there is) simply can't adequately answer why we feel this sense of right and wrong. Instead, Lewis reasons that there must be Someone out there guiding us and giving us direction, and that Someone is God.

Christianity in a Nutshell

God designed humanity for love, happiness, peace, and goodness. A core part of that design is God himself. He's what makes all these qualities possible. People break down when they're separated from God; this connection exists not because God doesn't want you to have it some other way but rather because there just isn't any other way. Think of this connection in everyday terms: With gasoline so expensive, you'd save a lot of money by putting water in your car instead. But, of course, your car wouldn't run if you replaced gas with water. Lewis points out that "God cannot give us a happiness and peace apart from himself, because it is not there. There is no such thing."

Despite the fact that God is part of the human design, all people — starting with Adam and Eve and going down the line — have chosen to live their lives on their own, to use some alternative source of fuel, so to speak. But, although God can't just overlook this rebellion (see Chapter 15), his goodness and love don't allow him to leave the world in its present messed up state. In that light, Lewis sums up Christianity in a nutshell:

- ✔ God instilled a conscience, the sense of right and wrong, in every person. Yet, try as they may, no one is able to consistently live up this standard existing inside their heads.

- ✔ God gave people what Lewis calls "good dreams," stories about a god who dies and is resurrected again. In some mysterious way, the god's death gives life to humanity. These stories are scattered through various religions and myths. (Chapter 3 discusses the impact these myths had on Lewis's conversion to Christianity.)

- ✔ God chose one particular group of people (the ancient Hebrews) and spent considerable time and energy trying to "[hammer] into their heads the sort of God He was — that there was only one of Him and that He cared about right conduct."

✔ Within that group of people, a man (Jesus Christ) entered the scene. He claimed that he was God, that he had always existed, and even that he could forgive sins. He said he was the means by which humanity can be restored with God himself.

Lewis understands two claims — that Jesus Christ is God and that He forgives sins — to be those that force men to either embrace Jesus as the Christ, the Son of the living God, or to completely reject Him. The truth of these claims is the pivotal point upon which all of Lewis's apologetics rest.

In *Mere Christianity,* Lewis says that if Jesus had stepped into human history out of a pantheistic religion, then claiming to be God would have been no big deal. Everyone is one with God in pantheism. But, Jesus was a Jew, and Jews have never been pantheistic. Instead, they have always believed in one distinct God who created the world but is completely separate from his creation. Based on these beliefs, Lewis says, the claim of Jesus to be God "was, quite simply, the most shocking thing that has ever been uttered by human lips."

According to Lewis, Jesus paints himself into a corner by making his radical claims. You can't simply call him a great teacher and a wonderful moral example. Instead, you have to deal head-on with his claims to be God. Lewis comments:

> *A man who was merely a man and said the sort of things Jesus said would not be a great moral teacher. He would either be a lunatic — on a level with a man who says he is a poached egg — or else he would be the Devil of Hell. You must make your choice. Either this man was, and is, the Son of God: or else a madman or something worse. You can shut him up for a fool, you can spit at Him and kill Him as a demon; or you can fall at His feet and call Him Lord and God. But let us not come with any patronizing nonsense about His being a great human teacher. He has not left that open to us. He did not intend to.*

How sin homogenizes people

According to the tenets of Christianity, everyone is created by God. And all the countless millions of personalities that exist in the world should prove to any doubters that God isn't interested in sameness. God wants everyone's real personalities to shine. In *Mere Christianity,* Lewis argues that "our real selves are all waiting for us in Him." Pride, which Lewis points out is "the anti-God state of mind," has a way of causing all governed by it to eventually be the same so that our personalities get swallowed up in a faceless mask of selfishness. Lewis reflects on pride and sameness, "How monotonously alike all the great tyrants and conquerors have been."

What's It Mean to Be a Christian?

Throughout *Mere Christianity,* Lewis describes to the reader what it means to be a Christian. This section highlights several of his key discussions.

Getting a "good infection" from Jesus Christ

Christianity holds that Jesus's sacrificial death on the cross

- Saves people who believe in Christ from punishment for their sins.
- Offers the free gift of eternal life in Heaven.

Lewis says that there are many theories on the mechanics of how Jesus's death saves someone, but he insists that none of those theories are crucial to Christianity: "They are explanations about how it works . . . The central Christian belief is that Christ's death has put us right with God." In other words, Lewis believes it doesn't matter *how* it works, just that it does work.

The focus on the end result is similar to one's understanding of the healing power of antibiotics. Unless you're in the medical field or have studied biology, you probably don't understand the science behind antibiotics and how they cure infection. Nonetheless, when you take an antibiotic, it cures your infection regardless of your level of intellectual understanding.

Christians talk about their salvation in many different ways. Some say "God has forgiven us because Christ has done for us what we ought to have done." Others say "Jesus's blood washes us clean." Still others say that death has been beaten by Christ. Lewis doesn't split hairs on this issue. He argues that "they are all true. If any of them do not appeal to you, leave it alone and get on with the formula that does. And, whatever you do, do not start quarrelling with other people because they use a different formula than yours."

Although Lewis doesn't argue the different theological theories on how Jesus's death works to save people, he does give his own thoughts on the matter. He explains that God becoming human — really human — gave us the man that "all men are intended to be." He lived a life that everyone should live but can't because of sin. He lived a life in which his natural human tendencies were surrendered constantly, so that his will became his Father's will. This surrender was so complete that it even included sacrificial death. But following that death was resurrection.

As a result, the change God wants people to experience — the natural becoming the spiritual, the old becoming the new — "has been done for us." Lewis says that salvation has been accomplished for humanity, and it's left up to individuals to "appropriate" it. Lewis refers to this as a "good infection." Jesus, he says, has this "new life" God wants us to have, and "if we get close to Him we will catch it from Him."

But Lewis cautions against thinking that this "new life" will grow in us simply because we mentally acknowledge the truth that Jesus was the Son of God and died for us. That's not what faith is, reasons Lewis. Instead, he explains, "Fallen man is not simply an imperfect creature who needs improvement: he is a rebel who must lay down his arms." Becoming a Christian thus involves surrendering yourself to God, admitting you were going the wrong way, and turning toward God's way.

Becoming "little Christs"

Lewis says that at the point that we become Christians, a "Christ-life" begins to grow in us and helps us continue to repent and believe. God's goodness calls us to a new life; God's love helps us get it. As this "Christ-life" grows in us, "We shall love the Father as [Jesus] does and the Holy Ghost will rise in us." As a result, Lewis says that Christians become "little Christs."

When Lewis says that Christians become "little Christs," he doesn't mean that people somehow become divine. Christianity isn't about being absorbed into God the way a river is absorbed into the ocean. What you give up in becoming a Christian is your natural self, which is "a bundle of self-centered fears, hopes, greeds, jealousies, and self-conceit, all doomed to death." What you get in return is your real self, which is the perfect self. Lewis says that "the more we get what we now call 'ourselves' out of the way and let Him take us over, the more truly ourselves we become."

More than being nice

In describing the process of becoming a Christian, the New Testament uses such imagery as "having the mind of Christ," "putting on Christ," "being born again," and Christ "being formed in us." Throughout *Mere Christianity*, Lewis reminds readers that this change doesn't mean Christians are to read the teachings of Jesus and try to follow them on their own strength to become good or nice people.

"Being a nice guy" isn't the same thing as being redeemed. Yes, God's redemption helps transform us and make us "nicer" folks, but niceness isn't God's ultimate goal. Lewis explains, "It costs God nothing, as far as we know, to create nice things: but to convert rebellious wills cost Him crucifixion." Lewis continues by contrasting the difference between niceness and true salvation:

> *Try every medical, educational, economic, and political means in our power, to produce a world where as many people as possible grow up 'nice' . . . But we must not suppose that even if we succeeded in making everyone nice we should have saved their souls. A world of nice people, content in their own niceness, looking no further, turned away from God, would be just as desperately in need of salvation as a miserable world — and might even be more difficult to save.*

Surrendering to Jesus Christ

The followers of Jesus Christ are often called disciples, named after the original twelve disciples that followed Jesus during his three-year earthly ministry. Jesus instructed people who believed in him to be disciples as well, telling to them in Mark 8:34, "Whoever wants to come after me, let him deny himself, and take up his cross, and follow me." In this passage, Jesus is saying he wants all of you, not just the part of you that goes to church once a week. In *Mere Christianity*, Lewis says that everything — the good, the bad, and the ugly — must be given to Christ. He isn't interested in pruning our bad behavior, but instead he wants "to have the whole tree down." Only then, can Jesus give us a new self, namely himself. Our old selves, as good as they may have been, are still sick from the disease of sin. He wants to cure us, but the cure can only come when we surrender and let him do the curing.

Although God's cure is real, we can't expect it to be completed in an instant. God's intention is for us to "be perfect," but the process of the cure will, as Lewis understands, "be long and in parts very painful." After all, when God created us originally, the transformation from fetus to baby wasn't instant. We started in our mothers' wombs and passed through many stages before birth. Lewis writes, "Something the same is now happening at a higher level . . . The [change] will not be completed in this life: but he means to get us as far as possible before death."

However, the more we surrender, the faster Christ can accomplish his work. Above all, no matter how hard we try, we can't cure ourselves. Lewis writes, "If I am a grass field that contains nothing but grass seed, I cannot produce wheat. Cutting the grass may keep it short; but I shall still produce grass and no wheat. If I want to produce wheat, the change must go deeper than the surface. I must be ploughed up and re-sown."

Examining Three Major Virtues of the Christian Life

In *Mere Christianity*, Lewis identifies two sets of virtues in the life of a Christian:

- ✓ **Cardinal virtues,** which all civilized people embrace. They are prudence, temperance, justice, and fortitude.
- ✓ **Theological virtues,** which are unique to the life of a believer. They are charity, hope, and faith.

According to Lewis, the three theological virtues are especially significant because of their connection to believers. These three virtues are explored in this section.

Loving your neighbor as yourself

In this day and age, charity has a very narrow definition: We think of it in terms of giving to those in need. But Lewis points out that its original meaning was far broader (as discussed further in Chapter 18). According to Lewis, charity is tied to what some people call the *golden rule:* Love your neighbor as yourself — or do unto others as you would have them do unto you.

When it comes to charity, loving your neighbor isn't an emotion; in fact, it has nothing to do with the emotional act of *liking* your neighbor. Lewis writes, "Do not waste time bothering whether you love your neighbor, act as if you did." Lewis believes that the action (loving), if done from a pure heart, leads eventually to the emotion (liking). The Christian, "trying to treat every one kindly, finds himself liking more and more people as he goes on."

In the teaching of his earthly ministry, Jesus Christ was very clear that neighbors include people you just plain dislike, can't stand being around, or who have hurt you in the past. As a result, part of loving your neighbor as yourself involves forgiving him as well. And this, Lewis says, may be the most unpopular of all Christian teaching. It can't be ignored, however, because it came from Jesus. In the Lord's prayer, Jesus said, "Forgive us our sins as we forgive those who sin against us" (Luke 11:4), and to the disciples, Jesus said, "If you do not forgive others, how will your father who is in heaven forgive you?" (Matthew 6:15). In fact, the nature of Christ's message is so challenging to Lewis that he writes, "I am not telling you in this book what I could do — I can do precious little — I am telling you what Christianity is. I did not invent it."

Being hopeful

Hope is the second virtue that exists in the life of a Christian. To a believer, hope is far more than the dream-like wishful thinking of a child. Instead, Lewis sees Christian hope as a constant expectation of what God has in store for us in eternity. By living with such a hope, Christians can to bring real good to the present world. Lewis cites the Apostles converting the Roman Empire and the English Evangelicals abolishing the slave trade as examples of how "minds occupied with heaven" can change things here on earth. Put simply, Lewis says, "Aim at heaven and you will get earth 'thrown in': aim at earth and you will get neither."

Living a life of faith

The third theological virtue that Lewis discusses in *Mere Christianity* is faith. On one level, faith simply means to believe as true the essential doctrines of Christianity. Yet, just because a person makes a sincere decision to embrace Christianity doesn't mean that his faith is on autopilot for the rest of his life. Instead, given our fallen nature, our belief-o-meter changes when our moods and emotions change. Perhaps your child becomes suddenly ill, you lose your job, or your spouse leaves you. The raw emotions that you feel at the time can convince you that Christianity can't possibly be true. At this point, your emotions start attacking your beliefs, and faith becomes a virtue. Faith is, as Lewis says, "the art of holding onto things your reason once accepted, in spite of your changing moods. For moods will change, whatever view your reason takes." In other words, faith is what the Christian uses to keep on believing in spite of mood swings and circumstances.

Three In One: The Doctrine of the Trinity

Christians hold the belief that God is a Trinity: the Father, the Son, and the Holy Spirit. He is one God in three persons. To explain this concept in *Mere Christianity,* Lewis compares it to a three-dimensional cube. A cube is composed of six distinct and separate squares, each of which has its own face and identity. Yet, the cube remains one cube. Similarly, with the Trinity, God is three distinct "persons" in one being.

The Trinity concept is important because it helps explain how God works on, and in, people to change them into new creatures. In describing the power of the Trinity, Lewis asks readers to imagine a man who is praying to God. The man is helped in his prayers by God, and the man can pray because of God.

Lewis explains, "God [The Father] is the Thing to which he is praying . . . God [The Spirit] is also the Thing inside of him which is pushing him on . . . God [The Son] is also the road or bridge along which he is being pushed to that goal."

Lewis believes the names given to each person of the Trinity perfectly describe who they are: You think of God the Father as "in front of you, and the Son as someone standing at your side . . . then you have to think of the third Person as something inside you."

The Apostle John says in 1 John 4:8 that "God is love." Lewis believes John's statement is further insight into the Trinity's mystery. According to Lewis, love is something shared between two persons, and God is love because, for all eternity, God the Son and God the Father have loved each other. This "living, dynamic activity of love" — Lewis calls it "Dance" — is what created the universe and all that's in it. The Dance (love) between God the Father and God the Son is more than a feeling — it's tangible, alive, and "dynamic, pulsating activity."

Chapter 17

How "To Each His Own" Leads to the Abolition of Man

....

....

*W*ant a great coffee drink? Go into your neighborhood coffee shop and order a *venti one pump soy extra whip mocha*. I receive strange looks every time I order that, but, trust me, it's the best coffee drink ever made. However, when I spend five minutes listening to other coffee orders from people behind me, I realize that the principle "to each his own" rules the coffee world. *Grande extra hot cappuccino. Tall Americano. Venti triple shot latte.* Menus aside, many of the drinks prepared by coffee shop baristas are tailor-made for the person ordering. To borrow a line from *Pirates of the Caribbean,* the menu offerings are "more what you'd call 'guidelines' than actual rules."

"To each his own" may be perfectly appropriate for ordering coffee, but post-modern society has concluded that you can apply that individualistic principle to all of life as well. In fact, nearly three out of four people believe that morality is a matter of personal opinion and circumstance. In other words, most of us believe that absolute right and wrong are "more what you'd call 'guidelines' than actual rules."

In *The Abolition of Man,* C.S. Lewis takes on this issue of relativism. He makes a compelling argument that not only is "to each his own" naive, but, if lived out, this principle ultimately causes people to lose their humanity, becoming nothing more than "trousered apes."

Background: Lewis's Desire to Debunk the Debunkers

When C.S. Lewis spoke regularly at Oxford's Socratic Club (see Chapter 2) in the early 1940s, one of the "hot topics" he debated against passionately was the idea that values are a matter of personal taste or circumstance. This belief, which I refer to in this chapter as *relativism,* holds that morality and values don't originate from God or anywhere else but rather arise within individuals based on instinct, intellect, or conditions in a person's life.

In 1942, Lewis came across two student textbooks that terrified and angered him — and became the motivation for *The Abolition of Man.* The two books were *The Control of Language* (1940) by Australian authors Alex King and Martin Ketley and *The Reading and Writing of English* (1936) by E.G. Biaggini. Lewis found the King and Ketley book particularly insidious. Under the guise of teaching English, the book's philosophical undertones held that values are simply statements of feeling by the speaker. Lewis observed that the authors taught "nothing of letters," and their cynicism and debunking cut the soul of the student. In a letter to author Dorothy Sayers in November of 1947, Lewis explains that he considered the book so dangerous because they "smuggled [relativism] in without argument in a book on a slightly different subject, for children, without probably being aware that it was controversial."

Lewis decided to use these two textbooks as the basis for three Riddell Memorial Lectures he presented at Durham University in February of 1943. These lectures were then published in book form the next year with yet another marketing-savvy title of Lewis's creation: *The Abolition of Man: Reflections on Education with Special Reference to the Teaching of English in the Upper Forms of Schools.* (Fortunately, everything after the colon is not typically used today!)

Because he goes into attack mode to address the two textbooks, Lewis decided to change the names of the authors and the books to protect the "not-so-innocent." He refers to King and Ketley as Gaius and Titius and calls their book *The Green Book.* He refers to Biaggini as Orbilius.

Although Lewis uses *The Green Book* as a springboard for discussing the relationship of teaching values in education, *The Abolition of Man* has far broader applications. It's more than just a critique of educational theory. The arguments that Lewis develops are just as applicable to today's postmodern society as a whole.

Anti-progress?

In 1944, Lewis received a humorous invitation to become a member of the Society for the Prevention of Progress. Along with his response, they asked him to list his credentials. Lewis responded by saying that he was honored by the membership invitation and hoped that "the unremitting practice of Reaction, Obstruction, and Stagnation would give [the society] no reason for repenting [their] favor."

He then suggested that *The Abolition of Man* be his credentials, one that they'd find worthy of admission to their "canon."

Because the society said that membership had been denied to such people as William Henry Beveridge, a social reformer in Britain, Lewis showed his wit by signing off his letter, "Beverages not Beveridges (my motto)."

The Abolition of Man is quite philosophical in nature and isn't written in the popular style of *Mere Christianity* or *The Screwtape Letters*. As a result, the book is perhaps one of Lewis's least approachable nonfiction works. (But hey, it's less than 100 pages, so that makes it easier to get through!) However, I, along with many others, suggest that this book is Lewis at the top of his game and shouldn't be missed. Some, in fact, argue that *The Abolition of Man* is the greatest defense of Natural Law (an absolute right and wrong) ever written. Lewis loved the book and considered it "almost my favorite among my books" even though it was largely overlooked by the public.

Understanding the Tao

One of the fundamentals that Lewis begins with in addressing relativism is the idea of the *Tao* (pronounced dow, as in Dow Jones or a dowel rod or Roddy McDowell or . . . well, you get the idea). The *Tao* is the belief in absolute values — that "certain attitudes are really true, and others really false." Lewis uses the Chinese term for this concept, but he's referring to the same thing as Traditional Values, Absolute Morality, or Natural Law.

In *The Abolition of Man* (specifically, in the book's appendix), Lewis provides compelling proof that until modern times, all peoples regardless of culture or geography believed there were good and bad — appropriate and inappropriate — ways to respond to life. What's more, all these cultures agreed quite closely on what's right and what's not. Lewis isn't just talking about Christianity or Judaism here. Instead, he documents the common ethical code that existed across Greek, Roman, Babylonian, Chinese, Sanskrit, Christian, Jewish, American Indian, and Australian aboriginal beliefs.

The *Tao* isn't just a veiled word for Christianity. In fact, Lewis never speaks directly of Christian theology in *The Abolition of Man*. Instead, the *Tao* is a basis of belief for *any* worldview that embraces absolute values, not just Christianity. Lewis points out the relationship between the *Tao* and Christianity in a letter to Martyn Skinner in March of 1943: "The relation between the *Tao* and [Christianity] is best seen from Confucius' remark 'There may be someone who has perfectly followed the way: but I never heard of one.'" In other words, Christianity explains

- ✔ Why the *Tao* exists (because God instilled it in the hearts of every human).

- ✔ How one person — Jesus Christ — followed the *Tao* perfectly.

- ✔ How it's possible to receive redemption from God (through Jesus Christ) for our failure to follow the *Tao*.

Comparing Relativism and the Tao

Throughout *The Abolition of Man,* Lewis pits relativism against the *Tao*. Just how different these two perspectives are becomes apparent when you start talking about statements of value. Consider the following statements about three Academy Award–winning films:

- ✔ In *Schindler's List,* Oskar Schindler is brave, and Nazi officer Amon Goeth is wicked.

- ✔ In *Braveheart,* William Wallace acts heroically, and Robert the Bruce acts cowardly.

- ✔ In *Gladiator,* Maximus dies an honorable death, and Commodus dies in disgrace.

On first take, these three statements seem rather benign and even plain obvious — or, to borrow an expression from my boys, "Well, duuuh!" But, when you look at these statements in light of these two worldviews, you can begin to see that perhaps these statements aren't so straightforward as one may initially believe.

Relativism: Right and wrong are subjective

Relativism holds that when you say "Oskar Schindler is brave," you may appear to be making a remark about the man, but you're actually commenting on your own emotions. Gaius and Titius confirm this perspective in *The*

Green Book (emphasis added): "We *appear* to be saying something very important about something: and actually we are *only* saying something about our own feelings." (Notice the not-so-subtle message communicated with the words "appear" and "only.") Lewis points out two conclusions you can draw from this perspective:

- All statements of value are about the emotional state of the person saying them.
- All statements of value are insignificant.

Therefore, from a relativistic perspective, people or things don't have values in and of themselves. In fact, emotion, feeling, and value have nothing to do with facts. Or as Lewis says: "The world of facts, without one trace of value, and world of feelings without one trace of truth or falsehood, justice or injustice, confront one another; and no *rapprochement* is possible."

In this light, Oskar Schindler isn't really brave, nor is Goeth truly wicked. Those statements are merely my emotional reactions after watching *Schindler's List*. The adjectives *brave* and *wicked* are "mere mists" between me and the real subjects.

Likewise according to relativism, in the film *Gladiator,* you can't call the death of Maximus *honorable* and Commodus' death *disgraceful;* all you can say is that they both died. Those are the cold hard facts. Everything else is the trivial, subjective feelings of onlookers.

The Tao: Right and wrong are objective

In contrast, the *Tao* holds that people and things have qualities that are true and false. Thus, you can say, for example, that William Wallace *really did* act bravely, and Robert the Bruce *really was* a coward. Those qualities — bravery and cowardice — were part of the two men's behavior and separate from any reaction I may have had to the film. In fact, the *Tao* holds that certain qualities in people or objects *demand* "a certain response from us whether we make it or not." And, in practice, we often don't respond the way the *Tao* calls us to.

For example, when I watch the classic Hitchcock film *Vertigo,* I realize Judy Barton is an accomplice to a murder and should be punished. But each time, at the movie's end, I always wish Scottie would overlook all that and they'd live happily ever after. Or, take the civil war film *Glory*. In the climax, Robert Gould Shaw volunteers his regiment to be the first soldiers to make a frontal attack on Fort Wagner — an act of almost certain death for he and his men. He does so out of honor and duty, yet, as much as I embrace his sense of duty, I care for Shaw and his troops by the film's end and wish they'd play it safe, stick to the rear, and survive. In both cases, I see my reactions as flawed and not living up to the *Tao*'s principles of justice and duty. As you can see, sometimes my impulses get the best of me.

How Society Produces the People We Most Despise

In *The Abolition of Man,* after Lewis clarifies the fundamental differences between relativism and the *Tao,* he talks about the inevitable implications on education and society.

While relativism holds that facts and feelings are always incompatible, the *Tao* sees emotions as sometimes in line with reason (Schindler is brave) and sometimes out of line, overpowered by impulse (Shaw should play it safe). According to the *Tao,* the purpose of teaching, therefore, is to train children to control their emotions and keep them in line with truth and reason.

"Trained emotions" become the critical factor in giving power to your "head" over your "impulses" — your intellect over your instincts and appetites. (Christianity maintains that when a Christian gives his life over to Christ, the Holy Spirit empowers him to have control over his appetites or "flesh.")

Head knowledge alone isn't enough to control your impulses. A simple example demonstrates this truth. Suppose you need someone to drive your brand new car home from the airport after dropping you off there. You can choose one of two neighbors: a theologian at a local college who teaches the Bible and Christian ethics but who has two DUI convictions and a history of speeding tickets for reckless driving, or a Scrooge-like man who has never set foot in church but who was taught from an early age to obey and respect laws. When the rubber meets the road (particularly if your new car is attached to the rubber), you'd rather have someone with trained emotions (Scrooge) than head knowledge (the out-of-control theologian).

Or consider the CEO of a Fortune 500 company. He doesn't run the company by himself. If the executive tried to do everything on his own, he'd fail miserably. He'd be spread too thin and forced to deal with subjects he has no expertise in. One person, no matter how capable, simply doesn't have the goods to do it alone. Instead, the CEO leads his company through an executive team. In the same way, your intellect must rule your impulses not on its own but through Trained Emotions (or what we may call our "moral compass").

Lewis writes, "The head rules the belly through the chest." You can think of the chest as the home base of our emotions, strengthened by discipline and proven habits so that as it matures, it's transformed into something as tough as nails. The chest is, therefore, the critical link between a person's intelligence and his or her appetites; it's what makes a person distinct from a "trousered ape." With just an intellect, you're a "mere spirit;" with just an appetite, you're a "mere animal." Lewis concludes, "The operation of *The Green Book* and its kind is to produce what may be called Men without Chests."

See the irony of our postmodern world? We cheer on Oskar Schindler, William Wallace, and Maximus in the movie theater but then walk out into a "to each his own" society that produces people like Amon Goeth, Robert the Bruce, and Commodus. We embrace heroism, bravery, and honor while insisting upon a system of belief that prevents a man from truly being heroic, acting brave, or dying with honor. Moreover, when people actually live out the principles of relativism and fail to use a moral compass to moderate their behavior, we have the gall to be outraged. We fume when a priest molests a child, an executive lies to stockholders for personal gain, and a baseball star cheats by taking steroids. Lewis memorably sums up the postmodern state:

> Such is the tragi-comedy of our situation — we continue to clamor for those very qualities we are rendering impossible . . . In a sort of ghastly simplicity we remove the organ and demand the function. We make men without chests and expect of them virtue and enterprise. We laugh at honor and are shocked to find traitors in our midst. We castrate and bid the geldings be fruitful.

Dealing with Rebellious Branches of the Tao

Something's out of whack: Three quarters of society dismiss the idea of absolute values, yet people really do see Oskar Schindler, William Wallace, and Maximus as heroes. Like Gaius and Titius, postmodern society has some sort of goal. Schindler's bravery, Wallace's heroism, and Maximus's honor must, therefore, be a means of making society better able to reach that goal. The *Tao* is debunked, but other values are proclaimed in its place. Many proponents of relativism insist that they're simply trimming the fat — sentimentalism, religious taboos, and cultural and historical baggage — from "real" or "base" values that are unsullied by tradition.

People, for example, who attack "traditional values" are quick to hold up their own values, such as tolerance, racial and gender equality, world peace, and personal freedoms. These values aren't meant as mere guidelines, however; with a religious fervor, they're proclaimed as a New Morality, a new right and wrong, that postmodern society must embrace as it continues into the 21st century.

Examining how relativists explain the rebellion

Relativists must look to a source apart from the *Tao* as the basis for the "real" values that replace "traditional" ones. So, they turn to reason and instinct as alternative sources.

"Reasonable" values

Some relativists argue that "real" values are defined from reason: You can deduce them based on facts around you. Therefore, Schindler's heroism is good because it's useful to society, and Goeth's wickedness is bad because it's harmful to society. Similarly, it's good and desirable that Shaw and his troops die for their country because it enables others to live without the bondage of slavery.

Yet, no matter how much practical benefit Schindler's and Shaw's behavior has for society, reason alone doesn't explain why they personally should put themselves at risk for the good of others. Lewis explains, "*This [action] will preserve society* cannot lead to *do this* except by the mediation of *society ought to be preserved.*" But, once you introduce the word *ought*, then you've gone full circle and are back to where you started. Reason can lead you to *is* but never to *ought*.

"Instinctive" values

For other relativists, "real" values come from our instincts — deep down inside of us is an instinctive drive to do or embrace certain behaviors and avoid others.

But why should you and I obey instinct? And, even tougher, *which* instincts should we obey? "Telling us to obey instinct is like telling us to obey 'people,'" says Lewis. "People say different things: so do instincts." If Schindler and Shaw both felt an instinct to preserve their species, why should this instinct be obeyed over the instinct to avoid risk, save their own skin, and live as long as possible?

Clearly, you need some authority to pick and choose between instincts. Lewis speaks to this point in *Mere Christianity*:

This thing that judges between two instincts, that decides which should be encouraged, cannot itself be either of them. You may as well say that sheet of music which tells you, at a given moment, to play one note on the piano and not another, is itself one of the notes on the keyboard. The [Tao] tells us the tune we have to play: our instincts are merely the keys.

Arguing the need for an arbitrator

Oskar Schindler ought to risk his life to save the Jews. Robert Gould Shaw ought to die for his country. Without an absolute right and wrong, you can't prove the *ought* in either of these statements. The *oughts* are starting points, not something you can derive from a rational calculation or conclude from an instinctive drive. If the *ought* isn't necessary for its own sake, says Lewis, then no *ought* is necessary at all.

Clearly, then, when you try to come up with values based on reason or instinct, you always come back to the same problem: the need for some sort of standard by which to judge the values. Lewis makes this same point in *Mere Christianity:*

> *If no set of moral ideas were truer or better than any other, there would be no sense in preferring civilized morality to savage morality, or Christian morality to Nazi morality. In fact, of course, we all do believe that some moralities are better than others . . . The moment you say that one set of moral ideas is better than another, you are, in fact, measuring them both by a standard . . . comparing them both with some Real Morality, admitting that there is such a thing as a real Right, independent of what people think and that some people's ideas get nearer to the real Right than others.*

Therefore, any effort to come up with "real" values only leads you back to the *Tao* again. In his essay entitled "On Ethics," Lewis explains, "Those who urge us to adopt new moralities are only offering us the mutilated or expurgated text of a book which we already possess in the original manuscript."

Lewis compares the drive by relativists to propose a new morality to that of a "rebellion of the branches against a tree: if the rebels could succeed they would find that they had destroyed themselves." Lewis adds in his essay "The Poison of Subjectivism:" "The human mind has no more power of inventing a new value than of planting a new sun in the sky or a new primary color in the spectrum."

Therefore, when people embrace "to each his own" while clinging to any sort of value system, they clumsily step all over themselves. They're just like a farmer who throws away his seeds in the spring yet tries to harvest crops in the fall from the barren ground. Seeped in self-contradictions, people try to find "real" values after they've thrown out the only possible source of values around.

Welcome to the Fallout

A postmodern society that has debunked traditional values (the *Tao*) has a choice of whether to irrationally cling to pseudo-values or to throw out any notion of right and wrong at all and simply do what it pleases. The latter — relativism — is the only intellectually honest alternative to the *Tao*.

True relativism, therefore, holds that nothing is good in and of itself. What's good is simply what suits me personally. In *The Abolition of Man*, Lewis sums up the relationship of the *Tao* and relativism as such: "When all that says 'it is good' has been debunked, what says 'I want' remains."

Most people familiar with the film *Schindler's List* would agree that Oskar Schindler is brave, and Nazi officer Amon Goeth is wicked. A relativist would argue that people go along with that value statement because they'd rather live in a world of Schindlers than Goeths. However, consider the right-wing supremacists who wish Hitler had come out on top. They could just as validly express an opposite value statement: Oskar Schindler is a traitor and sympathizer with the enemy, and Nazi officer Amon Goeth is heroic. People may argue that such a wacky position is wrong because it's dangerous to society and must be controlled, but their leverage is on grounds of power alone, not on any innate superiority of democratic values over Nazi values. Lewis provides an example in *Mere Christianity*:

> *What was the sense in saying the Nazis were in the wrong unless Right is a real thing which they at bottom knew as well as we did and ought to have practiced? If they had no notion of what we mean by right, then, though we might still have had to fight them, we could no more have blamed them for that than for the color of their hair.*

In the end, when society debunks the *Tao* and lives out relativism, there are three major fallouts:

- ✔ **A democratic and free society isn't possible.** According to Lewis, the *Tao* is "necessary for any idea of a rule which isn't tyranny or obedience which isn't coercion or slavery." Otherwise, you have no values that extend beyond the rulers and people being ruled; democracy and freedom are simply defined by the ones with the power.

- ✔ **Self-control isn't possible.** The *Tao* enables people have control over themselves as they build up their Trained Emotions and strengthen their moral compass. But, the moment you live by "I want," impulse, by definition, becomes the sole driver of your decisions.

✔ **Humanity isn't possible.** When you eliminate the *Tao,* Nature — our animal-like instincts and impulses — becomes the ultimate controller of humans. In a grand irony, "Man's final conquest has proved to be the abolition of Man," argues Lewis.

The well-known relativist psychologist B.F. Skinner didn't argue with Lewis's conclusion concerning the fallout of relativism. Instead, he writes in *Beyond Freedom and Dignity* that Lewis is wrong to object to the abolition of Man and that, in fact, the abolition of autonomous Man is long overdue.

Postmodern society wants it both ways. We love to flirt with "to each his own" relativism while we continue to hold back a small group of values as being valid for all people. But this half-hearted view is the one option not available to humanity. As Lewis writes in *The Abolition of Man,* there are simply two options: "Either we are rational spirit obliged to forever obey the absolute values of the *Tao,* or we are mere nature" ruled by instinct and natural impulses.

Chapter 18

C.S. Lewis on the Hot Seat

In This Chapter

▶ Exploring the nature of love, marriage, sex, and death

▶ Chiming in on worldly topics, including war, capital punishment, and politics

▶ Touching on spiritual topics, including the Bible and prayer

▶ Exploring the cardinal problem with naturalism

*T*urn on *Larry King* or *Oprah* and you're bound to find someone interesting giving his or her opinion on the issues of day. There's an almost universal curiosity about what famous people think about today's important issues.

Had C.S. Lewis lived in the 21st century, he'd surely be one of those sought-after opinion givers that frequent CNN or FOX News — and justifiably so, given his academic prowess, logical mindset, and top-notch debating skills. *Larry King* and *Oprah* aren't viable options for getting Lewis's two cents' worth, but you can turn to his library of published works and letters to discover his thoughts on timely issues, including marriage, sex, war, the Bible, politics, and more. That's what this chapter is all about: exploring Lewis's opinions on wide-ranging topics based on what we know from his many writings.

Love: Experiencing Its Four Flavors

Early in his Christian life, C.S. Lewis thought love was limited to only what most resembled "that love which is God." But, he eventually came to recognize four distinct types of love. He writes about this quartet in his 1960 book entitled, appropriately enough, *The Four Loves*. Using the original Greek words, the four loves are as follows:

- ✔ *Storge* (affection)
- ✔ *Philia* (friendship)
- ✔ *Eros* ("being in love")
- ✔ *Agape* (charity)

Lewis considers *storge*, *philia*, and *eros* to be human or natural loves and *agape* to be divine love. Because the human loves aren't "self sufficient," says Lewis, God desires to infuse natural loves with *agape* — but not in a way that causes them to lose their unique identities or distinctness. Without *agape* to align them with God, human loves become cancerous. Lewis writes, "They become gods: then they become demons . . . For natural loves that are allowed to become gods do not remain loves." In *The Great Divorce,* Lewis adds, "No natural feelings are high or low, holy or unholy, in themselves. They are all holy when God's hand is on the rein. They all go bad when they set up on their own and make themselves into false gods."

Each type of love is explored in the sections that follow. In each description, I point out the dangers of each love existing apart from *agape*.

Storge: Affectionately yours

According to C.S. Lewis, the first type of love is *storge,* which he describes as "affection, especially of parents to offspring." Lewis considers *storge* the human love that allows for so much closeness and acceptance between people who otherwise would struggle to find either. In fact, Lewis sees *storge* as "responsible for nine-tenths of whatever solid and durable happiness there is in our natural lives." Perhaps pastor and author Hugh Prather had *storge* in mind when he said, "Love should be as effortless as breathing and as indiscriminate as falling snow."

To Lewis, the indiscriminate nature of *storge* allows completely incompatible people to be compatible. He writes, "It is Affection *[storge]* that creates this taste, teaching us first to notice, then endure, then to smile at, then to enjoy, and finally to appreciate, the people who happen to be there." And even better, *storge* allows us to be loved even when we're most unlovable.

The biggest weakness of *storge* lies in its ability to dominate relationships and squeeze out *agape* love. As Lewis warns, "If we try to live on Affection alone, Affection will go bad on us." Because *storge* is so freely given and so willing to see past the objects that hinder the other human loves, people can lose focus and start to believe that they deserve *storge*. As such, Lewis refers to *storge* as "an affair of old clothes." In other words, because of *storge,* you can wear old clothes with those closest to you and they don't mind your appearance. However, Lewis notes, "Old clothes are one thing; to wear the same shirt till it stank would be another."

Without the balance that *agape* brings, *storge* becomes selfish and self-absorbed.

Giving and taking, love-style

Lewis believes each of the four loves are expressed in two distinct ways, which he calls "gift-love" and "need-love." *Gift-love* is selfless, meaning sacrificing or doing whatever is necessary for the other person. As Lewis writes in *The Four Loves,* it "moves a man to work and plan and save for the future well being of his family [even though] he will die without sharing or seeing." *Need-love,* on the other hand, is best illustrated by "that which sends a lonely or frightened child to its mother's arms."

Lewis doesn't attempt to paint gift-love as always being morally superior to need-love. Gift-love is certainly "most God-like," but need-love is natural for humans given the Creator-creature relationship that we have with God. In fact, our need for God and his love is what motivates us to seek him out in the first place.

Philia: Forever friends

"The greatest of worldly goods," according to Lewis, is *philia,* or friendship love. "Certainly to me it is the chief happiness of life," he writes. Lewis describes *philia* in his book *Present Concerns: Essays by C.S. Lewis:* "Friends are not primarily absorbed in each other. It is when we are doing things together that friendship springs up — painting, sailing ships, praying, philosophizing, fighting shoulder to shoulder. Friends look in the same direction. Lovers look at each other: that is, in opposite directions."

Lewis finds *philia* to be highly spiritual in nature. But, like *storge,* when *philia* tries to go it alone without *agape,* it can become harmful in two ways. First, friendship can be dangerous because, by its nature, it doesn't demand that friends have a passion for something good. Lewis believes that *philia* "makes good men better, and bad men worse." A second danger is the risk of pride forming in the friendship and a sense of smugness that ensues. To some extent, friendship naturally excludes others, but this exclusion can be "innocent and necessary." However, as Lewis explains, "From the innocent and necessary act of excluding to the spirit of exclusiveness is an easy step . . . We shall be a . . . little self-elected (and therefore absurd) aristocracy, basking in the moonshine of our collective self-approval."

See Chapter 3 for more on Lewis's views on friendship and its influence in his life.

Eros: Far more than just sex

Although *eros* is usually thought of as synonymous with sexual love, Lewis defines it more broadly, thinking of it as the "complex state of being in love." Sexual love is a certainly a part of *eros,* but so is non-sexual romance and desire. Sex also exists apart from *eros* when the sex becomes an end in itself. In contrast, *eros* is centered on the other person. "*Eros* wants the beloved," says Lewis.

Of the three human loves, Lewis believes *eros* is closest to divine love *(agape)* because of its passionate desire of the other. So too, when a person is "in love" with another, he or she is capable of selflessness at a very high degree. During the intensity of that moment, we're able to go without food, sleep, happiness, safety, or any other personal comfort if it means we can be with the one we love.

Eros is magnificent, believes Lewis, but its magnificence is what makes this type of love so dangerous and destructive without the restraint that *agape* brings. Without God, *eros* "becomes a demon" because it wants more than anything to become God itself. Lewis writes that *eros* "always tends to turn 'being in love' into a sort of religion." Its very nature echoes of redemption; for a brief and shining moment, a person "in love" thinks only of the beloved. But, there's a catch: "Eros is drawn to promise what Eros Himself cannot perform," says Lewis. When *eros* tries to live for itself (apart from God), it dies.

Agape: The love from above

The fourth and final love is *agape,* or charity. *Agape* is a divine, selfless, and all-giving love. It's the kind of love that God has for humans, best expressed in the familiar biblical passage John 3:16: "For God so loved the world, that he gave his one and only Son, that whoever believes in him should not perish, but have eternal life."

When infused with *agape,* the human loves are transformed into something heavenly:

- *Agape* returns *storge* to a level at which its "aim of giving is to put the recipient in a state where he no longer needs our gift."

- *Agape* focuses *philia* on good passions rather than evil ones and prevents *philia* from turning into a "mutual admiration society."

- *Agape* tempers the fires of *eros* and prevents it from becoming an idol or god in a person's life.

In the end, Lewis concludes that "natural loves can hope for eternity only so far as they have allowed themselves to be taken into the eternity of [*agape* love]."

Marriage: Far More than a Love Parade

To Lewis, marriage is far more than a mutual partnership between people in love with each other. Instead, marriage is the act of two persons becoming "one flesh." This concept of "one flesh" isn't some sentimental ideal to Lewis but rather a literal fact "just as one is stating a fact when one says that . . . a violin and a bow are one musical instrument." He writes in *A Grief Observed* that in this oneness a man and a woman are most fully human, which helps explain why Christianity holds that marriage isn't a temporary partnership but a lifelong union.

Lewis refuses to believe that marriage is designed for people only when they're "in love" and that divorce is acceptable when they fall "out of love." At the same time, he never declares that divorce is always wrong. After all, he did everything he could to get Joy Davidman Gresham out of an abusive marriage (see Chapter 2). Lewis is saddened that different views on divorce permeate the Christian Church, but he finds solace in the fact that even though some parts of the Church allow divorce and others don't, all "regard divorce as something like cutting up a living body . . . more like having your legs cut off than it is like dissolving a business partnership."

As seen in romantic films and books, modern society has deluded itself into thinking that if you can just find and marry the *right* person, you can count on being in love forever. Lewis scoffs at this romantic sentimentality: "They lived happily ever after" was never meant to mean they "felt for the next fifty years exactly as they felt the day before they were married." At the same time, this loss of feeling in love doesn't mean that you no longer love your spouse. In fact, this change of love from an emotion to an act isn't bad, Lewis recognizes, but rather is a necessary step toward a lifelong union. The act of love, not the feeling of "being in love," gives a married couple the ability to keep their promises to each other. As Lewis sums up, "It is on this love that the engine of marriage is run: being in love was the explosion that started it."

In a poignant letter to his friend Sheldon Vanauken, whose young wife passed away at a time in their marriage when the couple was still very much in love, Lewis shares a poignant insight into the change of love. He writes:

> *I sometimes wonder whether bereavement is not, at bottom, the easiest and least perilous of the ways in which men lose the happiness of youthful love. For I believe it must always be lost in some way: every merely natural love has to be crucified before it can achieve resurrection and the happy old couples have come through a difficult death and re-birth. But far more have missed the re-birth.*

Missing the "re-birth" (or perhaps not even knowing about a re-birth) is what Lewis feels to be the underlying cause of the collapse of marriage as a permanent covenant. Jesus said that unless a thing dies it cannot truly live. Lewis believes human love follows the same cycle: When the powerful feelings go away, it can be re-born as a true and lasting love, a permanent covenant that he believes marriage was designed, by God, to be.

For more discussion on marriage and its permanence, see *Mere Christianity* (which is explored in Chapter 16) and *A Grief Observed.*

Sex: Intended for Good Pleasure

Through the years, Christianity has gotten the reputation of being a "no-fun" religion when it comes to sex. I suspect that's partly due to the fact that Christian teaching places limits on sexual activity — saying that it must occur only within the context of a marital relationship. Perhaps Christianity also got this reputation because of misguided Christian groups and cultural movements in history that considered any physical pleasure to be somehow evil.

Yet, as Lewis argues across his writings, these misconceptions have no basis in the reality of Christian truth. Instead, when you look at the Christian and secular views of sex, Lewis contends that it's actually the secular view of sex that turns out to be "no fun."

Contrasting God's and Satan's perspectives on sex

Biblical Christianity never teaches that sex is bad. In fact, Christianity says the exact opposite. Lewis argues that "Christianity is almost the only one of the great religions which thoroughly approves of the body." He believes "sex is nothing to be ashamed of" when you talk about it as an act of pleasure and an act by which humans reproduce.

God's positive view of the body and pleasure and Satan's opposing view are illustrated by one of the principle plotlines of Lewis's *That Hideous Strength* (see Chapter 12). In the story, the ultimate goal of the evil organization called N.I.C.E. is to get rid of the human body altogether and gradually transform the human race into bodiless intelligences. Achieving this goal will have the effect of isolating human beings from all wholesome sensual pleasures.

Lewis uses this storyline to reveal how God loves and blesses sex, marriage, and fertility. God also rejoices in good pleasures experienced by humans. On the other hand, Satan offers only damaged goods, which are designed to destroy the body and soul. So too, Satan promotes perversion and sterility in order to derail humans from experiencing all that God has designed for them.

In *That Hideous Strength,* Lewis memorably illustrates these contrasting perspectives. Filostrato, an evil physiologist, talks about his admiration of the moon's barrenness and the lunar masters who were able to sterilize their world and progress to living without bodies or organic food. In contrast, Ransom, the hero of the space trilogy, observes that the Earth-facing side of the moon is cursed: "The womb is barren and the marriages [are] cold." He adds that sex as such does not exist on the moon, saying that their "children they fabricate by vile arts in a secret place."

Sex as a harbinger of things to come

In his 1941 sermon, "The Weight of Glory," Lewis makes it clear that sensual pleasures, when properly enjoyed, are earthly reflections of the transcendent joys of Heaven, echoes of "God's creative rapture." In "Transposition," a sermon from 1944, Lewis adds that people's existence in Heaven "will differ from the sensory life we know here . . . as a flower differs from a bulb or a cathedral from an architect's drawing."

Good instincts gone bad

In spite of the pleasures that God intended when he created sex, Lewis believes that the sexual instinct has gone bad in fallen humans. In fact, he concludes that the striking difference between human sexual practice (instinct) and the Christian teaching on sex means that one of them has to be wrong. As an illustration, in *Mere Christianity* Lewis compares the obsession that people have for sex to a striptease act with food:

> *Suppose you came to a country where you could fill a theater by simply bringing a covered plate on to the stage and then slowly lifting the cover so as to let every one see, just before the lights went out, that it contained a mutton chop or a bit of bacon, would you not think that in that country something had gone wrong with the appetite for food? And would not anyone who had grown up in a different world think there was something equally [skewed] about the state of the sex instinct among us?*

Lewis dismisses the notion that such a reaction occurs simply because people don't get enough sex. Instead, he argues, "Starving men may think much about food, but so do gluttons."

Lewis believes sex has become spoiled and tainted in the postmodern world. After all, if you compare sexual desire with the natural desire to eat food, you can see how skewed sexual desire as become in comparison. Very few people, if any, become obsessed with eating something other than food. But, if today's sex instinct is normal, Lewis wonders why perversions are so "numerous, hard to cure, and frightful." Some suggest that perversions arise from the fact that society has hushed up talk of sex. Lewis, who realized even in his lifetime that sex was no longer silenced, counters, "I think the human race originally hushed it up because it had become such a mess." Now, fast-forward fifty years to the 21st century and sex is discussed everywhere — in schools, on TV, in movies, and on the radio. It's used to sell everything from books to beer to baseball. Yet despite the openness, sexual behavior has become even more deviant, not healthier. As Lewis would say, it's not the Christian teaching on sex that's bad, but it's the condition of our sexual instincts.

Why illicit sex is bad but isn't the supreme vice

Marriage is the union of two persons into one being. Lewis points out that God's design for sex in marriage is based on his design of marriage itself. Lewis explains, "The monstrosity of sexual intercourse outside marriage is that those who indulge in it are trying to isolate one kind of union (the sexual) from all the other kinds of union which were intended to go along with it and make up the total union. The Christian attitude does not mean that there is anything wrong about sexual pleasure . . . It means that you must not isolate that pleasure and try to get it by itself."

However, Lewis doesn't think that sexual immorality is the absolute worst sin. "If anyone thinks that Christians regard unchastity as the supreme vice, he is quite wrong," says Lewis. The sins of the flesh are bad, but Lewis believes that the sins of the spirit are far worse. Pride, hatred, spite, maliciousness, and the like have a greater tendency to destroy a person and those around him than does sexual sin.

Death: The Final Frontier?

For many people, death is the great unknown. It incites fear, trepidation, and anxiety, and the world spends literally billions of dollars trying to prevent death or at least to slow its certain approach. Most people prefer not to even think about death, and when they do, it's usually because some relative or acquaintance has passed away. Not surprisingly, even these moments of forced consideration are kept purposefully short. How soon after losing a loved one do well-intentioned people start telling the mourner to "get on with it"? They're trying, as best as they know how, to bring comfort, but unconsciously they're really trying to minimize death. Trying, if you will, to push death back into the closet where it's out of sight and out of mind.

Rebirth for the believer

In contrast to those who ignore it, C.S. Lewis, like many great thinkers and writers, often muses on death. He recognizes that without some frame of reference, some belief (not necessarily religious) in the purpose of life, death becomes a black hole. In an essay on *Hamlet,* Lewis writes that death's an "unknown" with "infinite uncertainties," likely explaining why so few people actually concern themselves with death except when it forces itself into their lives.

For the greater part of his life, Lewis reflected on death from a distance. He came to view it as necessary and even a miracle of mercy to those who believe in the Christian faith. He believes that immortality for fallen man would be "the one utterly hopeless destiny." But in stark contrast, Christians believe that through death they're finally able to leave all the horrors of a fallen world behind. Death is a door through which they enter eternity. Or as Aslan says in *The Last Battle,* "The term is over: the holidays have begun."

Lewis embraces death as a haunting yet wonderful paradox. He knows it to be both the very worst that man faces and that moment in a man's life that's filled with infinite possibility. Lewis writes of death's duality, "It is holy and unholy; our supreme disgrace and our only hope."

Although death comes to people because of the Fall of Man, it's overcome through the sacrificial death of Jesus. In this way, death ironically becomes, for those who believe, our very "means of redemption."

A horrible experience for those left behind

Lewis did more than just write about death, however. He also experienced the effects of death when his newlywed wife died after just four years of marriage (see Chapter 2). During this experience, Lewis found death to be a most horrible thing, dubbing it "the triumph of Satan." This agonizing period is candidly presented to readers in his book *A Grief Observed* (see Chapter 15). In one poignant passage, he recalls with obvious bitterness the shallow attempts at comfort made by the statement, "She will live forever in my memory." He responds with disdain to such an attempt by saying, "Live? That is exactly what she won't do."

In the end, Lewis found that death, though a thing to be welcomed by a believer for the believer himself, is still a thing to be fought against by those who are left behind. Consider, for example, the fact that Jesus wept at the grave of Lazarus. Lewis believed Jesus wept "because death, the punishment of sin, is even more horrible in His eyes than in ours." However, in spite of the sting of death of loved ones, Lewis remained full of hope and expectation for the "morning after."

Lewis has much to say on the subject of death. Check out Chapters 8, 11, and 15 for more.

War: Why Pacifism Doesn't Work

C.S. Lewis believes that, as undesirable as war is, it can be justified and is sometimes even necessary. In 1940, Lewis gave a talk called "Why I am not a Pacifist" to, of all things, a pacifist society in Oxford. (Lewis was a lot of things, but obviously he wasn't shy!) The full text of this talk can be found in the book *The Weight of Glory and Other Addresses*. In typical Lewis fashion, he systematically argues his position based on a step-by-step analysis of the pacifist position, namely the beliefs that:

- ✔ Wars always do more harm than good.
- ✔ Love is better than hate.
- ✔ Jesus Christ is anti-war.

First, pacifists believe that wars always do more harm than good. But the problem with that belief, according to Lewis, is that it's not provable; it's mere speculation. He questions how anyone can know if an alternative would have been better than what actually took place. Would the world be a better place today if England and the United States hadn't fought Nazi Germany? Or what about the Iraq War — would goodness have been better served if the U.S. hadn't invaded Hussein's Iraq? Maybe. Maybe not. In the end, there's no way to know for certain either way.

Second, pacifists claim their position based on the universally held belief that "love is good and hatred is bad." Although Lewis doesn't argue with this view, he does say that there are difficulties with applying that principle in the real world. To love or to do good to a neighbor may eventually mean not doing good to someone else — it may mean actually doing *harm* to another person. Lewis uses the example of a person — I call him good ol' Gilligan — who's being hurt by someone else — I call him mean ol' Skipper. It's universally accepted that to love is to help Gilligan. But helping Gilligan may require actually doing ill to Skipper because doing nothing makes you complicit in hurting Gilligan. Pacifism, if strictly adhered to, eventually leaves you in a moral quagmire if you sit by and watch evil occur.

Third, pacifists, at least Christian ones, argue that Jesus was the ultimate anti-war pacifist. However, Lewis dismisses the idea that pacifists can use Jesus's teachings to support their views. He insists that when Jesus said, "If someone hits you on one cheek, let him hit you on the other cheek also," he wasn't establishing an anti-war position. Lewis believes Christ's teaching applies to individuals, not nation-states. Furthermore, he points to Jesus's unqualified praise of a Roman centurion (see Matthew 8:8–13) without insisting the officer give up his profession. If war and warriors were absolute evils, Lewis argues that such praise would have been inconsistent and out of place.

If you want to know more about Lewis's views on war, check out *The Weight of Glory; God in the Dock* and *Present Concerns: Essays by C.S. Lewis* also explore specific questions that are raised by war.

Capital Punishment: Certainly Gray Territory

Like most great thinkers, Lewis isn't afraid of the gray areas in life. He recognizes that the world isn't always black-and-white, and it's necessary at times to live within the mix. Capital punishment is a gray area issue for Lewis: He doesn't commit to the opinion that it's always right but says that "it is certainly not wrong."

His views on capital punishment are influenced by his views on death. Christianity claims that life is eternal. Remember, for Lewis, death is the transition from one life to another; it's the passing from a temporary to an eternal home. He feels that even a horrible person, a murderer for example, who experiences conversion realizes Heaven after death. And to Lewis's thinking, there's much greater possibility of such a person finding conversion at execution time than of finding it while in prison for 20 or 30 years.

The heart of Lewis's argument that capital punishment isn't "certainly wrong" centers on the well-being of the community. He maintains that if a person commits a violent crime against another, "the only efficient method of restraint" may be the death penalty. He cites not only the fact that such punishment can act as a deterrent but also that it serves "as an expression of the moral importance of certain crimes." In other words, when society establishes a death penalty for murder and rape, it communicates a very "valuable" lesson: Murder and rape are evil, and they will not be tolerated.

Of course, Lewis is aware of the arguments against capital punishment based on the Christian grounds that we're to love our enemies. But in his opinion, this argument lacks a true understanding of that Christian teaching. We love ourselves, but that doesn't mean we shouldn't "subject" ourselves to punishment when we do wrong. He reasons, "If one had committed murder, the right Christian thing to do would be to give yourself up to the police and be hanged."

Lewis is just as unmoved by the argument against capital punishment based on the Bible's instruction, "Thou shalt not kill." He points out that the Greek language has two words for kill: One means to kill and the other to murder. In the Gospels, Jesus used the word for murder. As Lewis explains, "All killing is not murder any more than all sexual intercourse is adultery."

Finally, even the argument that capital punishment may kill innocent people if they were wrongly convicted doesn't convince Lewis. He agrees that you can't undo a wrongful execution, but he maintains "neither can you give back the years which wrongful imprisonment has eaten."

In the end, Lewis holds capital punishment as a gray area with reasons for and against it, and he recognizes that "good men" can disagree on this topic. He cautions only that even in the act of killing "we must not hate." Just as we're so quick to forgive ourselves when we do wrong, so should we be forgiving toward our enemies. We should "wish that he were not bad, to hope that he may, in this world or another, be cured."

For further understanding of Lewis's position on capital punishment, refer to *Mere Christianity*, *The Weight of Glory*, and *God in the Dock*.

Politics: Necessary, But Nothing to Get Too Excited About

During his life, C.S. Lewis was never a "political animal," one who relishes talking of politics and hot issues of the day. Politics and government were necessary evils, not something to write home about. In words that echo Thomas Jefferson's immortal opening lines of *The Declaration of Independence*, Lewis writes, "The State exists simply to promote and to protect the ordinary happiness of human beings in this life." Being able to sit with friends at the local pub, stroll through an open field, or write a letter to a close friend are examples of what Lewis would probably consider privileges that government should afford its citizens, privileges that government exists to protect.

The apolitical nature of Lewis has to do not only with his personality but also with his Christian faith. Lewis recognizes that Jesus Christ said little, if anything, on the topic of politics.

From what Lewis does write on the topic of politics, we know that he believes that if man had not fallen, "Patriarchal Monarchy would be the sole lawful government." But because of the Fall of Man (see Chapter 16), democracy is the best alternative. This point of view isn't the product of any "romantic" notions of democracy, however. Lewis certainly makes it clear that democracy isn't preferred because all men are "good" enough and "wise" enough to "share in government." It's really quite the opposite. He believes that, because of the Fall, people are "so wicked that not one of them can be trusted with any irresponsible power over his fellows." And this is exactly why, despite his deep religious convictions, he despises theocracy. If men are fallen, Lewis reasons, they simply add "thus saith the Lord" to give divine authority to what are merely human laws. And, for Lewis, that's a dangerous development for the Christian Church.

Lewis doesn't sympathize with those Christians who hold that government needs a Christian political party. His insistence against this proposal is based on three reasons:

- ✔ **Such a party would claim its "favorite opinions" as God's truth.**
  The very existence of a "Christian Party" would suggest that this party represents all Christianity when, in truth, it only represents a part of Christianity: the part its particular members represent. A Christian political party would, in turn, "accuse all Christians who do not join it of apostasy and betrayal."

- ✔ **Christians should not try to legislate all Christian teaching.** Lewis's reasoning on this point is quite straightforward: "The Church should frankly recognize that the majority of the people are not Christians and, therefore, cannot be expected to live Christian lives." While Lewis was alive, Christians in Britain tried to influence society by changing the divorce laws to reflect the Christian position. Lewis was opposed to that movement based on his argument against legislating biblical teaching.

- ✔ **The only way Christians can truly influence society is by following the great Commission, not by becoming a political party.** Jesus's last words to His disciples are known as the Great Commission: "Go ye into all the world and make disciples of all men." On this instruction, Lewis writes, "He who converts his neighbor has performed that most practical Christian political act of all." According to Lewis, if you really want a moral society, you don't change the laws, you find a way to change the people in society — and only God can do that.

Lewis's clearest writings on politics can be found in *God in the Dock*. Of course, *Mere Christianity* and *The Abolition of Man* offer glimpses on the topic as well.

The Bible: More than Mere Literature

C.S. Lewis finds nothing in the Bible that, apart from its origins in God's inspiration, can cause it to be called a *great* book. "Stripped of its divine authority," he probably wouldn't even call it a *good* book. Lewis thinks that people who say it's just a piece of literature and actually claim to enjoy its "literary charms" aren't actual people; at least, he's never met such a person. It's painfully obvious to Lewis that, from beginning to end, the Bible is a spiritual book making claims that are sacred and holy. It's impossible to read the Bible and not notice how often the various writers prefaced their lines with "Thus saith the Lord." Lewis, so well-learned in the classics, argues that even Aeschylus and Virgil didn't begin their poetry with "Thus say the gods." And furthermore, a book with so many different literary styles and writing, which at times is quite good but at other times quite bad, would never be able to capture someone's interest, at least from a literary perspective, for very long. Therefore, the Bible itself demands to be approached from a different perspective — as the authoritative word of God, not as literature.

Thumbs up to modern biblical translations

Lewis believes that modern translations of the Bible are not only welcomed but very necessary. Language grows and changes with time. As a result, Lewis argues, "if we are to have translation at all we must have periodical re-translation."

The Bible is for all persons, Lewis believes, so it makes sense that it should be translated in such a way as to communicate its message to all people.

Prayer: God's Transformative Tool

To C.S. Lewis, prayer is nothing magical. It's simply talking with God. But, at the same time, prayer is far more than a one-sided conversation in which people read off a wish list to a Santa Claus–like figure in the sky.

According to Lewis, prayer's greatest significance is that it helps change people into what God wants them to be. Lewis sees the importance of other reasons for prayer, but the weighty sense of change that he experienced while communicating with God is what drove him to his knees. He discovered in his prayer life that the greatest blessing was when God, in mercy, broke down false perceptions of who Lewis believed God to be. Lewis experienced much joy when he rose from his knees saying to himself ". . . but I never knew before."

Jesus gave the Lord's Prayer (also known as the Our Father) in Matthew 6:9–13 as a model for his disciples. At the heart of this prayer, Jesus tells us to ask that God's will "be done on earth as it is in Heaven." Lewis argues that this goal is achieved one believer at a time — with God's will being born, through prayer, into a believer and the believer thereby becoming the vehicle through which God's will is accomplished.

Prayer is used to transform believers and enable them to surrender to God's will, but Lewis also believes that prayer involves asking God for your needs and desires. However, he reminds readers that the very nature of request "is that it may or may not be granted." For Lewis, the idea that our requests may not be answered in the manner that we hope for doesn't indicate anything bad or wrong about God. Instead, it's an issue with "finite and foolish creatures" asking for things that may, if we could possibly know the beginning from the end, be exactly the opposite of what we really think we're asking for. Lewis asks, "If God had granted all the silly prayers I've made in my life, where should I be now?"

As important as the Lord's Prayer is to one's understanding of prayer, Lewis believes that Jesus's prayer in the garden of Gethsemane on the night before he was crucified (see Matthew 26:36–46) is an even better model for Christians. Lewis points to Jesus's submission of his own will to that of his Father's as the transformative power of prayer. It's this transforming effect that allows the person praying to say "Thy will be done" and add to it the words "by me — now"!

Christ's prayer in Gethsemane is the cornerstone of Lewis's beliefs on prayer. He even suggests that "for most of us [it] is the only model." In his opinion, any teaching on answers to prayer, purpose of prayer, or effects of prayer has to take into account this prayer of Christ's.

According to Lewis, the prayer of Gethsemane also offers a response to those who believe God will answer any prayer so long as you have enough faith. How can you expect your every wish to be fulfilled, asks Lewis, if the person who had the most faith of all prayed three times and was denied each time? Likewise, Lewis uses the same argument against those who think answered prayer is a sign that the person praying is in favor with God. Surely Christ being refused "in Gethsemane is answer enough to that."

Most of the thoughts that C.S. Lewis makes on prayer can be found in two writings, his final book *Letters to Malcolm: Chiefly on a Prayer* and a little-known essay titled "The Efficacy of Prayer," which has been published both individually and as part of a larger collection titled *The World's Last Night and Other Essays.* However, *God in the Dock* also takes up the subject in some detail as does, in a much more subtle way, *The Screwtape Letters.*

Reason: Naturalism's Nasty Problem

In his apologetic book *Miracles,* Lewis explores how God intervenes in the world he created. However, one of the most timely arguments Lewis makes is his strong refutation of naturalism (at the start of the book). *Naturalism* is the belief that nature is all there was, is, and ever will be. Lewis's contention is that the nastiest problem that naturalism can never successfully overcome is what goes on inside that gray matter between your ears.

According to Lewis, because all possible knowledge depends on our ability to think, reason must be the starting point in assessing the validity of naturalism. "Unless human reasoning is valid no science is true," says Lewis. Therefore, if a naturalist claims that our reasoning powers are not real, then his position is dead in the water. Lewis quotes J.B.S. Haldane's *Possible Worlds* to prove his point: "If my mental processes are determined wholly by the motions of atoms in my brain, I have no reason to suppose that my beliefs are true . . . and hence I have no reason for supposing my brain to be composed of atoms."

Lewis sets his sights on dealing with the idea that our reasoning power could have come from purely natural means — Darwinian natural selection. According to evolutionary theory, the reasoning power of humans evolved from non-reasoning matter. Humans' thoughts, therefore, began simply as responses to the environment around them. Lewis, however, argues that it's impossible for a gradual improvement of responses to evolve into acts of insight by way of natural selection. The relationship between "response and stimulus is utterly different from that between knowledge and the truth known." Similarly, suppose you have an unlimited pass to the local cinema to watch movies any time you want. You watch three movies a day, every day, for a year. After all that time spent watching all the movies Hollywood produces, you know a lot about the films' stories, but you're no closer to understanding how film processing and projection technology works than you were on Day One. Lewis adds:

> *Our physical vision is a far more useful response to light than that of the cruder organisms which have only a photo-sensitive spot. But neither this improvement or any possible improvements we can suppose could bring it an inch nearer to being a knowledge of light . . . It is not men with specially good eyes who know about light, but men who have studied the relevant sciences.*

Lewis then dismisses the idea that human reasoning could have been acquired by making inferences based on human experiences. A child, for example, learns not to stick her finger into a light socket because after she tries it once, she realizes how much it hurts. Therefore, "If I stick my finger in light socket, I get an ouchie" is an inference based on experience. But Lewis believes not all experience-based inferences are right. For example, suppose the child burns her finger on a hot kettle. She'd be confused, looking around to find the light socket. Lewis says of inferences:

> *Such expectations are not inferences and need not be true. The assumption that things which have been conjoined in the past will always be conjoined in the future is the guiding principle not of rational but of animal behavior. Reason comes in precisely when you make the inference 'Since always conjoined, therefore probably conjoined.'*

Part V
The Part of Tens

The 5th Wave — By Rich Tennant

CS LEWIS HAS HIS FAITH TESTED AGAIN.

"There you go, governor. A piece of me own homemade steak and kidney pie."

In this part . . .

You've had the appetizer and main course in this "Lewis feast;" now it's time for dessert. No, the Part of Tens doesn't mean that you get ten helpings of chocolate mousse or ten chocolate chip cookies. But it does mean that you get ten nuggets of information in each of these chapters to help round out your understanding of Lewis and his works. Find out where to go on the Web and in the real world to get more Lewis. Pick your favorite from among ten great quotes from the master. Find out who Lewis the booklover would recommend you tackle in your next literary adventure. Finally, if you find Lewis a challenge to read, check out ten tips that make reading his works easier.

Chapter 19

Ten C.S. Lewis and Narnia Resources

In This Chapter

▶ Enjoying *The Chronicles of Narnia:* Movies, videos, and audio dramas

▶ Attending C.S. Lewis festivals and conferences

▶ Checking out fun and useful C.S. Lewis Web sites

The lasting influence of C.S. Lewis becomes crystal clear the moment you look around and see how just much "Lewis stuff" is going on today, decades after his death. In fact, the legacy of C.S. Lewis seems to grow with each passing year — from Narnia on the silver screen to Lewis conferences worldwide to new fan-based Web sites launching every week.

In this chapter, I highlight ten of the many resources available to you if you want to delve deeper into C.S. Lewis and *The Chronicles of Narnia.*

Narnia on the Big Screen, Small Screen, and Somewhere in Between

You can experience the world of Narnia in ways other than the printed page. *The Chronicles of Narnia* is dramatized in several different mediums, including

✔ **Film.** Most noteworthy is the major feature film release by Walden Media and Disney of *The Lion, the Witch and the Wardrobe* (and likely the other Narnia books, as well). You can visit the film's official Web site at www.narnia.com, or head to www.narniaweb.com to explore NarniaWeb, a fan-based site providing the inside scoop and latest details on Narnia films.

✔ **Audio drama.** Family Radio Theater, a ministry of Focus on the Family, has dramatized each of the seven Narnia books as radio theater. Available on both audio CDs and cassette tapes, these versions are extremely well-made and feature top voice talents, including Paul Scofield and David Suchet. Douglas Gresham, Lewis's stepson, is the series host. For more information, go to radiotheatre.org.

✔ **TV video.** In the late 1980s and early 1990s, four of the Narnia books — *The Lion, the Witch and the Wardrobe, Prince Caspian and the Voyage of the "Dawn Treader"* (combined into one), and *The Silver Chair* — aired on television (BBC and PBS). These productions, available on DVD and VHS, remain faithful to the books and are generally well-acted, but they were obviously done on limited budgets.

C.S. Lewis Foundation

www.cslewis.org

Founded in 1986, the C.S. Lewis Foundation offers a variety of conferences, programs, resources, and other opportunities for those interested in discovering more about C.S. Lewis as well as Christian scholarship in the contemporary university.

The C.S. Lewis Foundation restored and maintains the Kilns, Lewis's Oxford residence for much of his life. The foundation hosts a Study Centre at The Kilns, providing a variety of summer seminar opportunities.

C.S. Lewis Institute

www.cslewisinstitute.org

The C.S. Lewis Institute, created in 1976, sponsors conferences and lectures, provides fellows programs, and publishes the periodical *Knowing & Doing*. The Washington, D.C.–based Christian organization is chiefly devoted to supporting those who "like Lewis, articulate, defend, and live faith in Christ through personal and public life."

Be Eventful: C.S. Lewis Conferences, Seminars, and Festivals

A variety of organizations sponsor annual or periodic events relating to Lewis and his literary legacy. Highlights include

- **Oxbridge conference.** The C.S. Lewis Foundation hosts an annual Oxbridge conference at Oxford and Cambridge that regularly features top Lewis speakers and lecturers. For details, visit `www.cslewis.org/programs`.

- **C.S. Lewis Institute conferences.** The C.S. Lewis Institute sponsors a variety of conferences each year featuring well-known and respected speakers. Check out details at `www.cslewisinstitute.org/pages/upcomingEvents/index.php`.

- **Lewis Workshop Weekends.** Lewis expert Dr. Bruce Edwards gives churches and schools the opportunity to host workshops in which he introduces attendees to the author. For details, visit `personal.bgsu.edu/~edwards/lewis.html`.

- **C.S. Lewis Festival.** If you're near Petoskey, Michigan, check out the city's annual C.S. Lewis Festival in the summer. Activities include seminars, discussion groups, and other presentations. You can find more information at `www.cslewisfestival.org`.

- **The Frances White Ewbank Colloquium on C. S. Lewis and Friends.** The Center for the Study of C.S. Lewis and Friends at Taylor University sponsors this Biennial Colloquium as well as other events. For more information, visit `www.taylor.edu/cslewis`.

Into the Wardrobe

`cslewis.drzeus.net`

Into the Wardrobe, created by Lewis fan John Visser, is one of the most useful C.S. Lewis and Narnia sites on the Web. In addition to Lewis and Narnia FAQs, news, and book summaries, Visser also supplies visitors with excellent links to Lewis-related papers and essays.

The Definitive Lewis Launching Pad on the Web

`ic.net/~erasmus/RAZ26.HTM`

It's nothing fancy, but if you want a launching pad for exploring C.S. Lewis on the Web, check out this Web site, entitled *C.S. Lewis: 20th-Century Christian Knight.* Compiled by Dave Armstrong, this site serves as the definitive reference source for Lewis Web links, photographs, bibliographies, essays, and more.

C.S. Lewis and the Inklings Resources

personal.bgsu.edu/~edwards/lewis.html

Dr. Bruce L. Edwards, Professor of English at Bowling Green State University and a renowned expert on Lewis, maintains this site, which provides a variety of information and resources on Lewis and the Inklings.

The Stone Table

www.thestonetable.com

This fan-based Web site is devoted to providing news and resources on C.S. Lewis, his books, and the Narnia films.

C.S. Lewis Societies

Several C.S. Lewis Societies are scattered throughout the United States, Britain, Germany, and other countries. One of the most noteworthy is the New York C.S. Lewis Society, which can be found on the Web at www.nycslsociety.com. To find a C.S Lewis Society in or near your community, check out *Into The Wardrobe*'s listings at cslewis.drzeus.net/other/contacts.html.

Making a Pilgrimage: C.S. Lewis Tours

www.cslewistours.co.uk

If you would like to make a pilgrimage to the world of C.S. Lewis, contact C.S. Lewis Tours and hop a plane to England. You can take a three-hour guided tour through Oxfordshire, stopping by places of interest for Lewis fans, including the Kilns (his home) and Holy Trinity Church (his final resting place).

Chapter 20

Ten Classic Lewis Quotes

In This Chapter

▶ Expounding on Christianity and Christian belief

▶ Commenting on human nature and the bigger picture

1 love quotes. Like a nugget of gold, a great quote packs something priceless into a small package. As a writer, I'm always on the hunt for unforgettable quotes, whether they be from books, movies, TV shows, or songs. Over the years, I've undoubtedly quoted one creative source in my writing and speaking more than any other — C.S. Lewis. (Although the film *The Princess Bride* and the television series *Seinfeld* run awfully close in second and third places!)

Trying to select the ten best quotes from Lewis's library of work is much like the curator of the Louvre trying to identify the ten greatest paintings in his gallery — you just can't choose a definitive set. Yet, certain memorable quotes from Lewis jump out to me — ones that combine a clever, witty style, God-breathed wisdom, and brilliant logic. Therefore, in this chapter of tens, I list ten Lewis quotes that I consider to be among his best in terms of presenting Christian truth in a classic fashion.

On Calling Jesus Merely a Great Human

One of today's popular descriptions of Jesus Christ is that he was a great moral teacher. Yet, in *Mere Christianity*, Lewis says that a great teacher is the one thing that Christ could *not* have been. Instead, he says that Jesus Christ either had to be a crazy man, a deceiver, or God in the flesh. He writes:

> *I am trying here to prevent anyone saying the really foolish thing that people often say about [Jesus Christ]: "I'm ready to accept Jesus as a great moral teacher, but I don't accept His claim to be God." That is the one thing we must not say. A man who was merely a man and said the sort of things Jesus said would not be a great moral teacher. He would either be a lunatic — on a level with the man who says he is a poached egg — or else he would be the*

Devil of Hell. You can shut Him up for a fool; you can spit at Him and kill Him as a demon; or you can fall at His feet and call Him Lord and God. But let us not come with any patronizing nonsense about His being a great human teacher. He has not left that open to us. He did not intend to.

On Comparing Aslan to Jesus Christ

In *The Lion, the Witch and the Wardrobe,* Susan and Lucy first learn about Aslan and ask Mr. and Mrs. Beaver about who he is and what he's like. Lewis created Aslan to symbolize Jesus Christ in Narnia, and in this dialogue, Lewis offers a vivid picture of the good, yet untamed quality of Jesus Christ:

"Who is Aslan?" asked Susan.

"Aslan?" said Mr. Beaver, "Why don't you know, He's the king . . ."

"Is — is he a man?" asked Lucy.

"Aslan a man!" said Mr. Beaver sternly. "Certainly not. I tell you he is the King of the wood and the son of the great Emperor-Beyond-the-Sea. Don't you know who is the King of Beasts? Aslan is a lion — the Lion, the great Lion."

"Ooh!" said Susan. "I'd thought he was a man. Is he — quite safe? I shall feel rather nervous about meeting a lion."

"That you will, dearie, and no mistake," said Mrs. Beaver, "if there's anyone who can appear before Aslan without their knees knocking, they're either braver than most or else just silly."

"Then he isn't safe?" said Lucy.

"Safe?" said Mr. Beaver. "Don't you hear what Mrs. Beaver tells you? Who said anything about safe? 'Course he isn't safe. But he's good. He's the King, I tell you."

On the Cost of Throwing Out Moral Absolutes

Throughout *The Abolition of Man,* Lewis deals with the inevitable consequences of living in a world of relativism. However, perhaps nowhere does he express the cost more succinctly than when he writes:

When all that says "it is good" has been debunked, what says "I want" remains.

On Human Behavior When Everything is Relative

Lewis believes that when you throw out moral absolutes, people are ultimately dehumanized. Yet, at the same time, society still expects people to act decently to each other. In *The Abolition of Man,* Lewis addresses this inconsistency:

> *The Chest — Magnanimity — Sentiment — these are the indispensable liaison officers between cerebral and visceral man. It may even be said that it is by this middle element that man is man: for by his intellect he is mere spirit and by his appetite mere animal. The operation [of relativism] is to produce what may be called Men without Chests . . . Such is the tragi-comedy of our situation — we continue to clamor for those very qualities we are rendering impossible . . . In a sort of ghastly simplicity we remove the organ and demand the function. We make men without chests and expect of them virtue and enterprise. We laugh at honor and are shocked to find traitors in our midst. We castrate and bid the geldings be fruitful.*

On What's Fundamentally Wrong with Atheism

In *Mere Christianity,* Lewis points out a fundamental flaw in atheism:

> *[When I was an atheist] my argument against God was that the universe seemed so cruel and unjust. But how had I got this idea of* just *and* unjust? *A man does not call a line crooked unless he has some idea of a straight line. What was I comparing this universe with when I called it unjust? If the whole show was bad and senseless from A to Z, so to speak, why did I, who was supposed to be part of the show, find myself in such violent reaction against it? . . . Thus in the very act of trying to prove that God did not exist — in other words, that the whole of reality was senseless — I found I was forced to assume that one part of reality — namely my idea of justice — was full of sense. Consequently atheism turns out to be too simple. If the whole universe has no meaning, we should never have found out that it has no meaning.*

On the Effectiveness of Small Sins

In *The Screwtape Letters,* a senior devil instructs a junior devil on the effectiveness of small sins:

> *Like all young tempters, you are anxious to be able to report spectacular wickedness. But do remember, the only thing that matters is the extent to which you separate the man from [God]. It does not matter how small the sins are provided that their cumulative effect is to edge the man away from the Light and out into the Nothing. Murder is no better than cards if cards can do the trick. Indeed the safest road to Hell is the gradual one — the gentle slope, soft underfoot, without sudden turnings, without milestones, without signposts.*

On True Love

Lewis describes in *The Four Loves* the difference between romantic love and a deeper, agape love:

> *Love as distinct from "being in love" is not merely a feeling. It is a deep unity, maintained by the will and deliberately strengthened by habit; reinforced by the grace which both partners ask, and receive from God . . . "Being in love" first moved them to promise fidelity: this quieter love enables them to keep the promise. It is on this love that the engine of marriage is run: being in love was the explosion that started it.*

On the Immortality of Humans

In *The Weight of Glory,* Lewis dismisses the idea that people you see around you are just plain folks who live a certain number of years and then die:

> *There are no ordinary people. You have never talked to a mere mortal. Nations, cultures, arts, civilizations — these are mortal, and their life is to ours as the life of a gnat. But it is immortals that we joke with, work with, marry, snub, and exploit — immortal horrors or everlasting splendors.*

On People's Thoughts about Heaven and Earth

In *The Weight of Glory*, Lewis speaks about what Heaven is like and explains how you and I dismiss that future glory for something more tangible already around us:

> *We are half-hearted creatures, fooling about with drink and sex and ambition when infinite joy is offered us, like an ignorant child who wants to go on making mud pies in a slum because he cannot imagine what is meant by the offer of a holiday at the sea. We are far too easily pleased.*

On Life in Heaven

To close out *The Chronicles of Narnia*, Lewis ends *The Last Battle* with a description that is identical to the experience of a Christian as he or she enters Heaven:

> *We can most truly say that they all lived happily ever after. But for them it was only the beginning of the real story. All their life in this world and all their adventures in Narnia had only been the cover and the title page: now at last they were beginning Chapter One of the Great Story, which no one on earth has read: which goes on for ever: in which every chapter is better than the one before.*

Chapter 21

Ten Authors Recommended By C.S. Lewis

In This Chapter

▶ Looking at who influenced Lewis

▶ Appreciating the authors Lewis simply enjoyed

*I*f you could travel back in time and ask C.S. Lewis for a list of "must-read" authors, you would quickly get his full attention. Without missing a beat, I suspect he'd quickly rattle off a long list of his favorites with a smile that smacked of a boy talking about his new toys under the Christmas tree.

The problem is, unless your name is Marty McFly, you aren't able to travel back in time to Lewis's day and ask him firsthand. So, in this chapter, I try to do the next best thing: I list ten of Lewis's favorite authors. Among Lewis's favorite writers are those who were highly influential to his thinking or writing (foundational reading), those whose work he found great joy in reading again and again (pleasure reading), and those who were his contemporaries and fellow members of the Inklings. If you love reading Lewis, you may develop a similar affection for these other authors as well.

Several of Lewis's favorites are so-called classical writers who have works available in the public domain. Many of these works are available for free download at www.gutenberg.org. Throughout the chapter, I note which recommendations you can access through this Web site. Note that the more popular titles from these authors remain in print and are also available in modern editions.

Influential Authors

The authors introduced in this section are ones who were highly influential to Lewis's thinking or writing.

George MacDonald

Recommended works: *Phantastes, Lilith, Diary of an Old Soul, Unspoken Sermons, The Princess and the Goblin, The Princess and Curdie, The Golden Key, What's Mine's Mine,* and *Sir Gibbie*

No author was as influential to C.S. Lewis as Scottish minister and author George MacDonald (1824–1905). Of MacDonald, Lewis had the highest of praises, referring to him as "my master." Not only is MacDonald one of the main characters in *The Great Divorce,* but most of Lewis's other books include quotes from the Scottish author as well. (Flip to Chapter 11 for coverage of *The Great Divorce.*) In fact, Lewis once remarked that he believed he never wrote a book in which he didn't quote MacDonald either directly or indirectly.

MacDonald's book *Phantastes* was perhaps the most significant book Lewis ever read, encountering it first as an adolescent when he was turning away from his Christian faith. In spite of the Christian undertones of *Phantastes,* Lewis loved the book and found it stuck with him throughout his life. Even though it didn't lead him to Christianity right away, Lewis looked back later in life and felt MacDonald's book "baptized his imagination" and helped prepare the way for his conversion.

In addition to *Phantastes,* Lewis considered one of MacDonald's final books, *Lilith,* among his most powerful. Apart from the Bible, Lewis said of *Lilith,* "I know of no book that is in a spiritual sense more deeply moving."

Lewis found MacDonald sometimes clumsy in his writing but believed "the gold is so good it carries off the dross." In the end, he concluded, "I know nothing that gives me such a feeling of spiritual healing, of being washed, as to read George MacDonald."

You can find most of George MacDonald's books available for download at www.gutenberg.org. In addition, they're also available from Johannesen Printing and Publishing (www.johannesen.com).

Edmund Spenser

Recommended work: *The Faerie Queene*

Sixteenth-century poet Edmund Spenser (1552–1599) was another favorite author of Lewis, who was particularly fond of his classic, *The Faerie Queene.* When he was at Great Bookham (see Chapter 2), Lewis was so captivated by *The Faerie Queene* that he read it in one sitting. Throughout his life, he never lost his enthusiasm for the classic work; in fact, he wrote in an updated edition of Spenser's *Images of Life,* "Once you have become an inhabitant of [*The Faerie Queene*'s] world, being tired of it is like being tired of London, or of life."

Spenser undoubtedly influenced the writings of Lewis, in particular *The Chronicles of Narnia.* In *Reading the Classics with C.S. Lewis,* scholar Doris Myers even goes so far as to say that you can think of *The Chronicles of Narnia* series as a "miniature *Faerie Queene.*"

You can download *The Faerie Queene* online at www.gutenberg.org/etext/6930.

Dante Alighieri

Recommended work: *The Divine Comedy*

Dante Alighieri (1265–1321) was a medieval Italian poet best known for his classic *The Divine Comedy,* a three-part poem that describes Dante's journey through Hell *(Inferno),* Purgatory *(Purgatorio),* and Heaven *(Paradiso).* Lewis had a lifelong passion for *The Divine Comedy* and boldly held up *Paradiso* as the best literary work in history. The same enthusiasm carried over to Dante himself; in *Selected Literary Essays,* Lewis claims, "Dante has not only no rival, but none second to him."

Dante's influence is clearly evident in *The Great Divorce,* which involves a similar fictional journey to Hell and Heaven. In addition to the overall topical similarities, Lewis pays homage to Dante's encounter with his love Beatrice in *Paradiso* by crafting a similar scenario with a husband and wife. (See Chapter 11 for more information on *The Great Divorce.*)

The Divine Comedy is available for download at www.gutenberg.org/etext/8800.

G.K. Chesterton

Recommended works: *The Everlasting Man, Orthodoxy, The Man Who Was Thursday*

G.K. Chesterton (1874–1936) was a popular early 20th-century British writer and novelist and an influential voice for Christianity. When Lewis was still an atheist, he read Chesterton's *The Everlasting Man* and was influenced by the arguments that Chesterton makes concerning Christianity's view of history. In *Surprised by Joy,* Lewis recalls his reaction at the time: "I already thought Chesterton the most sensible man alive 'apart from his Christianity.' Now, I veritably believe, I thought that Christianity itself was very sensible 'apart from its Christianity.'" And, while the book alone did not convert him, Lewis held up *The Everlasting Man* as the contemporary work that most influenced him toward Christianity.

In addition to the affect that Chesterton had on Lewis personally, he also appears to have impacted the way in which Lewis approached his popular apologetic books. For example, the popular theology expressed in *The Everlasting Man* is reminiscent of what Lewis tried to accomplish with books such as *Mere Christianity* and *The Problem of Pain*.

E. Nesbit

Recommended works: *The Story of the Treasure Seekers, Five Children and It, The Phoenix and the Carpet, The Story of the Amulet,* and *The Railway Children*

Edith Nesbit (1858–1924) was a prolific British children's author who published under the name E. Nesbit. Lewis enjoyed Nesbit's works when he was young, and the literary approach Nesbit used in her stories seems to have influenced Lewis in penning *The Chronicles of Narnia.* The Bastable family featured in several of Nesbit's stories is even paid homage to in *The Magician's Nephew* when Lewis begins, "In those days Mr. Sherlock Holmes was still living in Baker Street and the Bastables were looking for treasure in the Lewisham Road."

Honorable mentions

Hardly anything gave C.S. Lewis greater joy than reading a great book. And with such a passion for literature, it's no surprise that his list of favorite authors is extensive. In addition to those profiled in this chapter, Lewis also thoroughly enjoyed the work of Homer, Virgil, John Milton, John Bunyan, Matthew Arnold, Charlotte Brontë, John Keats, Percy Shelly, Leo Tolstoy, James Stephens, and Beatrix Potter.

Many of E. Nesbit's books are available for download at www.gutenberg.org.

Enjoyable Authors

This category of writers were perhaps less influential to Lewis's thinking than those covered in the previous section, but Lewis found great joy in reading these authors' books again and again.

Sir Walter Scott

Recommended works: *Waverly, Ivanhoe, Rob Roy*

Sir Walter Scott (1771–1832) is known as the father of the historical novel, being the first to set a fictional story within the context of real historical events. His work was widely popular in the 19th century but fell out of favor in academic circles in the 20th century.

Lewis was a lifelong fan of the "Waverly novels" (*Waverly* and the series of novels that followed with a similar theme). Although Lewis acknowledged the deficiencies in Scott's style and his sometimes paper-thin plots, he could easily look beyond these weaknesses. In particular, Lewis liked the way Scott taught the "feeling of period," or the ability to be transported back to a particular point and time in history. Lewis also admired the way that Scott's writing embodied "virtues of which no age is in more desperate need than our own."

Sir Walter Scott's works are available for download at www.gutenberg.org.

William Morris

Recommended works: *The Well at the World's End, The Wood Beyond the World*

William Morris (1834–1896) was a novelist, poet, and early leader of the socialist movement in 19th-century Britain. Lewis was introduced to Morris's writing at Great Bookham (see Chapter 2), and Morris quickly became another lifelong favorite. Although Morris had socialist leanings, he's described as a "romantic socialist," and Lewis, in fact, distanced Morris's socialist beliefs from the secular socialism of the modern era.

Lewis loved the highly romantic fantasies that Morris wrote, such as *The Wood Beyond the World*. Morris's fantasies seem to have influenced both Lewis and J.R.R. Tolkien. In fact, there are some amazing parallels between *The Well at the World's End* and Tolkien's Middle-earth.

Modern readers tend to find Morris's archaic style of writing to be an acquired taste, so if you choose to explore his work, the style's something that you have to get used to.

Many of William Morris's books (including those recommended in this section) are available for download at www.gutenberg.org.

Jane Austen

Recommended works: *Persuasion, Pride and Prejudice, Emma, Sense and Sensibility, Northanger Abbey, Mansfield Park*

Jane Austen (1775–1817) was an British novelist in the early 19th century whose works were well received on publication and whose popularity has continued into the 21st century. C.S. Lewis read her books again and again over his lifetime, though his personal favorite was *Persuasion.*

You can download Jane Austen's books at www.gutenberg.org. In addition, many of her books have been made into films for both theatrical and television release, most notably *Pride and Prejudice* (A&E, 1995), *Emma* (1996), and *Sense and Sensibility* (1995).

Contemporary Authors (Contemporaries of Lewis, That Is)

Lewis would likely round out his author recommendations with a few of his contemporaries and fellow members of the Inklings, a literary group that Lewis and J.R.R. Tolkien formed in the 1930s. The following would be at the top of Lewis's list.

J.R.R. Tolkien

Recommended works: *The Hobbit, The Lord of the Rings*

J.R.R. Tolkien (1892–1973) was many things to Lewis: a dear friend, a colleague at Oxford, and a fellow member of the Inklings. Tolkien's influence on both Lewis's faith and his writings are discussed in detail in Chapter 3.

Ten most influential books, according to Lewis

In 1962, *Christian Century* magazine asked C.S. Lewis to name the books that most significantly shaped his "vocational attitude and philosophy of life." Lewis responded with the following list:

✔ *Phantastes,* George MacDonald (available at www.gutenberg.org/etext/325)

✔ *The Everlasting Man,* G.K. Chesterton

✔ *The Aeneid,* Virgil (available at www.gutenberg.org/etext/228)

✔ *The Temple,* George Herbert

✔ *The Prelude,* William Wordsworth

✔ *The Idea of the Holy,* Rudolf Otto

✔ *The Consolation of Philosophy,* Boethius (available at www.gutenberg.org/etext/14328)

✔ *Life of Samuel Johnson,* James Boswell (available at www.gutenberg.org/etext/1564)

✔ *Descent into Hell,* Charles Williams

✔ *Theism and Humanism,* Arthur James Balfour

Lewis was a huge fan of Tolkien's work, and he followed the step-by-step construction of *The Hobbit* and *The Lord of the Rings* as chapters were read aloud during Inklings sessions. In *On Stories,* Lewis writes of *The Lord of the Rings,* "Here are beauties which pierce like swords or burn like cold iron; here is a book that will break your heart."

Charles Williams

Recommended works: *Descent into Hell, The Place of the Lion*

Charles Williams (1886–1945) was a British novelist and fantasy writer who became a close friend to Lewis and member of the Inklings after they corresponded about books the other had written. Lewis loved Williams's work and especially favored *The Place of the Lion* and *Descent into Hell.* On first reading *The Place of the Lion,* Lewis wrote to his friend Arthur Greeves, "It is not only a most exciting fantasy, but a deeply religious and (unobtrusively) a profoundly learned book . . . Do get it, and don't mind if you don't understand everything the first time. It deserves reading over and over again. It isn't often now-a-days you get a *Christian* fantasy."

Chapter 22

Ten Tips for Reading C.S. Lewis

In This Chapter
- ▶ Getting in the right frame of mind to read Lewis
- ▶ Trying some suggestions for getting through difficult text

*O*ne problem that many modern readers face is that Lewis's notion of what's "easy-to-understand" doesn't always match their own. I've had glaze-eyed readers approach me about their struggles in trying to make it through such books as *Miracles*, *Mere Christianity,* and even *The Screwtape Letters.* They tell of frequently needing to read a page multiple times in order to truly "get it." Some readers I talk to make it to the end of the book, but others get frustrated and simply give up.

If you struggle with Lewis or simply want to know how to get more out of his books, check out the ten tips provided in this chapter. You get practical advice for reading Lewis as well as discover some of the key approaches that Lewis uses in his writing.

Accept the Perspective of a "Mere Christian"

Whether or not you share Lewis's Christian faith, his work will make more sense to you if you recognize that everything he wrote after his conversion to Christianity was written from the perspective of a Christian worldview. This underlying belief shows up in his writings in three different ways:

✔ **Lewis's works reflect a Christian view of the world.** Except for his early poetry written prior to his conversion, all Lewis's works are steeped in Christianity. His faith wasn't just something he took out of his closet and wore for an hour on Sunday; it was a fundamental part of who he was and — by extension — his writings as well.

✔ **Lewis expresses beliefs that are common among all Christians.** Like most Christians in England in his day, Lewis was an Anglican Protestant. Yet, although the Church of England was the arm of the Church in which Lewis worshipped, he wrote about his faith in a much broader manner. He aims his focus on "mere" Christianity — the core beliefs that Protestant, Catholic, and Orthodox Christians could all embrace without disagreement. In *The Problem of Pain,* for example, Lewis underscores this point, saying, "I have tried to assume nothing that is not professed by all baptized and communicating Christians."

✔ **Lewis writes as a "mere" layman.** Lewis may have been deemed a popular theologian by some, but he always was careful to qualify himself a *layman,* a churchy term that means any Christian who is not a pastor or priest. In fact, he often goes out of his way to qualify himself as such. For example, prefacing *The Problem of Pain,* he notes, "If any real theologian reads these pages he will very easily see that they are the work of a layman and an amateur." At the same time, he sees his place as a "translator" as critical, noting in *The God in the Dock,* "If the real theologians had tackled this laborious work of translation about a hundred years ago, when they began to lose touch with the people (for whom Christ died), there would have been no place for me."

Acknowledge Lewis's "Real Deal" Idealism

As you read Lewis, notice how he combines cold, calculating rationalism with the Christian hope of Heaven. Recognizing this delicate balance will help you understand many of the positions that come out in his writings.

Before he was a Christian, Lewis sat firmly in the realist camp. From his tutoring under William Kirkpatrick (see Chapter 2), Lewis developed a skeptic view of the world, along with a quick wit and keen intellect. But, this combination of intellectual qualities ultimately led him to question his atheism and turn to the Christian faith. When he became a believer, Lewis mixed his logic and realism with the promise claimed by Christianity.

To Lewis, faith and reason both point towards identical truth. In *Miracles,* he refers to God as the "ultimate Fact." Heaven, the focus of hope for the Christian, is expressed as "reality itself" in *The Great Divorce.* But perhaps nowhere is Lewis's "real deal" idealism expressed better than in *The Problem of Pain:*

We are afraid of the jeer about 'pie in the sky,' and of being told that we are trying to 'escape' from the duty of making a happy world here and now into dreams of a happy world elsewhere. But either there is a 'pie in the sky' or there is not. If there is not, then Christianity is false, for this doctrine is woven into its whole fabric. If there is, then this truth, like any other, must be faced.

Keep Lewis's Audience in Mind

Lewis wrote for the average person in the mid-20th century, not the 21st century, so if you're used to page-turners and quick reads, then some of Lewis's books, particularly his nonfiction, may be a bit of an adjustment. You quickly discover that books like *The Abolition of Man* can be fairly dense to read, with one paragraph often spanning more than one page.

If you find yourself struggling, stretch yourself even if the book is different than what you're normally used to reading. Also, I recommend reading the corresponding chapter in this book, as applicable, in conjunction with Lewis's book to get the most out his text.

Remember that Lewis Wrote at Various Reading Levels

Lewis targeted his books for the average reader, but you should be aware that not all Lewis books are created equally.

Obviously, *The Chronicles of Narnia* — written as a children's series — is the easiest to read of all his work. But fictional books such as *The Screwtape Letters* and *The Great Divorce* are also not difficult for most readers to make it through. The most approachable apologetic book is *Mere Christianity,* followed by *The Problem of Pain.*

Some of Lewis's other works are much more challenging. Fictional works including *Till We Have Faces* and *The Pilgrim's Regress* are less user-friendly for the modern reader unless you understand the classic stories upon which these books are based. So too, *The Abolition of Man* and *Miracles* are more philosophical than Lewis's other popular apologetic writings.

If you're just starting out, I recommend sticking with his more approachable works. See the following "Intimidated? Try the Tour de Lewis Road Map" section for a suggested reading strategy.

Intimidated? Try the Tour de Lewis Road Map

Perhaps you started reading a Lewis book in the past and gave up. If so, I recommend that you take the Tour de Lewis approach: Start out with the easier reads and save the more challenging books for later, when you're more familiar with Lewis's subject matter and writing style. The lists below include of some of the author's most well-known books. I've divided them into three groups, divvied up according to level of difficulty and overall must-read status. (Within each group, I order the books from the least to the most difficult.)

Start off by reading the "essential" Lewis books:

- *The Chronicles of Narnia*
- *The Screwtape Letters*
- *The Great Divorce*
- *Mere Christianity*

Move on to other works of Lewis that are more complex but still highly understandable:

- *Perelandra* (or the entire space trilogy, if you're into fantasy)
- *The Problem of Pain*
- *The Four Loves*
- *Letters to Malcolm: Chiefly on Prayer*
- *Surprised by Joy*
- *A Grief Observed*

If you've made it this far, keep going! With a solid Lewis foundation, you can tackle his most challenging works:

- *The Abolition of Man*
- *The Weight of Glory and Other Addresses*

- ✔ *The World's Last Night and Other Essays*
- ✔ *Till We Have Faces*
- ✔ *Miracles*

By following the Tour de Lewis approach, you familiarize yourself with Lewis's writing style and vocabulary slowly, so that by the time you get to *Miracles,* you may even be philosophizing with your friends and family!

Seeking Truth? Try the Conversion Road Map

Perhaps you're new to Lewis and are curious about his personal path from atheism to Christianity and the reasons that lead to his conversion. If so, I offer a suggested road map through several of Lewis's meatiest works to explore his arguments for the truth of Christianity. The list starts with the following:

- ✔ *Mere Christianity*
- ✔ *The Abolition of Man*
- ✔ *The Problem of Pain*
- ✔ *Miracles*
- ✔ *Surprised by Joy*

After you've tackled the five core books above, I recommend rounding out your exploration of Lewis by reading, along with other classics, his fictional books that help underscore the truth of Christianity:

- ✔ *Out of the Silent Planet, Perelandra,* and *That Hideous Strength*
- ✔ *The Chronicles of Narnia*
- ✔ *The Screwtape Letters*
- ✔ *The Great Divorce*
- ✔ *The Weight of Glory and Other Addresses*
- ✔ *The World's Last Night and Other Essays*
- ✔ *The Pilgrim's Regress*
- ✔ *Till We Have Faces*

Read 'Em Again

C.S. Lewis once said that a sure sign of a non-reader is that he uses "I've read it already" as a good excuse against reading a book. Lewis added, "Those who read great works, on the other hand, will read the same work ten, twenty, or thirty times during the course of their life." Although Lewis would have been far too humble to consider his books "great," his "read 'em again" principle most certainly applies to his work. Each time I read Lewis's books, I pick up on ideas that I overlooked before, and I gain a deeper understanding of his reasoning and imagination. The same can happen for you; just keep at it, and keep an open mind each time you open that cover.

Read Lewis Aloud to Your Children

As I explain in Chapter 1, *The Chronicles of Narnia* is a series that appeals to children of all ages, from preschoolers to teenagers (and adults, too). For a more educational exercise, *The Great Divorce* can offer great discussion material for children 9 years and older. If your older children or teens like science fiction, then check out the space trilogy (flip to Chapter 12 for the lowdown). Finally, *The Screwtape Letters* (see Chapter 10) may not be ideal for cover-to-cover reading with your children, but older kids and teenagers can gain a great understanding of temptation and tactics used by Satan if you select and read certain chapters to them.

Depending on your child, don't shy away from Lewis's apologetic works, either. *Mere Christianity,* while challenging for kids, can be understood, especially if you explain Lewis's logic as you read it aloud. (And to get a handle on that logic, turn to Chapter 16.)

Hang In There

If you ever feel overwhelmed when reading a Lewis book, simply hang in there and keep reading. Be persistent and do your best to follow Lewis's logic; it will gradually make more and more sense. Honestly!

Remember that Lewis's Works Are Great, But They're Not Scripture

A close friend and fellow Lewis fanatic approached me recently in excitement: After twenty years of studying Lewis, he finally found an issue about which he believed Lewis was wrong. As I thought later about his "coming of age" thrill of standing up to Lewis, I realized that my friend's reaction reveals a phenomena among many Christians today. Because of Lewis's brilliance, persuasive arguments, and embrace of biblical Christianity, believers can fall in the trap of subconsciously treating everything he writes as "infallible," as almost an extension of the Bible itself.

Lewis was a brilliant author, but you should always remember that he was human and could occasionally be wrong about things. Undoubtedly, Lewis would be the first person to admit this vulnerability.

Complete List of Works by C.S. Lewis

$\bullet \bullet$

*W*hen you read through his bibliography of works, you see that not only was C.S. Lewis a brilliant writer, communicator, and debater, but he was amazingly prolific as well. What's more, he wrote on a wide spectrum of topics, in various literary styles, and to a variety of different audiences, ranging from children to academics.

In this appendix, I provide an annotated bibliography to the works of Lewis and organize them into six categories.

Although decades have passed since his death, it's worth noting that many of Lewis's works remain not only in print but also appear perennially on lists of top-selling books.

Fictional Works

Lewis loved fiction and wrote many novels and stories over the course of his life, all of which have underlying Christian themes.

The Pilgrim's Regress (1933)

The Pilgrim's Regress was a book of firsts for Lewis. It was his first published work since becoming a Christian, and it was his first prose work. Based on Lewis's real-life spiritual journey, the story is an allegory in which the main character, John, searches for Joy and truth and ultimately discovers both in his faith.

Out of the Silent Planet (1938)

Out of the Silent Planet is the first book in Lewis's famed science fiction "space trilogy." In the story, the main character, Dr. Ransom, is kidnapped and taken in a spaceship to a planet called Malacandra (Mars). After discovering that he's intended as a human sacrifice, Ransom escapes and befriends the planet's native creatures.

The Screwtape Letters (1942)

The Screwtape Letters follows a senior devil named Screwtape as he instructs a junior devil named Wormwood in the art of temptation. Both are in the civil service of Hell, charged with tempting humans. The book is presented as a collection of letters from Screwtape to Wormwood, giving tips and techniques on how Wormwood can derail the Christian faith of a British man living during the height of World War II.

Perelandra (1943)

Perelandra is the second installment of the space trilogy. This time around, the main character, Dr. Ransom, travels to Perelandra (Venus). While there, he must save the "Green Lady" (the Eve of Venus) by fighting the Devil, who has taken over the body of Weston, the evil scientist from *Out of the Silent Planet*.

That Hideous Strength (1945)

The third and final part of the space trilogy, *That Hideous Strength* concludes the story of Dr. Ransom, who fights an evil organization, called N.I.C.E., which is attempting to bring back Merlin to accomplish its schemes.

The Great Divorce (1945)

The Great Divorce is a dream fantasy that follows a group of ghosts from Hell who board a bus and visit Heaven. The passengers not only discover how different Heaven looks and feels compared to Hell, but they also get to decide whether or not they want to stay. The narrator of the story is a passenger on the bus, and all the events that take place are seen through his eyes.

The Lion, the Witch and the Wardrobe (1950)

Certainly the most celebrated of *The Chronicles of Narnia, The Lion, the Witch and the Wardrobe* tells the story of four British children (Peter, Susan, Edmund, and Lucy Pevensie) who enter an enchanted world called Narnia through a magic wardrobe. Once there, the children discover that the White Witch has cast an evil spell on Narnia, holding it in an endless winter.

Prince Caspian (1951)

In *Prince Caspian,* the four Pevensie children return to Narnia to help Prince Caspian of Narnia and his army of Talking Beasts defeat the invading Telemarines.

The Voyage of the "Dawn Treader" (1952)

The Voyage of the "Dawn Treader" focuses on the journey that Edmund and Lucy Pevensie and their cousin Eustace Scrubb take into Narnia. As they enter Narnia, they find themselves on a ship (called the *Dawn Treader*) headed by the Prince-turned-King Caspian. The King and his crew are on a voyage to sail to the End of the World.

The Silver Chair (1953)

In *The Silver Chair,* Aslan charges Eustace Scrubb and his cousin Jill Pole to find and rescue Rilian, the true and rightful heir to the Narnian throne.

The Horse and His Boy (1954)

In *The Horse and His Boy,* a boy Prince named Shasta and a talking horse help save Archenland and Narnia from invasion.

The Magician's Nephew (1955)

The Magician's Nephew tells the story of how Aslan creates Narnia and its Talking Beasts. Magic rings transport two British children named Digory and Polly into another world where they encounter an evil queen.

The Last Battle (1956)

The final chapter in the Narnian Chronicles, *The Last Battle* centers on Shift the Ape, who disguises a gullible donkey as Aslan in order to deceive Narnia. As events unfold, Narnia is attacked by the Calormenes and is threatened by ultimate destruction.

Till We Have Faces (1956)

Till We Have Faces is a retelling of the myth of Cupid (the god of love) and the princess Psyche. The story, narrated by Psyche's sister Orual, describes Orual's struggle with the gods and with her own, less than perfect loves.

This book is one for which readers tend to have polarizing attitudes: They either "get it" or don't. Those who "get it" regard *Till We Have Faces* as among Lewis's best work. (Lewis himself considered it his best work of fiction.) But those who don't understand it just end up confused, wondering what exactly they've read.

Christian Nonfiction Works

Lewis spent much of his writing energies in the 1940s writing books that articulate and defend the truth of Christianity. His attention shifted to fiction in the 1950s, but he continued to write periodically on various Christian topics.

The Problem of Pain (1940)

The first of Lewis's great Christian apologetic works, *The Problem of Pain* explores the problem of how an all-powerful and all-loving God can allow evil to exist.

The Abolition of Man (1943)

The Abolition of Man explores the inevitable, damaging consequences of moral relativism on education as well as on all of society. This book is one of Lewis's most challenging apologetics works to read, but it's also one of the most forceful.

Miracles (1947)

In *Miracles,* Lewis argues on the reasonableness of miracles, which he defines as supernatural interventions in the natural world. The book starts by looking at whether there's a good reason for believing in the supernatural in the first place. Then it provides a philosophical exploration of miracles, including the claim by Christians of the "Great Miracle" — that God took the form of a human in Jesus Christ.

Mere Christianity (1952)

Lewis's best known Christian apologetics book, *Mere Christianity,* provides a philosophical yet approachable defense of Christianity and explanation of common Christian beliefs. The book originated as a popular series of broadcast talks given by Lewis on BBC radio during World War II. These talks were originally published as three separate books (*The Case for Christianity, Christian Behavior,* and *Beyond Personality*), but they were combined into one book as *Mere Christianity* a decade later. This is Lewis's best and clearest rational defense of the Christian faith.

Reflections on the Psalms (1958)

Reflections on the Psalms is an exploration by Lewis of the Book of Psalms. Lewis also provides great Christian insight on Judaism in the time of the Old Testament.

The Four Loves (1960)

In *The Four Loves,* Lewis examines different types of love, centering on four that were defined by the ancient Greeks: *storge* (affection), *philia* (friendship), *eros* (erotic love), and *agape* (charity, or unconditional love).

The World's Last Night and Other Essays (1960)

This book contains seven essays that focus on key challenges that test the faith of Christians in the modern world. Topics include prayer, life on other planets, and the Second Coming of Jesus Christ. Also featured in this book is "Screwtape Proposes a Toast," an essay that's now often included with more recent editions of *The Screwtape Letters*.

Letters to Malcolm: Chiefly on Prayer (1964)

His final book, *Letters to Malcolm: Chiefly on Prayer,* is a collection of "letters" written by Lewis to a fictitious correspondent named Malcolm. Lewis uses this correspondence-style structure to explore the nature of prayer.

The Weight of Glory (1949, an expanded version in 1980)

The Weight of Glory is a collection of addresses that Lewis gave during World War II. The most notable is "The Weight of Glory," in which Lewis talks about the glory of Heaven and the glimpses that people can get of that glory here on earth.

Autobiographical Works

Lewis blesses his readers with two compelling autobiographical works. Read these and you should feel as though you're getting to know who C.S. Lewis was and what made him tick.

Surprised by Joy (1955)

Surprised by Joy, Lewis's spiritual autobiography (rather than general biography), focuses on his search for Joy. In the book, Lewis tells how this quest ultimately led him to Christianity.

A Grief Observed (1961)

A Grief Observed shares the suffering and spiritual struggles Lewis faced after the tragic death of his wife Joy. Lewis originally published this heart-wrenching work under the pseudonym N.W. Clerk.

Early Poetry

Lewis's original dream was to be a poet, and his first two published works were, in fact, poems. Although his poetry received generally positive reviews, the response by the general reading public was never to Lewis's liking. He eventually moved away from poetry and into the world of prose.

Spirits in Bondage: A Cycle of Lyrics (1919)

Spirits in Bondage is the first published work of Lewis and was published under the pseudonym Clive Hamilton. Written prior to becoming a Christian, the pessimistic collection of poems, according to Lewis, is centered on the notion "that nature is wholly diabolical and malevolent and that God, if He exists, is outside of and in opposite to the cosmic arrangement."

Spirits in Bondage is available online at www.gutenberg.org/etext/2003.

Dymer (1926)

Originally published under the pseudonym Clive Hamilton, *Dymer* is a poem written by Lewis (before his conversion) about a man who begets a monster. The monster, when it kills his father, becomes a god.

Literary Criticism and Academic Writings

Lewis's "day job" was an instructor in the literature department at Oxford and later Cambridge. He was widely recognized as an expert and scholar in British and Western European literature and wrote several titles in these areas.

The Allegory of Love (1936)

The Allegory of Love examines the tradition of allegorical love poetry in Western Europe from Ovid in ancient Rome through Edmund Spenser.

Rehabilitations and Other Essays (1939)

This work is a collection of specialized essays on literary criticism.

The Personal Heresy (1939)

Coauthored by E.M.W. Tillyard, *The Personal Heresy* debates the question of whether poetry should be an expression of a poet's personality.

A Preface to Paradise Lost (1942)

Taken from lectures he delivered at Oxford, *A Preface to Paradise Lost* explores epic poetry but focuses mostly on John Milton's classic *Paradise Lost*.

English Literature in the Sixteenth Century Excluding Drama (1954)

This reference work is Lewis's tome on 16th-century British literature, of interest chiefly to scholars and others eager to know more about that academic field of study.

Studies in Words (1960)

Studies in Words is an exploration of language. Lewis takes 11 words and examines changes to their meaning and usage through the centuries. The words are *nature, sense, sad, wit, free, simple, conscience, conscious, world, life,* and the expression *I dare say.*

An Experiment in Criticism (1961)

In *An Experiment in Criticism,* Lewis provides an exploration on how to best critique literature, music, and art. He argues that you can't judge art as inherently "good" or "bad" but instead should assign value to it based on the joy you receive from it.

Works Published After His Death

Because of the massive popularity of C.S. Lewis, it's quite natural that readers have been interested in discovering other writings that Lewis left unpublished at the time of his death. Over the years, several books have been released as compilations of his letters, diary entries, essays, and unfinished works.

Over the years, Lewis's essays have been assembled and published in many different books, leaving readers somewhat confused. Not only are there occasional differences between U.S. and UK releases with the same title, but some individual essays also appear in multiple books.

Poems (1964)

This is a collection of poems that Lewis wrote over the course of his life.

The Discarded Image: An Introduction to Medieval and Renaissance Literature (1964)

The Discarded Image is based on lectures that Lewis gave at Oxford examining medieval and Renaissance literature.

Of Other Worlds: Essays and Stories (1966)

Of Other Worlds focuses on the importance of Story in literature. It's an assortment of nine essays, three short science fiction stories, and a portion of a novel left unfinished.

On Stories: And Other Essays on Literature (1966)

A compilation by Walter Hooper (see Chapter 2) after Lewis's death, *On Stories* provides nine essays and eleven other writings that deal with the importance of Story, particularly in fantasy and science fiction literature. This book serves as a companion to *The Dark Tower and Other Stories.*

Studies in Medieval and Renaissance Literature (1966)

This book provides several of Lewis's academic-oriented essays on literature.

Letters to an American Lady (1967)

Letters to an American Lady is a collection of letters that Lewis wrote between 1950 and 1963 to an American woman that he never met face-to-face.

God in the Dock: Essays on Theology and Ethics (1970)

God in the Dock is a collection of 48 essays and 12 other writings that Lewis wrote between 1940 and 1963.

The Dark Tower and Other Stories (1977)

Four of the six stories in this book were published in *Of Other Worlds.* The other two stories are new, and "The Dark Tower" is an unfinished work.

They Stand Together: The Letters of C.S. Lewis to Arthur Greeves (1914–1963) (1979)

In this work, readers are privy to the correspondence between Lewis and Arthur Greeves, one of Lewis's closest, lifelong friends.

Boxen: The Imaginary World of the Young C. S. Lewis (1985)

Boxen and Animal-Land were fantasy worlds created by C.S. Lewis when he was still a boy. Later, in 1927, he decided to go through his earlier writings and write an "Encyclopedia Boxoniana." This work provides access to some of Lewis's earliest writings, though it should be noted that Boxen carries no resemblance to Narnia nor are there any overarching morals to the stories.

C.S. Lewis' Letters to Children (1985)

This work is a compilation of letters Lewis wrote to children over the years, most of which deal with Narnia.

All My Road Before Me: The Diary of C. S. Lewis, 1922–1927 (1991)

This book provides a diary of C.S. Lewis's life while he was a student at Oxford from 1922 to 1927. The diary entries are a window into the mind of Lewis at the time of his life when he was still an atheist.

Letters of C. S. Lewis (1994)

This work is a compilation of Lewis's letters, diary entries, and other items he wrote throughout his life, both before and after his conversion.

Collected Letters of C.S. Lewis (2000–)

This massive, three-volume compilation of letters by C.S. Lewis is in the process of being published. As of this writing, the first two volumes are available: *C. S. Lewis: Collected Letters,* Vol. I [Family Letters 1905–1931] (2000) and *C. S. Lewis: Collected Letters,* Vol. II [Books, Broadcasts, and the War 1931–1949] (2004).

Index

• •